Pharmacy and Medicines Law in Ireland

Pharmacy and Medicines Law in Ireland

Edited by
Peter Weedle BPharm, LLM, PhD, MRPharmS, MPSI
Community Pharmacist
Adjunct Professor of Clinical Pharmacy
University College Cork

Leonie Clarke BSc(Pharm), MSc, CDipAF, Dip Legal Studies,
Cert EU Law, MPSI
Pharmaceutical Consultant

London • Chicago   **Pharmaceutical Press**

Published by Pharmaceutical Press

1 Lambeth High Street, London SE1 7JN, UK
1559 St. Paul Avenue, Gurnee, IL 60031, USA

© Pharmaceutical Press 2011

(PP) is a trade mark of Pharmaceutical Press

Pharmaceutical Press is the publishing division of the Royal Pharmaceutical Society of Great Britain

First published 2011

Typeset by Thomson Digital, Noida, India
Printed in Great Britain by TJ International, Padstow, Cornwall

ISBN 978 0 85369 882 1

A catalogue record for this book is available from the British Library.

Contents

8   Misuse of Drugs Acts and Regulations   119

L Sahm and P Weedle

Foreword

In Ireland, attempts to separate the practice of pharmacy from medicine began in the early 1600s. By 1741 it was proposed to have a separate category of trained person to make, sell, compound and dispense prescriptions.[1] The entitlement of apothecaries to practise in the traditional manner was also to be limited to 'cases of engaging, with restrictions, in the sale of potent substances' and the Apothecaries' Hall Act 1791 provided for the first regulation of the profession of pharmacy.[2]

Over the centuries there has been much tension between surgeons, physicians and apothecaries. For example, in 1833, the College of Surgeons charged the apothecaries as a whole with the neglect of their business. The main charges were that apothecaries had become medical practitioners instead of compounders and that shops were left in the charge of unqualified persons. An example of this tension is illustrated by an extract from a memorandum submitted to the British House of Commons:[3]

> By this same Act, a surgeon, however highly educated, or competent he may be, to act as an apothecary, cannot do so, unless he has been apprenticed to an apothecary in a similar manner [a five year apprenticeship] and whilst the physician and surgeon, of the highest possible attainments, are thus treated by the Apothecaries' Society, like toads under a harrow, the Master and all the Society of Apothecaries who have prosecuted these physicians and surgeons to their ruin . . . for making up a pill, necessary after an operation, may, if they please, physic the same person to death; do the same operation, if they have not killed him before; and make up the same pill with perfect impunity.

---

1. Weedle P, Cahill J. *Medicines and Pharmacy Law in Ireland*. Dublin: Kenlis Publications, 1991, Chapter 3.
2. Ibid., p.15.
3. S.C.M.E., 1834 (602-II) XIII, Part II, Q.4944, p. 48: Memorandum submitted to the Select Committee of the House of Commons on the Apothecaries' Bill. pp. 48–50.

The 1875 Act established the first Pharmaceutical Society of Ireland and ensured that the profession of pharmacy was effectively regulated.[4] The Pharmacy Act 1962[5] made it a criminal offence to take or use the name or title of pharmaceutical chemist, dispensing chemist and druggist, registered druggist or to use any title implying that the holder was a registered pharmacist, unless he or she was so registered. It also became illegal to use descriptions such as pharmacy, medical stores, drug store or chemist unless the person who was involved in selling, dispensing or compounding possessed the requisite qualification. Since the enactment of the 1875 and 1962 Acts the Council of the Pharmaceutical Society of Ireland has had statutory accountability and responsibility in respect of the education, training and granting of qualifications for pharmacists.

It is of note that the Pharmaceutical Society of Ireland had lobbied for a new Pharmacy Act since the 1920s,[6] and while there were Acts in 1951 and 1962, it was widely accepted that legislation regulating the profession of pharmacy was in serious need of updating. This was finally achieved by the passing of the Pharmacy Act 2007.[7]

Parliament has recognised that pharmacy is a safe, viable and sustainable way to effectively distribute medicines because of their potency and more importantly, because of the contribution medicines have made and will continue to make to the health and well-being of patients and the public. One hundred and thirty-two years after the original Pharmacy Act, Ireland's parliament formally enacted on 5 April 2007, the most important piece of legislation in the history of Irish pharmacy, the Pharmacy Act 2007, passing all stages in Dáil Éireann and Seanad Éireann unanimously.[8] All or most of the amendments sought by the old Pharmaceutical Society of Ireland and other pharmacy bodies were very much welcomed by both Houses of the Oireachtas and were incorporated into the final draft of the legislation in accordance with the advice of the Attorney General. Uachtaráin na hÉireann, Mary McAleese, signed the legislation on 21 April 2007 and the implementation of this legislation commenced, on a phased basis, on 22 May 2007 by order of the Minister for Health and Children, Mary Harney TD.[9] The new Council of the PSI took office on 12 June 2007 and the Minister directed that the Pharmacy Act be implemented in full, but in any event not later than mid-summer of 2009.

The Pharmacy Act 2007 is an Act that makes new provisions for the regulation of pharmacy, including provision for the dissolution of the old Pharmaceutical Society of Ireland and the setting up of a new Pharmaceutical

---

4. Pharmacy Act (Ireland) 1875. 38 & 39 Vict., c. 57.
5. No. 14 of 1962.
6. Carroll J. Unpublished history of PSI, 1997.
7. No. 20 of 2007. Copyright Houses of the Oireachtas 2007.
8. Bill No. 21 of 2007.
9. S.I. No. 243 of 2007.

Society of Ireland (PSI); for the establishment, constitution and functions of the new Society's Council; for a new system of registration of pharmacists, druggists and pharmaceutical assistants, and of pharmacies; for the creation of certain offences relating to pharmacy; for the setting up of new procedures to ensure that pharmacists are, and continue to be fit to practise; to prevent pharmacists, pharmacy owners and medical practitioners from entering into certain inappropriate relationships; and to provide for other related matters.

Registered pharmacists and pharmacies are effectively given a monopoly in the Pharmacy Act 2007 in relation to the sale and supply of most medicinal products. This is backed up by way of criminal sanctions and also a system of professional conduct and fitness to operate. An effective and robust system of regulation and registration is an essential safeguard, in such a sensitive and important area as pharmacy services. These are frontline services which must be compliant with medicines law and pharmacy law in the interests of patient safety and public protection.

The Pharmacy Act 2007 and regulatory system, including a statutory code of conduct,[10] and statutory standards which it underpins, requires all pharmacists and pharmacies in the State to be compliant with the legislation. The PSI has primary responsibility for inspection and enforcement of pharmacy law and secondary responsibility for enforcement of medicines law. It also has obligations under the Pharmacy Act 2007 in relation to accreditation, continuing professional development (CPD), practice guidelines, public and patient information, complaints and the development of pharmacy education and the practice of pharmacy in Ireland. Section 14 of the Pharmacy Act 2007 sets out procedures and criteria for registration of pharmacists; Section 16 sets out qualifications for practice for pharmacists; Section 17 establishes criteria for registration of retail pharmacy businesses; and Section 18 establishes the regulation of retail pharmacy businesses. The registration system provides for an EU route of registration for pharmacists and also a non-EU route for pharmacists. It is absolutely essential in the interest of patient safety that only those properly registered as pharmacists are in jurisdiction and in control of pharmacies in the State.

On 29 November 2008, the Minister signed regulations and rules[11] relating to pharmacies and pharmacists and, in particular, established supervising and superintendent pharmacists who are accountable for the proper conduct of their practice. The new system of registration for pharmacists, pharmaceutical assistants, druggists and pharmacies came into operation on 1 January 2009, a comprehensive and robust system as had been sought by the old PSI and pharmacy representative bodies for over a century.

10. Section 7(2)(a)(iii). Pharmacy Act 2007.
11. S.I. No. 488 of 2008, S.I. No. 492 of 2008, S.I. No. 493 of 2008, S.I. No. 494 of 2008, S.I. No. 495 of 2008, S.I. No. 496 of 2008.

The main functions of the PSI are set out as follows:[12]

a   to regulate the profession of pharmacy in the State having regard to the need to protect, maintain and promote the health and safety of the public;

b   to promote and ensure a high standard of education and training for persons seeking to become pharmacists;

c   to ensure that those persons and pharmacists obtain appropriate experience;

d   to ensure that pharmacists undertake appropriate continuing professional development, including the acquisition of specialisation;

e   otherwise to supervise compliance with the Act and the instruments made under it.

The key responsibility for the PSI was the putting in place of the new pharmaceutical registration system. In line with the international experience, it is a serious offence to act outside the parameters of this regulatory system. The PSI has statutory accountability for complaints systems, inquiries and disciplinary matters relating to pharmacists and pharmacies. The PSI has powers of investigation, entry, search, seizure and the penalties range up to and including, on indictment, a sentence of up to ten years in prison and/or a €320 000 fine (at the time of writing). The Pharmacy Act 2007, and rules and regulations underpinning it, are designed to ensure that pharmacy in Ireland is properly and effectively regulated, that registered pharmacists, druggists, pharmaceutical assistants and owners of pharmacies are held accountable in a fair and equitable manner.

The creation of certain offences relating to pharmacy and the setting up of new procedures to ensure pharmacists meet professional statutory conduct requirements and that pharmacy owners are fit to operate pharmacies, is clear evidence that pharmacy is seen by policy makers and our political leaders as a safe, effective and proper channel to distribute medicines to patients and the public. The Oireachtas has moved to prevent pharmacy owners and medical practitioners and others from entering into certain inappropriate relationships, and to provide for related matters to protect patients and the public interest.[13] The fees approved by statutory rule by the Minister for Health and Children pay for the professional conduct regime and the bringing of criminal prosecutions by the PSI. This safeguards not only the public but reputable pharmacists and reputable pharmacy owners from those who would act improperly and bring the profession into disrepute.

The PSI places a high priority on the development of pharmacy practice in the coming years. Pharmacists are highly educated and skilled professionals. It is the PSI's statutory obligation to keep these standards up to date and to

---

12. Section 7(1)(a)–(e). Pharmacy Act 2007.
13. Sections 63 and 64. Pharmacy Act 2007.

advise government to expand the area of pharmacy practice, so that the State can avail of this important, if under-utilised, resource in terms of the skills and abilities of registered pharmacists. The development of pharmacy services in Ireland offers potential to deliver significant enhanced patient and public value. Expanded areas of practice will mean increased opportunities for pharmacists and pharmacies, as well as direct cost-effective benefits to patients, tax payers and third-party funders.[14]

The PSI is working towards a professional development and learning programme to deal with the education of pharmacists including mandatory continuing professional development. The new system of registration, professional conduct and overall regulatory system will ensure a raising of standards in the profession. The new system ensures that every pharmacy in the State has, at a minimum, a superintendent pharmacist and a supervising pharmacist, who have to ensure a high level of compliance with the Code of Conduct for Pharmacists and the statutory standards.

Major scandals in the health sector in Ireland, the UK and across the world, and emerging scandals in other sectors, including the current regulatory deficits in the financial sector, have generated public expectations that effective regulation would apply to all critical services. In healthcare, we are dealing with matters of life and death, where the outcome of patient care and treatment are critical to the quality of life. So it is absolutely essential that there be an effective regulatory system in pharmacy as was sought by the profession and the Oireachtas for many years.

The PSI is accountable to the Minister for Health and Children, the Government and the Oireachtas in respect of its delivering effectively on the regulatory system. If the PSI were to fail to deliver on this remit, it would face public ridicule, severe criticism and the possibility of being abolished by the Oireachtas. This in turn would have a severe impact on public confidence in pharmacists and pharmacies.

This textbook will enable and support pharmacists and other readers to develop a comprehensive understanding of this regulatory system which has a huge impact on the public, patients and the profession of pharmacy and also the broader regulatory system for medicinal products. This textbook will prove most valuable to those in pharmacy practice, in health service management, in academia and those who study pharmacy and medicines law across the world.

Dr A McLoughlin, Registrar/CEO,
Pharmaceutical Society of Ireland

---

14. Pharmacy Ireland 2020. Working group. Interim Report April 2008. 'Advancing clinical pharmacy services to deliver better patient care and added value services.'

Acknowledgements

This book would not have been possible but for the help, expertise and hard work of many people. We are particularly grateful to our co-authors for providing their expertise to facilitate the production of this book; they are, in alphabetical order:

Dr Stephen Byrne
Mr Frank Crean
Mr Dominic Dowling
Professor Paul Gallagher
Ms Damhnait Gaughan
Dr Suzanne McCarthy
Dr Michael Morris
Dr Laura Sahm

This book would not have seen the light of day but for their efforts and expertise.

We are very appreciative to Dr Ambrose McLoughlin, Registrar of the Pharmaceutical Society of Ireland for writing the Foreword.

We acknowledge the help and advice we have received from numerous sources. In particular, Mr Tom McGuinn (former Chief Pharmacist of the Department of Health and Children) for his extraordinary insight and understanding of the legislation, of which he gave freely. We would like to thank Dr J Gabriel Beechinor, Director of Veterinary Medicines, Irish Medicines Board, for his comments and corrections to the chapter on veterinary medicines.

We are grateful to the Copyright Officer for the Houses of the Oireachtas for kind permission to reproduce extracts of legislation including statutory instruments enacted as and from 2001 and acknowledge the Houses of the Oireachtas' copyright in the relevant acts, orders and statutory instruments. We also acknowledge the copyright of the Government in all legislation including statutory instruments enacted prior to 2001.

On a personal note we wish to thank both our families for their continuing forbearance and support as we disappeared for hours on end drafting, writing and editing the various chapters. In particular, we would like to thank Rebecca Weedle for her work on proofing this manuscript.

While every effort has been made to ensure accuracy of information contained in this book, we accept no liability for errors or omissions or responsibility for loss or damage occasioned by any person acting or refraining from acting as a result of this material. This book is a summary of legislation and where necessary reference should be made to the relevant acts, regulations, and orders as published by the Stationary Office and available on the Irish Statute Book website (www.irishstatutebook.ie) and to the relevant EU directives and regulations. EU pharmaceutical legislation is published by the European Commission in *The Rules Governing Medicinal Products in the European Union*, which is available on the Commission website at http://ec.europa.eu/health/documents/eudralex/index_en.htm.

Any views or opinions expressed are those of the relevant authors.

We have endeavoured to state the law as at 1 March 2011.

Leonie Clarke
Peter Weedle
March 2011

About the editors

Peter Weedle, BPharm, LLM, PhD, MRPharmS, MPSI is a community pharmacist and adjunct Professor of Clinical Pharmacy at University College Cork. He is a former Registrar of the Pharmaceutical Society of Ireland (PSI) and was a member of the Council from 2002–2009. Peter was the first chairman of the PSI Registration Committee. Peter has a wide range of interests in the area of pharmacy but in particular, medicine use by the elderly, drug interactions, legal and ethical matters. He is co-author of two previous books: Medicines and Pharmacy Law in Ireland and Medicines: A guide for everybody.

Leonie Clarke, BSc(Pharm), MSc, CDipAF, Dip Legal Studies, Cert EU Law, MPSI runs a pharmaceutical consultancy advising on issues such as compliance with medicines legislation, quality management, education and corporate governance. She is a former Assistant Registrar of the PSI. She has several years' experience in the pharmaceutical industry and also spent time in academia. She has been an examiner to the PSI Professional Registration Examination for a number of years. Other appointments include membership of the PSI Council and the Poisons Council.

Contributors

Stephen Byrne BSc(Hon) Pharmacy, PhD, Dip Stat, Cert Health Econ, Cert Clin Pharm, MPSI, is Senior Lecturer, Clinical Practice, School of Pharmacy, University College Cork.

Frank Crean BSc(Pharm), MPSI, Barrister-at-Law, Law Library, Four Courts, Dublin 7.

Dominic Dowling BCL, Dip Arb, MCIArb, Commissioner for Oaths, Solicitor, Dalkey, Co. Dublin has acted as legal adviser to the Pharmaceutical Society of Ireland for nearly three decades.

Paul Gallagher BSc(Pharm), PhD, MPSI, Head of School of Pharmacy and Associate Professor of Pharmacy, Royal College of Surgeons in Ireland, Dublin. Member of the Pharmaceutical Society of Ireland (PSI) Council and Chair of PSI Professional Development and Learning Committee.

Damhnait Gaughan BSc(Pharm), MPSI, is Head of Registration and Qualification Recognition for the Pharmaceutical Society of Ireland, Dublin.

Suzanne McCarthy MPharm, PhD, is a Lecturer in Clinical Practice, School of Pharmacy, University College Cork.

Ambrose McLoughlin BDS, MBA, CPA, is Registrar and CEO of the Pharmaceutical Society of Ireland, Dublin. Dr McLoughlin is a former CEO of the North Eastern Health Board and has been a key advisor to the Department of Health and Children on a number of patient safety and public health matters.

John Michael Morris   BSc(Pharm), PhD, MRPharmS, MPSI, is Senior Scientific Advisor at the Irish Medicines Board, Dublin. He was president of the European Pharmacopoeia Commission, 2004–2007.

Laura Sahm   BSc(Pharm)(Hons), PhD, MPSI. Lecturer in Clinical Practice, School of Pharmacy, University College Cork, and Consultant Pharmacist, Department of Pharmacy, Mercy University Hospital, Cork.

Abbreviations

1,4 BD	butan-1,4-diol
ADR	alternative dispute resolution
AIDS	acquired immune deficiency syndrome
BP	British Pharmacopoeia
BPC	British Pharmaceutical Codex
BZP	benzylpiperazine
CAM	companion animal medicine
CD	controlled drug(s)
CD1	controlled drugs listed in Schedule 1 to the Misuse of Drugs Regulations 1988 as amended
CD2	controlled drugs listed in Schedule 2 to the Misuse of Drugs Regulations
CD3	controlled drugs listed in Schedule 3 to the Misuse of Drugs Regulations
CD4	controlled drugs listed in Schedule 4 to the Misuse of Drugs Regulations
CD5	controlled drugs listed in Schedule 5 to the Misuse of Drugs Regulations
CHMP	Committee for Medicinal Products for Human Use
CPD	Continuing Professional Development
CPMP	Committee for Proprietary Medicinal Products
DNA	deoxyribonucleic acid
DPR	Dual Pack import Registration
DTC	direct-to-consumer
EC	European Community
ECHR	European Convention on Human Rights
ECJ	European Court of Justice
EDQM	European Directorate for the Quality of Medicines & HealthCare
EEA	European Economic Area
EEC	European Economic Community

EFTA	European Free Trade Association
EMA	European Medicines Agency
EPAR	European Public Assessment Report
EU	European Union
GBL	gamma-butyrolactone
GCP	good clinical practice
GDP	good distribution practice
GMP	good manufacturing practice
GMS	General Medical Services
HoR	Homeopathic Registration
HSE	Health Service Executive
IMB	Irish Medicines Board
INN	international non-proprietary name
LM	licensed merchant
LSD	lysergic acid diethylamide
MD	maximum dose
MDD	maximum daily dose
MDPV	methylenedioxypyrovalerone
MPS	maximum pack size
MPSI	member of the Pharmaceutical Society of Ireland
MPT	maximum period of treatment
MS	maximum strength
NDAB	National Drugs Advisory Board
OTC	over the counter
PA	product authorisation
PCC	Professional Conduct Committee
Ph Eur	European Pharmacopoeia
PHECC	Pre-Hospital Emergency Care Council
PIL	patient information leaflet (also known as package leaflet or PL)
PL	product licence (term used in UK for marketing authorisations); package leaflet
PO	post office
POM(E)	prescription-only medicine (exempt)
POM	prescription-only medicine
PPA	parallel product authorisation
PPC	Preliminary Proceedings Committee
PS	pharmacy only
PSI	Pharmaceutical Society of Ireland
PSUR	periodic safety update report
RPSGB	Royal Pharmaceutical Society of Great Britain

S1A	First Schedule to the Medicinal Products (Prescription and Control of Supply) Regulations 2003 as amended, Part A
S1B	First Schedule to the Medicinal Products (Prescription and Control of Supply) Regulations, Part B
S1C	First Schedule to the Medicinal Products (Prescription and Control of Supply) Regulations, Part C
SmPC	summary of product characteristics, sometimes abbreviated to SPC
SPC	See SmPC
UK	United Kingdom
UN	United Nations
USA/US	United States of America
VPA	veterinary product authorisation
VPO/VPO-1	veterinary practitioner only animal remedy.

Latin terms

bona fide 'in good faith,' means good, honest intention (even if producing unfortunate results) or belief. It is the mental and moral state of honesty; conviction as to the truth or falsehood of a proposition or body of opinion; or as to the rectitude or depravity of a line of conduct.

de facto 'by the fact,' means 'in practice but not necessarily ordained by law' or 'in practice or actuality, but without being officially established'.

ex parte 'from (by or for) one party' An *ex parte* decision is one decided by a judge without requiring all the parties to the issue to be present. *Ex parte* means a legal proceeding brought by one person in the absence of and without representation or notification of other parties.

expressio unius est exclusio alterius means 'The express mention of one thing excludes all others'. Items not on the list are assumed not to be covered by the statute. Sometimes a list in a statute is illustrative, not exclusionary. This is usually indicated by a word such as 'includes' or 'such as'. However, even words such as 'includes' and 'including' may be defined as terms in legislation and no longer retain their common meaning.

in camera 'in a chamber' – means 'in private'. It is also sometimes termed 'in chambers' or *in curia*. *In camera* describes court cases (or portions thereof) that the public and press are not admitted to. *In camera* is the opposite of trial in open court where all the parties and witnesses testify in a public courtroom.

indicia 'signs, indications'. Circumstances that point to the existence of a given fact as probable, but not certain.

inter alia 'among other things' is a term used in formal extract minutes to indicate that the minute quoted has been taken from a fuller record of other matters, or in other documents when alluding to the parent group after quoting a particular example.

in utero in the womb.

locus classicus means a passage from a classic or standard work that is cited as an illustration or instance.

locus standi   is the term for the ability of a party to demonstrate sufficient connection to and harm from the law or action challenged to support that party's participation in a case.

nemo debet bis puniri pro uno delicto   means that nobody ought to be punished twice for the same offence.

novus actus interveniens   'new act intervening'. Even if the defendant has been shown to have acted negligently there will be no liability if some new intervening act breaks the chain of causation.

prima facie   'on its first appearance', or 'at first sight'. The literal translation would be 'at first face'. It is used in modern legal English to signify that on first examination, a matter appears to be self-evident from the facts. In common law jurisdictions, *prima facie* denotes evidence which – unless rebutted – would be sufficient to prove a particular proposition or fact.

res judicata   'a matter [already] judged', and may refer to two things: in both civil law and common law legal systems, a case in which there has been a final judgment and is no longer subject to appeal; the term is also used to refer to the legal doctrine meant to bar (or preclude) continued litigation of such cases between the same parties, which is different between the two legal systems.

simpliciter   'simply, plainly' without any qualification or conditions.

stare decisis   'doctrine of precedent'. This is the legal principle by which judges are obliged to respect the precedents established by prior decisions. The words originate from the Latin phrase *stare decisis et non quieta movere*: stand by decisions and do not disturb the undisturbed. In a legal context, this is understood to mean that courts should generally abide by precedents and not revisit settled matters.

ultra vires   'beyond the powers'. The *ultra vires* doctrine typically applies to a corporate body, such as a limited company, a government department or a local council so that any act done by the body which is beyond its capacity to act (and not *intra vires*) will be considered void.

vires   powers.

vis-à-vis   'with regard to' or 'in relation to'.

Citation of legislation and cases

Acts

The title of the Act is followed by the year of enactment and the Act number of that year, e.g. Pharmacy Act 2007 (No. 20 of 2007). Each act is divided into 'sections' and 'subsections'.

Statutory instruments (e.g. regulations, orders)

The title of the statutory instrument is followed by the year in which it was made and the statutory instrument number of that year, e.g. Medicinal Products (Control of Advertising) Regulations 2007 (S.I. No. 541 of 2007). Each individual numbered section within a set of regulations is called a 'regulation', e.g. Regulation 1. In older regulations, the term 'article' may be used to describe these individual sections, e.g. Article 2.

EU directives and regulations

Directives and regulations are cited with reference to the name of the institution from which they originated, i.e. the Commission, Council and/or Parliament, nature (i.e. Regulation, Directive, etc.), the number, year, treaty under which they were made (e.g. European Community (EC), European Economic Community (EEC), European Union (EU)) and the date.

In a regulation, the name of the treaty comes before the number and year and title in the following format: Regulation (EC) No. 726/2004 of the European Parliament and of the Council of 31 March 2004 laying down Community procedures for the authorisation and supervision of medicinal products for human and veterinary use and establishing a European Medicines Agency.

Directives are cited by reference to year, number and name of treaty and title in the format: Directive 2001/83/EC of the European Parliament and of the Council of 6 November 2001 on the Community code relating to medicinal products for human use.

Cases

When citing cases, the names of parties are followed by the year, the volume number (if relevant) and the abbreviation of the law report where the case is reported, followed by the page number, e.g. *Donoghue* v. *Stevenson* [1932] A.C. 562 at 603. All law report series have abbreviations, e.g. IR – Irish Reports, ILRM – Irish Law Reports Monthly. For an unreported judgment, the format is: *Hughes* v. *Staunton* Unreported, High Court, Lynch J, 16 February 1990 at p. 53.

1

Introduction

P Weedle and L Clarke

In the predecessor to this book (published in 1991) the then authors concluded in a postscript:

> we were warned at the outset that the time was not opportune for producing a book dealing with the legislation affecting medicines. Too many directives and national regulations were still in the pipeline to enable the subject to be covered with any degree of finality. While there was, and is, much truth in that proposition, we were more convinced by a different viewpoint: there will never be an opportune time.

Much has happened in the intervening years with a significant updating of the body of legislation relating to medicines and pharmacy, as was predicted. Major developments have occurred, in particular in the last decade, largely driven by the evolving regulatory system for human and veterinary medicines at European Union (EU) level. The enactment of the Pharmacy Act 2007 has been another highly significant development and a major catalyst in developing the current book.

This book is designed primarily as a reference source for healthcare professionals, in particular, pharmacists, to ensure that they have easily accessible information on legislation relevant to their practice. It is considered, therefore, that only a brief outline of the legal systems giving rise to this legislation is appropriate (Chapter 2). Law students have complete courses of lectures and access to numerous textbooks on legal systems. Chapter 2 is not designed for lawyers, but for those involved with medicines who need to know, in simple terms, the basis of their legal controls.

Following the legal system chapter, a brief historical background is given to the development of medicines and pharmacy legislation over the centuries and an analysis provided of the evolution of EU law on human medicines since the 1960s (Chapter 3). The purpose of the law then was, as it still is today, to protect the public. The first law controlling medicines was enacted in the sixteenth century; many administrative controls developed much earlier. It was not until the latter part of the nineteenth century that the law took a major and sustained interest in controlling medicines.

The first modern Irish legislation controlling the purity and quality of medicines was the Therapeutic Substances Act 1932. The worldwide concern which followed the tragedy of the teratogenic effects of thalidomide led to controls in the 1960s on the placing of medicinal products on the market in Europe (Chapter 4). Initially these controls took the form of a licensing system to ensure the quality, safety and efficacy of such products. Over the years, other aspects have been regulated, including manufacturing and testing, wholesaling, labelling, advertising, monitoring of side-effects (pharmacovigilance), supply classification and clinical trials, largely driven by EU requirements. The EU is also proactively taking steps to encourage the licensing of medicines for children (paediatric medicines), for rare diseases (orphan medicines) and cell, gene and tissue therapies (advanced therapies). The advent of the EU centralised procedure and the mutual recognition and decentralised procedures for the authorisation of medicinal products have reduced the duplication of work between national regulatory authorities, ensured a growing role for the European Medicines Agency and its Committee for Medicinal Products for Human Use and faster access for European patients to new medicines. The controls on placing medicinal products on the market are reinforced by the rigorous obligations placed on those who manufacture and wholesale such products (Chapter 5) and the controls applicable to their advertising and promotion (Chapter 6).

The law also controls the availability of certain medicines which are considered to require professional selection and advice on their use. The Medicinal Products (Prescription and Control of Supply) Regulations 2003 as amended describe the controls applicable to medicines that may only be supplied on prescription and to those exempted from prescription control. It is noteworthy that the right to prescribe medicinal products has been extended in recent years to nurses, albeit with some restrictions (Chapter 7). Certain drugs which are liable to be abused because of their psychoactive effects (e.g. morphine) are very strictly controlled by the Misuse of Drugs Acts (Chapter 8) to ensure that they are available only for *bona fide* medical purposes.

In the past, controls on the supply of human and veterinary medicines imposed by poisons legislation were a crucial element of the regulatory system for such products. However, as the body of human and veterinary medicines legislation evolved, the need for such controls diminished. Poisons legislation has been totally updated in the last few years and human and veterinary medicines are now completely removed from its scope. The legislation still has some relevance to modern-day pharmacy practice in terms of poisons sold and supplied for use in agriculture, horticulture etc., albeit far more limited than previously (Chapter 9).

Veterinary medicines are controlled in a manner similar to medicines for human use (Chapter 10). Additional controls apply because certain animals are used as a food source for humans and therefore the law is concerned with ensuring that residues in meat, milk and other animal produce do not pose a threat to public health. Most of the controls over medicines for veterinary use originate from the EU in the form of directives and regulations.

Other areas of the law that affect medicines and their supply to the public by pharmacists are also covered, namely the Pharmacy Act (Chapter 12) and Regulations and Rules (Chapter 13) and the Disciplinary System (Chapter 14). Controls on the sale of methylated spirits are also detailed (Chapter 11). Finally, the increasingly important areas of the tort of negligence and the EU Directive on product liability in the provision of medical and pharmaceutical care to patients are discussed (Chapter 15).

There are many other areas of legislation that may impact on a pharmacist in practice (e.g. data protection, employment law, etc.) that could be included in this book. However, the volume of legislation which would need to be covered to comprehensively deal with all these topics is beyond the scope of this book.

A number of conclusions can be drawn from the many legislative developments that have occurred in recent years:

- A comprehensive legal framework now exists through the Pharmacy Act and its accompanying regulations, rules and code of conduct, for the regulation of the pharmacy profession in Ireland. It will be interesting to see how the profession expands and develops within this new regulatory framework in the years ahead.
- In terms of human and veterinary medicines, the regulatory environment created by the EU's pharmaceutical directives and regulations is comprehensive and appropriate given the EU's twin objectives of safeguarding of public health, while at the same time facilitating the development of industry and trade in medicines within the EU. The one aspect of the EU regulatory system that could be rationalised is the system available for the authorisation of medicinal products which comprises three different mechanisms for medicines to be marketed in more than one country (centralised, mutual recognition and decentralised procedures) as well as national systems for medicines that will be marketed in only one member state.

- The expansion in EU regulation has been mirrored by a diminution of controls emanating at national level and, on occasion, some real complexity where it is necessary to marry EU requirements with those in place in national legislation. For example in the area of medicines for use in animals, the Animal Remedies Acts 1993 and 2006 as amended sit alongside various regulations made under the European Communities Acts to implement EU law on veterinary medicinal products. The definition of animal remedy is actually broader than that of the EU's 'veterinary medicinal product'. Another example is the Irish Medicines Board Act 1995 which has been amended by four separate European Communities regulations, primarily to designate the Irish Medicines Board as competent authority for various classes of medical devices. The Irish Medicines Board (Miscellaneous Provisions) Act 2006, as would be expected, amended the 1995 IMB Act but it is interesting to note that it also amended six other acts[1] as well as amending or revoking six statutory instruments; the changes covering matters as diverse as nurse prescribing and dental health services for children. Another example of complexity in legislation is the system for supply classification of medicinal products which is covered in both the Medicinal Products (Control of Placing on the Market) Regulations 2007 and the Medicinal Products (Prescription and Control of Supply) Regulations 2003 as amended. The latter regulations had to be amended by the former to reconcile the requirements of the two sets of regulations.

This complicated approach to legislation, while it may achieve the desired legislative controls and compliance with Ireland's obligations as a member of the EU, gives rise to a body of acts and statutory instruments which are difficult to navigate without expert knowledge of the relevant legislation. The authors believe that this is an area which would benefit from review and streamlining.

It is hoped that this textbook will help those with an interest in pharmacy and medicines law in Ireland to find their way through the maze of legislation as it currently exists. To assist the reader, details of relevant EU directives and regulations have been covered in addition to the relevant national provisions.

Given the vast legislative change that has occurred in the last 20 years, there is a hope that there may be a degree of stability for the foreseeable future. However, given the speed of technical and scientific advances in therapeutics and the ever-expanding reach of the EU, this is probably an unrealistic wish.

---

1. Misuse of Drugs Act 1977, Control of Clinical Trials Act 1987, Health Acts 1947, 1970 and 1994 and Animal Remedies Act 1993.

2

Sources of Irish law

F Crean and P Weedle

The law in Ireland derives from four major sources. The first of these is the Constitution, Bunreacht na hÉireann, which takes precedence over all other sources of law. This supremacy is tempered insofar as is necessary to ensure that Ireland can fulfil its obligations pursuant to membership of the European Union (EU). Legislation enacted by the organs of the EU within its sphere of legislative competence is of increasing importance as a source of law in Ireland. The other important sources of Irish law are legislation that is enacted by the Oireachtas and the accumulation of decisions of judges that constitutes the common law.

Irish legal history

In ancient times, Ireland was governed by a sophisticated indigenous system of law which was administered by judges called brehons. This system was replaced by the Anglo-Norman common law system after the Anglo-Norman invasion in 1169.

Ireland was part of the United Kingdom prior to 1922 and until then the system of law which operated in the country was controlled by the government based in London. The Anglo-Irish Treaty of 1921 formed the basis of the Irish Free State. In 1922 the Constitution of the Irish Free State (Saorstát Éireann) was approved by Dáil Éireann.[1] In 1937 a new Constitution (Bunreacht na hÉireann) was put to the people in a referendum and passed. Bunreacht na hÉireann is the source of legal authority in Ireland and all other laws derive their validity from it.

The two Constitutions did not break completely with the legal order which existed prior to 1922. It was not feasible to establish a totally new system of law and, therefore, the rules which applied in Saorstát Éireann were largely

---

1. Constitution of the Irish Free State (Saorstát Éireann) Act 1922 (No. 1 of 1922) was passed.

those which had operated prior to 1922. A considerable number of legal rules were transferred to the new system. In this regard, the Adaptation of Enactments Act 1922[2] adapted the legislative regime previously in force and applied it to the new institutions of the nascent Irish Free State.

For laws in operation before the introduction of Bunreacht na hÉireann, Article 50 provides that such laws continue to have full force and effect 'subject to this Constitution and to the extent to which they are not inconsistent therewith'.

The law prior to 1922 continues to be of relevance today. A considerable number of the laws which operate in the State pre-date the establishment of Saorstát Éireann in 1922. Until recently, certain provisions of the Apothecaries' Hall Act 1791,[3] the Pharmacy Act (Ireland) 1875[4] and the Pharmacy Act (Ireland) 1875 Amendment Act 1890[5] remained in force. The existing court system also owes much to its antecedent.

The Constitution

Bunreacht na hÉireann sets out the framework and the principal functions of the organs of government of the State and prescribes the manner in which those parts of government must discharge their functions. Bunreacht na hÉireann is founded on the tripartite division of the powers of government into legislative, executive and judicial functions. It defines the nature, extent and powers of the nation and of the State and declares the sovereignty of the people. In addition, Bunreacht na hÉireann declares that each individual is possessed of certain fundamental rights; though many of these rights are expressly guaranteed, 'there are many personal rights of the citizen which follow from the democratic nature of the State which are not mentioned'[6] in the Constitution.

Bunreacht na hÉireann was adopted by the people of Ireland by referendum on 1 July 1937. Accordingly, it constitutes and ordains the system of law by which the people of Ireland have agreed to be governed. Since the Constitution was enacted by the people, amendments to it must be enacted in a like manner. A Bill to amend Bunreacht na hÉireann must be submitted to the people in a referendum. Any proposed amendment will only take effect if a majority of votes are cast in favour of the amendment. It is the function of the Referendum Commission, which was established pursuant to Section 2 of the

---

2. No. 2 of 1922.
3. 31 Geo. 3., c. 34.
4. 38 & 39 Vict., c. 57.
5. 53 & 54 Vict., c. 48.
6. *Ryan* v. *Attorney General* [1965] 1 I.R. 294 at 313.

Referendum Act 1998,[7] to explain the proposed amendment and set out the arguments for and against the amendment concerned.

Legislation

Legislation is the laying down of rules by a competent authority.[8] Article 15.2 of the Constitution provides that the sole and exclusive right to make laws for the State is vested in the Oireachtas, which consists of the President and two houses, Dáil Éireann (house of representatives) and Seanad Éireann (senate). Article 15.4 of the Constitution provides that the Oireachtas shall not enact any legislation that is repugnant to any provision of the Constitution.

Acts of the Oireachtas are referred to as primary legislation. Primary legislation often contemplates the need to prescribe more detailed rules in order to give effect to the principles and policies contained therein. To this end, secondary legislation is enacted by bodies or individuals given this power by statute. The exercise of the power to enact secondary legislation is subject to the scrutiny of the courts to ensure that it does not stray beyond the power, or *vires*, which was granted by the statute in question. The power to legislate can only be delegated by the Oireachtas for the purpose of implementing the principles and policies declared in primary legislation.[9] Any attempt to exceed this constitutional limitation will constitute an impermissible delegation by the Oireachtas of its legislative function.[10]

For example, Section 18 of the Pharmacy Act 2007[11] empowers the Minister for Health and Children to make regulations concerning certain aspects of the practice of pharmacy. This power is expressed to be for the purposes of the 'health, safety and convenience of the public'. Any regulations that are made pursuant to this power must be exercised for this purpose and can only relate to the matters specified in subsections 18(1)(a)–(o). In exercise of the powers conferred by this section, the Minister made the Regulation of Retail Pharmacy Businesses Regulations 2008.[12]

Common law

Common law is the ancient unwritten law of England, so called because it was made common to the whole of England and Wales after the Norman

---

7. No. 1 of 1998.
8. Doolan B. *Principles of Irish Law*. 7th edn. Dublin: Gill and Macmillan, 2007, p. 22.
9. *Cityview Press* v. *An Chomhairle Oiliúna* [1980] I.R. 381.
10. *O'Neill* v. *Minister for Agriculture* [1998] 1 I.R. 539.
11. No. 20 of 2007. Copyright Houses of the Oireachtas 2007.
12. S.I. No. 488 of 2008.

Conquest in 1066.[13] The common law consists of the body of law that has accumulated by decisions of the courts over many years.

The Irish legal system is in the common law tradition and, therefore, many of the legal rules which operate were developed originally by judges and are still being refined. Indeed, the common law was for many years the primary source of Irish law and remains 'an integral portion of our jurisprudence'.[14]

While the Oireachtas has the power to make law, judges have an important role to play in determining the manner in which existing laws, including common law rules, are actually applied.

The common law governs any aspect of the law that is not the subject of legislation. In addition, judges are assigned the function of interpreting legislation and of determining the precise nature of the rights and liabilities that flow from it. This function is exercised when a dispute as to the application of the law is brought before the courts in the context of litigation. A system of judicial precedent has evolved in many common law countries, including Ireland. According to this system, a court, in arriving at a decision, will be guided by past decisions. In addition, lower courts are bound to follow the decisions of higher courts. The doctrine of precedent, or *stare decisis*, ensures a degree of consistency in judicial decisions. Many branches of law today, for example, contract law and the law of torts, still rely heavily on common law principles.

Through the interplay of these rules and the demands of the doctrine of precedent, the common law has developed into a coherent body of law that gives a degree of predictability to citizens.

European law

Since Ireland's accession to the European Economic Community (EEC) (now known as the European Union or EU) on 1 January 1973, the Irish legal system has been profoundly influenced by the provisions of the various European treaties and by legislation passed by the EU. The EU possesses its own legal system, which is presided over by the European Court of Justice. The treaties are the fundamental documents from which the various institutions of the EU derive their competence and powers. In order to implement the provisions of the treaties and to make their aims manifest, the institutions of the EU act in concert to enact legislation. Membership of the EU required Ireland to subscribe to this new legal order; EU law enjoys supremacy over domestic law where the two appear to conflict.[15] The EU treaties and some

---

13. Doolan B. *Principles of Irish Law*. 7th edn. Dublin: Gill and Macmillan, 2007, p. 2.
14. *Cook v. Carroll* [1945] I.R. 515 at 522.
15. *Costa v. ENEL* [1964] E.C.R. 74.

other aspects of EU law create legal rights that can be relied on by citizens of member states in national courts.[16]

In order to facilitate accession to the EU, or the EEC as it then was, the people of Ireland voted in a referendum in 1972 to amend Bunreacht na hÉireann. The Constitution, while remaining the paramount domestic law, was amended to provide that no provision of it could be invoked to invalidate any acts required by membership of the EU, or to prevent any EU law from having full force and effect in Irish law.[17]

Accession to the EU does not give the government authority to ratify every amendment to the founding EU treaties. Any amendment to those treaties of the European Union requires approval by referendum if it exceeds the original scope and objectives of the treaty that was ratified by Ireland on accession in 1973.[18]

The two principal types of legislation enacted by the EU are directives and regulations. The salient difference between directives and regulations is that, while regulations are binding in their entirety and are directly effective in member states, directives are binding only insofar as the result to be achieved and also require specific implementation in national legislation.[19] The European Court of Justice is assigned the function of interpreting the provisions of the EU treaties and it is the arbiter of disputes that arise concerning the interpretation and application of the laws governing the EU.

Directives are the main mechanism used to achieve harmonisation of laws across the EU. The basic purpose of a directive is set out in its preamble and the substance of it must be implemented in the member states by a date specified therein. However, a measure of discretion is afforded to each member state in the detailed implementation of a directive. The state's obligations are satisfied as long as the aims of the directive are made manifest. If the specified implementation date has passed, the Commission may bring a case before the European Court to force its introduction by the defaulting state. Certain directives, even when they have not been implemented by a member state, in fact become law once the deadline passes; this usually applies to directives which confer rights on individuals.[20]

---

16. *Van Gend en Loos* v. *Nederlandse Belastingenadministratie* [1963] E.C.R. 1.
17. Bunreacht na hÉireann, Art. 29.4.10. This amendment was originally contained in Art. 29.4.3 of Bunreacht na hÉireann. Subsequent constitutional amendments consequent on the ratification or otherwise of various treaties, prototols, decisions, etc. have since displaced the numbering of this provision.
18. *Crotty* v. *An Taoiseach* [1987] 1 I.R. 713.
19. Article 249 of the Treaty. It is noteworthy that directives may be directly effective, but only in limited circumstances.
20. *Francovich* v. *Italian Republic* [1991] E.C.R. I-5357.

Other types of European law include EU regulations which have a general application, are binding in their entirety and are directly applicable in all the member states. EU decisions are binding on those to whom they are addressed. There are also recommendations and opinions which do not have legal effect.

Alternative dispute resolution

Certain provisions of the Pharmacy Act 2007 envisage a role for bodies outside of the court system in the resolution of disputes. In particular, the fitness to practise provisions of Part 6 of the Act provide for the resolution of complaints against pharmacists or registered retail pharmacies by mediation or other forms of alternative dispute resolution (ADR). The principal difference between mediation and adjudicative processes such as hearings is that the emphasis in the former is on agreement rather than on decisions. Recourse to resolution of complaints through ADR aims to supplement the Pharmaceutical Society of Ireland's disciplinary powers and to provide greater remedial flexibility and satisfaction. The PSI Council may issue guidelines[21] regarding the appropriateness of recourse to ADR in professional disciplinary complaints to ensure that the interests of all parties involved and the public interest are vindicated. It is not envisaged that all complaints made can be suitably resolved by mediation or other ADR mechanisms. In this regard, it would appear that mediation will not be appropriate where the process can vindicate the private interest of the parties in the resolution of a complaint but not the public interest in the proper conduct of the profession.

Mediation is essentially a process of negotiation that is structured and influenced by the intervention of a neutral third party, who seeks to assist the parties to reach a settlement that is acceptable to them.[22] Whether an agreement results depends on the parties, rather than something that is imposed by a judge or an arbitrator. A mediator will attempt to identify the interests behind the positions adopted by the parties and produce a range of options to address those interests. The success of mediation as a process is substantially founded on the principle that what takes place in the mediation is, and remains, inaccessible for the purposes of subsequent hearings if the mediation does not result in settlement.[23] Accordingly, this provides an opportunity for the respondent to a complaint to offer an apology or propose certain remedial steps where appropriate to do so.

---

21. Section 37(1)–(2) of Pharmacy Act 2007.
22. Mackie K, Miles D, Marsh W. *Commercial Dispute Resolution: An ADR Practice Guide*, 3rd edn. London: LexisNexis, 2007, para.1.3.3.
23. Section 37(7) of the Pharmacy Act 2007 ensures that this applies to mediation for the purposes of the Act.

3

Historical development of medicines and pharmacy law

P Weedle, F Crean and L Clarke

The regulation of dealings with medicinal products and drugs is currently achieved by the interplay of an array of complex enactments. The need for such regulation is eloquently expressed by the learned authors of *Bell and O'Keefe's Sale of Food and Drugs*,[1] who stated the following:

> The act of debasing a food or drug with the object of passing it off as genuine, or the substitution of an inferior article for a superior one to the detriment of the purchaser, whether done in fraud or in negligence, appears to be as old as trade. These practices, in an organized society, naturally lead to official suppressive action (by the twin needs to protect the purchaser and the honest trader) and in various forms such action has existed since the thirteenth century.

The provisions of the Misuse of Drugs Acts 1977 to 2006,[2] the Irish Medicines Board Acts 1995 and 2006,[3] the Animal Remedies Acts 1993 and 2006,[4] and the Pharmacy Act 2007 as amended[5] all have a role to play in the current regulatory regime. In addition, the research, manufacture, marketing, distribution and promotion of medicinal products are regulated

1. O'Keefe JA. *Bell and O'Keefe's Sale of Food and Drugs*, 14th edn. London: Butterworths, Shaw and Sons, 1968.
2. No. 12 of 1977 as amended by Misuse of Drugs Act 1984 (No. 18 of 1984) and by Irish Medicines Board (Miscellaneous) Provisions Act 2006 (No. 3 of 2006).
3. No. 29 of 1995 as amended by S.I. No. 304 of 2001, S.I. No. 444 of 2001, S.I. No. 576 of 2002, Act No. 3 of 2006 and S.I. No. 542 of 2007.
4. No. 23 of 1993 as amended by Irish Medicines Board (Miscellaneous) Provisions Act 2006 (No. 3 of 2006).
5. No. 20 of 2007 as amended by European Communities (Recognition of Professional Qualifications Relating to the Profession of Pharmacist) (No. 2) Regulations 2008 (S.I. No. 489 of 2008).

by European Union (EU) legislation, which has been implemented by various regulations and orders made under the European Communities Act 1972[6] and the Irish Medicines Board Acts.

While the manufacture, sale, supply and use of medicinal products are now subject to extensive regulation, this was not always the case. The proliferation of laws enacted to control medicinal products since the dawn of the twentieth century reflects to some extent the enormous increase in knowledge and understanding of the modes of action of medicinal products, their potential for good if used appropriately and their potential to cause grave harm if misused or abused.

In this chapter, the development of laws governing medicinal products in Ireland is outlined. It might be observed that these laws reflect a number of legislative aims such as:

a   to ensure the purity of drugs;
b   to raise revenue from the sale of drugs;
c   to prevent the misuse of drugs;
d   to protect the public;
e   to regulate the sale and supply of medicines.

Accordingly, a brief summary of the history of salient legislative developments governing the sale and supply of medicines is provided under these headings.

To ensure the purity of drugs

Up until 1800 there was considerable adulteration in foods and drugs commonly consumed. It was the duty of the Guilds to maintain the purity of the commodities with which their members dealt. The early history of regulation of quality of food and drugs is succinctly summarised by the authors of *Bell and O'Keefe's Sale of Food and Drugs* as follows:

> Anciently, pepper was highly valued and used to preserve meat and other foods. A Guild of Pepperers flourished in the reigns of Henry II and Henry III, and the Crown granted it the responsibility of garbling (i.e. sifting) spices. The garblers' duty was to detect and remove impurities for a fee. In 1429, the Grocers Company was incorporated and garblership was vested in its wardens. The garblers' powers were extended by various Acts between the reigns of Mary Tudor and William and Mary, until they dealt with the goods of grocers, confectioners, tobacconists, sugar refiners and (until 1617) druggists.

---

6. No. 27 of 1972 as amended.

In 1448 the Grocers' Company was empowered to inspect certain drugs that were offered for sale and was allowed to confiscate any adulterated samples.[7] As there were no chemical or microscopic techniques available, testing consisted of the viewing, tasting and smelling of the products. This role was taken over by the Society of Apothecaries in 1617.[8]

The Apothecary, Wares, Drugs and Stuffs Act 1540[9] was enacted after Henry VIII was persuaded by the physicians of the day that adulterated drugs were being sold and used by apothecaries.[10] Section 2 of the Act provided for the appointment of physicians to visit apothecaries' shops in London in order to inspect their 'Wares, Drugs and Stuffs' and destroy any adulterated medicines that were 'defective, corrupted and not meet nor convenient to be ministered for the Health of Man's Body'. The Act was amended in 1727 to allow representatives of the Society of Apothecaries to accompany the physicians.[11]

The Adulteration of Food and Drugs Act 1872[12] required local authorities to appoint persons 'possessing competent medical, chemical, and microscopical knowledge'[13] as analysts 'of all articles of food and drugs' purchased within the local authority's functional area. The Act did not specify standards for drugs nor did it specify standard methods for their analysis, but merely required the analysts to report the number of articles tested by them and to specify 'the nature and kind of adulterations detected in… drugs' to the local authority on a quarterly basis.[14] Sections 1 and 2 of the 1872 Act imposed penalties on persons who adulterated food or drugs and on those who sold adulterated food or drugs.

During the twentieth century, products derived from bacteria or from the endocrine organs of animals began to be used as medicines. Such products differed from other medicinal products used at the time in that they were required to be sterile but could not be heat sterilised. Furthermore, they had to be assayed by biological as opposed to chemical methods. The unfortunate consequences of the administration of defective batches made and used elsewhere resulted in the enactment of the Therapeutic Substances Act 1925[15] in

---

7. Ditchfield PH. *The City Companies of London and Their Good Works: A Record of Their History, Charity and Treasure*. London: JM Dent, 1904.
8. Chapman WSC. The Worshipful Society of Apothecaries of London 1617–1967. *BMJ* 1967; 4: 540–541.
9. 32 Hen. 8, c. 40.
10. Griffin JP. Venetian treacle and the foundation of medicines regulation. *Br J Clin Pharmacol* 2004; 58(3): 317–325.
11. Clark G. *History of the Royal College of Physicians*, Vol. 2. London: Clarendon Press, 1970, pp. 1704–1735.
12. 35 & 36 Vict., c. 74.
13. Section 5.
14. Section 7.
15. 15 & 16 Geo. 5, c. 60.

the United Kingdom and the Therapeutic Substances Act 1932[16] in Ireland. The object of these acts was to ensure that vaccines, sera, toxins, antitoxins and antigens were manufactured under appropriate conditions and tested to ensure quality, safety and efficacy prior to marketing. This aim was achieved by a licensing system which imposed very strict conditions on manufacturers and importers as regards manufacturing procedures, facilities, expert staff, testing and assay procedures. The licences required a product to be manufactured and tested in accordance with any conditions applicable to the product.

To raise revenue from the sale of drugs

In the seventeenth century, 'patent' medicines began to appear on the market.[17] Patented remedies gained respectability from association with ancient royal letters patent, granted to give an individual sole manufacturing rights for a unique product. To obtain the patent the ingredients of the remedy had to be declared. By contrast 'secret', branded or trademarked remedies could cloak their, often very ordinary, formulae in mystery by registering and protecting just the product's name.[18] The latter category was known as 'proprietary medicines'. In order to raise revenue from the sale of all such medicines, the Medicines Stamp Act 1802,[19] the Medicines Stamp Act 1804,[20] and the Medicines Stamp Act 1812[21] were enacted. Pursuant to the provisions of those acts, sellers of proprietary medicines required a licence[22] and a medicines stamp had to be attached to the container of the medicine when sold to show the tax had been paid.[23] The value of the stamp was related to the sale price of the medicine.

The categories of medicines subject to charge under the acts were:

- occult or secret remedies;
- proprietary remedies;
- patented remedies;
- remedies which in certain terms were 'held out or recommended to the public by the makers, vendors or proprietors thereof as nostrums or proprietary medicines, or as specifics, or as beneficial to the prevention, cure or relief of any distemper, malady, ailment or complaint incident to or in any way affecting the human body'.[24]

---

16. No. 25 of 1932.
17. Aronson JK. Patent medicines and secret remedies. *BMJ* 2009; 339: b5415.
18. Museum of the Royal Pharmaceutical Society of Great Britain, Information Sheet: 10, Patent and Brandname Medicines. My drops and my pills – will cure all your ills.
19. 42 Geo. 3, c. 56.
20. 44 Geo. 3, c. 98.
21. 52 Geo. 3, c. 150.
22. 42 Geo. 3, c. 56, Section 6.
23. 42 Geo. 3, c. 56, Section 11.
24. Schedule to the 1812 Act.

These acts facilitated the sale of proprietary medicines and substances recommended as beneficial for the cure or relief of any ailment affecting the human body by qualified and unqualified vendors. The requirement for medicines to be 'stamped' was challenged in a 1903 test case where it was held that, provided ingredients of medicines were disclosed so as to show they were known and approved medicines, they could be sold by chemists without affixing a stamp.[25] The Medicines Stamp Acts have long since been repealed but manifest the inception of legislative intervention to ensure that the sale and supply of drugs resulted in revenue to the State.

To prevent the misuse of drugs

Medicinal products have long been known to be liable to misuse and to be apt to cause serious harm if administered in excessive doses. The potential for use of medicinal products for criminal ends has been recognised by legislative bodies for many years. The Arsenic Act 1851[26] regulated the sale and supply of arsenic and arsenious compounds because, as the preamble to the act recognises, 'the unrestricted sale of arsenic facilitates the commission of crime'.

The Arsenic Act 1851 restricted the sale of arsenic in a number of ways. Arsenic could not be sold except to a purchaser who was known to the seller or in the presence of a witness known to both the seller and the purchaser.[27] Before they could be sold, arsenic and arsenious compounds had to be mixed with soot or indigo to prevent their later admixture with food[28] and all such transactions had to be recorded.[29] The sale of designated poisons was also restricted by various enactments. For example, under Section 30 of the Pharmacy Act (Ireland) 1875,[30] poisons could only be sold by pharmaceutical chemists registered under that act.

The Dangerous Drugs Act 1920 was enacted to control the possession and use of addictive drugs such as cocaine and raw and prepared opium.[31] The sale and dispensing of these substances was already controlled because they were classed as poisons. The 1920 Act required the keeping of records of sales and supplies of these drugs by pharmacists, doctors, dentists and veterinarians and also prohibited their sale or supply except on prescription. Their manufacture, import and export were similarly strictly controlled by a licensing system established under the provisions of the act. The Dangerous Drugs Act

---

25. *Farmer* v. *Glyn-Jones* [1903] 2 K.B. 6.
26. 15 & 15 Vict. c. 3.
27. Section 2.
28. Section 3.
29. Section 2.
30. 38 & 39 Vict., c. 57.
31. 10 & 11 Geo. 5, c. 46.

1920 was repealed by the Dangerous Drugs Act 1934, which remained in force until the Misuse of Drugs Act 1977 was enacted.

To protect the public

Notwithstanding the tremendous advances that have been made in the treatment and management of diseases, there are ailments which remain incurable. It would appear that the public has always been susceptible to claims made by vendors of medicinal products regarding the potential benefits associated with their consumption.

In 1912, the British Medical Association began a campaign to control the sale and advertising of proprietary medicines and published some startling facts about their composition and efficacy.[32] The House of Commons set up the Select Committee on Patent Medicines in April 1912, and directed it to study the situation with regard to medicines and medical appliances, including advertisements of same, and to report any amendments to the law which were necessary or desirable. The committee took evidence from various bodies such as the Pharmaceutical Society of Great Britain and the British Medical Association in the course of its deliberations.[33]

The select committee summarised the situation regarding legal controls over the sale and advertisement of patent medicines as follows:[34]

> For all practical purposes British law is powerless to prevent any person from procuring any drug, or making any mixture, whether potent or without any therapeutical activity whatever (so long as it does not contain any scheduled poison), advertising it in any decent terms as a cure for any disease or ailment, recommending it by bogus testimonials and the invented opinions and facsimile signatures of fictitious physicians, and selling it under any name he chooses, on the payment of a small stamp duty, for any price he can persuade a credulous public to pay.

At that time there was a large and rapidly growing market for the various types of remedies available, as was shown by the revenue collected. The income from stamp duties in respect of the sale of such remedies was £327 856 in 1912; £328 318 in 1913; and £360 376 in 1914.[35] The select

---

32. British Medical Association. *More Secret Remedies: what they cost and what they contain.* London: BMA, 1912.
33. Turner ES. *The Shocking History of Advertising.* London: Michael Joseph, 1952, pp. 142–176.
34. Secret Remedies: Report of the Select Committee. *BMJ* 1914; 2: 404–405.
35. Report from the Select Committee on Patent Medicines. House of Commons paper 414, 1914.

committee reported that advertising was often the major cost in the production of these remedies.

The Medicines Stamp Acts which facilitated the marketing of secret and proprietary medicines have long since been repealed. The select committee's concerns regarding misleading advertising have also been addressed. Such practices now attract the scrutiny of the Consumer Protection Act 2007. In Ireland, specific legislative controls on the advertising of medicines first came into place in 1958.[36]

To regulate the sale and supply of medicines

The profession of pharmacy as it is currently constituted has evolved from a number of related disciplines. Over the centuries, medicines were being compounded and dispensed by apothecaries and by chemists before the inception of the profession of pharmaceutical chemists. Though a full history of the evolution of the pharmacy profession is outside the scope of this work, some of the salient developments are recorded below. In broad terms, the earliest antecedent of the modern pharmacist was the apothecary. Over time, the role of apothecaries developed and they were recognised to possess a broad range of clinical skills in addition to their expertise in compounding and dispensing medicines. Chemists and druggists, whose role was confined to the compounding and supply of medicines, emerged some time later. It will be seen that the role fulfilled by pharmacists in modern times has expanded considerably on the duties formerly carried out by chemists and druggists.

The Society of Apothecaries was incorporated by Royal Charter in 1617[37] as 'the Master, Wardens, and Society of the Art and Mystery of Apothecaries in the City of London'. An apothecary in former times was a compounder of prescriptions, that being, in the view of the legislature, his most important function.[38] Subsequently, apothecaries became known as persons who professed to diagnose internal disease by its symptoms and applied themselves to cure such disease by medicine.[39] Gradually, the right of apothecaries to attend patients and to diagnose and treat their diseases was recognised by the law. Indeed, the preamble to the Exemptions of Apothecaries Act 1694[40] suggests that it was at that time part of the duty of an apothecary to attend and advise the sick as well as make up and sell medicines.

The Governor and Company of the Apothecaries' Hall of the city of Dublin were incorporated by the Apothecaries' Hall Act 1791,[41] an act of

---

36. Medical Preparations (Advertisement and Sale) Regulations 1958 (S.I. No. 135 of 1958).
37. See www.apothecaries.org (accessed 1 March 2011).
38. *Apothecaries' Co. v. Warburton* (1819) 3 B. & Ald. 40, p. 43.
39. *Apothecaries' Co. v. Lotinya* (1843) 2 Mood. & R. 495.
40. 6 & 7 Will. & Mar., c. 4.
41. 31 Geo. 3, c. 34.

the Parliament in Ireland to regulate practice of and entry into the profession of apothecaries in Ireland. That act also established the Apothecaries' Hall in Dublin and provided for the regulation of the profession. Attempts to separate the practice of pharmacy from medicine were made from early in the seventeenth century. Apothecaries and barber surgeons joined together to introduce apprenticeship as a method of training under the aegis of the Guild of St Mary Magdalene.[42] They practised medicine and compounded and dispensed prescriptions written by physicians.

In *Attorney General (at the relation of the King and Queen's College of Physicians in Ireland)* v. *The Governor and Company of the Apothecaries' Hall*,[43] the College of Physicians attempted to restrain the Apothecaries' Hall from joining in holding a qualifying examination in medicine jointly with the College of Surgeons. It was held that the Apothecaries' Hall was a medical corporation, capable of granting a diploma in medicine within the meaning of the Medical Act 1866.[44]

Whereas an apothecary selected the medicines and determined what ought to be given, a chemist sold medicines which were asked for.[45] A chemist could prepare and sell, but could not prescribe nor administer medicine.[46]

The Pharmaceutical Society of Ireland was established by the Pharmacy Act (Ireland) 1875 which provided for a Council to manage the affairs of the Society. The need for the Act, as recited in the preamble, was as follows:

> And whereas a great deficiency exists throughout Ireland of establishments and shops for the sale of medicines and compounding of prescriptions, and great inconvenience thereby arises to the public in many parts of the country.

> And whereas to remedy such inconvenience it is expedient to amend the Act of 1791, and to enable persons who, although they do not desire to practise the art and mystery of an apothecary, desire and are qualified to open shop for the retailing, dispensing, and compounding of poisons and medical prescriptions, to keep open shop for the purposes aforesaid.

The 1875 Act also provided for the registration of pharmaceutical chemists and prescribed the qualifications necessary to be registered as such. Pharmaceutical chemists were legally entitled to keep open shop for the retailing, dispensing and compounding of poisons and medical preparations

---

42. McNee J. Barber-surgeons in Great Britain and Ireland. Thomas Vicary lecture delivered at the Royal College of Surgeons of England, 1958.
43. (1888) 21 L.R. Ir. 253.
44. 49 & 50 Vict., c. 48.
45. *Apothecaries' Co.* v. *Lotinya* (1843) 2 Mood. & R. 495, 500.
46. *Allison* v. *Haydon* (1826) 4 Bing. 619, 621.

pursuant to Section 30 of the 1875 Act. The Pharmacy Act (Ireland) 1875 (Amendment) Act 1890[47] provided for the registration of druggists who were entitled to mix and sell poisons, but not to dispense or compound prescriptions. Under the Pharmacy Act 1951,[48] a register of dispensing chemists and druggists was established. Although a register of druggists is maintained by the Pharmaceutical Society of Ireland established under the Pharmacy Act 2007, druggists have not been trained in the State for many years and that profession is now all but extinct.

From the 1960s to the present day

Two developments provided the stimulus for the major changes in the law governing medicinal products in the 1960s and have played a key role in the evolution of the regulatory system that currently applies to such products in Ireland.

First, the thalidomide disaster focused attention on the lack of safeguards in relation to the marketing of medicines and led the World Health Organization to recommend in the early 1960s that a central agency be established in each country to monitor drug usage. This resulted in the establishment of the National Drugs Advisory Board (NDAB) in Ireland in 1966 to handle various matters relating to drug safety, including collection, assessment and dissemination of adverse reaction reports, obtaining and assessing information about the safety of new and reformulated drugs and advising the Minister for Health on controls on the sale and supply of medicines.[49]

The regulation of medicines also became an important issue for the European Economic Community (EEC) (now the European Union or EU) during the 1960s as it recognised that harmonising standards was an essential step towards achieving a single market in pharmaceuticals. It was also intended that the increasing level of harmonisation would ensure the highest possible degree of protection of public health.

The first 'framework' Directive 65/65/EEC was adopted in response to both of these developments. Its objectives were to set out rules to safeguard public health concerning the production and distribution of medicinal products, to attain this by means that did not hinder the pharmaceutical industry, and to eliminate disparities which affected the internal market in the Community. Directive 65/65/EEC laid down the basic principle that certain minimum controls, including prior authorisation, should apply to medicinal products placed on the market anywhere in the Community. It established a framework of pharmaceutical regulation and defined the products to which it

---

47. 53 & 54 Vict., c. 48.
48. No. 30 of 1951.
49. The National Drugs Advisory Board (Establishment) Order 1966 (S.I. No. 163 of 1966).

applied by providing a definition of the term 'medicinal product'. This was followed by further directives in 1975,[50] which introduced specific requirements regarding the testing of medicinal products in order to establish their efficacy, safety and quality; established the Committee for Proprietary Medicinal Products (CPMP) comprising scientific experts from all member states; established a multistate procedure to enable member states to cooperate in the assessment of applications for marketing authorisation in more than one member state; and introduced the requirement for manufacturers of medical products to be licensed.

A voluntary licensing system for medicines that had been introduced for medicines in Ireland in December 1967 became mandatory with the passing of the European Communities (Proprietary Medicinal Products) Regulations 1975.[51] Around the same time, national licensing systems for manufacturers and wholesalers of medicines were introduced.[52]

Technological developments, in particular in the area of biotechnology, resulted in a new range of pharmaceutical products which all member states were struggling to evaluate by the mid-1980s. In response, a mandatory Community procedure, known as the concertation procedure, was established,[53] whereby the CPMP agreed a common position on applications for such products prior to the granting of a marketing authorisation by individual member states.

In the late 1980s, the pace of harmonisation of EU pharmaceutical legislation picked up as the Community's 1992 deadline for completion of the single market loomed. Products such as immunologicals (vaccines, toxins, serums, allergens), radiopharmaceuticals, and blood and plasma products, which were initially exempted from the provisions of European rules, were brought within the definition of medicinal product by the 1989 'extension directives' (Directive 89/342/EEC, Directive 89/343/EEC and Directive 89/381/EEC, respectively). Homeopathic medicines were incorporated by Directive 92/73/EEC.

The 1992 'rational use' package of directives focused on areas not previously regulated at EU level: wholesaling, legal classification, labelling and package leaflets, and advertising of medicinal products.[54]

The next stage of development of the EU regulatory system was the establishment of the European Agency for the Evaluation of Medicinal Products,

---

50. Directive 75/318/EEC and Directive 75/319/EEC.
51. S.I. No. 301 of 1975.
52. Medical Preparations (Licensing of Manufacture) Regulations 1974 (S.I. No. 225 of 1974) and Medical Preparations (Wholesale Licences) Regulations 1974 (S.I. No. 333 of 1974).
53. Directive 87/22/EEC.
54. Respectively Directive 92/25/EEC, 92/26/EEC, 92/27/EEC and 92/28/EEC.

now known as the European Medicines Agency (EMA), in London in 1995.[55] In tandem, the concertation and multistate procedures were replaced with two significantly more streamlined procedures: the centralised procedure and the mutual recognition procedure[56] (see Chapter 4, Placing medicines on the market, for details.)

In Ireland, the NDAB was replaced by the Irish Medicines Board (IMB) in 1996. The main difference between the two organisations was that the IMB was empowered to grant product authorisations and manufacturing and wholesaling licences, a role which was previously undertaken by the Minister for Health acting on the advice of the NDAB and was empowered to raise revenue by charging fees for such activities. The IMB also assumed responsibility for the authorisation of most animal remedies from the Minister for Agriculture.

The focus of the EU's regulatory efforts in recent years has been on streamlining the regulatory system to enhance access for European patients to new medicines, to guarantee a high level of health protection for European citizens, and to complete the internal market for pharmaceutical products in a context that favours the competitiveness of the European pharmaceutical industry and meets the needs of globalisation. To this end, the majority of pharmaceutical directives were consolidated in 2001 into two 'codified directives' relating to human medicines (Directive 2001/83/EC) and veterinary medicines (Directive 2001/82/EC) respectively and in 2004, a package of measures[57] was adopted to update the EU's pharmaceutical legislation.

Special efforts have also been made to address the needs of particular groups of patients such as children and those with rare diseases, with the passing of the paediatric medicines regulation[58] and the orphan medicines regulation.[59] More recently the EU has adopted legislation to regulate new advanced therapies based on cells, tissues and genes.[60]

In tandem, there has been a growing focus on the safety of medicines and particular efforts to enhance pharmacovigilance across the region, which was a key focus of the 2004 review. The pharmacovigilance system will be further strengthened when additional EU legislation adopted in November 2010

---

55. Regulation (EEC) No. 2309/93 of 22 July 1993 laying down Community procedures for the authorisation and supervision of medicinal products for human and veterinary use and establishing a European Agency for the Evaluation of Medicinal Products.
56. Directive 93/39/EEC of 14 June 1993 amending Directive 65/65/EEC, Directive 75/318/EEC and Directive 75/319/EEC in respect of medicinal products.
57. Directives 2004/24/EC and 2004/27/EC amending Directive 2001/83/EC, Directive 2004/28/EC amending Directive 2001/82/EC and Regulation (EC) No. 726/2004 which replaced Regulation (EEC) No. 2309/93.
58. Regulation (EC) No. 1901/2006.
59. Regulation (EC) No. 141/2000.
60. Regulation (EC) No. 1394/2007.

comes into operation in July 2012.[61] Two directives have been adopted to harmonise the requirements for clinical trials in all the member states.[62]

At the time of writing, proposals to address information to patients about prescription medicines and the problem of counterfeit medicines are also being considered at EU level.

These regulations, the codified directives and all other EU legislation on human and veterinary medicines, are published by the European Commission in Volume 1 (Human Medicines) and Volume 5 (Veterinary Medicines) of *The Rules Governing Medicinal Products in the European Union* which is modified periodically to account for updates in the legislation. This and other volumes of the same series are available on the Commission's website.[63]

The role and functions of the IMB have also expanded in recent years and in addition to medicinal products for human and veterinary use, it is now the competent authority for medical devices, blood and blood components and also for tissues and cells. It is also responsible for the authorisation of clinical trials conducted in Ireland[64] and was recently designated as the competent authority for cosmetics.[65] It currently carries out various licensing functions in relation to controlled drugs on behalf of the Minister for Health and Children.[66]

Not all legislation relating to medicinal products in Ireland has its origins in EU directives; for example the Misuse of Drugs Acts and Regulations largely have their basis in United Nations (UN) conventions. However, Ireland, like all other EU member states, is obliged under the Technical Standards Directive 98/34/EC (as amended by Directive 98/48/EC) to notify technical regulations of this nature to the European Commission in draft and then wait for at least three months before adopting the regulation, in order to allow other member states and the Commission an opportunity to raise concerns about potential barriers to trade. An 'emergency procedure' applies where, for defined urgent reasons, e.g. protection of public health or safety, a member state is obliged to prepare regulations in a very short space of time in order to enact and introduce them immediately, without any consultations being possible. This emergency procedure was availed of by the Government when it passed legislation in May 2010 to bring within the remit of the Misuse of Drugs Acts substances with psychoactive effects (known as 'legal highs')

---

61. Regulation (EU) No. 1235/2010 and Directive 2010/84/EU.
62. Clinical Trial Directive 2001/20/EC and Good Clinical Practice Directive 2005/28/EC.
63. See http://ec.europa.eu/health/documents/eudralex/index_en.htm (accessed 1 March 2011).
64. European Communities (Clinical Trials on Medicinal Products for Human Use) Regulations 2004 to 2007 (S.I. No. 190 of 2004 as amended by S.I. No. 878 of 2004, S.I. No. 374 of 2006 and S.I. No. 540 of 2007).
65. Irish Medicines Board (Miscellaneous Provisions) Act 2006 (Certain Provisions) Commencement Order 2010 (S.I. No. 441 of 2010).
66. See www.imb.ie (accessed 1 March 2011).

that had previously been legally sold from 'head shops'. The Commission agreed that the legislation in question could be implemented without the need to await the expiry of the three-month period (see Chapter 8, Misuse of drugs acts and regulations, for further details).

It is noteworthy that the term 'medical preparation' as originally defined in the Health Act 1947 as amended[67] continued to be used in Ireland until the mid-1990s, even though the concept of a 'medicinal product' was used in EEC/EU legislation since the 1960s. The two terms were defined in similar but not identical terms. This anomaly was resolved when the Irish Medicines Board Act 1995 repealed the Health Act 1947 insofar as it defined medical preparations and introduced the concept of medicinal product as defined in EU legislation. Section 32 of the Irish Medicines Board Act gives the Minister for Health and Children extensive powers to make regulations to regulate the manufacture, production, preparation, importation, distribution, sale, supply, placing on the market, advertisement or promotion of medicinal products. Since 1995, several regulations relating to medicinal products have been made under Section 32, primarily to implement relevant EU directives in Irish law.

In the sphere of pharmacy, a major milestone was achieved with the passing of the Pharmacy Act 2007, the first significant overhaul of pharmacy legislation in 130 years. It introduced new standards of governance, fitness to practise and registration for pharmacists and pharmacies, with the emphasis on having a modern, accountable and efficient system of regulation. Many other health professions in Ireland have or are about to have a new statutory framework for the same reasons, including doctors,[68] allied health professionals (e.g. physiotherapists, occupational therapists, social workers[69]), and nurses and midwives.[70]

---

67. Section 65 of No. 28 of 1947 as amended by Section 7 of Health (Family Planning) (Amendment) Act 1992 (No. 20 of 1992).
68. Medical Practitioners Act 2007 (No. 25 of 2007).
69. Health and Social Care Professionals Act 2005 (No. 27 of 2005).
70. Nurses and Midwives Bill 2010 (No. 16 of 2010).

4

Placing medicines on the market

L Clarke and JM Morris

The legal framework in relation to placing medicinal products on the market in the European Union (EU) is highly complex. The key pieces of legislation are Regulation (EC) No. 726/2004 as amended[1] which deals with centrally authorised medicinal products and the operation of the European Medicines Agency (EMA), and Directive 2001/83/EC as amended,[2] which focuses on nationally authorised medicinal products (including those authorised through the mutual recognition and decentralised systems). This legislation is supported by a wide range of EU guidance documents.

EU legislation relating to medicinal products is published by the European Commission in Volume 1 of *The Rules Governing Medicinal Products in the European Union*, which is modified periodically to account for updates in the legislation. This and other volumes of the same series are available on the Commission website.[3]

Like all other EU regulations, Regulation (EC) No. 726/2004 as amended is directly applicable throughout the EU, including Ireland. The provisions of Directive 2001/83/EC as amended as they relate to placing medicines on the market and related topics such as labels and leaflets, supply classification and

1. Regulation (EC) No. 726/2004 of the European Parliament and of the Council of 31 March 2004 laying down Community procedures for the authorisation and supervision of medicinal products for human and veterinary use and establishing a European Medicines Agency, as amended (Consolidated version dated 20.4.2009).
2. Directive 2001/83/EC of the European Parliament and of the Council of 6 November 2001 on the Community code relating to medicinal products for human use as amended by Directive 2002/98/EC, Directive 2003/63/EC, Directive 2004/24/EC, Directive 2004/27/EC, Directive 2008/29/EC, Directive 2009/53/EC, Directive 2009/120/EC, Regulation (EC) No. 1901/2006 and Regulation (EC) No. 1394/2007.
3. http://ec.europa.eu/health/documents/eudralex/vol-1/index_en.htm (accessed 1 March 2011).

pharmacovigilance, are implemented in Irish law by the Medicinal Products (Control of Placing on the Market) Regulations 2007 as amended (the 'Control of Placing on the Market Regulations').[4]

This chapter focuses primarily on the content of the Control of Placing on the Market Regulations. Those regulations extensively cross refer to Directive 2001/83/EC as amended and, where necessary, the relevant provisions of the directive are discussed. A summary of the different routes by which medicines may be authorised in Europe is provided for the information of the reader, but it is beyond the scope of this chapter to analyse the EU regulatory framework in detail.

The chapter concludes with a brief overview of the role of the pharmacopoeias and the European Directorate for the Quality of Medicines & HealthCare in the quality control of medicines in Europe.

Key definitions and terms

A 'medicinal product' is defined as (a) any substance or combination of substances presented as having properties for treating or preventing disease in human beings; or (b) any substance or combination of substances which may be used in or administered to human beings either with a view to restoring, correcting or modifying physiological functions by exerting a pharmacological, immunological or metabolic action, or to making a medical diagnosis.[5] The Control of Placing on the Market Regulations and Directive 2001/83/EC as amended deal with human medicinal products only. Related products intended for use in humans such as medical devices, cosmetics, foods (e.g. food supplements containing vitamins) and biocides, are subject to parallel systems of regulation under EU law. The question of which category certain products fall into may often be a matter for interpretation; such products are commonly known as 'borderline products'. Directive 2001/83/EC as amended states that in the case of doubt as to whether a product is deemed to be a medicinal product or falls into another category, then the default position is that it is classified as a medicinal product.[6]

The term 'competent authority' is used to denote the body assigned responsibility at national level for the discharge of the responsibilities assigned to the competent authority in the relevant EU legislation. The Irish Medicines Board (IMB) is the designated competent authority in Ireland for medicinal products insofar as Directive 2001/83/EC as amended is concerned.

---

4. S.I. No. 540 of 2007 (Copyright Houses of the Oireachtas 2007) as amended by S.I. No. 3 of 2009 (Copyright Houses of the Oireachtas 2009) and S.I. No. 287 of 2010 (Copyright Houses of the Oireachtas 2010).
5. Article 1 of Directive 2001/83/EC as amended.
6. Article 2.2.

It should also be noted that certain functions of the member state as provided for in that directive are also assigned to the IMB as the competent authority in Ireland. Certain other functions have been retained by the Minister for Health and Children, including the right to authorise the use of unlicensed medicines in an emergency situation.[7]

Bodies such as the IMB are sometimes called 'regulatory authorities' or 'national authorities', although these terms are not defined in national or EU medicines legislation.

The 'European Economic Area (EEA)' was established on 1 January 1994 following an agreement between the member states of the European Free Trade Association (EFTA) and the European Community (later the EU). Specifically, it allows Iceland, Liechtenstein and Norway to participate in Europe's single market without having to join the EU. In exchange, they are obliged to adopt certain EU internal market legislation.

The term 'member state' is used to denote any country that is a member of the EEA. 'Third country' is used to denote any country which is not an EEA state.

Registration systems for medicines in Europe

Within the EU, medicines may be authorised either in one member state only, through the national authorisation procedure of that country, or in more than one member state simultaneously, through one of three procedures: the centralised procedure, the mutual recognition procedure, or the decentralised procedure.

The centralised procedure is compulsory for human medicinal products derived from biotechnology, for orphan and advanced therapy medicinal products and for all new medicines for the treatment of AIDS, cancer, neurodegenerative disorders, diabetes, autoimmune disorders and viral diseases. It is optional for other human medicinal products containing new active substances not authorised in the EU before 20 May 2004 or for products which constitute a significant therapeutic, scientific or technical innovation or for which a community marketing authorisation is in the interests of patients at EU level. Applications for authorisation via this route are made directly to the EMA which is located in London. The scientific assessment in relation to human medicines is undertaken by the Committee for Medicinal Products for Human Use (CHMP), which comprises experts from regulatory authorities in all the member states and operates under the auspices of the EMA. When the CHMP has issued a positive opinion on the application and a further short consultation has been completed with all member states, a single marketing authorisation is issued by the European Commission which is binding

---

7. Regulation 5, Control of Placing on the Market Regulations.

throughout the EEA. The CHMP's assessment report is published as the European Public Assessment Report (EPAR) on the EMA's website.[8]

All other medicinal products intended to be marketed in more than one member state must be authorised via the mutual recognition procedure or the decentralised procedure. The details of how these procedures operate are set out in Directive 2001/83/EC as amended and the Control of Placing on the Market Regulations provide the legal basis for their implementation in Ireland.

The mutual recognition procedure is based on the principle of recognition by one or more member states of a national marketing authorisation previously granted by another member state. Since 1 January 1998, the mutual recognition procedure is compulsory for any medicinal product to be marketed in a member state other than that in which it was first authorised. Any national marketing authorisation granted by an EU member state's national authority can be used to support an application for its mutual recognition by other member states.

The decentralised procedure is used when a product is being placed on the market in any EU member state for the first time. Through this procedure, an application for the marketing authorisation of a medicinal product is submitted simultaneously in two or more member states, one of which undertakes the assessment on behalf of the others who have an input prior to the application being finalised.

With both procedures, a separate marketing authorisation is granted in each of the relevant member states.

If a company wishes to market a product in only one member state, the option remains to apply to the competent authority in that member state for a national marketing authorisation.

The changes in the European registration systems are manifesting themselves in every member state including Ireland. Increasingly, the focus of national regulatory authorities is shifting from national to European activities, as the new system relies heavily on utilising the expertise available within those authorities. The new systems have posed considerable challenges for regulators and industry alike, and significant efforts have been undertaken by both groups separately and jointly to ensure that the procedures work smoothly and that there is consistency in decision making. The main drawback has been a loss of flexibility and autonomy at national level, but this has been offset by a significant reduction in the duplication of effort in assessing applications for marketing authorisations throughout the EU and faster access by European patients to new medicines.

---

8. www.ema.europa.eu (accessed 1 March 2011).

Requirement for medicinal products to be licensed

A medicinal product cannot be placed on the market in Ireland unless it has a marketing authorisation (granted by the IMB), a community marketing authorisation (granted by the European Commission), or a certificate of registration or a certificate of traditional-use registration (granted by the IMB).[9]

Similarly, a person in the course of a business cannot sell, supply, manufacture or procure the sale, supply or manufacture or have in his or her possession, a medicinal product unless he or she reasonably believes that it has been or is intended to be placed on the market on foot of a marketing authorisation or certificate as described in the previous paragraph, or is intended to be placed in the market in another EEA state on foot of equivalent licensing provisions in that State. This requirement does not apply to products intended for export to a third country.[10]

Marketing authorisations may be granted by the IMB or by the European Commission. In the latter case, they are known as community marketing authorisations and the marketing authorisation number will be in the format: EU/1/10/111/001. The term 'product authorisation' or 'PA' is used to denote marketing authorisations granted by the IMB, with the number format 'PA11/11/1'. It is important to note that the marketing/product authorisation granted by the IMB is the same legal document irrespective of whether the application was considered under the mutual recognition or decentralised procedure or assessed by the IMB purely as a 'national' application. The equivalent term to 'PA' in the UK is 'product licence' or PL. Products which have a marketing authorisation are commonly described as having been 'authorised' or 'licensed'. The marketing authorisation category includes parallel import licences[10] (see section on Parallel imports).

Certificates of traditional-use registration are granted in respect of traditional-use herbal medicinal products that have undergone a simplified registration procedure (see below).

Certificates of registration are granted in respect of homeopathic medicinal products that have undergone a simplified registration procedure (see below).

Herbal medicines

There are two options available in relation to placing herbal medicinal products on the market. An application may be submitted for a marketing authorisation based on the submission of the standard dossier of data confirming quality, safety and efficacy for the proposed indications. In the case of traditional herbal medicinal products, application may be made

---

9. Regulation 6, Control of Placing on the Market Regulations.
10. Regulations 6(2) and 6(3), Control of Placing on the Market Regulations.

instead for a certificate of traditional-use registration instead. Under this procedure, the standard proof of efficacy for medicinal products (e.g. large-scale clinical trials) does not apply. Instead, sufficient data regarding the traditional use of the product for the proposed indication must be provided to show that the product is not harmful in the specified conditions of use, and that the pharmacological effects and claims of efficacy are plausible on the basis of longstanding use and experience. This registration procedure is only open to herbal medicines intended for oral use, external use and/or inhalation, without medical prescription or supervision. In terms of verifying the traditional use of the product for the proposed indication, the product must have been so used anywhere in the world for at least 30 years prior to the application for the certificate and within the EU for at least 15 years.[11] Products registered through this procedure are confined to certain minor indications which do not require medical diagnosis and supervision.

Homeopathic medicines

There are three different ways in which homeopathic medicinal products may be approved for sale or supply in Ireland:

i   An application may be submitted for a marketing authorisation based on the submission of the standard dossier of data confirming quality, safety and efficacy for the proposed indications;

ii Application may be made for marketing authorisation under the 'national procedure for authorisation of homeopathic medicinal products'. This is operated by the IMB as the 'homeopathic medicinal products national rules scheme' and the data requirements for proof of efficacy and safety are not so stringent in that preclinical and clinical data are not mandatory. This procedure is only open to products that are typically used in homeopathy in Ireland and which do not require medical prescription or supervision. The proposed indication(s) must be appropriate to such a homeopathic medicinal product. Efficacy is established on the basis of evidence that the particular class of homeopathic medicinal product has been in use in the State as a homeopathic medicine for the indication sought. Safety is assessed with reference to published literature or original data (if available) and the degree of dilution of the product. Additional labelling requirements apply to products authorised via this route, for example, they must state that evidence of efficacy is not based on the outcome of clinical trials and must

---

11. Article 16a–16i of Directive 2001/83/EC as amended.

advise the user to consult a doctor or other healthcare professional if symptoms persist;[12]

iii The applicant may apply for a certificate of registration under a special simplified registration procedure. Under this procedure, there is no requirement to submit data to prove efficacy but, in turn, no indications for use may appear on the product's label or leaflet. This procedure is only open to homeopathic medicines intended for oral or external use and which have a sufficient degree of dilution to guarantee safety.[13] Such products must not make any medicinal claims and are not marketed under a 'brand name'.

Use of unauthorised medicines on temporary authorisation of the Minister

The Minister for Health and Children may temporarily authorise the distribution of an unauthorised medicine in response to the suspected or confirmed spread of pathogenic agents, toxins, chemical agents or nuclear radiation, which could cause harm. The regulations give specific immunity from liability that might result from the use of such products to the marketing authorisation holder and the manufacturer or anyone acting on their behalf, and also to healthcare professionals. Liability for defective products is unaffected by this provision.[14]

Exemptions from requirement for products to be licensed

The requirement for products to be licensed does not apply to:[15]

a investigational medicinal products (see section on Clinical Trials for further information);

b the sale or supply of a medicinal product in accordance with any exception or exemption set out in Directive 2001/83/EC as amended;

c the importation of a medicinal product from outside the EEA by a person for his or her own personal use, other than on a mail order basis;

d the sale or supply of an 'exempt medicinal product' (i.e. the sale or supply of an unauthorised product, in response to a *bona fide* unsolicited order, formulated in accordance with the specification of a registered medical practitioner or registered dentist for use by his or her individual patients under his or her direct responsibility in order to fulfil the special needs of

---

12. Regulation 11, Control of Placing on the Market Regulations.
13. Article 14 of Directive 2001/83/EC as amended.
14. Regulation 8, Control of Placing on the Market Regulations.
15. Schedule 1, paragraphs 1–6, Control of Placing on the Market Regulations.

those patients). A number of conditions apply, for example, the product must be supplied to a practitioner or for use in a pharmacy under the supervision of a pharmacist. Advertisements for such products may only include the trade name, pack size, price and dose. If manufactured in the State, the manufacturer's authorisation must specifically permit the manufacture of such products;

e   a registered medical practitioner or registered dentist preparing or procuring the manufacture of a stock of medicinal product for administration to one or more of his or her patients. The maximum amount of stock covered by this exemption is 3 litres of fluids or 1 kg of solids;

f   any activities in a pharmacy in relation to procuring the manufacture of a stock of medicinal products with a view to dispensing them as 'exempt medicinal products'. All such activities must be conducted by or under the supervision of a pharmacist;

g   the supply of non-prescription medicines to a person exclusively for use in the course of his or her business for the purpose of administration to one or more human beings, other than by selling it;

h   the preparation of a medicinal product that is a radiopharmaceutical at the time at which it is intended to be administered, by or under the responsibility of the person by whom it is to be administered, in accordance with the manufacturer's instructions, exclusively from an authorised kit, generator or precursor in an establishment that is licensed by the Radiological Protection Institute of Ireland to use such products.

A person who sells or supplies a medicinal product in accordance with any of paragraphs (d) to (h) shall maintain, and keep for a period of at least five years, records detailing:

a   the source from which that person obtained the product;
b   the person to whom, and the date on which, the sale or supply was made;
c   the quantity of each sale or supply;
d   the batch number of the batch of that product from which the sale or supply was made;
e   details of any suspected adverse reaction to the product of which he or she is aware.

He or she must make these records available for inspection at all reasonable times by the IMB and notify the IMB of any serious suspected adverse reaction of which he or she is aware in relation to such products.[16]

---

16. Schedule 1, paragraphs 7 and 8, Control of Placing on the Market Regulations.

Overview of licensing process

Within the EU, all medicines must fulfil specific scientific requirements before they can be authorised for sale. As part of the marketing authorisation application process, the applicant company must provide evidence that the medicine adheres to clear and predefined standards of quality, safety and efficacy, relevant to its proposed therapeutic use. This takes the form of a dossier including details of all trials and studies undertaken of the drug substance and the final pharmaceutical product, including preclinical studies, clinical trials and manufacturing and analysis data. The format of the dossier and the type of data to be submitted is set out in Directive 2001/83/EC as amended and various EU guidelines. The Control of Placing on the Market Regulations set out the administrative requirements for applications to the IMB for a marketing authorisation in Ireland[17] and the procedure to be followed by the IMB in assessing such applications, including the steps to be taken if it proposes to refuse an application or grant it other than in accordance with the application. The IMB is required to provide its reasons in writing to the applicant in that instance.[18]

Approval is given on the basis of a favourable benefit versus risk balance for specific therapeutic indication(s) having regard to the quality, safety and efficacy of the product for the proposed conditions of use.[19] The IMB approves the final wording of the summary of product characteristics (SmPC) and wording and appearance of the product label and package leaflets.

The IMB may refuse to grant a market authorisation outright. More commonly, it will grant a different marketing authorisation to what was applied for with, for example, fewer or more restricted indications than those sought by the company, different precautions and warnings etc. Post-authorisation obligations or conditions may be imposed on the applicant, such as the requirement to undertake post-marketing studies to further investigate the safety of the product in particular groups of patients or to undertake longer term stability studies of the finished product.[20]

The marketing authorisation document issued by the IMB states the marketing authorisation number, the date on which the authorisation was granted or last renewed, the name and address of the marketing authorisation holder, the names and addresses of all manufacturers of the product (including those involved in the intermediate stages of manufacture, e.g. tableting, packaging, etc.), the supply classification (e.g. prescription-only medicine), the method of promotion and incorporates the final approved SmPC.

---

17. Regulation 9.
18. Regulation 10 and Schedule 2.
19. Articles 17–26 of Directive 2001/83/EC as amended.
20. Regulation 10, Control of Placing on the Market Regulations.

A marketing authorisation or certificate is valid for a maximum of five years, after which the holder must apply to have it renewed. After one renewal, it remains valid indefinitely, unless the IMB decides that one further renewal after five years is justified on grounds of pharmacovigilance.[21]

Once a medicine has been granted a marketing authorisation or certificate, any changes (e.g. new indications, updated safety information, pharmaceutical changes) require approval by the IMB on foot of a formal application to vary the authorisation or certificate (a 'variation') and the submission of relevant supporting data. This usually involves a change to the content of the SmPC. In practice, SmPCs are updated regularly as new data comes to light from ongoing clinical trials and pharmacovigilance activities.

The IMB has the power to revoke or vary a marketing authorisation or certificate at the request of holder and also on its own initiative on justified grounds. Similarly, it may suspend an authorisation or certificate, suspend the marketing of a product and/or order the authorisation or certificate holder to recall the product.[22]

The IMB may also impose an 'urgent safety restriction' on the holder of an authorisation or certificate, which may take the form of an instruction to amend the SmPC, labels or leaflets, restrict the marketing of the product, etc. The authorisation or certificate holder is required to take whatever steps are necessary to comply with the urgent safety restriction, including applying to vary the authorisation or certificate, within 15 days of the urgent safety restriction being imposed.[23]

An authorisation or certificate ceases to be valid if the product to which it relates is not actually placed on the market in Ireland within three years from the date of grant of the authorisation or certificate. Similarly in the case of the products previously placed on the market, if they are no longer actually present on the market for a period of three consecutive years, the authorisation or certificate lapses. The IMB may in exceptional circumstances and on grounds of public health, grant exemptions to these requirements. Collectively, these provisions are known as the 'sunset clause'.[24]

Summary of product characteristics

The summary of product characteristics (often abbreviated to SmPC or SPC) is a legal document that is part of the marketing authorisation. An application for a marketing authorisation or certificate must include a draft SmPC, which outlines the proposed prescribing information (therapeutic use(s), dosage,

---

21. Regulation 10(3) and 10(5), Control of Placing on the Market Regulations.
22. Regulation 14, Control of Placing on the Market Regulations.
23. Regulation 13, Control of Placing on the Market Regulations.
24. Regulation 10(6)–10(8), Control of Placing on the Market Regulations.

safety in use, etc.), based on the applicant's analysis of the data submitted. This is evaluated by the IMB during the assessment process, along with the scientific data provided, and final marketing authorisation approval will be on the basis of a legally binding SmPC, which has been agreed between the applicant and the IMB.

The format of the SmPC is laid down in Directive 2001/83/EC as amended[25] and is the exactly the same for all medicines authorised in the EU:

1 name, form and strength;
2 composition: list and quantities of active ingredients. It is also necessary to list excipients, knowledge of which is essential for the correct administration of the product;
3 pharmaceutical form (e.g. tablet, capsule, solution for infusion);
4 clinical particulars:
    4.1 indications (what the product is to be used for);
    4.2 posology (dose) and method of administration for adults and, where necessary, children;
    4.3 contraindications (situations where the product must not be used in any circumstances);
    4.4 special precautions and warnings relating to the use of the product;
    4.5 interactions with other medicines and other interactions (e.g. interactions with alcohol, food, if any);
    4.6 use in pregnancy and lactation;
    4.7 effects on ability to drive and use machines;
    4.8 undesirable effects (frequency and seriousness);
    4.9 overdose (symptoms, antidotes, emergency procedures);
5 pharmacological properties:
    5.1 pharmacodynamics;
    5.2 pharmacokinetics;
    5.3 preclinical safety data (i.e. details of animal studies, toxicity studies);
6 pharmaceutical particulars:
    6.1 list of excipients;
    6.2 major incompatibilities (information on physical and chemical incompatibilities with other products likely to be administered simultaneously);
    6.3 shelf life (including shelf life after reconstitution if applicable);
    6.4 special precautions for storage;
    6.5 nature and contents of container;
    6.6 special precautions for disposal;
7 name and address of marketing authorisation holder;

---

25. Article 11.

8   marketing authorisation number;

9   date of first authorisation and last renewal of authorisation;

10   date of revision of the text (i.e. date of any variations to the SmPC since the marketing authorisation was originally granted or last renewed).

Labelling and package leaflets

There are many reasons why medicines have to be labelled with certain information, the most important being that the patient can use the medicine effectively and safely. Furthermore, labelling is vital to the identification of the product, thus ensuring that the pharmacist dispenses the right medicine on foot of a particular prescription and as a means of verifying what medication a patient is taking should the need arise.

As recently as the 1970s it was not unusual for patients to receive prescription medicines labelled with 'The Tablets – Take one tablet x times daily' or similar, on the basis that they wouldn't understand and didn't need to know what they were taking. As patient knowledge and power has grown, this has changed dramatically and detailed information must now appear on all medicines, both prescription and non-prescription.

The labelling requirements that apply to medicinal products placed on the market in Ireland are almost exclusively derived from EU legislation, specifically Directive 2001/83/EC as amended.[26] The Medicinal Products (Prescription and Control of Supply) Regulations 2003 as amended set out the additional labelling requirements that apply to dispensed medicines. These requirements are covered in detail in Chapter 7, Prescription and control of supply of medicines.

Regulation 16 of the Control of Placing on the Market Regulations refers to Directive 2001/83/EC as amended as the source of the detailed requirements that apply to labels and leaflets of medicinal products and makes it an offence to place on the market, sell, supply, offer or keep for sale any product that does not comply with those requirements. In addition, a package leaflet that also meets the requirements of Directive 2001/83/EC as amended must be provided unless all the information required to be included on the leaflet appears on the outer or immediate packaging.

The following information must appear on the label of a medicine:

a   name of the medicine followed by its pharmaceutical form and strength and, if appropriate, whether intended for adults, children, or babies. In the case of a product containing up to three active substances, the international non-proprietary name (INN) or common name must also be included;

---

26. Title V Labelling and Package Leaflet, Articles 54–69.

b   qualitative and quantitative details of active ingredients, using common names;
c   pharmaceutical form and contents by weight, volume or number of doses of the product;
d   list of those excipients with a recognised action or effect (all excipients must be listed in the case of injectable, topical or eye preparations);
e   method and, if necessary, route of administration. Space must be provided for the prescribed dose to be indicated;
f   warning to store the product out of the reach and sight of children;
g   any special warnings necessary for the product;
h   expiry date in clear terms (month/year);
i   special storage requirements, if any;
j   special precautions for disposal of the product, if any, as well as reference to any appropriate collection system in place;
k   name and address of marketing authorisation holder and, where applicable, his or her representative;
l   marketing authorisation number;
m   manufacturer's batch number;
n   instructions for use in the case of non-prescription medicines.

The above information must appear on the outer packaging or, where there is no outer packaging, on the immediate packaging. The label information must be clearly legible, easily comprehensible and indelible.

As part of the regulatory approval process, authorisation holders are required to submit label text and label artwork (in the form of mock-ups) for approval, and any changes made at a later date (change of text, fonts, layout, etc.) must be approved also.

In recognition of size constraints on smaller packaging, there are reduced labelling requirements for blister packs and other smaller packs (e.g. ampoules), provided they are supplied in outer packaging labelled with the full requirements.

Blister packs need only include:

a   name of the medicine as required to appear on the label;
b   name of marketing authorisation holder;
c   expiry date;
d   batch number.

Small immediate packaging where it is not feasible to print all the details (e.g. ampoule) need only include:

a   name of the medicine as required to appear on the label;
b   method of administration and if necessary, route of administration;
c   expiry date;

d   batch number;
e   contents by weight, volume or unit.

The package leaflet (PL; also known as patient information leaflet, PIL) supplied with a medicine must be drawn up in accordance with the SmPC. In essence, the leaflet restates the technical scientific information in the SmPC in patient-friendly language. The package leaflet must include the information set detailed below, in the specific order listed:

a   for the identification of the product:
    i   name of the medicine followed by its pharmaceutical form and strength and, if appropriate, whether it is intended for adults, children or babies. The common name must be included if there is only one active ingredient and its name is an invented name;
    ii pharmacotherapeutic group or type of activity in terms easily comprehensible by patients;
b   the therapeutic indications;
c   a list of information which is necessary before the product is taken:
    i   contraindications;
    ii   appropriate precautions for use;
    iii interactions with other medicines, food, alcohol, if relevant;
    iv   special warnings, e.g. use in pregnancy and breastfeeding; effects on ability to drive and operate machinery, excipients;
d   necessary instructions for use, in particular:
    i   dose;
    ii   method and, if necessary, route of administration;
    iii frequency of administration, specifying, if necessary, the time at which the medicine may or must be administered;
    and, as appropriate, depending on the nature of the product;
    iv   duration of treatment, where it should be limited;
    v   action to take in event of overdose (such as symptoms, emergency procedures);
    vi   what to do if one or more doses have not been taken;
    vii indication, if necessary, of the risk of withdrawal effects;
    viii specific recommendation to consult doctor or pharmacist for any clarification on the use of the product;
e   a description of adverse reactions which may occur with normal use of the product and, if necessary, the action to take in such a case. The patient should be expressly asked to communicate to their doctor or pharmacist any adverse reaction not listed in the leaflet;
f   reference to expiry date indicated on the label with:
    i   a warning against use after expiry date;
    ii   where appropriate, special storage precautions;

iii if necessary, a warning concerning visible signs of deterioration;

iv for each presentation of the product, the full qualitative composition (active substances and excipients) and the quantitative composition in active substances using common names;

v for each presentation, the pharmaceutical form and content in weight, volume or units of dosage;

vi name and address of marketing authorisation holder and, if applicable, their representative in the State;

vii name and address of the manufacturer;

g in case of a product authorised under the mutual recognition or decentralised procedure under different names in the member states concerned, a list of the names authorised in each member state;

h date on which leaflet was last revised.

The contents of the leaflet must reflect the results of user testing with patients to ensure that it is legible, clear and easy to use, and the results of that user testing must be included when submitting the leaflet to the regulatory authority for approval.

Symbols or pictograms to clarify information and other information compatible with the SmPC may be included on labels or leaflets, provided they are not promotional in nature. Examples would include contact details for relevant patient support groups.

If a product is not intended to be handed directly to a patient, for example, it is one that must be administered by a healthcare professional, the regulatory authority assessing the application may grant an exemption from some of the requirements for labels and leaflets.

The authorisation holder is required to provide package leaflets on request from patient organisations in formats suitable for the blind and partially sighted (e.g. Braille, large-print and audio versions). The name of the product must also be included in Braille on every pack.

In addition to a clear mention of the words 'homeopathic medicine', the labelling and, where appropriate, the package insert for a homeopathic medicinal product that is the subject of a certificate of registration shall include the following, and no other, information:

a the scientific name of the stock or stocks followed by the degree of dilution. If the homeopathic medicinal product is composed of two or more stocks, the scientific names of the stocks on the labelling may be supplemented by an invented name;

b name and address of the registration holder and, where appropriate, of the manufacturer;

c method of administration and, if necessary, route;

d expiry date, in clear terms (month, year);

e pharmaceutical form;

f contents of the sales presentation;

g special storage precautions, if any;

h a special warning, if necessary, for the medicinal product;

i manufacturer's batch number;

j registration number;

k the statement 'homeopathic medicinal product without approved therapeutic indications';

l a warning advising the user to consult a doctor if the symptoms persist.

In addition to the general requirements for labels and leaflets, traditional herbal medicinal products must also state that the product is a traditional herbal medicinal product for use in specified indications based exclusively on long-standing use and that the user should consult their doctor/practitioner if symptoms persist or if adverse effects not mentioned in the leaflet occur.[27]

As part of its general powers in relation to the supervision of medicinal products, the IMB has the power to request changes to the labels and leaflets of medicines, either individually or across a class or classes of medicinal products, and to order the recall of incorrectly labelled products that pose a risk to patients.

Supply classification

In the past, major divergences between the member states in respect of the legal classification for supply assigned to individual medicinal products were commonplace and it was frequently the case that a product that was prescription-only in one state would be a non-prescription product in another state. This was the driving force behind moves to harmonise classification at EU level. The 1992 classification directive[28] (now incorporated in 2001/83/EC as amended) defined standard supply categories throughout the EU and specified the criteria which were to be used in assigning a medicinal product to a particular category. Notwithstanding, it is interesting to note that considerable variability remains in relation to supply classification throughout Europe, particularly in terms of those products that may be sold without prescription. The outlets where medicinal products may be sold is a matter for the individual member states to determine.

The IMB assigns one of the following classifications as part of the assessment of an application for the grant or renewal of a marketing authorisation or certificate: (a) supply on prescription, either for renewable or non-renewable supply or (b) not subject to medical prescription, for a supply either from

---

27. Article 16(g) of Directive 2001/83/EC as amended.

28. Directive 92/26/EEC.

a pharmacy only or on general sale. Strict criteria are laid down in the Control of Placing on the Market Regulations in order to guide the IMB in its assignment of the various classifications for supply that may be applied to medicinal products that it authorises, and the IMB is obliged to follow those criteria in the course of its assessments.[29]

The Control of Placing on the Market Regulations state that prescription-only status will be assigned to any product that:

a   is likely to present a danger either directly or indirectly to human health, even when used correctly, if used without the supervision of a practitioner;

b   is frequently and to a wide extent used incorrectly, and as a result is likely to present a direct or indirect danger to human health;

c   contains substances whose actions or adverse reactions require further investigation;

d   is normally prescribed for parenteral administration (i.e. injectable products).

The IMB is also required to take into account other factors such as whether the product contains a drug controlled by international conventions on narcotic and psychotropic drugs; is likely to be abused or to lead to addiction or be used illegally; is only suitable for use in hospital or under specialist supervision; or is intended for the treatment of a condition which requires special diagnostic facilities.

In determining whether a prescription-only medicine should be available for renewable supply, the IMB is required to consider the reasonable need for patients to have access to repeat supplies of the product, which may be prescribed by their practitioner for the treatment of an ongoing, intermittent or recurring condition and in circumstances where it is safe to do so and where the practitioner concerned has not directed that such repeat supply shall not be made.

The IMB may decide to classify a medicine as suitable for supply without prescription having regard to the maximum single dose of the product concerned; the maximum daily dose; the strength of the product; its pharmaceutical form; its packaging; or any other circumstances relating to its use as the IMB may consider appropriate, for example, for a particular indication only.

In determining if a product should be classified as general sale, the IMB must have regard to the nature and purpose of the product and must be satisfied that the product concerned can with reasonable safety be sold or supplied other than under the supervision of a pharmacist.

The IMB is required to publish details of the supply classifications of medicines at least annually.

---

29. Regulation 12.

Because the legal classification of medicines in Ireland was traditionally assigned by way of the regulations governing prescription supply, the Control of Placing on the Market Regulations[30] amended the Medicinal Products (Prescription and Control of Supply) Regulations 2003 to align the requirements of the two sets of regulations. For details of those amendments and a more comprehensive discussion of the changes in the supply classification system since 2007, see Chapter 7, Prescription and control of supply of medicines.

Obligations of marketing authorisation and certificate holders

The Control of Placing on the Market Regulations[31] and Directive 2001/83/EC as amended place various obligations on the holders of marketing authorisations and certificates.

The overriding requirement is to continually monitor all new information that comes to light about the product which could affect its benefit–risk balance. Other requirements include the need to:

a   comply with all duties imposed by EU legislation including in particular, obligations relating to pharmacovigilance, labelling and package leaflets, to providing or updating information, to making changes and to applying to vary the authorisation or certificate;

b   keep full records of adverse reactions and make these available to the IMB. This does not apply to holders of certificates of registration (see section on Pharmacovigilance for further information);

c   keep appropriate records to enable recalls to be carried out if required;

d   update any information in the product's dossier as required;

e   take account of scientific and technical progress in the manufacturing and testing of the product and vary the authorisation or certificate as necessary;

f   notify the IMB of any prohibitions or restrictions placed on the product in other countries and of any other new information which might affect the evaluation of the benefits and risks of the product;

g   provide the IMB on request with data on the volume of sales and prescriptions for the product;

h   notify the IMB of the date of placing on market of the product and, if relevant, the date of cessation of marketing;

i   inform the IMB of any defects that could result in the recall or abnormal restrictions on the supply of the product.

To ensure that the needs of patients are catered for, authorisation or certificate holders or anyone acting on their behalf in placing the product

---

30. Regulations 20–24.
31. Part 3 Regulations 15–19.

on the market are required to ensure within the limits of their responsibility, appropriate and continued supplies of the product to pharmacies and other persons authorised to supply such products.[32] This continuity of supply provision and the 'sunset clause' discussed previously both originate from Directive 2001/83/EC as amended,[33] and were introduced in an attempt to address the problem of shortages of certain off-patent medicines.

Pharmacovigilance

Once a new medicine is authorised and placed on the market, its safety continues to be monitored throughout its entire life cycle through the EU system of pharmacovigilance. This system ensures that any product which presents an unacceptable level of risk is rapidly withdrawn from the market.

Pharmacovigilance is the process and science of monitoring the safety of medicines and taking action to reduce the risks and increase the benefits of medicines. It comprises collecting and managing data on the safety of medicines, looking at the data to detect 'signals' (any new or changing safety issue), evaluating the data and making decisions with regard to safety issues, acting to protect public health (including regulatory action), communicating with stakeholders and audit, both of the outcomes of action taken and of the key processes involved.

The current legal framework of pharmacovigilance for drugs marketed within the EU is provided for in Regulation EC No. 726/2004 as amended with respect to centrally authorised medicinal products, and in Directive 2001/83/EC as amended with respect to nationally authorised medicinal products (including those authorised through the mutual recognition and decentralised systems).[34]

Key definitions in pharmacovigilance are as follows:[35]

- **Adverse reaction:** A response to a medicinal product which is noxious and unintended and which occurs at doses normally used in humans for the prophylaxis, diagnosis or therapy of disease or for the restoration, correction or modification of physiological function.
- **Serious adverse reaction:** An adverse reaction which results in death, is life-threatening, requires inpatient hospitalisation or prolongation of

---

32. Regulation 19, Control of Placing on the Market Regulations.
33. Article 81 and Article 24(4)–(6).
34. European Commission Pharmaceuticals Unit 'The EU Pharmacovigilance System' http://ec. europa.eu/health/human-use/pharmacovigilance/index_en.htm (accessed 1 March 2011). New EU legislation adopted in November 2010 will further strengthen the pharmacovigilance system when it comes into operation in July 2012 (Directive 2010/84/EU and Regulation (EU) No. 1235/2010).
35. Article 1, Directive 2001/83/EC as amended.

existing hospitalisation, results in persistent or significant disability or incapacity, or in a congenital anomaly/birth defect.

• **Unexpected adverse reaction:** An adverse reaction, the nature, severity or outcome of which is not consistent with the summary of product characteristics.

The Control of Placing on the Market Regulations require a person placing a medicine on the market in Ireland to:[36]

a   have a qualified person for pharmacovigilance;
b   keep detailed records of all suspected adverse reactions that come to their attention;
c   report serious suspected adverse reactions within fifteen days, to the IMB or EMA as appropriate;
d   submit details of all adverse reactions that come to their attention in the form of a periodic safety update report (PSUR) which includes a scientific evaluation of the benefit-risk balance of the product. This must be submitted to the IMB at defined intervals as follows or on request at any time: every six months prior to and for two years after the product has been placed on market; then, annually for the next two years; and thereafter, every three years;
e   collect any specific additional pharmacovigilance information requested by the IMB or EMA;
f   notify the IMB or EMA as appropriate when releasing pharmacovigilance information to the public. Such information must be presented objectively and not mislead the public.

Particular categories of medicinal products

Generics

A 'generic medicinal product' is a medicinal product which contains the same active ingredients in the same quantities and has the same pharmaceutical form as an originator or 'reference' medicinal product. To receive market approval, a generic medicine must be 'bioequivalent' to the originator product (i.e. it must work in essentially the same way in the patient's body). The applicant is not required to provide the results of preclinical and clinical studies for a generic medicine; instead appropriate evidence of bioequivalence to the reference product is supplied. More stringent data requirements apply to generic biological products. In cases where the medicinal product does not fall within the definition of a generic medicinal product, or where bioequivalence cannot be demonstrated through bioavailability studies, or in the case

---

36. Regulations 17 and 18.

of changes in the active substance(s), therapeutic indications, strength, pharmaceutical form or route of administration, *vis-à-vis* the reference medicinal product, data from preclinical tests or clinical trials must be submitted.[37]

To allow companies who develop new medicinal products a reasonable period of time to recoup their investment in research and development, generics cannot be placed on the market for ten years after the marketing authorisation for the reference product was granted, although the generic application may be submitted to the IMB after eight years. The ten year period is extended to eleven years if one or more significant new indications are approved for the reference product during the first eight years after it was authorised.[38]

Parallel imports

Parallel imports are products imported into one member state from another and placed on the market in the destination member state outside the manufacturer's or its licensed distributor's formal channels. European Court of Justice (ECJ) rulings have played a key role in defining how parallel imports are to be handled and the European Commission has published a Communication, based mainly on the ECJ's rulings, clarifying how the principle of free movement of goods within the EU applies in practice to parallel imports of medicinal products in the EU.[39]

In order to legally place a parallel import which is not a centrally authorised product on the Irish market, application must be made to the IMB for a parallel import licence. A 'parallel import licence' means a marketing authorisation or a certificate of traditional-use registration granted by the IMB under the Control of Placing on the Market Regulations in respect of a medicinal product which is imported into Ireland from another EEA state, in accordance with the rules of Community law relating to parallel imports.[40]

The IMB operates two schemes in relation to the granting of parallel import licences.[41] Where the product to be imported differs in any respect from that on the Irish market, a parallel import licence termed a 'parallel product authorisation' (PPA) must be obtained. Where the product to be imported is identical in all respects (including identical packaging, labels and leaflets) to the product on the Irish market, a parallel import licence termed a dual pack import registration (DPR) may be obtained. The IMB has developed these schemes on the basis of the aforementioned Commission Communication, which states that a medicinal product may be imported in

---

37. Article 10, Directive 2001/83/EC as amended.
38. Regulation 7, Control of Placing on the Market Regulations.
39. Commission Communication on parallel imports of proprietary medicinal products for which marketing authorisations have already been granted (COM(2003)839, 30.12.2003).
40. Regulation 3(1), Control of Placing on the Market Regulations.
41. IMB Guide to Parallel Imports – Human Medicines, AUT-G0006-6, 11 February 2010.

parallel on the basis of a licence granted according to a 'simplified' procedure, under which the applicant needs to provide less information than is required for an application for a marketing authorisation.

Distributors wishing to parallel distribute a centrally authorised product in any member state must notify the EMA and the national authority of the member state concerned, but a further authorisation at national level is not required as they are already authorised for sale or supply in all member states by virtue of their community marketing authorisations.[42]

Advanced therapies

Advanced therapy medicinal products are medicines based on genes (gene therapy), cells (cell therapy) and tissues (tissue engineered products). The 2007 advanced therapies regulation[43] puts in place an EU-wide framework for the licensing and control of advanced therapies to make safe, novel treatments available to patients as quickly as possible. The lack of an EU-wide regulatory framework in the past led to divergent national approaches which hindered patients' access to products and hampered the development of this emerging sector. The advanced therapies regulation recognised that many advanced therapies could not be regulated as 'conventional' medicines and need adapted requirements.

Advanced therapies now have automatic access to the centralised procedure and the licensing process has been adapted to deal with the particular characteristics of these products. A new committee has been set up in the EMA (the Committee for Advanced Therapies) whose function is to assess advanced therapies and follow scientific developments in the field.

The Control of Placing on the Market Regulations were amended in 2009[44] to facilitate the operation of the advanced therapies regulation in Ireland. Provisions were included to ensure the traceability of advanced therapy medicinal products. The holder of the marketing authorisation for an advanced therapy is required to have a system to trace the product, starting with raw materials, from sourcing through to the hospital, institution or private practice place where the product is used, and these data have to be kept for at least 30 years. The hospital, institution or private practice where the product is used must also have a system to enable traceability to patient level.[45]

The standard labelling and leaflet requirements for medicinal products are modified to reflect the special characteristics of advanced therapies and the

---

42. Commission Communication on parallel imports of proprietary medicinal products for which marketing authorisations have already been granted (COM(2003)839, 30.12.2003).
43. Regulation (EC) No. 1394/2007.
44. S.I. No. 3 of 2009.
45. Regulations 19A and 19B, Control of Placing on the Market Regulations.

requirements of EU legislation;[46] for example, in the case of tissue therapy, unique donation and product codes must appear on the label to facilitate traceability from donor to recipient. In the case of products for autologous use (i.e. products based on patient's own cells), the unique patient identifier and the statement 'For autologous use only' must appear on the label.

The updated regulations provide for controls in respect of 'exempt' advanced therapy medicinal products which are prepared on a non-routine basis according to specific quality standards, and used within the State in a hospital under the exclusive professional responsibility of a medical practitioner, to comply with an individual medical prescription for a custom-made product for an individual patient.[47]

Orphan medicines

Orphan medicinal products are intended for the diagnosis, prevention or treatment of life-threatening or very serious conditions that affect not more than 5 in 10 000 persons in the EU.[48]

Since only a very small proportion of the population is affected by these diseases, the pharmaceutical industry has been reluctant in the past to invest in the research and development of medicinal products to treat them, as costs are extremely high and do not allow for these medicines to be supplied at normal prices. The orphan medicinal products regulation that was introduced by the EU in 2000 aimed to incentivise research into and licensing of orphan medicinal products. The supports on offer reflect the fact that most orphan medicinal products are developed by small to medium enterprises rather than by big international pharmaceutical companies, and include the provision of assistance to applicants in developing clinical trial programmes and applications for marketing authorisation and access to the centralised procedure but with waived or reduced fees. Up to ten years' market exclusivity is granted to the holder of a marketing authorisation for an orphan medicinal product to maximise his or her ability to recoup the development costs. Finally, it is important to note that the standard requirements for quality, safety and efficacy also apply to these products.

Paediatric medicines

Concerns about the small number of medicines available in Europe being specifically tested and authorised for use in children, leading to 'off-label' use of adult products, was the driving force behind the EU's paediatric

---

46. Regulation 16(4)–16(6), Control of Placing on the Market Regulations.
47. Schedule 1A.
48. EU orphan medicinal products regulation, Regulation (EC) No. 141/2000.

medicines regulation.[49] This regulation aimed to ensure high-quality research into the development of medicines for children, so that eventually the majority of medicines used by children would be specifically tested and authorised for such use and also to ensure the availability of high-quality information about paediatric medicines.

The key provisions in the paediatric medicines regulation include:

a marketing authorisation applications for new medicines and new forms and/or strengths of existing patent-protected medicines must include data on the use of the medicine in children unless the medicine is unlikely to benefit children. In return, an additional six months' patent protection is granted;

b ten years' data protection is given for new paediatric indications for established products which means that a generic version cannot claim paediatric use during that time unless they conduct their own paediatric studies;

c more robust pharmacovigilance has been introduced for children;

d member states are required to take steps to encourage research into medicines in children.

Clinical trials

In the broadest sense, the term 'clinical trial' means a biomedical or health-related research study in humans that follows a predefined protocol.

In relation to medicinal products, a clinical trial is any investigation that aims to study the pharmacological or clinical impact of an investigational medicinal product on human subjects. This includes pharmacokinetic studies and studies designed to investigate the safety of a medicinal product in volunteers and in patients alike.

Requirements for the conduct of clinical trials in the EU are set out in Directive 2001/20/EC (the 'Clinical Trial Directive') and Directive 2005/28/EC (the 'Good Clinical Practice Directive') which are implemented in Ireland by the European Communities (Clinical Trials on Medicinal Products for Human Use) Regulations 2004 to 2007 (the 'Clinical Trial Regulations').[50]

The Clinical Trial Regulations set out various measures relating to the conduct of clinical trials and replace the controls that previously applied under the Control of Clinical Trials Acts 1987 and 1990.

---

49. Regulation (EC) No. 1901/2006.
50. S.I. No. 190 of 2004 (Copyright Houses of the Oireachtas 2004) as amended by S.I. No. 878 of 2004 (Copyright Houses of the Oireachtas 2004), S.I. No. 374 of 2006 (Copyright Houses of the Oireachtas 2006) and S.I. No. 540 of 2007 (Copyright Houses of the Oireachtas 2007).

Any medicinal product used in a clinical trial – either an active substance or placebo, whether being tested or used as a reference – is known as an 'investigational medicinal product'. Also falling within this category is a medicinal product that is already the subject of a marketing authorisation which is used, formulated or packaged differently from the authorised form, is used for an indication that is not included in the SmPC for the product, or is being used to gain further information about the form of the authorised product.

Before commencing a clinical trial, it is necessary to obtain a favourable ethics committee opinion and approval from the IMB to conduct the trial. There are also provisions in the Clinical Trial Regulations regarding the manufacture, importation, supply and labelling of investigational medicinal products, pharmacovigilance and the need to comply with standards of good clinical practice (GCP) and good manufacturing practice (GMP).

The Clinical Trial Regulations set out rules regarding the establishment, recognition and operation of ethics committees. They must be independent, consist of healthcare professionals and lay members, and be responsible for protecting the rights, safety and well-being of those taking part in a trial. They are required to confirm the suitability of the trial protocol and investigators, the adequacy of the facilities, the availability of appropriate insurance, indemnity or compensation and the suitability of information used to inform trial subjects and to obtain their informed consent. In the case of clinical trials which take place in more than one centre ('multicentre trials'), one single ethics committee opinion given in Ireland will cover all the centres.

Clinical trials included in any marketing authorisation application in the EU must be conducted in accordance with GCP. GCP is a set of internationally recognised ethical and scientific quality requirements that must be observed for designing, conducting, recording and reporting clinical trials that involve the participation of human subjects.

Conditions and principles for the protection of clinical trial subjects are set out in Schedule 1 to the Clinical Trial Regulations and are consistent with the principles contained in the Declaration of Helsinki.[51] The regulations also set out the detailed conditions that apply to the giving of consent by trial subjects, including minors and incapacitated adults.

Non-interventional studies or trials are specifically exempted from the controls set out in the Clinical Trial Regulations. A non-interventional study is one where the medicinal product(s) is (are) prescribed in the usual manner, in accordance with the terms of the marketing authorisation. The assignment of the patient to a particular therapeutic strategy is not decided in advance by a trial protocol but falls within current practice, and the prescription of the

---

51. Published by the World Medical Association and available at http://www.wma.net/en/
30publications/10policies/b3/index.html (accessed 1 March 2011).

medicine is clearly separated from the decision to include the patient in the study. No additional diagnostic or monitoring procedures are applied to the patients, and epidemiological methods are used for the analysis of collected data.

Pharmacopoeias and European Directorate for the Quality of Medicines

The European Pharmacopoeia is a single reference work for quality control of medicines in Europe.[52] It was set up in 1964 as a Convention under the Council of Europe proposed by the then six EEC member states together with the UK and Switzerland, all countries with a long tradition of their own national pharmacopoeias. The Convention was subsequently adopted by other European countries and the EU itself joined the Convention in 1993. Currently there are 37 member signatories to the European Pharmacopoeia Convention: 36 member states, including all 30 EEA member states, and the EU, which speaks with a single voice on behalf of its individual member states on non-technical matters.

In 1992, the European Directorate for the Quality of Medicines & HealthCare (EDQM) was established as a standalone institute of the Council of Europe and the activities of the European Pharmacopoeia and its secretariat were lodged in the EDQM. The EDQM also developed activities in relation to providing the European Union Official Medicines Control Laboratory Network and subsequently the European Pharmacopoeia Certification of Suitability system for assessing data on those active substances and excipients which are covered by specific monographs of the European Pharmacopoeia. The EDQM is located in Strasbourg, the headquarters of the Council of Europe and continues to develop its activities and range of responsibilities. The EDQM therefore participates with the EU regulatory authorities at national level and the European Commission and the EMA in completing the network of the regulatory system for medicines control in the EU. However, the role of the EDQM covers a wider audience than EU because it is an institution of the Council of Europe, which currently has 47 member states.

European Pharmacopoeia (Ph Eur) monographs are mandatory for signatories of the European Pharmacopoeia Convention, and are given a particular importance in the EU directives relating to medicinal products. For example, Annex 1 to Directive 2001/83/EC as amended[53] sets out the formal position that all substances covered by monographs of the European Pharmacopoeia

---

52. See www.edqm.eu (accessed 1 March 2011).
53. Annex 1 to Directive 2001/83/EC as substituted by Directive 2003/63/EC.

must meet these quality criteria before being used in medicinal products marketed in the EU.

The British Pharmacopoeia (BP) was designated as the official pharmacopoeia for Ireland by the Pharmacopoeia Act of 1931.[54] Subsequently, in 1976, Ireland signed the European Pharmacopoeia Convention and the European Pharmacopoeia became also the official pharmacopoeia for Ireland.

As the role and the authority of the European Pharmacopoeia has strengthened and widened, most of the national pharmacopoeias simply reproduce the specific monographs of the European Pharmacopoeia, but they may have additional monographs which are valid in their respective territories. For example, the BP includes some specific dose form monographs for formulated products, a type of monograph that does not appear in the European Pharmacopoeia.

The IMB provides the secretariat for the Irish Pharmacopoeia as well as the membership of the Ireland delegation to the European Pharmacopoeia Commission in association with the Department of Health and Children. Dr JM Morris from the IMB is a past chairman of the European Pharmacopoeia Commission, the first person elected from Ireland to the role.

---

54. No. 22 of 1931.

5

Manufacturing and wholesaling of medicines

JM Morris and L Clarke

This chapter reviews the requirements for the manufacture and wholesale distribution of medicinal products in Ireland. It also covers the importation of medicinal products from third countries (i.e. from outside the European Economic Area (EEA)), as this activity is regulated under the same legislation as manufacturing.

Manufacture of medicinal products

The rules governing the manufacture of medicinal products in Ireland are almost exclusively derived from European Union (EU) law, specifically Directive 2001/83/EC as amended.[1] The relevant requirements of that Directive are implemented in Irish law via the Medicinal Products (Control of Manufacture) Regulations 2007 as amended (the 'Manufacturing Regulations').[2]

These regulations also govern the manufacture and importation from a third country of investigational medicinal products.

The Irish Medicines Board (IMB) is responsible for the regulation of manufacturers of medicinal products in Ireland. At the time of writing there

---

1. Directive 2001/83/EC of the European Parliament and of the Council of 6 November 2001 on the Community code relating to medicinal products for human use as amended by Directive 2002/98/EC, Directive 2003/63/EC, Directive 2004/24/EC, Directive 2004/27/EC, Directive 2008/29/EC, Directive 2009/53/EC, Directive 2009/120/EC, Regulation (EC) No. 1901/2006 and Regulation (EC) No. 1394/2007. Title IV of this directive deals with manufacture and importation of medicinal products.
2. S.I. No. 539 of 2007 (Copyright Houses of Oireachtas 2007) as amended by S.I. No. 4 of 2009 (Copyright Houses of Oireachtas 2009) and S.I. No. 288 of 2010 (Copyright Houses of the Oireachtas 2010).

are 88 authorised manufacturers of human medicinal products in Ireland. In addition, 53 manufacturers of investigational medicinal products, for which a separate manufacturer's authorisation is required, are authorised.[3]

Requirement for manufacturer's authorisation

A manufacturer's authorisation is required by a person who manufactures medicinal products for supply in the EEA or for export to a third country (i.e. outside the EEA) or who imports a medicinal product from a third country.[4] The term 'manufacture' includes total and partial manufacture and the various processes of dividing up, packaging and presentation.[5]

An authorisation is not required for the manufacture of an active substance used in a medicinal product; however, there is an obligation on the manufacturer of a medicinal product sourcing such substances to ensure that the substance has been manufactured in accordance with the EU guidelines on good manufacturing practice (GMP) for starting materials.[6]

An application for a manufacturer's authorisation in Ireland must be made in writing to the IMB[7] and include the information specified in Schedule 1 to the Manufacturing Regulations. In addition to the details of the products to be manufactured or imported, type of operations to be carried out, premises to be used, arrangements for storage and distribution of products manufactured, recall procedures and so on, the applicant must also provide full details of the proposed qualified person. Additionally, if manufacturing operations are to be carried out, details of the production manager at each premises, as well as the name of the person who will be in charge of quality control, must be supplied.

For each valid application, the IMB may grant or refuse an authorisation, usually within 90 days of the date of receipt of a valid application, but this time may be extended to allow for the submission of additional information, following inspection of the premises. The IMB also has the option to grant the authorisation other than in accordance with the application or to impose certain obligations or restrictions on the authorisation holder.[8]

The manufacturer's authorisation granted sets out the specific classes of medicinal products and pharmaceutical forms that it applies to, the

3. Irish Medicines Board, personal communication.
4. Regulation 4, Manufacturing Regulations.
5. Regulation 3(1), Manufacturing Regulations.
6. Schedule 2, paragraph 16 and Schedule 3, paragraph 23, Manufacturing Regulations.
7. Regulation 6, Manufacturing Regulations.
8. Regulations 7 and 8, Manufacturing Regulations.

manufacturing or importation operations that may be undertaken and the premises where these may be carried out.[9]

Exemptions from requirement for manufacturer's authorisation

The Manufacturing Regulations provide for a number of exemptions from the requirement to have a manufacturer's authorisation as follows:[10]

a   the extemporaneous manufacture of a medicinal product in response to a *bona fide* unsolicited order to fulfil a special need which is carried out:

    i   in a pharmacy by or under the personal supervision of a pharmacist in accordance with the specifications of a registered medical practitioner or registered dentist for use by his or her individual patients on his or her direct personal responsibility or to maintain a stock of a medicinal product for dispensing exclusively in that pharmacy to meet the orders of the aforementioned practitioners, or in accordance with the prescriptions of a pharmacopoeia for supply to patients attending that pharmacy;

    ii   by or under the personal supervision of a registered medical practitioner or registered dentist for use by his or her individual patients on his or her direct personal responsibility, provided the product is not advertised in any way and no other suitable authorised product is available;

b   the preparation, dividing up, changes in packaging or in the presentation of a medicinal product in (i) a pharmacy by or under the supervision of a pharmacist for supply from the pharmacy or (ii) by a doctor or dentist for supply to patients under his or her care;

c   in the case of a herbal medicinal product not industrially produced, provided it is supplied without a written recommendation for use and without a trade name. The processes of drying, crushing or comminuting herbal plants are not considered to be 'industrial';

d   in the case of homeopathic medicines not industrially produced and which are supplied without any written recommendation for use and without a trade name. The processes of dilution and succussion or potentisation of homeopathic stocks for individual patients are not considered to be 'industrial';

e   the preparation of a radiopharmaceutical product at the time when it is due to be administered by or under the supervision of the person who will administer it, in accordance with the manufacturer's instructions from an

---

9. Regulation 9, Manufacturing Regulations.
10. Regulation 5.

authorised kit, generator or precursor and in an establishment licensed by the Radiological Protection Institute of Ireland to use such products.

To a certain extent these exemptions mirror the exemptions from the requirement for products to be authorised as detailed in Schedule 1 to the Medicinal Products (Control of Placing on the Market) Regulations 2007 as amended[11] (see Chapter 4, Placing medicines on the market).

Requirements applicable to holders of manufacturer's authorisation

All manufacturing or importation operations must be conducted in accordance with the principles of good manufacturing practice (GMP), as laid down in the EU GMP directive.[12] In addition, all holders of manufacturer's authorisations must comply with a series of general requirements which are applicable to all holders and with any further conditions or obligations attached to their authorisation by the IMB.[13]

The general requirements that apply to an authorisation holder who manufactures medicinal products are extensive and include:[14]

a   providing and maintaining such staff, premises and facilities, as set out in the application to the IMB, as are necessary for the manufacturing operations carried out, and notifying the IMB of any material changes in these;

b   carrying out manufacturing operations to ensure that products produced comply with the applicable standards of quality, strength and purity, for example, those specified in a marketing authorisation or pharmacopoeia;

c   keeping batch records and samples of each batch of product manufactured for prescribed periods of time (minimum five years);

d   having a system for recording and investigating complaints about the products manufactured;

e   keeping records to facilitate recalls if required and complying with any instructions of the IMB to recall products. The IMB must be notified if the manufacturer has any grounds to believe a recall may be required or if any abnormal restrictions have been applied to the supply of a particular product imported by him or her;

f   in the case of products that he or she manufactures which have a marketing authorisation, only supplying these to authorised wholesalers in Ireland or in another EEA state, to persons lawfully entitled to supply

---

11.   S.I. No. 540 of 2007 (Copyright Houses of Oireachtas 2007) as amended by S.I. No. 3 of 2009 (Copyright Houses of Oireachtas 2009) and S.I. No. 287 of 2010 (Copyright Houses of the Oireachtas 2010).
12.   Directive 2003/94/EC.
13.   Regulation 10, Manufacturing Regulations.
14.   Schedule 2, Manufacturing Regulations.

such medicines to the public or to administer the product in the course of a professional practice or in a hospital. This provision does not apply to the supply of investigational medicinal products for use in clinical trials;

g providing any information required by the IMB and permitting it to inspect any premises, and take samples and copies of any records;

h complying with specific requirements in relation to the wholesale supply of any medicines that they manufacture, for example, complying with good distribution practice. (A manufacturer is permitted to wholesale medicines manufactured or imported in accordance with the manufacturer's authorisation but must have a separate wholesaler's authorisation for the wholesale supply of any other medicines).

Similar general requirements apply to authorisation holders engaged in the importation of medicinal products from a third country, but with the focus on the handling, storage and distribution of those products. In addition, the authorisation holder is required to ensure, within the limits of their responsibility as a distributor, appropriate and continued supplies of the product to pharmacies and other persons authorised to supply such products.[15]

Variation of manufacturer's authorisation

The IMB may vary a manufacturer's authorisation, either on application by the holder, or on its own initiative to change (a) the medicinal products or pharmaceutical forms, premises or equipment or the manufacture, control or storage facilities or (b) any other details in relation to the authorisation.[16] Such changes are known as 'variations'.

Revocation or suspension of manufacturer's authorisation

A manufacturer's authorisation is valid indefinitely until otherwise revoked or suspended. The IMB has the power to suspend or revoke the authorisation on various grounds, including the fact that the holder is not carrying out or has indicated in writing that he or she is no longer intending to carry out the operations to which the authorisation relates. Other grounds for revocation or suspension include the submission of false or incomplete information in the original application, a material change in relation to any of the particulars in the application, a material failure to comply with the obligations applicable to the authorisation holder, the manufacture or importation of medicinal products other than in accordance with the authorisation and the

---

15. Schedule 3, Manufacturing Regulations.
16. Regulation 11, Manufacturing Regulations.

authorisation holder not having the staff, premises, equipment or facilities necessary to properly carry out the handling, storage or distribution activities to which the authorisation relates. The revocation or suspension of the authorisation may be total or may be limited to certain medicinal products or to certain premises covered by the authorisation.[17]

Schedule 4 to the regulations sets out the procedure to be followed by the IMB if it proposes to vary or revoke a manufacturer's authorisation, other than on the request of the holder, or if it intends to suspend an authorisation. The holder/applicant has the opportunity to make representations regarding the proposed course of action, and must be given reasons in writing for the IMB's final decision on the matter. The same procedure applies if the IMB intends to reject an application for a manufacturer's authorisation or to grant the application subject to certain conditions.

Qualified person

It is a fundamental condition of the granting of a manufacturer's authorisation that the manufacturer or importer has at its disposal at least one 'qualified person'.[18] The qualifications and experience required by individuals nominated as qualified persons are detailed in Schedule 5 to the regulations. These requirements necessitate the qualified person to have studied one of the following disciplines: pharmacy, medicine, veterinary medicine, chemistry, pharmaceutical chemistry and technology or biology; and to have covered specific basic subjects. In addition, there is a requirement to have at least two years' experience in a pharmaceutical manufacturing operation, this period being reduced if the applicant's university course is of five years' duration or more. Schedule 5 also contains a 'grandfather clause', setting out exceptions to these requirements for persons with previous experience in a manufacturing operation who began their course of studies prior to the introduction of the qualified person requirement and whose qualifications do not meet the prescribed standards.

The Manufacturing Regulations specify the functions and duties of the qualified person. In particular, it is his or her responsibility to certify in a register that each batch of product has been manufactured in accordance with applicable laws, the terms of the manufacturer's authorisation and the relevant marketing authorisation or certificate applicable to the product, or in the case of investigational medicinal products, the product specification file.[19]

---

17. Regulation 12, Manufacturing Regulations.
18. Regulation 13, Manufacturing Regulations.
19. Regulation 13(3)–13(5).

In the case of products imported from outside the EEA, the qualified person must certify that these products have been manufactured in accordance with GMP and have undergone appropriate tests and analyses on importation to ensure that their quality is in accordance with the terms of the relevant marketing authorisation or certificate of registration or certificate of traditional-use registration. This obligation for re-testing on importation does not apply in respect of products imported from a third country with which the EU has entered a Mutual Recognition Agreement that confirms that the GMP standards are at least equivalent in that country to those in place in the EU and that the relevant control steps have been carried out in that country.

Medicinal products that have undergone the controls described above in another EEA state may be imported into and marketed in Ireland without any further release by a qualified person here, provided they are accompanied by the relevant control reports from the EEA country in question. In the case of investigational medicinal products, they must be accompanied by the batch release certificates signed by the qualified person in the other EEA state.

If the IMB is of the opinion that a qualified person is failing to carry out his or her functions and duties, it can refuse to allow the person concerned to continue in that role, either temporarily or permanently.

Importation of exempt medicinal products from third country

An 'exempt medicinal product' is a medicinal product to which paragraph 2 of Schedule 1 to the Medicinal Products (Control of Placing on the Market) Regulations 2007 as amended (i.e. an unauthorised product sold or supplied in response to a *bona fide* unsolicited order, formulated in accordance with the specification of a doctor or dentist for use by his or her individual patients under his or her direct responsibility in order to fulfil the special needs of those patients), or any equivalent legislation in another EEA state, applies (see Chapter 4, Placing medicines on the market, for further information on exempt medicinal products).

A manufacturer's authorisation is required to import exempt medicinal products from third countries and the authorisation must have this type of activity specified. Such products may only be imported in response to an order which meets the requirements of the Control of Placing on the Market Regulations as set out above.[20]

A manufacturer who imports exempt medicinal products from a third country does not have to comply with all of the obligations normally

---

20. Schedule 3, paragraph 25, Manufacturing Regulations.

applicable to authorised manufacturers, in particular the requirement to have a qualified person.[21]

The following records must be kept by the importer in respect of each exempt medicinal product imported:

a   name of the product, and any other name under which it is to be sold or supplied in Ireland;
b   dosage form;
c   trading style or name of product's manufacturer;
d   list of active ingredients;
e   quantity imported;
f   batch number;
g   name and address of the manufacturer of that medicinal product in the form in which it was imported and, if the person who supplied the product is not the manufacturer, the name and address of such supplier.

These records must be retained for at least five years and be available for inspection by the IMB.

For every exempt medicinal product sold or supplied by the importer, the following details must also be recorded: batch number and details of any suspected adverse reaction or quality defect relating to the product of which they become aware. The importer must notify the IMB of any such adverse reaction or quality defect reports.

The importer may not issue any advertisement, other than one that states only the trade name, pack size, price and dose, relating to an exempt medicinal product or make any representations in respect of such product.

The importer must notify the IMB of each importation of an exempt medicinal product. Except in exceptional circumstances, this must be done electronically, no later than two working days from the date of importation. This notification requirement does not apply to manufacturing or compounding of exempt medicinal products.

The importer must cease importing or supplying an exempt medicinal product if he or she has been directed by the IMB in writing that a particular product or class of products may no longer be imported or supplied from a particular date. Similarly, if having been informed by the IMB or by the manufacturer or person who supplied the medicinal product for importation that there is a safety, quality or efficacy issue with the product, they must immediately withdraw any supplies of that product held by them and immediately recall all supplies already sold or distributed.

---

21. Regulation 13(8)(a), Manufacturing Regulations.

Manufacture of advanced therapies

Advanced therapy medicinal products are medicines based on genes (gene therapy), cells (cell therapy) and tissues (tissue engineered products). The Manufacturing Regulations were amended in 2009[22] to facilitate the operation of the EU advanced therapies regulation in Ireland.[23] The manufacturer of an advanced therapy medicinal product is required to operate a system to enable the individual product and its starting and raw materials to be traced through sourcing, manufacturing, packaging, storage, transport, the whole way through to the hospital, institution or private practice where the product is used. These data have to be kept for at least 30 years by either the manufacturer or the marketing authorisation holder.[24] If the advanced therapy contains human cells or tissues, the manufacturer is also required to ensure that the traceability systems are complementary to and compatible with those required by the EU cells and tissues directive 2004/23/EC and the blood directive 2002/98/EC as appropriate.

Wholesale Supply of Medicinal Products

As with manufacturing, the rules governing the wholesaling of medicinal products in Ireland are almost exclusively derived from Directive 2001/83/EC as amended.[25] The relevant requirements of that directive are implemented in Irish law by the Medicinal Products (Control of Wholesale Distribution) Regulations 2007 as amended (the Wholesaling Regulations).[26]

The IMB is responsible for regulation of wholesalers of medicinal products in Ireland.

At the time of writing, there are 208 authorised wholesalers in Ireland, 136 general wholesalers and 72 specialising in supply of general sale medicines only, for example, to grocery and allied trade, according to the IMB.

Requirement for wholesaler's authorisation

A wholesaler's authorisation is required by any person who keeps or offers for sale, or sells a medicine by wholesale.[27] 'Sale by wholesale' means sale or supply for the purposes of sale in the course of a business or for administration to patients in the course of a professional practice. The term also includes all

---

22. S.I. No. 4 of 2009.
23. Regulation (EC) No. 1394/2007.
24. Schedule 2, paragraph 32, Manufacturing Regulations.
25. Title VII of this directive deals with wholesale distribution of medicinal products.
26. S.I. No. 538 of 2007 (Copyright Houses of Oireachtas 2007) as amended by S.I. No. 2 of 2009 (Copyright Houses of Oireachtas 2009) and S.I. No. 286 of 2010 (Copyright Houses of the Oireachtas 2010).
27. Regulation 5, Wholesaling Regulations.

activities consisting of the procuring, holding or exporting of medicinal products other than activities involving the sale and supply of such products to the public.[28]

The procedures for applying for a wholesaler's authorisation and the IMB's consideration of the application[29] are similar to those for a manufacturer's authorisation. Schedule 1 to the Wholesaling Regulations sets out the particulars which should accompany the application. In addition to the details of the products to be sold by wholesale, the type of operations involved, details of each premises where products will be stored and distributed from, the arrangements for storage and distribution of products and so on, the applicant must also provide details of the proposed recall, record-keeping and stock control procedures as well. Details of the 'responsible person' and the people responsible for supervision of wholesaling operations at each premises must also be supplied.

In addition to granting or refusing the application, the IMB also has the option to grant the authorisation other than in accordance with the application or to require certain obligations to be carried out by the authorisation holder.[30]

The wholesaler's authorisation granted sets out the specific classes of medicinal products that may be sold by wholesale, the wholesaling operations that may be undertaken and the specific premises where these may be carried out.[31]

Exemptions from requirement for wholesaler's authorisation

The Wholesaling Regulations set out various exemptions from the requirement for a wholesaler's authorisation:[32]

a   sale by wholesale of a medicinal product by a person who has manufactured or imported it from a third country in accordance with the provisions of a manufacturer's authorisation;

b   supply of an investigational medicinal product for use in a clinical trial;

c   sale by or under the personal supervision of a pharmacist of a medicine to a doctor, dentist, dispensing optician, optometrist, veterinary surgeon or pre-hospital emergency care provider for administration to patients in the course of a professional practice or service;

---

28. Regulation 4(1), Wholesaling Regulations.
29. Regulations 7 and 8, Wholesaling Regulations.
30. Regulation 9, Wholesaling Regulations.
31. Regulation 10, Wholesaling Regulations.
32. Regulation 6.

d   sale by or under the personal supervision of a pharmacist of a medicine to a person lawfully entitled to obtain such products for administration to patients in the course of a business as a hospital.

Requirements applicable to holders of wholesaler's authorisation

A number of requirements are specified in Schedule 2 to the Regulations with regard to wholesaler's authorisations, in particular, the requirement for compliance with good distribution practice (GDP) as set out in the EU GDP guidelines.[33] Good distribution practice is that part of quality assurance which ensures that products are consistently stored, transported and handled under suitable conditions as required by the marketing authorisation or product specification and that traceability is ensured. It covers all aspects of distribution such as premises, storage facilities, personnel, equipment, procedures and record-keeping. The authorisation holder must provide and maintain such staff, premises and facilities, procedures, etc. as are necessary for the wholesaling operations carried out to avoid any deterioration of the products involved. To verify that the appropriate systems are in place, IMB inspectors monitor compliance with the principles of GDP through regular on-site inspections of wholesalers.

The wholesaler is required to have a 'responsible person'[34] who in the opinion of the IMB has the appropriate knowledge and experience of GDP to take charge of this function, although the specific education and experience requirements for this role are not specified in legislation in contrast to the role of the manufacturer's qualified person. The role of the responsible person is to ensure all conditions relating to the wholesaler's authorisation are complied with and that the quality of the products handled by the wholesaler is maintained in accordance with the relevant marketing authorisation. If the IMB is of the opinion that the responsible person is failing to carry out his or her functions and duties, it may refuse to allow the person concerned to continue in that role, either temporarily or permanently.

A wholesaler must only obtain his supplies of medicinal products from authorised manufacturers or other authorised wholesalers within the EEA. He or she may only sell products covered by the authorisation. The products sold must have a marketing authorisation, certificate of registration or certificate of traditional-use registration and be sold in accordance with the terms of that authorisation. In addition, a wholesaler may only sell medicinal products to wholesalers who are entitled to sell them, to manufacturers for use in the manufacture of products covered by their manufacturer's authorisation, or to

---

33. Guidelines on Good Distribution Practice of Medicinal Products for Human Use (94/C 63/03).
34. Schedule 2, paragraph 6, Wholesaling Regulations.

individuals who are lawfully entitled to supply the products in question to the public, for example, pharmacists, or to administer the products to their patients in the course of a professional practice or business in a hospital.

Holders of wholesaler's authorisations must permit officers of IMB to conduct such inspections and make available such information as may be required to satisfy the IMB that the conditions of the authorisation are being complied with and give, without payment, adequate samples of the medicine to any person authorised to take such a sample.

The wholesaler is required to keep records of all products received or dispatched, which at a minimum must include the date of receipt or supply, the name of the product, the quantity received or supplied and the name and address of the supplier or consignee, as appropriate. These records must be kept for at least five years. It is interesting to note that while there is no legal requirement for wholesalers to record batch numbers, the records must be capable of identifying products or product batches which might not conform with the provisions of relevant marketing authorisation, are of inappropriate quality or have been found to give rise to concerns regarding their safety or efficacy, to permit the withholding or recall of such products, in accordance with the directions of the IMB.

Medicines sold by wholesale to persons entitled to sell them to the public or to persons lawfully entitled to administer the product in the course of a professional practice or in a hospital must be accompanied by a dispatch note stating the date of sale, the name and pharmaceutical form of the product, the quantity of product supplied and the name and address of the supplier and consignor.

A wholesaler who proposes to parallel import a medicinal product from another member state in respect of which he or she is not the marketing authorisation holder or is not acting on their behalf, must notify the marketing authorisation holder and the IMB of his or her intention to import the product.

To ensure that the needs of patients are catered for, a wholesaler is required to ensure, within the limits of his or her responsibility as a distributor, appropriate and continued supplies of the product to pharmacies and other persons authorised to supply such products.

Revocation, suspension and variation of wholesaler's authorisation

The provisions and procedures in the Wholesaling Regulations relating to the variation, revocation and suspension of a wholesaler's authorisation[35] mirror those set out in the Manufacturing Regulations in relation to manufacturer's authorisations.

---

35. Regulations 12 and 13.

Like a manufacturer's authorisation, a wholesaler's authorisation is valid indefinitely unless otherwise revoked or suspended. The IMB may suspend or revoke an authorisation on various grounds, including the fact that the holder is not carrying out or has indicated in writing that he or she is no longer intending to carry out the wholesaling operations to which the authorisation relates. Other grounds for revocation or suspension include the submission of false or incomplete information in the original application, a material change in relation to any of the particulars in the application, the sale by wholesale of medicines other than in accordance with the authorisation and the authorisation holder not having the staff, premises, equipment or facilities necessary to carry out properly the handling, storage or distribution activities to which the authorisation relates. The revocation or suspension of the authorisation may be total or may be limited to certain medicinal products or certain premises covered by the authorisation.

The IMB may also vary a wholesaler's authorisation, either on application by the holder, or otherwise, to change (a) the description of medicinal products, the wholesaling operations, premises, installations and equipment or (b) any other details in relation to the authorisation.

Importation of exempt medicinal products from within EEA

Authorised wholesalers may import exempt medicinal products from another EEA state for distribution in Ireland provided this activity is specifically covered by their authorisation. Such importation is subject to the same requirements and conditions that apply to the importation of such products from third countries by the holder of a manufacturer's authorisation, as discussed earlier in this chapter, in terms of the circumstances where such importation is permitted, the records to be kept, the notifications to be made to the IMB, etc.[36]

Wholesaling of advanced therapies

The Wholesaling Regulations were amended in 2009[37] to facilitate the operation of the EU advanced therapies regulation in Ireland by extending their scope to include such products.

---

36. Schedule 2, paragraph 17, Wholesaling Regulations.
37. S.I. No. 2 of 2009.

6

Advertising of medicines

L Clarke

Unrestricted advertising of goods and services is not permitted in any sphere of life. By its nature, advertising is about presenting products and services in a positive light in order to attract consumers to purchase or use them, and it is important that this is not done in a way that exaggerates the properties or benefits of the product or service on offer and/or misleads the target audience.

The advertising of medicinal products is subject to a greater range of restrictions than apply to so-called other 'normal items of commerce'. The details of these restrictions will be discussed later in this chapter, but the most striking one is the ban in Europe on the advertising of prescription-only medicines to the public (including patients).

There are many reasons why these additional restrictions exist, the main one being to protect consumers from unreasonable and/or misleading claims of efficacy and safety. Furthermore, these controls complement the restrictions that apply to the distribution of medicines, the vast majority of which are only available on prescription or confined to sale from pharmacies. In addition, there is a particular need in the case of medicines to encourage their rational use so that they are only used by those who need them.

The rules governing the advertising of medicinal products in Ireland are almost exclusively derived from European Union (EU) law, specifically, Directive 2001/83/EC as amended.[1] The relevant requirements of that

---

1. Directive 2001/83/EC of the European Parliament and of the Council of 6 November 2001 on the Community code relating to medicinal products for human use as amended by Directive 2002/98/EC, Directive 2003/63/EC, Directive 2004/24/EC, Directive 2004/27/EC, Directive 2008/29/EC, Directive 2009/53/EC, Directive 2009/120/EC, Regulation (EC) No. 1901/2006 and Regulation (EC) No. 1394/2007. Title VIII of this directive deals with advertising of medicinal products.

directive are implemented in Irish law by the Medicinal Products (Control of Advertising) Regulations 2007 (the 'Advertising Regulations').[2] The rest of this chapter will focus on the detail of the Advertising Regulations.

Scope of Advertising Regulations

It is important at the outset to understand what is meant by the term 'advertising' so as to understand what falls within the scope of the Advertising Regulations. To this end, it is worth reproducing the definition given in the regulations:[3]

> Advertising, in relation to a medicinal product, includes any form of door-to-door information, canvassing activity or inducement designed to promote the prescription, sale, supply or consumption of medicinal products and including in particular:
>
> a   the advertising of medicinal products to the general public;
> b   the advertising of medicinal products to persons entitled to prescribe or supply them;
> c   visits by medical sales representatives to persons qualified to prescribe them;
> d   the supply of samples of medicinal products;
> e   the provision of inducements to prescribe or supply medicinal products by the gift, offer or promise of any benefit or bonus, whether in money or in kind;
> f   the sponsorship of promotional meetings attended by persons qualified to prescribe or supply;
> g   the sponsorship of scientific congresses attended by persons qualified to prescribe or supply medicinal products and in particular payment of their travelling and accommodation expenses in connection therewith;
>
> and cognate words shall be construed accordingly.

It can be seen from the above definition that the term advertising applies in the broadest sense and extends well beyond the general notion of advertising as a written or audiovisual means of communication.

---

2. S.I. No. 541 of 2007. Copyright Houses of the Oireachtas 2007.
3. Regulation 4(1).

The Advertising Regulations also set out various exemptions (i.e. activities to which the regulations do not apply):[4]

a labelling and package leaflets of medicinal products, which are subject to separate controls under the Medicinal Products (Control of Placing on the Market) Regulations 2007 (see Chapter 4, Placing medicines on the market);

b correspondence, accompanied by material of a non-promotional nature, needed to answer a specific question about a medicinal product. This exemption allows a pharmaceutical company's medical information department to answer queries from pharmacists, prescribers and others about the company's products, including those relating to off-label indications, dosages, etc.;

c factual informative announcements and reference material relating to pack changes, adverse drug warnings, trade catalogues and price lists provided they include no product claims ('Dear Healthcare Professional' letters dealing with safety matters would fall into this category);

d books, journals, etc. imported into Ireland which contain advertising not intended for or directed at people resident in the State. This exemption covers, for example, American editions of women's magazines which typically contain advertisements for prescription medicines that would not be permitted to appear in Irish publications;

e information relating to human health or diseases, provided there is no reference, even indirect, to medicinal products. This exemption provides the basis for the growing number of public disease awareness campaigns run by pharmaceutical companies.

General provisions on advertising

A medicinal product may not be advertised unless a marketing authorisation or certificate of traditional-use registration has been granted.[5] Certificates of traditional-use registration are granted to herbal medicinal products which are permitted to make claims of efficacy based on their traditional use as herbal medicines. The above advertising restriction will not apply to the traditional-use herbal medicines or homeopathic medicines until 30 April 2011, which is the deadline for the mandatory registration or authorisation of all such products in Ireland.

Advertisements must comply with all parts of the relevant product's summary of product characteristics (SmPC).[5] For example, a product can only be promoted for the indications listed in its current SmPC; even if a significant new study confirming efficacy in another indication had been published in a

---

4. Regulation 5.
5. Regulations 6 and 7.

peer-reviewed journal, that new indication could not be mentioned in any advertising until such time as the SmPC was updated to include it.

Finally, advertising for a medicinal product must encourage the rational use of the product by presenting it objectively and without exaggerating its properties and must not be misleading.

Advertising to the general public

Part 3 of the Advertising Regulations deals with the advertising of medicines to the general public.

The following categories of medicines may not be advertised to the general public: (i) prescription-only medicines and (ii) those containing drugs listed in Section 2 of Misuse of Drugs Act 1977 (e.g. codeine). This latter prohibition applies regardless of whether or not the product is available on prescription.[6]

The ban on advertising prescription-only medicines to the general public is an EU-wide ban. Direct-to-consumer (DTC) advertising of prescription-only medicines is only allowed in the United States and New Zealand. Pharmaceutical companies in the United States have considerable freedom in terms of the media that can be used, including radio, TV, press and methods which include celebrity endorsement of their products. The question of allowing pharmaceutical companies greater freedom to communicate with the public in relation to prescription medicines has been debated at EU level since 2001. At the time of writing, legislative proposals are under discussion which would clarify the circumstances in which companies may provide non-promotional information (but not advertising) to patients.[7] It is clear, however, that there is no appetite in Europe to follow the US DTC model.

The only exception to the ban on advertising prescription-only medicines in Ireland relates to advertisements for vaccines undertaken as part of a vaccination campaign that has been approved by the Minister for Health and Children. With vaccines it is public policy to maximise uptake rates in order to achieve herd immunity and eradicate disease, and it is deemed appropriate in that context to provide some leeway in relation to the advertising of vaccines to the public.[8]

It is noteworthy that marketing authorisations granted by the Irish Medicines Board (IMB) specify the promotion status of the product. The IMB has on occasion restricted the advertising of non-prescription medicines to healthcare professions only, for example, in the case of products that have

---

6. Regulations 9 and 10.
7. See European Commission's 'Information to Patients' website for further information, http://ec.europe.eu/health/human-use/information-to-patient/index_en.htm (accessed 1 March 2011).
8. Regulation 13.

been recently switched from prescription to non-prescription status or for certain products that require a prior medical diagnosis of the condition for which they are indicated.

Requirements for advertisements aimed at the general public

There are a number of restrictions on what may appear in an advertisement aimed at the general public which reflect the fact that the products being advertised are non-prescription medicines, typically intended for the short-term relief of symptoms and without the need for a formal diagnosis by a prescriber. Advertising to the general public must not contain any material which:[9]

a   gives the impression that a medical consultation or surgery is unnecessary, in particular by offering a diagnosis or by suggesting treatment by post, telephone, e-mail and other electronic means of communication;
b   suggests that the effects of taking the medicinal product are guaranteed, are unaccompanied by adverse reactions or are better than, or equivalent to, those of another treatment or medicinal product;
c   suggests that the health of the subject can be enhanced by taking the medicinal product;
d   suggests that the health of the subject could be affected by not taking the medicinal product (this does not apply to approved vaccination campaigns);
e   is directed exclusively or principally at children;
f   refers to a recommendation by scientists, health professionals or people who because of their celebrity status, could encourage the consumption of medicinal products;
g   suggests that the medicinal product is a foodstuff, cosmetic or other consumer product;
h   suggests that the safety or efficacy of the medicinal product is due to the fact that it is natural;
i   might, by a description or detailed representation of a case history, lead to erroneous self-diagnosis;
j   refers, in improper, alarming or misleading terms, to claims of recovery;
k   uses, in improper, alarming or misleading terms, images of changes in the human body caused by disease or injury, or of the action of a medicinal product on the human body.

In all advertising aimed at the general public, it must be clear that the message is an advertisement and that the product is clearly identified as a

---

9. Regulation 11.

medicinal product. The following minimum information must appear in such advertisements:[10]

a   name of the medicinal product;

b   if it contains only one active ingredient, the common name of the medicinal product (i.e. the generic name);

c   information necessary for the correct use of the medicinal product;

d   an express and legible invitation to read carefully the instructions on the package leaflet or on the label, as the case may be;

e   in the case of traditional herbal medicinal products, the following additional statement: 'Traditional herbal medicinal product for use in' followed by one or more of the registered indications for the product, followed by the words 'exclusively based upon long-standing use'.

The Advertising Regulations also regulate 'reminder' advertisements aimed at the general public; these are advertisements which include the name of the medicine but no claims or indications. Reminder advertising is often used as part of a broader marketing campaign for a medicine to supplement so-called 'full' or 'decision' advertisements. Reminder advertisements may only contain the following details: (a) the name of the product, or its international non-proprietary name, where such exists, or the trademark (or, in the case of a homeopathic medicinal product that is the subject of a certificate of registration, the scientific name of the stock or stocks or its invented name), and (b) advice to read carefully the instructions on the leaflet contained within the package, or on the label, as the case may be.[11]

Homeopathic medicines

The Advertising Regulations include specific provisions in relation to the advertising of registered homeopathic medicines that reflect the fact that such products are not permitted to state any indications or make claims on their labelling:[12]

a   the words 'homeopathic medicinal product';

b   scientific name of the stock or stocks followed by the degree of dilution; where the homeopathic medicinal product is composed of two or more stocks, the scientific names of the stocks may be supplemented by an invented name;

c   name and address of the holder of the certificate of registration and, where different, the name and address of the manufacturer;

d   method of administration and, if necessary, the route;

---

10. Regulation 12(1).
11. Regulation 12(3).
12. Regulation 12(2) and Schedule to the Advertising Regulations.

e   expiry date of the product in clear terms, stating the month and year;
f   pharmaceutical form;
g   contents of the sales presentation;
h   any special storage precautions;
i   any special warning necessary for the product concerned;
j   manufacturer's batch number;
k   registration number allocated by the IMB preceded by the letters 'HoR';
l   the words 'Homeopathic medicinal product without approved therapeutic indications';
m   warning advising the user to consult a doctor if symptoms persist.

Advertising to persons entitled to prescribe or supply medicinal products

Part 4 of the Advertising Regulations set out the requirements for advertisements for medicinal products that are directed wholly or mainly at persons qualified to prescribe or supply medicinal products i.e. doctors, dentists, nurses and pharmacists. In particular, these advertisements must include:[13]

a   essential information compatible with the SmPC;
b   name of the product and a list of the active ingredients immediately adjacent to the most prominent display of the name of the product;
c   classification for sale or supply of the product (e.g. 'Prescription-only medicine');
d   one or more of the indications as per the marketing authorisation or certificate of traditional-use registration;
e   details of adverse reactions, precautions and relevant contraindications as per the SmPC;
f   dosage and method of use relevant to the indications shown and the method of administration, where this is not obvious;
g   name and address of the holder of the marketing authorisation, certificate of registration or certificate of traditional-use registration or the business name and address of the part of the business responsible for placing the medicinal product on the market;
h   marketing authorisation, certificate of registration or certificate of traditional-use registration number of the product;
i   if it is a traditional herbal medicinal product, the words 'Traditional herbal medicinal product for use in' followed by one or more of the registered indications for the product, followed by the words 'exclusively based upon long-standing use'.

---

13. Regulation 16.

The details required at (e) and (f) above must be clear and legible and be placed in such a position in the advertisement that their relationship to the claims and indications for the product can readily be appreciated by the reader. Typically this information and also much of the other mandatory information detailed above appears as a block of text at the bottom of the advertisement commonly known as 'prescribing information'.

Reminder advertisements aimed at persons entitled to prescribe or supply medicinal products must contain:[14]

a   essential information compatible with the SmPC;
b   name of the product, or its international non-proprietary name or the trademark;
c   classification for sale or supply of the product;
d   name and address of the holder of the marketing authorisation, certificate of registration or certificate of traditional-use registration or the business name and address of the part of the business responsible for placing the medicinal product on the market;
e   a statement which clearly indicates that further information is available on request to the holder of the authorisation or certificate, or in the product's SmPC;
f   if it is a traditional herbal medicinal product, the words 'Traditional herbal medicinal product for use in' followed by one or more of the registered indications for the product, followed by the words 'exclusively based upon long-standing use'.

In essence, a reminder advertisement may not include any claims nor does it include the detailed prescribing information that will appear in a full or decision advertisement.

Promotional aids

Promotional aids are defined as non-monetary, inexpensive gifts that are relevant to the practice of medicine or pharmacy and are made for a promotional purpose by a commercially interested party.[15] Examples include pens bearing product names that are distributed to persons qualified to prescribe or supply medicinal products by pharmaceutical companies. The following conditions apply to advertisements on promotional aids:

a   the advertisement may only include the name of the product or its international non-proprietary name or the trademark (or in the case of a homeopathic medicinal product that is the subject of a certificate of

---

14. Regulation 17.
15. Regulation 18.

registration, the scientific name of the stock or stocks or its invented name);

b   it must be intended solely as a reminder;

c   the promotional aid must be intended for supply only to persons qualified to prescribe or supply medicinal products.

Written promotional material

Any written promotional material provided to persons qualified to prescribe or supply medicinal products must as a minimum include:

a   essential information compatible with the SmPC;

b   the supply classification; and

c   the date on which the document was drawn up or last revised.[16]

The information included in such material must be accurate, up-to-date, verifiable and sufficiently complete to enable the recipient to form his or her own opinion of the therapeutic value of the medicinal product to which the material relates. Any quotation, tables or other illustrations taken from medical journals or other scientific works must be accurately reproduced and the precise sources of the information indicated.

Medical sales representatives

The Advertising Regulations regulations set out various requirements in relation to the conduct and training of medical sales representatives.[17] Representatives visiting persons entitled to prescribe or supply medicinal products are required to have available or give a copy of the SmPC for each product promoted during the visit. The only exception to this is where the relevant SmPC is included in a compendium or other such reference publication which has been delivered within the last twelve months to the relevant group of health professionals (including electronic versions of same) and provided that the product has been on the market for at least twelve months.[18] In this case, the representative should draw the health professional's attention to the relevant entry in the compendium or other reference publication. Representatives are also required to report to the company's scientific service, any information about the use of such products obtained during the visit, in particular any adverse reactions reported to them.

---

16. Regulation 19.
17. Regulation 20.
18. Regulation 23.

Marketing authorisation holders have various responsibilities under the regulations in relation to their medical representatives.[19] In particular, they must ensure that representatives are given adequate training and have sufficient scientific knowledge to enable them to provide information which is as precise and as complete as possible about the products that they promote. If the IMB is of the opinion that this responsibility is not being met, it may specify the training and scientific knowledge required. The marketing authorisation holder is also required to ensure that representatives have available the appropriate SMPC during visits and that they transmit adverse reaction reports to the company's scientific service.

Gifts and hospitality

The Advertising Regulations recognise that certain inducements and hospitality may be provided to health professionals in the course of promoting medicinal products, but place restrictions on how this is to be done.[20]

Any gift, pecuniary (i.e. monetary) advantage or benefit in kind supplied, offered or promised in the course of promoting medicines to persons qualified to prescribe or supply such products must be inexpensive and relevant to the practice of medicine or pharmacy.

Companies are permitted to offer hospitality to persons entitled to prescribe or supply such products at their own promotional events or at other professional or scientific events (including those organised by health professionals) provided the hospitality is:

a   reasonable in level;
b   strictly limited to the main purpose or scientific objective of the event; and
c   not extended to persons other than health professionals (e.g. spouses, partners, children).

Health professionals are prohibited from soliciting or accepting any prohibited inducement, hospitality or sponsorship.

It is recognised that health professionals such as pharmacists may have business relationships with pharmaceutical companies and the regulations state that the provisions relating to inducements and hospitality are not intended to prejudice the negotiation of prices, margins and discounts in the ordinary course of business. However, any agreed prices, margins or discounts must be incorporated in the relevant sales invoice.

---

19. Regulation 24.
20. Regulation 21.

Free samples of medicinal products

It is illegal for pharmaceutical companies, manufacturers or wholesalers or anyone acting on their behalf to sell or supply medicines for promotional purposes to the general public. This means that the giving of free samples of medicines to the public is prohibited.[21]

Free samples of medicinal products may be provided to persons entitled to prescribe such products but not to those entitled to supply them (e.g. pharmacists). Certain conditions apply to such samples:[22]

a   the sample may be provided on an exceptional basis only and for the purpose of acquiring experience in dealing with that product;
b   a maximum of six samples per year may be provided to each recipient;
c   a written request for the sample, signed and dated by the recipient is required;
d   the supplier of such samples must maintain an adequate system of control and accountability. The regulations do not specify exactly how this system should operate but in practice, the expectation is that sufficient information will be recorded to be able to track the number of samples provided to a given prescriber, to verify that the relevant written request has been obtained and to facilitate a full recall of all samples distributed to prescribers if the need arises;
e   the sample pack must be no larger than the smallest pack available on the market;
f   the sample must be labelled 'Free medical sample – not for sale' or similar;
g   each sample must be accompanied by the relevant SmPC (not required if the product has been available for twelve months or more and the relevant SmPC appears in a compendium or other reference publication delivered to or freely accessible by the relevant prescribers).

The regulations prohibit the giving of free samples of controlled drugs, antidepressants, hypnotics, sedatives or tranquillisers in any circumstances.

Duties of marketing authorisation and certificate holders

The Advertising Regulations place a wide range of obligations on the holders of marketing authorisations, certificates of registration and certificates of traditional-use registration in respect of medicinal products that they place on the market.[23] These include the requirement to establish a scientific service to compile and collate all information relating to those products received from

---

21. Regulation 14.
22. Regulation 22.
23. Regulation 24.

any source. In practice, this service is provided by the medical department within a pharmaceutical company and comprises medical information and pharmacovigilance activities.

It is also necessary to keep samples of all advertising emanating from the undertaking, together with information indicating the persons to whom it is addressed, the method of dissemination and the date of first dissemination. There is also a requirement to provide details of any advertisement or proposed advertisement, samples or representative training requested by an officer of the IMB and also to ensure that any IMB decision in relation to advertising is immediately and fully complied with.

Self-regulation and enforcement

Directive 2001/83/EC as amended recognises that self-regulation has a role to play in relation to the advertising and promotion of medicines and this is reflected in the Irish Advertising Regulations, which permit the Minister for Health and Children to approve voluntary codes of practice (in whole or in part) issued by self-regulatory bodies for the purpose of providing practical guidance to the regulations.[24]

Self-regulatory advertising and marketing codes of practice are commonplace across the EU and share the following features: they are usually administered by pharmaceutical industry trade associations; are binding on all member companies of such associations; include a complaints mechanism with sanctions for code breaches; and provide more detailed guidance on matters such as the content of advertisements and the provision of gifts and hospitality, in addition to reflecting the minimum legislative requirements for advertising. Many such codes also address matters not specifically covered in advertising legislation, such as public relations activities, interactions with patient organisations and advertising through electronic media such as the internet, e-mail, text messages, etc. The 'Code of Marketing Practice for the Pharmaceutical Industry' and the 'Code of Standards of Advertising Practice for the Consumer Healthcare Industry' published by the Irish Pharmaceutical Healthcare Association are two such codes.[25]

Alongside the self-regulatory system, breaches of the regulations may be prosecuted in the courts under Section 32 of the Irish Medicines Board Acts 1995 and 2006.[26] Penalties that may be applied by the courts include

---

24. Regulation 26.
25. Available at www.ipha.ie (accessed 1 March 2011).
26. No. 29 of 1995 as amended by S.I. No. 304 of 2001, S.I. No. 444 of 2001, S.I. No. 576 of 2002, Act No. 3 of 2006 and S.I. No. 542 of 2007.

orders to withdraw misleading advertising and/or publish corrective statements, fines and additionally in the case of repeated offences, prison sentences. The IMB also has the power to order the withdrawal of misleading advertising and the publication of appropriate corrective statements.

7

Prescription and control of supply of medicines

P Gallagher, L Sahm and L Clarke

It is generally accepted that medicines must be used correctly. Controls over the distribution of human medicines are designed to protect the public and reflect the fact that medicines are not ordinary commercial items. They are supplied to the public on a normative need basis (a need identified according to a set of standards) rather than on a perceived need basis, as often pertains with items of commerce.

There are essentially three reasons for restricting medicines that are not on a general sales list, to supply on prescription or through retail pharmacy business, namely:

a   to prevent the individual from initiating self-treatment for more serious or prolonged conditions by restricting access to treatments which require healthcare professional supervision;
b   to protect the health of the public by restricting the availability of drugs with the potential to cause serious side-effects or to be misused and also those products whose indiscriminate use could lead to the emergence of resistant microorganisms; and
c   to ensure patient safety by determining that the pharmacist reviews the medicine therapy and counsels the patient appropriately.[1]

The principal regulations are the Medicinal Products (Prescription and Control of Supply) Regulations 2003 which were further amended in 2005,

---

1. As required by Regulations 9 and 10 of the Regulation of Retail Pharmacy Businesses Regulations 2008, S.I. No. 488 of 2008. Copyright Houses of the Oireachtas 2008.

2007, 2008 and 2009 (the 'Prescription Regulations').[2] These regulations have also been amended by the Irish Medicines Board (Miscellaneous Provisions) Act 2006[3] and the Medicinal Products (Control of Placing on the Market) Regulations 2007.[4]

The main purpose of the 2003 Regulations is to consolidate and update previous outdated regulations applicable to prescription medicines. In addition, they facilitate the control of certain medicines as pharmacy-only medicines.

The regulations regulate both prescription writing and dispensing requirements (Regulation 7); allow for the emergency supply of certain prescription medicines by pharmacists (Regulation 8); regulate the labelling of all dispensed medicines (Regulation 9); regulate the recording of supplies of prescription medicines (Regulations 10 and 11); regulate the sale, labelling and packaging of paracetamol in pharmacies and non-pharmacy outlets (Regulations 12–16); prohibit the sale of any medicine from vending machines (Regulation 17); prohibit the offering or keeping for sale of any medicine after its expiry date (Regulation 18); prohibit the supply of prescription medicines by mail order (Regulation 19); regulate for exemptions in which supply can be made without prescription (Regulation 20) and also for the supply of certain medicines to ambulance personnel (Regulation 20A). In addition the regulations extend the right to prescribe certain prescription medicines, provided specific conditions are met, to registered nurses and midwives, as provided for in the Irish Medicines Board (Miscellaneous Provisions) Act 2006 (Regulations 5A and 5B).

Key definitions

For the purpose of the Prescription Regulations, the term 'prescription' includes those issued by doctors, dentists and nurses registered in Ireland, as well as those issued by doctors and dentists practising in other European Union (EU) member states. The conditions that apply to the dispensing of the latter prescriptions are that the doctor or dentist in question is not practising in Ireland, their address in the other member state is shown on the prescription and the prescription has not been issued with a view to facilitating mail order supply of a medicinal product.[5]

In recognition of Ireland's position as part of the EU internal market, the term 'supply' is defined in the Prescription Regulations in the broader context,

---

2. S.I. No. 540 of 2003 Copyright Houses of the Oireachtas 2003; S.I. No. 510 of 2005 Copyright Houses of the Oireachtas 2005; S.I. No. 201 of 2007 Copyright Houses of the Oireachtas 2007; S.I. No. 512 of 2008 Copyright Houses of the Oireachtas 2008; S.I. No. 442 of 2009. Copyright Houses of the Oireachtas 2009.
3. No. 3 of 2006. Copyright Houses of the Oireachtas 2006.
4. S.I. No. 540 of 2007. Copyright Houses of the Oireachtas 2007.
5. Regulation 4.

so that the controls apply equally to supplies made to persons in the State and to persons who may at the time be in another member state of the EU. The term 'supply' also encompasses selling, distributing or offering or keeping for sale, supply or distribution.

'Supply by mail order' means any supply made, after solicitation of custom by the supplier, or by another person in the chain of supply whether inside or outside of the State, without the supplier and the customer being simultaneously present and using a means of communication at a distance, whether written or electronic, to convey the custom solicitation and the order for supply.

'Supply by way of wholesale dealing' means the supply of a medicinal product to a person who obtains the product for one or more of the following purposes: (a) supply in the course of a pharmaceutical business, (b) administration in the course of a professional practice, or (c) for or in connection with a service provided by a hospital.

'External use' is construed very broadly in the regulations and is defined as application to the skin, hair, teeth, mucosa of the mouth, throat, nose, ear, eye, vagina or anal canal when a local action only is intended and extensive systemic absorption is unlikely to occur. It is interesting to note that the definition of 'external use' specifically excludes transdermal delivery systems, throat sprays, throat pastilles, throat lozenges, throat tablets, nasal drops, nasal sprays, nasal inhalations and teething products.

'New chemical molecule' means a substance not listed in any of the schedules to the regulations and which was not contained as an active substance in a medicinal product lawfully on the market in the State on, or before, 19 January 1987.

In this chapter, the term 'doctor' should be taken to mean 'registered medical practitioner,' similarly 'dentist' to mean 'registered dentist,' 'pharmacist' to mean 'registered pharmacist,' 'nurse' to mean 'registered nurse' and 'midwife' to mean 'registered midwife.' The term 'radiopharmaceuticals' is used throughout the chapter as a generic term to cover medicinal products that on administration emit radiation, or which contain or generate any substance that emits radiation, in order that radiation may be used.

Medicines confined to supply on prescription

The Medicinal Products (Prescription and Control of Supply) Regulations 2003 as amended specify classes of medicines which may only be supplied on prescription as follows:[6]

a   any medicinal product in respect of which a Community marketing authorisation or marketing authorisation has been granted (respectively a

---

6. Regulation 5(1).

marketing authorisation granted by the European Commission or by the Irish Medicines Board (IMB)) and such authorisation contains a statement that the product is to be available only on medical prescription;

b   any medicine which does not have a Community marketing authorisation or marketing authorisation but which consists of a substance listed in Column 1 of the First Schedule to the regulations or a substance which is a new chemical molecule;

c   medicines intended for parenteral use i.e. injectable medicines;

d   radiopharmaceuticals.

The supply of prescription-only medicines must be made by a person lawfully conducting a retail pharmacy business (i.e. from a pharmacy), by or under the personal supervision of a registered pharmacist.

All medicines subject to prescription-control under these regulations are listed in Column 1 of the First Schedule. Column 2 indicates whether they fall into Part A (S1A), Part B (S1B) or Part C (S1C) which dictates how they are to be dispensed. Columns 3, 4 and 5 indicate the circumstances under which certain medicines are exempt from prescription-control.

Administration of medicinal products

It is not an offence for any person to administer to another person any medicinal product which is not subject to prescription-control under the regulations.[7] Similarly, a doctor or dentist may administer to a patient any medicinal product subject to control under the regulations, including prescription medicines. Any person, other than a doctor or dentist, may likewise administer a prescription medicine to a patient provided they do so in accordance with the directions of a doctor or dentist. The references to 'dentist' should be construed as a dentist acting in the course of his or her practice.

Exemptions from prescription-control

The Prescription Regulations provide for exemption from prescription-control for medicines containing substances listed in the First Schedule in the following circumstances:[8]

i   a   medicines having a maximum strength (MS), maximum pack size (MPS) or maximum period of treatment (MPT) not exceeding that indicated in Column 3 of the First Schedule and which are labelled, if applicable, not to exceed the maximum period of treatment;

---

7. Regulation 4A.
8. Regulation 5(2).

b   medicines having a specified use only, a specified pharmaceutical form or a specified manner of administration only as indicated in Column 4 of the First Schedule and which are supplied, if applicable, for such use or manner of administration only; or

c   medicines labelled with a maximum dose (MD) and/or a maximum daily dose (MDD) not exceeding the limits specified in Column 5 of the First Schedule and which are labelled with a dose not exceeding the relevant MD and/or MDD and the statement 'Warning. Do not exceed the stated dose';

ii   medicines intended for veterinary use provided that they are labelled 'For Animal Treatment Only';

iii   medicines that are specified in Part 1 of the Second Schedule (see Appendix 7.1) and that have a product or marketing authorisation, are supplied in the manufacturer's original container and outer packaging and are clearly labelled to show that they may be supplied without prescription. Medicines falling into this category include a number of non-steroidal anti-inflammatory drugs, famotidine, nicotine, hydrocortisone and minoxidil.

Medicines that are exempt from prescription-control by virtue of their dose, pack size, indication, etc., and which have not been assigned a general sale supply classification by the IMB, may only be sold from a retail pharmacy business by or under the personal supervision of a registered pharmacist.[9] It is noteworthy that Sections 27–29 of the Pharmacy Act 2007 require the sale and supply of all medicines in retail pharmacy businesses (including general sale medicines) to be carried out by or under the personal supervision of a registered pharmacist. (See Chapter 12, The Pharmacy Act and Chapter 13 Pharmacy Act – regulations and rules, for further information on the controls that apply under pharmacy legislation to the sale and supply of medicines in pharmacies.)

General sale list medicines may be sold in retail outlets other than pharmacies. The origins of the general sale category are discussed further in the next section.

Supply classification system

Prior to 2007, medicinal products were legally classified as prescription-only medicines in Ireland by virtue of containing substances included in the First Schedule to the Prescription Regulations or were exempt from prescription-control by satisfying the criteria set out in those regulations and described in the previous section. The situation had become somewhat complicated by the

---

9. Regulation 6, Prescription Regulations.

IMB on occasion granting marketing authorisations which specified a more restrictive supply category than that provided for in the Prescription Regulations for the substance in question. As a result, if a marketing authorisation holder wished to change the supply classification of a product, for example, from prescription-only to pharmacy-only, an application had to be made to the IMB to change the supply classification in the marketing authorisation and then to the Minister for Health and Children to make the necessary amendment to the First Schedule to the Prescription Regulations.

At the same time, a small number of medicines such as cough bottles and antacids contained substances which were not classified in any medicines or poisons legislation, and could, by default, be sold anywhere, unless confined to pharmacy-only sale via their marketing authorisation. Amendments to the Irish Medicines Board Act in 2006 changed that position by providing that all medicines not subject to supply on prescription were by default to be supplied from pharmacies. That Act went on to provide the framework for the creation of a general sale category by giving the Minister for Health and Children power to make regulations to provide for an exemption from the default position, to permit non-prescription medicines to be sold from non-pharmacy outlets if deemed reasonably safe to do so.[10] This power was exercised in the passing of the Medicinal Products (Control of Placing on the Market) Regulations 2007, which set out the criteria to be applied by the IMB in assigning the general sale classification to a particular product.[11] The IMB publishes a list of products falling into the general sale category.[12]

More generally, the Control of Placing on the Market Regulations formalised the system whereby the legal category of a medicine was assigned by virtue of the marketing authorisation and determined on a case-by-case basis when an application for grant or renewal of a marketing authorisation was being considered, and set out a new classification system for medicines. The IMB is required under those regulations to have regard to classification criteria for prescription and non-prescription medicines that are derived from EU Directive 2001/83/EC as amended.[13] In addition, the Control of Placing on the Market Regulations define criteria for the assignment of subcategories of prescription-only supply (renewable and non-renewable supply) and non-prescription supply (pharmacy-only and general sale).

---

10. Section 32(2)(m) of Irish Medicines Board Act 1995 as substituted by Section 16(a)(viii) of the Irish Medicines Board (Miscellaneous Provisions) Act 2006.
11. S.I. No. 540 of 2007, Regulation 12.
12. www.imb.ie – see Product Listing (Human Medicines) (accessed 1 March 2011).
13. Directive 2001/83/EC of the European Parliament and of the Council of 6 November 2001 on the Community code relating to medicinal products for human use as amended by Directive 2002/98/EC, Directive 2003/63/EC, Directive 2004/24/EC, Directive 2004/27/EC, Directive 2008/29/EC, Directive 2009/53/EC, Directive 2009/120/EC, Regulation (EC) No. 1901/2006 and Regulation (EC) No. 1394/2007. Title VI deals with classification of medicinal products.

The Control of Placing on the Market Regulations inserted the following new provisions in the Prescription Regulations[14] to align the requirements of the two sets of regulations regarding the classification of medicines:

a   in the case of a medicine granted a marketing authorisation by the IMB after 23 July 2007 (when the Control of Placing on the Market Regulations came into operation), it is to be treated as an S1A medicine if the supply classification assigned in the authorisation is 'medical prescription for non-renewable supply' and as an S1B medicine if the supply classification assigned is 'medical prescription for renewable supply';

b   in the case of a medicine granted a Community marketing authorisation after 23 July 2007 whose authorisation contains a statement that the product is to be available only on medical prescription, it is to be treated as an S1B medicine unless it contains a substance listed in Part A of the First Schedule, in which case it must be treated as an S1A medicine;

c   in the case of a medicine authorised by the IMB or the European Commission prior to 23 July 2007 whose authorisation contains a statement that the product is to be available only on medical prescription, it is to be treated as an S1A medicine if it contains a substance listed in Part A of the First Schedule and as an SIB medicine if it contains a substance listed in Part B;

d   in the case of a medicine authorised prior to 23 July 2007 containing a new chemical molecule whose authorisation contains a statement that the product is to be available only on medical prescription, it is to be treated as an S1A medicine.

As a result, the supply classification assigned by the IMB in the marketing authorisation is now the legal classification without any further requirement to amend the First Schedule to the Prescription Regulations.

The moves to consolidate the classification system are welcome, but the changes have in reality caused confusion for healthcare professionals. Previously, it was possible to ascertain the legal classification of a medicine simply by checking the relevant entry in the First Schedule to the Prescription Regulations, whereas now more extensive research is required. In the case of products authorised by the IMB, the precise supply and dispensing status (e.g. non-renewable or renewable prescription) can be found on the Product Listing section on the IMB website. In the case of products authorised by the European Commission, a review of the product's details on the European Medicines Agency website[15] will reveal if the product is 'subject to medical prescription' or 'not subject to medical prescription' or 'subject to restricted

---

14. Regulation 7(10), Prescription Regulations.
15. www.ema.europa.eu (accessed 1 March 2011).

prescription'. However, subclassifications such as renewable or non-renewable prescription are not assigned by the Commission and the determination of the applicable subcategory in Ireland has to be done on a case-by-case basis with reference to the aforementioned new provisions inserted in the Prescription Regulations in 2007.

Nurse prescribing

Up until 2007, only medical practitioners and dentists were permitted to issue prescriptions for medicinal products intended for human use. Nurse and midwife prescribing was introduced into Ireland with the aim of enhancing the health system's capacity to respond to service needs by maximising nurse and midwife prescribing as a key competency in collaboration with the multidisciplinary team. The introduction of nurse and midwife prescribing has been accomplished by a twin-track approach encompassing the amendment of Irish medicinal products and controlled drugs legislation and the introduction of new professional nursing regulations[16] by the statutory regulator of nurses and midwives, An Bord Altranais.

The Irish Medicines Board (Miscellaneous Provisions) Act 2006 provided for amendments to medicines regulations by ministerial order to allow for nurse and midwife prescribing. The Medicinal Products (Prescription and Control of Supply) (Amendment) Regulations 2007[17] and the Misuse of Drugs (Amendment) Regulations 2007[18] gave prescriptive authority to nurses and midwives and specified the legislative requirements for the prescribing of medicinal products (including those containing controlled drugs) by nurses and midwives.

The Prescription Regulations impose the following conditions on registered nurses and midwives who wish to prescribe:[19]

a   the nurse must be employed by a health service provider in a public or private health service setting;
b   the medicine is one which would normally be provided as part of the health service setting where the nurse is employed;
c   the prescription is in fact issued in the usual course of the provision of that health service.

A health service provider may choose to restrict the prescribing authority of nurses employed by it or impose additional conditions on nurse prescribing over and above those set out in the Prescription Regulations.

---

16. Nurses Rules 2007; now replaced by Nurses Rules 2010 (available at www.nursingboard.ie)
17. S.I. No. 201 of 2007.
18. S.I. No. 200 of 2007.
19. Regulations 5A and 5B.

If a person supplying a medicine on foot of a nurse's prescription, such as a pharmacist, has reasonable cause to believe that not all of the above conditions have been met, he or she may refuse to supply the medicine.

It should be noted that An Bord Altranais requires registered nurses and midwives to complete an accreditation process before they can become registered prescribers and has published practice standards to guide their prescribing activities.[20]

As health service providers move towards greater accessibility for prescription medicines to the general public, the extension of prescriptive authority to nurses is to be welcomed. The success of its implementation will determine, at least in part, whether the extension of prescriptive authority will be considered for other healthcare professionals, including pharmacists, in the future.

Prescription writing requirements

Prescriptions issued by doctors, dentists and nurses must:[21]

a   be in ink;
b   be signed by the prescriber with his or her usual signature and be dated by him or her;
c   clearly indicate the prescriber's name;
d   specify the prescriber's address, except in the case of a health prescription (i.e. General Medical Services (GMS) prescription). In this case, the prescriber's GMS number and name and address are pre-printed on the prescription form given to the patient;
e   state whether the prescriber is a doctor, dentist or nurse and in the case of a nurse, his or her registration number. It is noteworthy that the Medical Council's 'Guide to Professional Conduct and Ethics for Registered Medical Practitioners'[22] states that prescriptions must include a doctor's registration number, although this is not a legal requirement;
f   specify the name and address of the patient;
g   state the age of the patient if under twelve years.

While this list may seem exhaustive, it is interesting to observe that the regulations do not specify that the prescription must contain the name of the medicinal product to be supplied or strength, dose, etc. The determination may

20. An Bord Altranais. Practice Standards and Guidelines for Nurses and Midwives with Prescriptive Authority, 2nd edition, September 2010.
21. Regulation 7(1), Prescription Regulations.
22. Medical Council. *Guide to Professional Conduct and Ethics for Registered Medical Practitioners*, 7th edn. 2009, paragraph 59.1.

have been that this requirement was intuitive and did not have to be included in the regulation, or indeed that a prescription without a specified product is in itself without legal value. It is also noteworthy that there is no imperative for prescribers to write prescriptions generically (i.e. using non-proprietary or generic names for medicines rather than proprietary or brand names).

The requirement for a prescription to be signed by the prescriber means that those sent by e-mail, facsimile or by other electronic means are not valid. Therefore, this regulation will have to be amended if there is to be a move to the electronic issuing of prescriptions in Ireland in the future.

A pharmacist may dispense a prescription in the absence of one of the above prescription writing requirements if he or she is satisfied that it is safe to do so.[23]

In the case of a medicine listed in Schedule 1, 2 or 3 to the Misuse of Drugs Regulations 1988 as amended, the more stringent prescription writing requirements of those regulations apply (see Chapter 8, Misuse of drugs acts and regulations).

Except in the case of the three monthly repeatable prescription forms issued under the GMS scheme (comprising the original and two duplicates), the prescription must be the original as issued by the prescriber.[24]

Dispensing rules

The rules governing the dispensing of prescriptions are specified in the Prescription Regulations.[25] They do not apply to prescription medicines containing drugs listed in Schedules 1, 2 or 3 to the Misuse of Drugs Regulations 1988 as amended, as there are separate dispensing rules applicable to such products under those regulations (see Chapter 8, Misuse of drugs acts and regulations).[26]

A prescription is valid for a maximum period of six months irrespective of any alternative directions written by the prescriber such as 'repeat for twelve months'.

Repeat dispensing of prescriptions

Generally the rules of repeating with regard to S1A and S1B medicines are as follows.

With an S1A drug, the pharmacist is NOT allowed to repeat the dispensing of the prescription unless the prescriber specifically directs that this be done.

---

23. Regulation 7(7), Prescription Regulations.
24. Regulation 7(5)(b), Prescription Regulations.
25. Regulation 7.
26. Regulation 7(8), Prescription Regulations.

Therefore S1A medicines are more likely to be medicines which patients need on a once-off basis; those liable to lead to resistance problems if used repeatedly (e.g. antibiotics, antiviral drugs); medicines with a higher risk of side-effects (e.g. chemotherapeutic agents); misuse or abuse potential (e.g. benzodiazepines); or medicines which require close prescriber supervision. Conversely with S1B medicines, a pharmacist is allowed to repeat the prescription for up to six months from the date of issue, unless the prescriber specifically directs otherwise (e.g. with the words 'no repeats'). These medicines are usually those which are taken for long-term conditions (e.g. furosemide for use in congestive heart failure or hypertension), or medicines intended for short-term or occasional use, such as non-narcotic analgesics.

Where neither the number of occasions nor the intervals (e.g. 'monthly', 'weekly') at which a medicine may be repeated are specified on a prescription, the following rules apply:

a   S1A medicine: may be dispensed on one occasion only;
b   S1B medicine: may be supplied for up to six months at intervals deemed appropriate by the person dispensing it, having regard to the specified rate of dosage.

Where the number of intervals at which the medicine may be supplied is specified on the prescription but not the number of occasions, the following rules apply:

a   S1A medicine: may be dispensed on not more than three occasions (i.e. two repeats permitted);
b   S1B medicine: may be dispensed for up to six months at the stated intervals.

Where the number of occasions on which the medicine may be supplied is specified on the prescription but not the intervals, the prescription may be dispensed at such intervals as are considered appropriate by the person dispensing it, having regard to the specified rate of dosage. This applies to both S1A and S1B medicines.

Additional rules applicable to certain medicines

Prescriptions for medicines for parenteral administration (with the exception of insulin – see below) or for radiopharmaceuticals cannot be repeated unless the intervals of supply or the number of occasions of supply have been stated by the prescriber.

Prescriptions for radiopharmaceuticals and S1C medicines (e.g. specialist diagnostic medicines) may only be dispensed in a hospital.

A number of S1A medicines may be dispensed in accordance with the requirements for S1B medicines in certain circumstances. The medicines to which this applies are:

a   any product intended for external use which is or which contains a substance specified in Part 1 of the Third Schedule (see Appendix 7.2), typically corticosteroids;

b   any product for parenteral administration containing insulin;

c   any preparation intended for use as an oral contraceptive that contains a substance specified in Part 2 of the Third Schedule (see Appendix 7.2), e. g. cyproterone acetate. It is of note that newer pharmaceutical delivery systems of contraceptives (intravaginal and transdermal systems) are, because of their pharmaceutical form, scheduled as S1A and not S1B medicines and are therefore subject to more restrictive dispensing rules. It might reasonably be anticipated that future legislation would account for this discrepancy;

d   any preparation containing hydrocortisone sodium succinate or triamcinolone acetonide intended for treatment of ulceration of the mouth.

In the case of the above medicines, if a marketing authorisation is granted which assigns a supply classification other than one corresponding to S1B, then the medicine must be supplied in accordance with the category assigned in the authorisation.

Due to the concerns over the teratogenicity of oral isotretinoin, a new provision[27] was inserted into the Prescription Regulations by the 2005 amendment regulations to state that prescriptions for oral isotretinoin intended for a woman of childbearing potential should not be dispensed later than seven days after the date on the prescription and the treatment on foot of each prescription should not exceed 30 days.

One of the practical difficulties for prescribers is that they are required to have a clear understanding of what is intended legally by the classification of a medicine as SIA/non-repeatable or SIB/repeatable. Where this is not the case, pharmacists can be left in the position of having to determine what was actually intended by the prescriber and, if necessary, contacting them to clarify their intentions.

Repeating prescriptions issued by dentists

Prescriptions issued by dentists may be dispensed on one occasion only, except for prescriptions issued for sodium fluoride tablets.

---

27. Regulation 7(9).

Steps to be taken after dispensing is complete

When the dispensing of a prescription has been completed, namely, when no further repeats are permitted or the prescription has reached its six-month expiry date, the pharmacist must write or print prominently on the prescription the word 'dispensed' and the date of dispensing, and retain it for two years. When the dispensing of a prescription has been dispensed in part, the pharmacist shall record on the prescription the quantity of each product supplied by him or her and the date on which he or she supplied each such quantity, and the name and address of the person by whom such product was supplied.

Emergency supply of prescription medicines

In order to facilitate access to prescription medicines to patients in an emergency situation, the Prescription Regulations pragmatically allow for supply without a prescription in certain circumstances, including (i) supply at the request of a prescriber and (ii) supply at the request of a patient.[28] The conditions that apply to each category are set out below.

Emergency supply at the request of a doctor, dentist or nurse

The conditions that apply are:

a   the pharmacist is requested by a practitioner or nurse to supply a particular patient but the prescriber is unable to furnish a prescription immediately by reason of an emergency;

b   the practitioner or nurse undertakes to furnish a prescription within 72 hours;

c   the medicine is supplied in accordance with the prescriber's directions;

d   the medicine is not listed in Schedule 1, 2, 3 or 4 to the Misuse of Drugs Regulations 1988 as amended (except for methylphenobarbitone, phenobarbitone or phenobarbitone sodium for use in the treatment of epilepsy).

Notwithstanding these provisions, it is noteworthy that An Bord Altranais's practice standards for nurse and midwife prescribers do not permit them to issue or communicate a prescription verbally or by telephone, e-mail or fax in any circumstance.

---

28. Regulation 8.

Emergency supply at the request of a patient

The conditions that apply are:

a   the pharmacist, having interviewed the person requesting the medicine, is satisfied that there is an immediate need to supply it and that it is impracticable in the circumstances to obtain a prescription without undue delay;

b   a practitioner or nurse has prescribed treatment for the patient with that medicine on a previous occasion;

c   the pharmacist is satisfied that he or she can safely specify the appropriate dose for the patient;

d   the quantity supplied is not greater than what is required for five days' treatment, except in the case of an aerosol for the relief of asthma or a pre-packed ointment or cream, where the smallest available pack size may be supplied or, in the case of an antibiotic in liquid form for oral use, where the smallest quantity that will provide a full course of treatment may be supplied, or in the case of oral contraceptives, sufficient quantity for a full cycle may be supplied;

e   the medicine is not listed in Schedule 1, 2, 3 or 4 to the Misuse of Drugs Regulations 1988 as amended (except for methylphenobarbitone, phenobarbitone or phenobarbitone sodium for use in the treatment of epilepsy) or in the Fourth Schedule to the Prescription Regulations (see Appendix 7.3);

f   the product supplied is labelled with the following information:
   i   date of supply;
   ii   name of the product, either the proprietary (i.e. brand) name or non-proprietary (i.e. generic) name, in which case the name of the manufacturer (or the person placing the product on the market) must also be given;
   iii quantity and, except where it is apparent from the name, the pharmaceutical form and strength of the product;
   iv   name of the person requesting the product;
   v   name and address of the shop from which the product was supplied, and
   vi   the words 'Emergency Supply'.

The provision in relation to emergency supply at the request of a practitioner places an obligation on the prescriber to furnish a prescription within 72 hours, but there are no restrictions on further such supplies if he or she fails to do so. However, it is interesting to note that the legislation governing the supply of animal remedies in Ireland prohibits a pharmacist from making an emergency supply of a prescription-only animal remedy at the request of a veterinary surgeon if he or she has failed to provide a prescription within 72 hours for such a supply in the past.[29]

Labelling of dispensed medicines

The Prescription Regulations include provisions regarding the labelling of dispensed medicinal products.[30] In this context, the term 'dispensed medicinal product' is much broader than just medicines supplied by a pharmacist on foot of a prescription. It includes medicines supplied by a medical practitioner or dentist for or to a patient under his or her care and medicines supplied by a pharmacist on foot of a prescription or specification provided by the patient or in circumstances where the pharmacist exercised his or her own judgement as to the treatment required by the patient.

The following information must appear on the label of a dispensed medicinal product:

a   name of the patient;
b   name and the address of the pharmacy, doctor or dentist who supplied the product;
c   date of dispensing;
d   unless the prescriber directs otherwise, the name of the medicine, either the brand name or generic name, in which case the name of the manufacturer must also be given;
e   where the product is being supplied on foot of a prescription, the directions for use and precautions relating to the use of the product, as specified by the prescriber. Where a pharmacist is of the opinion that the prescriber's instructions are inappropriate, and has tried, but failed, to contact the prescriber, then the pharmacist should include such instructions that he or she deems appropriate;
f   where the product is not being supplied on foot of prescription, the directions for use;
g   'Keep out of the reach of children';
h   'For external use only' on products so intended;
i   any of the cautionary and warning notices specified in the Fifth Schedule (see Appendix 7.4) as deemed appropriate by the pharmacist.

---

29. Regulation 44(3) of European Communities (Animal Remedies) (No. 2) Regulations 2007 (S.I. 786 of 2007). Copyright Houses of the Oireachtas 2007.
30. Regulation 9.

It is not necessary to include the information specified in (d), (g), (h) and (i) above on the dispensing label if the product is supplied in the manufacturer's original pack accompanied by the relevant patient information leaflet (if any), provided that the information originally on the container has not been removed or obscured in the course of supply.

Indeed, in a number of EU member states, such original pack dispensing is mandatory. It could be argued that the supply of medicines in the original pack of the manufacturer is preferable from a patient safety perspective as the necessary information can be more effectively communicated to a patient in pack design rather than the information that can be contained in a dispensing label(s). Furthermore, supply in original packs permits more effective auditing of the source of medicines which is important as the EU considers more effective mechanisms to protect the integrity of the supply chain against counterfeit medicines. An additional benefit of original pack dispensing is that it more easily facilitates the process of automated dispensing as a growing number of pharmacists employ such technology to improve their risk-management systems and increase operational efficiency. Original pack dispensing, however, is not without its problems. An important consideration for such dispensing is that patients may be supplied with more medicine than is required for effective therapeutic treatment and there is also the problem of lack of standardisation of original pack sizes, for example, medicines intended for monthly dispensing may be available as a 28-day calendar pack or as a 30-day pack.

Pharmacy records

General requirements

Every pharmacy must keep a prescription register for recording all transactions involving the supply of prescription-only medicines to the public (i.e. prescriptions (including repeats), emergency supplies and wholesale-type transactions).[31] In practice, adhesive labels containing the required information may be used for recording purposes in the register and should be affixed in chronological sequence. Any required details not included in the label should be written into the register by the pharmacist. The requirement to record supplies is most commonly complied with through the use of computerised records and the regulations permit this, provided a daily printout of the relevant records is generated and signed and dated by the registered pharmacist managing the pharmacy within 24 hours.

---

31. Regulation 10, Prescription Regulations.

Information to be recorded

The following details must be recorded in the prescription register:

a   supply on prescription:
  i   date of supply;
  ii   name, quantity and, if not apparent from the name, form and strength of the medicine;
  iii   name of prescriber and, where he or she is not known to the pharmacist, their address;
  iv   name and address of person for whom product is prescribed;
  v   date of the prescription;
  vi   in the case of emergency supply at the request of a prescriber, the date on which the prescription is actually received;

b   repeat prescriptions:
  i   date of supply together with a reference to the original entry in the register OR all the particulars required for original prescriptions;
  ii   in the case of a prescription which was dispensed previously at another pharmacy, the name and address of that pharmacy together with the prescription reference number;

c   emergency supply at the request of a patient:
  i   date of supply;
  ii   name, quantity and, if not apparent from the name, form and strength of the medicine;
  iii   name and address of person requiring the medicine;
  iv   nature of the emergency;
  v   name of the prescriber who prescribed the medicine previously and, where he or she is not known to the pharmacist, his or her address;
  vi   where the previous sale or supply occurred at another pharmacy, the name and address of that pharmacy and the prescription reference number;

d   wholesale transactions where written orders or invoices are not retained:
  i   date of supply;
  ii   name, quantity and, if not apparent from the name, form and strength of the medicine;
  iii   name and address and trade, business or profession of the person to whom the product is supplied;
  iv   purpose for which the product is supplied.

All prescription registers, computerised records, daily printouts, prescriptions, duplicates of GMS prescriptions and orders or invoices relating to wholesale transactions must be kept on the premises from which the medicines concerned were supplied for two years from the date of the last entry, the date of sale or supply or the date of last dispensing.

Exemptions from recording requirements

The requirement to record details in the prescription register does not apply to the following:

a   health prescriptions (i.e. prescriptions issued under the GMS scheme where a pre-printed prescription form is used by the prescriber. A duplicate copy is retained by the dispensing pharmacy and the original is submitted for reimbursement);
b   the sale or supply of controlled drugs which require a separate record to be kept in the controlled drugs register (as per Article 16 of the Misuse of Drug Regulations 1988 as amended);
c   supply by wholesale where the order or invoice (or copy of same) is retained in the pharmacy;
d   supply to a sampling officer.

Mifepristone

Mifepristone, an S1C anti-progestogenic steroid, is subject to additional recording requirements.[32] A separate register must be kept for recording the supply and administration of mifepristone which must include the following details:

a   date of supply or administration;
b   name and address of the recipient;
c   dosage, form, strength and quantity of product supplied or administered;
d   purpose/circumstances of supply or administration;
e   signature of person who made the supply or administration.

This register should be kept for a period of two years from the date of last entry.

Mifepristone has a number of uses including that of abortifacient. However, it is illegal to use it for this purpose in Ireland because of the constitutional ban on abortion.[33] It has a number of other therapeutic uses (e.g. labour induction after foetal death *in utero*) which are not in breach of this constitutional ban and clearly the reason for having to record the purpose/circumstances of supply or administration is to ensure that its supply is lawful.

---

32. Regulation 11, Prescription Regulations.
33. Article 40.3.3 of Bunreacht na hÉireann (Constitution of Ireland).

Paracetamol supply

Paracetamol poisoning is an important public health issue. It is the most commonly enquired about drug to the National Poisons Information Centre.[34] Research has shown that the incidence of paracetamol poisoning is related to its ease of access.[35] A strong positive association has been found between trends in paracetamol use and trends in non-fatal paracetamol overdose.[36] This, added to the body of evidence that reductions in the quantity and presentation of paracetamol available as a single purchase might reduce suicide and fulminant liver failure related to paracetamol, created the impetus to restrict the availability of paracetamol without prescription.

In 1997 the IMB introduced guidelines for the supply and sale of paracetamol in pharmacy and non-pharmacy outlets. These guidelines were put on a statutory footing in the Medicinal Products (Control of Paracetamol) Regulations 2001 and subsequently the provisions in these regulations were incorporated into the current Prescription Regulations in 2003 and updated further by the 2008 amendment regulations.[37]

The regulations provide that the paracetamol may only be supplied without prescription from pharmacies and non-pharmacy outlets subject to certain restrictions on presentation and quantities supplied. The pack size restrictions that apply to products containing paracetamol intended for oral use, sold or supplied by pharmacies and non-pharmacy outlets are set out in Table 7.1.

Paracetamol products may only be supplied in a pharmacy by or under the personal supervision of a pharmacist. Notwithstanding the pack restrictions described above, if a pharmacist has interviewed the person requesting the product and is satisfied that it is safe to do so, then he or she may supply them with a total quantity of paracetamol-containing medicinal product not exceeding 50 dosage units or in the case of products other than tablets or capsules, two packs.

Paracetamol products sold in non-pharmacy outlets may not contain any other active analgesic substance and only one pack of the product may be sold in the course of any one retail transaction. Many retail outlets have adapted their cash registers to automatically detect the purchase of multiple packs of paracetamol.

---

34. Annual report of National Poisons Information Centre 2009, available at www.poisons.ie (accessed 1 March 2011).
35. Hawton K, Ware C, Mistry H et al. Why patients choose paracetamol for self-poisoning and their knowledge of its dangers. *BMJ* 1995; 310(6973): 164.
36. Laffoy M, Scallan E, Byrne G. Paracetamol availability and overdose in Ireland. *Ir Med J* 2001; 94(7): 212–214.
37. Regulations 12–16.

Table 7.1 Pack size restrictions on supply of non-prescription oral paracetamol products by pharmacies and non-pharmacy outlets

	Form and strength	Maximum pack size that may be sold in pharmacies	Maximum pack size that may be sold in non-pharmacy outlets
(a)	Dosage unit (e.g. tablet, capsule, sachet) containing more than 120 mg but not more than 500 mg of paracetamol	24 dosage units	12 dosage units
(b)	Dosage unit containing more than 500 mg but not more than 600 mg of paracetamol	20 dosage units	10 dosage units
(c)	Dosage unit containing more than 600 mg but not more than 1000 mg of paracetamol	12 dosage units	6 dosage units
(d)	Medicinal product intended for use in children under 6 years of age where: (i) each dosage unit contains not more than 120 mg of paracetamol or (ii) in the case of a liquid form of the product, each 5 mL dosage contains not more than 120 mg of paracetamol	24 dosage units 140 mL	12 dosage units 60 mL
(e)	Medicinal product in liquid form, intended for use in children over 6 years of age and under 12 years of age, where each 5 mL dosage unit contains not more than 250 mg of paracetamol other than a product to which (d) applies	140 mL	May not be sold in non-pharmacy outlets
(f)	Medicinal product in liquid form where each 5 mL dosage unit contains not more than 250 mg of paracetamol, other than a product to which (d) or (e) applies	240 mL	60 mL

Paracetamol presentation

Products containing paracetamol in solid unit dosage form (e.g. tablet, capsule) must be supplied in a blister pack or other equivalent form of packaging as specified in the relevant marketing authorisation (i.e. in the manufacturer's original pack). This restriction does not apply to paracetamol products intended for supply solely on prescription.

Warnings on labels and package leaflets

In order to provide greater information to the public and to highlight the dangers of paracetamol overdose and the associated risk of hepatotoxicity, the Prescription Regulations provide for explicit and specified information to be contained both on the outer packaging and package leaflets of paracetamol-containing medicines.

In particular, the following statements must appear clearly on the outer packaging of paracetamol products or, if there is no outer packaging, on the immediate packaging:

a   'Contains paracetamol';
b   'Do not take any other paracetamol-containing products';
c   'Do not exceed the stated dose';
d   'Immediate medical advice should be sought in the event of overdosage, even if you feel well. Please read the enclosed leaflet carefully' in cases where a package leaflet is supplied and the product is intended mainly for use in adults;
e   'Immediate medical advice should be sought in the event of overdosage, even if the child seems well. Please read the enclosed leaflet carefully' in cases where a package leaflet is supplied and product is intended mainly for use in children not over twelve years;
f   'Immediate medical advice should be sought in the event of overdosage, because of the risk of irreversible liver damage' in cases where no package leaflet is supplied with the product.

In addition the regulations provide that the following information should appear on the package leaflet:

a   'Contains paracetamol';
b   'Do not take any other paracetamol-containing products';
c   'Do not exceed the stated dose';
d   'Immediate medical advice should be sought in the event of overdosage, because of the risk of irreversible liver damage.'

These statements may be varied with the prior written approval of the IMB, provided the amendments do not alter the effect of the information that was to have been conveyed by the original statement. Whether these provisions of the regulations have any meaningful outcome for patient safety has yet to be fully determined.

Expiry dates

A person must not supply any medicinal product after its expiry date has passed.[38] The expiry date is defined by the manufacturer and printed on the outer and immediate packaging of all medicinal products. As the term 'supply'

---

38. Regulation 18, Prescription Regulations.

includes keeping or offering to supply, it is also a breach of the regulations to have expired medicines in stock. This prohibition does not apply to a medicinal product where the IMB has determined that the expiry date may be extended and the product is supplied for use within such extended period, and any condition or restriction relating to that determination is complied with.

Mail order supply

Mail order supply of prescription-only medicines is not permitted.[39] Supply by mail order is defined in very broad terms as 'any supply made, after solicitation of custom by the supplier, or by another person in the chain of supply whether inside or outside of the State [i.e. Ireland], without the supplier and the customer being simultaneously present and using a means of written communication at a distance, whether written or electronic, to convey the custom solicitation and the order.'[40] Internet sales therefore fall within this definition.

Anyone who owns or occupies a premises must not permit it to be used for the receipt, collection or transmission of orders or correspondence relating to mail order supplies. Furthermore if the address of the premises is not identifiable due to the use of a post office (PO) box, telephone number or e-mail address, the person making available the relevant PO box, phone number or e-mail address facility will be deemed to be the occupier of the premises.

This prohibition on the mail order selling of prescription-only medicinal products which applies in Ireland (and in many other EU member states) was upheld in the 2003 judgment of the European Court of Justice on the 'Doc Morris' case.[41] It is interesting to note that in Ireland, the blanket ban that had applied to mail order supplies of all medicinal products had to be modified in light of the Doc Morris judgment which did not extend to banning the mail order of non-prescription medicines.

Vending machines

The Prescription Regulations provide that medicines cannot be sold in a vending machine.[42]

---

39. Regulation 19, Prescription Regulations.
40. Regulation 4, Prescription Regulations.
41. Case C-322/01 *Deutscher Apothekerverband eV* v. *0800 DocMorris NV and Jacques Waterval.*
42. Regulation 17.

Exemptions from prescription requirements

General exemptions

Prescriptions are not required for the sale and/or supply of prescription medicines to the following:[43] to higher education institutions or scientific research institutes for the purposes of education or research; to sampling officers or officers of the IMB or public analysts in connection with the performance of their duties; to persons who are required by law to provide medical treatment to employees for the purposes of such treatment; or to persons involved in testing the quality or amount of drugs, medicines and appliances supplied for the purpose of Section 59 of the Health Act 1970[44] (Section 59 provides the basis for the GMS and other community drugs schemes which are now administered by the Health Service Executive).

The wholesale supply of prescription medicines is also exempt.

In addition to not requiring a prescription, the requirements for pharmacist supervision of the supply of medicinal products exempt from prescription control, the ban on mail order supplies and the pack size restrictions on paracetamol products do not apply to any of the above transactions.

Supply to registered optometrists and registered dispensing opticians

The Prescription Regulations allow for the supply by wholesale of certain medicinal products to registered optometrists for administration to patients in the course of their professional practice, subject to a number of restrictions.[45] First, the products in question are medicinal products which contain cyclopentolate hydrochloride, fluorescein sodium, oxybuprocaine hydrochloride or tropicamide and are not intended for parenteral use. Second, the optometrist is required to submit a signed order to the supplier for the purpose of each such supply.

Registered dispensing opticians who hold a certificate of entitlement to fit contact lenses issued by the Opticians Board may be provided with medicinal products containing fluorescein sodium which are not intended for parenteral use, for administration to patients in the course of their professional practice. Registered dispensing opticians are also required to provide signed orders in respect of such supplies.

---

43. Regulation 20(1), Prescription Regulations.
44. No. 1 of 1970.
45. Regulation 20(2) and 20(2A).

Supply in hospitals

Pharmacists or nurses may supply prescription medicines in hospitals in accordance with the written directions of a registered medical practitioner or dentist, notwithstanding that those directions do not meet the requirements for prescriptions set out in the regulations.[46] This exemption permits the use of medication charts such as the patient's bed card (drug kardex) or case sheet for inpatients in hospitals. In the case of hospitals providing community mental health services to patients (i.e. outpatients under the care of the hospital), nurses in the service may provide such patients with up to three days' supply of medication in accordance with the written directions of a registered medical practitioner in the service, notwithstanding that those directions do not meet the standard requirements for prescriptions.

Supply by doctors and dentists to patients under their care

Doctors and dentists may supply prescription and non-prescription medicinal products to their patients in the course of their professional practice.[47]

Supply to pre-hospital emergency care providers

The Prescription Regulations were amended in 2005[48] and 2008[49] in order to grant exemption from prescription control and give legal authority to supply certain medicinal products to specific ambulance personnel, namely the following grades of pre-hospital emergency care providers: advanced paramedics, paramedics and emergency medical technicians, for use in the course of their duties.[50]

The medicinal products that may be supplied to advanced paramedics, paramedics and emergency medical technicians are outlined in the Seventh Schedule to the regulations (see Appendix 7.5) along with the route and conditions of administration and the basis of their authority to administer, which is either on foot of clinical practice guidelines published by the Pre-Hospital Emergency Care Council (PHECC) or on the instructions of a registered medical practitioner. The PHECC is an independent statutory agency with responsibility for standards, education and training in the field of pre-hospital emergency care in Ireland. Clinical practice guidelines are published by PHECC for each grade of pre-hospital emergency care provider.[51]

---

46. Regulation 20(3)(a) and (b).
47. Regulation 20(3)(c).
48. S.I. No. 510 of 2005.
49. S.I. No. 512 of 2008.
50. Regulation 20(8).
51. Available at www.phecit.ie (accessed 1 March 2011).

Herbal medicinal products

The Prescription Regulations only permit the extemporaneous preparation and supply without prescription of products containing *Ginkgo biloba* L. and *Hypericum perforatum* L. (also known as St John's wort) in the following circumstances: the product must be prepared on the premises of the person making the supply, for administration to a particular person after being requested by or on behalf of that person, and with the person supplying it using his or her own professional judgement as to the treatment required. The premises concerned cannot be a shop or other retail premises and must not be freely accessible by the public.[52] In practice, these provisions apply to herbalists who prepare customised treatments for patients who consult them. In all other circumstances, medicinal products containing *Hypericum perforatum* for any use other than external use and medicinal products containing *Ginkgo biloba* are confined to supply on prescription.

Emergency circumstances

The provisions of the Regulations do not apply to the supply of a medicinal product to which Regulation 8 of the Medicinal Products (Control of Placing on the Market) Regulations 2007 applies. Regulation 8 permits the supply and use of an unauthorised medicine or a medicine outside the terms of its marketing authorisation on the direction of the Minister for Health and Children in response to the suspected or confirmed spread of pathogenic agents, toxins, chemical agents or nuclear radiation in emergency circumstances. The Prescription Regulations also exempt the supply of any other medicine for use in such an emergency situation.[53]

Supply of free samples to prescribers

The supply of free samples of medicinal products to prescribers in the course of product promotion is exempt from the requirements for prescription control and pharmacist supervision.[54] These samples are typically provided by medical representatives during visits to prescribers and their supply is subject to detailed controls under the Medicinal Products (Control of Advertising) Regulations 2007[55] (see Chapter 6, Advertising of medicines).

---

52. Regulation 20(5).
53. Regulation 20(9).
54. Regulation 20(6).
55. S.I. No. 541 of 2007.

Appendix 7.1 Substances which when contained in certain non-prescription medicinal products may only be supplied in the manufacturer's original container showing the legal classification for supply

(Medicinal Products (Prescription and Control of Supply) Regulations 2003 as amended, Second Schedule, Part 1[56])

Acyclovir

Diclofenac diethylammonium

Diclofenac sodium [inserted by
2005 Amendment Regulations]

Famotidine

Flurbiprofen

Hydrocortisone

Hydrocortisone acetate

Ibuprofen

Ketoprofen

Minoxidil

Naproxen

Nicotine

Nicotine resinate

Oxetacaine

Piroxicam

Appendix 7.2 Substances which are normally SIA but may be dispensed as SIB medicines in certain circumstances

(Medicinal Products (Prescription and Control of Supply) Regulations 2003, Third Schedule[57])

Part 1 – Substances which, when contained in medicinal products intended for external use, may be dispensed as SIB medicines

Alclomethasone dipropionate

Beclometasone dipropionate

Betametasone

Betametasone benzoate

Betametasone dipropionate

Betametasone sodium phosphate

Betametasone valerate

Clobetasol propionate

Clobetasone butyrate

Desonide

Desoxymethasone

Dexamethasone

Dexamethasone sodium
phosphate

Diflorasone diacetate

Diflucortolone valerate

Fluclorolone acetonide

Fludroxycortide

Flumethasone pivalate

Fluocinolone acetonide

Fluocinonide

Fluocortolone

---

56. S.I. No. 540 of 2003 (Copyright Houses of the Oireachtas 2003) as amended by S.I. No. 510 of 2005 (Copyright Houses of the Oireachtas 2005).
57. S.I. No. 540 of 2003 (Copyright Houses of the Oireachtas 2003).

Fluocortolone hexanoate
Fluocortolone pivalate
Fluorometholone
Fluprednidene acetate
Formocortal
Halcinonide
Hydrocortisone
Hydrocortisone acetate
Hydrocortisone butyrate

Medrysone
Methylprednisolone acetate
Mometasone furoate
Prednisolone
Prednisolone acetate
Prednisolone hexanoate
Prednisolone sodium phosphate
Prednisolone steaglate
Triamcinolone acetonide

Part 2 – Substances which, when contained in oral contraceptives, may be dispensed as SIB medicines

Cyproterone acetate
Drospirenone
Desogestrel
Estradiol valerate
Ethinylestradiol
Ethynodiol
Etynodiol diacetate
Gestodene

Levonorgestrel
Lynestrenol
Mestranol
Norelgestromin
Norethisterone
Norethisterone
  acetate
Norgestimate

Appendix 7.3 Medicines that cannot be supplied without a prescription in an emergency at the request of a patient

(Medicinal Products (Prescription and Control of Supply) Regulations 2003 as amended, Fourth Schedule[58])

Ammonium bromide
Calcium bromidolactobionate
Calcium bromide
Chlomethiazole edisilate
Chlomethiazole
Embutramide

Fluanisone
Hydrobromic acid
Isotretinoin [inserted by 2005
  Amendment Regulations]
Meclofenoxate hydrochloride
Mifepristone

---

58. S.I. No. 540 of 2003 (Copyright Houses of the Oireachtas 2003) as amended by S.I. No. 510 of 2005 (Copyright Houses of the Oireachtas 2005).

Piracetam   Strychnine hydrochloride
Potassium bromide   Tacrine hydrochloride
Sodium bromide   Thiopental sodium

Appendix 7.4 Cautionary and warning notices for dispensed medicinal products

(Medicinal Products (Prescription and Control of Supply) Regulations 2003, Fifth Schedule[59])

	Notice	Examples of medicinal products for which the notice appearing opposite may be appropriate
1	Warning. May cause drowsiness	Products for children containing antihistamines or other products given to children that can cause drowsiness
2	Warning. May cause drowsiness. If affected do not drive or operate machinery. Avoid alcoholic drink	Products for adults that can cause drowsiness thereby affecting the ability to drive and operate hazardous machinery
3	Warning. May cause drowsiness. If affected do not drive or operate machinery	Monoamine-oxidase inhibitors when 'Treatment Card' is supplied
4	Warning. Causes drowsiness which may continue the next day. If affected do not drive or operate machinery. Avoid alcoholic drink	Hypnotics and certain other products with sedative effects, prescribed to be taken at night
5	Warning. Avoid alcoholic drink	
6	Do not take indigestion remedies at the same time of day as this medicine	Products coated to resist gastric acid (e.g. enteric coated tablets). This is to avoid the possibility of premature dissolution due to the presence of an alkaline pH
7	Do not take indigestion remedies or medicines containing iron or zinc at the same time of day as this medicine	Products containing ciprofloxacin and some other quinolones, doxycycline, lymecycline, minocycline or penicillamine
8	Do not take milk, indigestion remedies or medicines containing iron or zinc at the same time of day as this medicine	Products containing norfloxacin, tetracyclines other than doxycycline and minocycline

---

59. S.I. No. 540 of 2003 (Copyright Houses of the Oireachtas 2003).

9	Do not stop taking this medicine except on your doctor's advice	Products (such as beta-adrenoceptor blocking drugs, anti-hypertensives, those for the treatment or prophylaxis of asthma or allopurinol) required to be taken over a prolonged period for a benefit to be noticed or where withdrawal is likely to be a particular hazard (e.g clonidine)
10	Take at regular intervals. Complete the prescribed course unless otherwise directed	Antimicrobial drugs given by mouth
11	Warning. Follow the printed instructions you have been given with this medicine	Products (such as anticoagulants, lithium and oral corticosteroids) in respect of which a treatment card or other written instructions are given to the patient
12	Avoid exposure of skin to direct sunlight or sun-lamps	Products which may cause photo toxic or photo allergic reactions
13	Do not take products containing aspirin while taking this medicine	Products containing salicylate derivatives
14	Dissolve or mix with water before taking	
15	This medicine may colour the urine	Products such as levodopa (dark reddish), phenolphthalein (pink), triamterene (blue), and rifampicin (red)
16	Caution flammable: keep away from fire or flames	
17	Allow to dissolve under the tongue. Do not transfer from this container. Keep tightly closed. Discard eight weeks after opening	Glyceryl trinitrate tablets
18	Not to be used for prolonged periods or at higher levels than those recommended without medical advice	Sympathomimetics for internal use
19	Do not take more than.....in 24 hours or......in any one week	Products containing ergotamine
20	Do not take more than......in 24 hours	Products for the treatment of acute migraine except for ergotamine (see above)
21	Take an hour before food or on an empty stomach	Certain oral antibiotics the absorption of which may be reduced by the presence of food and acid in the stomach
22	Take half to one hour before food	Products the action of which is thereby improved
23	To be swallowed whole, not chewed	Enteric coated or modified release products or in the case of products that taste very unpleasant or may damage the mouth
24	Take with plenty of water	

	Notice	Examples of medicinal products for which the notice appearing opposite may be appropriate
25	To be applied sparingly	Products for external use containing a corticosteroid or dithranol
26	To be dissolved under the tongue	Products intended for sublingual use
27	To be sucked or chewed	
28	Take with or after food	Products liable to cause gastric irritation or which are better absorbed with food
29	Warning. Do not exceed the stated dose	
30	Caution. It is dangerous to exceed the stated dose	Products that are recommended to be taken on an 'as required' basis
31	Do not take more than 2 at any one time. Do not take more than 8 in 24 hours	Dispensed tablets or capsules containing paracetamol labelled to be taken 'as required'
32	Contains paracetamol	Dispensed products containing paracetamol when the name on the label does not include the word 'paracetamol'
33	Contains aspirin and paracetamol	Dispensed products containing aspirin and paracetamol when the name on the label does not include the words 'aspirin' and 'paracetamol'
34	Contains aspirin	Dispensed products containing aspirin when the name on the label does not include the word 'aspirin'
35	Contains an aspirin-like medicine	Dispensed products containing a salicylate derivative
36	Not to be taken	
37	Shake the bottle	
38	Store in a cool place	
39	Do not use after . . .	
40	Discard . . . days after opening	
41	Not to be used for babies	
42	Not to be used for children under three years of age or for application to large areas of skin unless on medical advice	Products containing hexachlorophane
43	Not to be applied to broken skin and not to be used for children under three years of age	Products containing boric acid or borax

44	When taking this medicine and for 14 days after your treatment finishes you must observe the following instructions:	Monoamine-oxidase inhibitors – (Treatment Card Text)
	1 Do not eat cheese, pickled herrings or broad bean pods 2 Do not eat or drink Bovril, Oxo, Marmite or any similar meat or yeast extract 3 Eat only fresh foods and avoid food that you suspect could be stale or going off. This is especially important with meat, fish, poultry or offal. Avoid game 4 Do not take any other medicines whether purchased by you or previously prescribed for you by your doctor, without first consulting your doctor or your pharmacist 5 Avoid alcoholic drinks	
45	If the condition is not improved, consult your doctor	
46	Do not use in pregnancy without medical advice	

Note – Certain of these labels may be incorporated in the directions for use on the label of the product.

Appendix 7.5 Supply of medicines to pre-hospital emergency care providers

(Medicinal Products (Prescription and Control of Supply) Regulations 2003 as amended, Seventh Schedule[60])

Part 1 – Medicinal products that may be supplied for use by advanced paramedics

Medicinal product	Route of administration	Conditions of administration	Authority to administer
Adenosine solution for injection	Intravenous	Adults: Supraventricular tachycardias (SVT)	According to Clinical Practice Guidelines (CPG) or on registered medical practitioner's instructions
Amiodarone injection	Intravenous	Adults and children: Cardiac arrest	According to CPG or on registered medical practitioner's instructions

---

60. S.I. No. 540 of 2003 (Copyright Houses of the Oireachtas 2003) as amended by S.I. No. 512 of 2008 (Copyright Houses of the Oireachtas 2008).

Medicinal product	Route of administration	Conditions of administration	Authority to administer
Aspirin (various oral dosage forms)	Oral	Adults: Cardiac chest pain	According to CPG or on registered medical practitioner's instructions
Atropine injection	Intravenous Endotracheal	Adults and children: Cardiac arrest, bradycardia, poisoning	According to CPG or on registered medical practitioner's instructions.
Benzylpenicillin injection	Intravenous Intramuscular	Adults and children: Suspected or confirmed meningococcal sepsis	According to CPG or on registered medical practitioner's instructions
Cefotaxime powder for injection	Intravenous Intramuscular	Adults and children: Suspected or confirmed meningococcal sepsis	According to CPG or on registered medical practitioner's instructions
Ceftriaxone powder for injection	Intravenous Intramuscular	Adults and children: Suspected or confirmed meningococcal sepsis	According to CPG or on registered medical practitioner's instructions
Clopidogrel tablets	Oral	Adults: Myocardial infarction	According to CPG or on registered medical practitioner's instructions
Cyclizine injection	Intravenous	Adults and children: To prevent or treat opiate-induced nausea and vomiting. Anti-emetic	According to CPG or on registered medical practitioner's instructions
Dextrose 5% solution for infusion	Intravenous	Adults and children: Dilutant for medications	According to CPG or on registered medical practitioner's instructions
Dextrose 10% solution for infusion	Intravenous	Adults and children: Hypoglycaemia, dilutant for medications	According to CPG or on registered medical practitioner's instructions
Diazepam injection	Intravenous Intramuscular	Adults and children: Seizures, sedation	According to CPG or on registered medical practitioner's instructions
Diazepam rectal solution	Per rectum	Adults and children: Seizures	According to CPG or on registered medical practitioner's instructions
Enoxaparin sodium solution for injection	Intravenous Subcutaneous	Adults: ST-elevation myocardial infarction (STEMI)	According to CPG or on registered medical practitioner's instructions
Epinephrine (adrenaline) 1 mg/1 mL (1 : 1000) injection	Intramuscular	Adults and children: Anaphylaxis, bronchospasm	According to CPG or on registered medical practitioner's instructions

Epinephrine (adrenaline) 1 mg/10 mL (1 : 10 000)	Intravenous Endotracheal	Adults and children: Cardiac arrest, bradycardia, anaphylaxis	According to CPG or on registered medical practitioner's instructions
Ergometrine injection 500 micrograms/mL	Intravenous Intramuscular	Adults: Post-partum haemorrhage	According to CPG or on registered medical practitioner's instructions
Furosemide injection	Intravenous Intramuscular	Adults: Pulmonary oedema	According to CPG or on registered medical practitioner's instructions
Glucagon for injection	Intramuscular Subcutaneous	Adults and children: Hypoglycaemia	According to CPG or on registered medical practitioner's instructions
Glyceryl trinitrate aerosol	Sublingual	Adults: Cardiac chest pain, congestive heart failure	According to CPG or on registered medical practitioner's instructions
Haloperidol injection 5 mg/mL	Intravenous Intramuscular	Adults: Sedation	According to CPG or on registered medical practitioner's instructions
Hartmann's solution for infusion	Intravenous	Adults and children: Hypovolaemic shock, anaphylaxis, decompression illness, burns, cardiac arrest, bradycardia, dilutant for medications	According to CPG or on registered medical practitioner's instructions
Hydrocortisone powder for solution for injection	Intravenous Intramuscular	Adults and children: Bronchospasm	According to CPG or on registered medical practitioner's instructions
Ipratropium bromide nebuliser solution	Inhalation.	Adults and children: Bronchospasm in acute asthma	According to CPG or on registered medical practitioner's instructions
Ibuprofen (various oral dosage forms)	Oral	Adults and children: Pain	According to CPG or on registered medical practitioner's instructions
Lidocaine hydrochloride injection	Intravenous Endotracheal	Adults: Cardiac arrest	According to CPG or on registered medical practitioner's instructions
Lorazepam injection	Intravenous Intramuscular	Adults and children: Seizures	According to CPG or on registered medical practitioner's instructions
Lorazepam tablets	Oral	Adults and children: Sedation	According to CPG or on registered medical practitioner's instructions

Medicinal product	Route of administration	Conditions of administration	Authority to administer
Magnesium sulphate injection BP	Intravenous	Adults and children: Cardiac arrest, bronchospasm	According to CPG or on registered medical practitioner's instructions
Meropenem powder for injection	Intravenous	Adults and children: Suspected or confirmed meningococcal sepsis	According to CPG or on registered medical practitioner's instructions
Midazolam solution for injection	Intravenous Intramuscular Intranasal	Adults and children: Seizures, sedation	According to CPG or on registered medical practitioner's instructions
Midazolam solution (buccal)	Buccal	Adults and children: Seizures	According to CPG or on registered medical practitioner's instructions
Morphine injection	Intravenous Intramuscular	Adults and children: Moderate to severe pain	According to CPG or on registered medical practitioner's instructions
Morphine oral solution	Oral	Children: Pain	According to CPG or on registered medical practitioner's instructions
Naloxone for injection	Intravenous Intramuscular Subcutaneous Intranasal	Adults and children: Respiratory depression secondary to known or suspected narcotic overdose	According to CPG or on registered medical practitioner's instructions
Nifedipine capsules	Oral	Adults: Inhibition of labour	According to CPG or on registered medical practitioner's instructions
Nitrous oxide–oxygen mixture – medical gas	By inhalation	Adults and children: Pain relief	According to CPG or on registered medical practitioner's instructions
Ondansetron hydrochloride injection	Intravenous	Adults and children: To prevent or treat opiate-induced nausea and vomiting. Antiemetic	According to CPG or on registered medical practitioner's instructions
Oxytocin solution for injection	Intravenous Intramuscular	Adults: Post-partum haemorrhage	According to CPG or on registered medical practitioner's instructions
Paracetamol suppositories	Per rectum	Children: Pyrexia	According to CPG or on registered medical practitioner's instructions
Paracetamol (various oral dosage forms)	Oral	Adults and children: Pain, Pyrexia	According to CPG or on registered medical practitioner's instructions

Salbutamol for nebulisation	Inhalation	Adults and children: Bronchospasm in anaphylaxis and acute asthma	According to CPG or on registered medical practitioner's instructions
Salbutamol inhaled aerosol	Inhalation	Adults and children: Bronchospasm in anaphylaxis and acute asthma	According to CPG or on registered medical practitioner's instructions
Sodium bicarbonate injection BP	Intravenous	Adults and children: Crush injury, poisoning	According to CPG or on registered medical practitioner's instructions
Sodium chloride 0.9% for infusion	Intravenous	Adults and children: Hyperglycaemia, dehydration, cardiac arrest, crush injury, hypothermia, to keep vein open, cannula flush, dilutant for medications	According to CPG or on registered medical practitioner's instructions
Tenecteplase powder for injection	Intravenous	Adults: ST-elevation myocardial infarction (STEMI)	According to CPG or on registered medical practitioner's instructions
Tetracaine gel 4%	Topical	Adults and children: Anaesthesia prior to venepuncture	According to CPG or on registered medical practitioner's instructions

Part 2 – Medicinal products that may be supplied for use by paramedics

Medicinal product	Route of administration	Conditions of administration	Authority to administer
Aspirin (various oral dosage forms)	Oral	Adults: Cardiac chest pain	According to CPG or on registered medical practitioner's instructions
Cyclizine injection	Intramuscular	Adults and children: To prevent or treat opiate-induced nausea and vomiting	On registered medical practitioner's instructions
Dextrose 10% solution for infusion	Intravenous	Adults and children: Hypoglycaemia	According to CPG or on registered medical practitioner's instructions
Diazepam rectal solution	Per rectum	Adults and children: Seizures	On registered medical practitioner's instructions
Epinephrine (adrenaline) 1 mg/1 mL (1 : 1000) – injection	Intramuscular	Adults and children: Anaphylaxis	According to CPG or on registered medical practitioner's instructions

Medicinal product	Route of administration	Conditions of administration	Authority to administer
Glucagon for injection	Intramuscular Subcutaneous	Adults and children: Hypoglycaemia	According to CPG or on registered medical practitioner's instructions
Glyceryl trinitrate aerosol	Sublingual	Adults: Cardiac chest pain, congestive heart failure	According to CPG or on registered medical practitioner's instructions
Hartmann's solution for infusion	Intravenous	Adults and children: Hypovolaemic shock, anaphylaxis, decompression illness, burns, cardiac arrest, bradycardia, dilutant for medications	According to CPG or on registered medical practitioner's instructions
Ibuprofen (various oral dosage forms)	Oral	Adults and children: Pain	According to CPG or on registered medical practitioner's instructions
Midazolam solution for injection	Intranasal	Adults and children: Seizures	According to CPG or on registered medical practitioner's instructions
Midazolam solution (buccal)	Buccal	Adults and children: Seizures	According to CPG or on registered medical practitioner's instructions
Morphine injection	Intravenous Intramuscular	Adults and children: Moderate to severe pain	On registered medical practitioner's instructions
Naloxone for injection	Intramuscular Subcutaneous Intranasal	Adults and children: Respiratory depression secondary to known or suspected narcotic overdose	According to CPG or on registered medical practitioner's instructions
Nitrous oxide–oxygen mixture – medical gas	By inhalation	Adults and children: Pain relief	According to CPG or on registered medical practitioner's instructions
Paracetamol suppositories	Per rectum	Children: Pyrexia	On registered medical practitioner's instructions
Paracetamol (various oral dosage forms)	Oral	Adults and children: Pain, pyrexia	According to CPG or on registered medical practitioner's instructions
Salbutamol for nebulisation	Inhalation	Adults and children: Bronchospasm in anaphylaxis and acute asthma	According to CPG or on registered medical practitioner's instructions

Salbutamol inhaled aerosol	Inhalation	Adults and children: Bronchospasm in anaphylaxis and acute asthma	According to CPG or on registered medical practitioner's instructions
Sodium chloride 0.9% for infusion	Intravenous	Adults and children: Hyperglycaemia, dehydration, cardiac arrest, crush injury, hypothermia, to keep vein open, cannula flush, dilutant for medications	According to CPG or on registered medical practitioner's instructions
Tetracaine gel 4%	Topical	Adults and children: Anaesthesia prior to venepuncture	On registered medical practitioner's instructions

Part 3 – Medicinal products that may be supplied for use by emergency medical technicians

Medicinal product	Route of administration	Conditions of administration	Authority to administer
Aspirin (various oral dosage forms)	Oral	Adults: Cardiac chest pain	According to CPG or on registered medical practitioner's instructions
Cyclizine injection	Intramuscular	Adults and children: To prevent or treat opiate-induced nausea and vomiting	On registered medical practitioner's instructions
Epinephrine (adrenaline) injection 1 mg/1 mL (1 : 1000) – prefilled disposable syringe (auto)	Intramuscular	Adults and children: Anaphylaxis	According to CPG or on registered medical practitioner's instructions
Glucagon for injection	Intramuscular Subcutaneous	Adults and children: Hypoglycaemia	According to CPG or on registered medical practitioner's instructions
Glyceryl trinitrate aerosol	Sublingual	Adults: Cardiac chest pain	According to CPG or on registered medical practitioner's instructions
Morphine injection	Intravenous Intramuscular	Adults and children: Moderate or severe pain	On registered medical practitioner's instructions

Medicinal product	Route of administration	Conditions of administration	Authority to administer
Naloxone for injection	Intramuscular Subcutaneous Intranasal	Adults: Respiratory depression secondary to known or suspected narcotic overdose	On registered medical practitioner's instructions
Nitrous oxide–oxygen mixture – medical gas	By inhalation	Adults and children: Pain relief	According to CPG or on registered medical practitioner's instructions
Paracetamol (various oral dosage forms)	Oral	Adults and children: Pain, pyrexia	According to CPG or on registered medical practitioner's instructions
Salbutamol inhaled aerosol	Inhalation	Adults and children: Bronchospasm in anaphylaxis and acute asthma	According to CPG or on registered medical practitioner's instructions

8

Misuse of Drugs Acts and Regulations

L Sahm and P Weedle

The historical development of controls over drugs with a strong potential for abuse developed originally around the time of the First World War as an attempt to overcome the problems associated with cocaine use by servicemen. The law then developed through a series of international agreements, which effectively specified which substances were to be controlled and the means by which they would be controlled. The main purpose of the legislation is to criminalise the non-medical use of the substances listed, to authorise severe penalties for breaches of the law, and to ensure that countries including Ireland meet their obligations under various international conventions, in particular, the United Nations (UN) Single Convention on Narcotic Drugs 1961, and the UN Convention on Psychotropic Substances 1971. The primary objective of these conventions is to ensure the availability of controlled drugs for medical and scientific purposes and to prevent the non-medical use of those drugs.[1]

The Misuse of Drugs Acts

The Misuse of Drugs Acts 1977 to 2006,[2] and regulations and orders made thereunder, regulate and control the import, export, production, supply and

---

1. International Narcotics Control Board. Chapter 1 'The international drug control conventions: history, achievements and challenges' in *Report of the International Narcotics Control Board for 2008*. Vienna: International Narcotics Control Board, 2009.
2. Misuse of Drugs Act 1977 (No. 12 of 1977) as amended by Misuse of Drugs Act 1984 (No. 18 of 1984) and Part 2 of the Irish Medicines Board (Miscellaneous Provisions) Act 2006 (No. 3 of 2006) (Copyright House of the Oireachtas 2006).

possession of 'controlled drugs' (i.e. narcotic drugs and psychotropic substances listed in the Schedule to the 1977 act). An order of the Government is necessary to declare additional substances to be 'controlled drugs' for the purposes of the act. The Minister for Health and Children makes regulations to place controls on the import, export, production, supply and possession, which are appropriate to the substances classified as controlled drugs.

The Misuse of Drugs Act 1977 replaced the earlier Dangerous Drugs Act 1934.[3] The act prohibits the import, export, production, supply and sale, and possession of controlled drugs unless carried out in accordance with the terms of regulations made under the act. In addition, it creates a series of criminal offences and lays down penalties for such unlawful activity. The Misuse of Drugs Act 1984 made several amendments to the 1977 act and set out various procedural matters in relation to prosecution, penalties and offences. It also prohibited the printing, sale and distribution of publications containing any material or advertisements which advocate or encourage the illegal use of controlled drugs. The 1977 act was further updated by the Irish Medicines Board (Miscellaneous Provisions) Act 2006 to:

a   allow for the prescribing of controlled drugs by nurses;
b   transfer powers in relation to the issuing of licences for controlled drugs from the Minister for Health and Children to the Irish Medicines Board (IMB);
c   allow the IMB and Council of the Pharmaceutical Society of Ireland (PSI) to appoint inspectors for the purposes of enforcing the Misuse of Drugs Acts and any regulations made thereunder.

These changes only come into effect when the relevant sections of the Irish Medicines Board (Miscellaneous Provisions) Act 2006 are commenced and this has not happened in the case of (b) and (c) at the time of writing. The section of the 2006 act relating to the prescribing of controlled drugs by nurses was commenced in 2007 (nurse prescribing is discussed in more detail elsewhere in this chapter).

The Misuse of Drugs Acts are designed to prevent the abuse of certain dangerous drugs and to regulate the various professional activities associated with such substances. The acts themselves are of little immediate relevance to the healthcare professions since they deal, *inter alia*, with powers of arrest, search warrants, penalties, etc.

---

3. No. 1 of 1934.

The Misuse of Drugs Regulations

The principal regulations made under the Misuse of Drugs Acts are the Misuse of Drugs Regulations 1988 (the 'Misuse of Drugs Regulations'). They have been amended on several occasions, in 1993, 1999, 2006, 2007, 2009 (twice) and most recently in 2010.[4]

These regulations apply controls to the groups of controlled drugs specified in Schedules 1 to 5 to the regulations. They impose restrictions on the production, supply, importation and exportation of the drugs in question, which vary according to the extent to which these drugs are used for medical or scientific purposes, and having regard to the likelihood of their being abused.

The regulations permit the use by the healthcare professions of listed drugs, which are medical preparations, for the treatment of patients under their care, and also the use of controlled drugs by veterinary surgeons for the treatment of animals under their care. There are also some other groups of people who are allowed restricted use of those drugs. In order to ensure that their use is not abused, the regulations control such matters as the form of prescriptions required, records, labelling, recording and destruction of controlled drugs.

It should be noted that the term 'medical preparation' is used throughout the regulations to denote pharmaceutical products although it has now been legally replaced by 'medicinal product'.[5] This legislative change came after the passing of the principal regulations in 1988.

The schedules

The Misuse of Drugs Regulations classify controlled drugs into five schedules with different controls applying to each (see Appendix 8.1).

Schedule 1 includes raw opium, coca leaf, cannabis and the major hallucinogenic drugs (lysergic acid diethylamide (LSD), mescaline, psilocin, etc.) These are substances which have little, if any, therapeutic value but which have a strong potential for abuse. A special licence is required for any activity in respect of these drugs. In practice, such activities are strictly limited to scientific research or forensic analysis. They are, therefore, of little interest to the healthcare professions.

---

4. S.I. No. 328 of 1988 as amended by S.I. No. 342 of 1993, S.I. No. 273 of 1999, S.I. No. 53 of 2006 (Copyright Houses of the Oireachtas 2006), S.I. No. 200 of 2007 (Copyright Houses of the Oireachtas 2007), S.I. No. 63 of 2009 (Copyright Houses of the Oireachtas 2009), S.I. No. 122 of 2009 (Copyright Houses of the Oireachtas 2009) and S.I. No. 200 of 2010 (Copyright Houses of the Oireachtas 2010).
5. Irish Medicines Board Act 1995 (No. 29 of 1995) repealed Section 65 of the Health Act 1947 (which defined 'medical preparation') and gave effect to the EU concept of 'medicinal product'.

Schedule 2 includes opiates, such as morphine and heroin, major stimulants like the amphetamines, and synthetic narcotics such as pethidine, methaqualone, dextromoramide, methadone, hydrocodone, dihydrocodeine, buprenorphine and dipipanone. It should be noted that quinalbarbitone is also included. A licence is required for their import and export, and their destruction must be witnessed by appropriately authorised persons. Those entitled to produce, supply or possess them are listed in the regulations. A pharmacist may supply them to a patient only on the authority of a prescription in the prescribed form. Record-keeping and safe custody storage requirements (including the requirement to maintain a controlled drugs (CD) register) apply in full.

Schedule 3, to which less stringent controls apply, includes most barbiturates, some potent analgesics and minor stimulants. Flunitrazepam, temazepam and 4-hydroxybutanoic acid were added by the 1993 amendment regulations. Persons not covered by a general authority must be registered for the purposes of supply and possession, and licensed in the case of production. Controlled drugs safe custody and prescription requirements apply, but there is no requirement to maintain a CD register or for witnessed destruction of these drugs. Wholesalers and pharmacists must retain invoices or records issued in respect of any Schedule 3 drugs obtained or supplied by them for two years.

Schedule 4 includes benzodiazepines (with the exception of those listed in Schedule 3) and phenobarbitone preparations containing less than 100 mg or 0.5% calculated as base. Midazolam and selegiline were added by the 1993 amendment regulations. Control of these preparations under the Misuse of Drugs Acts is minimal and, in practice, they should be supplied in accordance with the requirements of the Medicinal Products (Prescription and Control of Supply) Regulations 2003 as amended (see Chapter 7, Prescription and control of supply of medicines).

Schedule 5 contains preparations exempt from most restrictions under the regulations. It should be noted that invoices must be retained for two years. Schedule 5 includes certain preparations (but not injections) containing codeine, nicocodeine, nicodicodeine, norcodeine, acetyldihydrocodeine, ethylmorphine and pholcodine mixed with other substances and containing less than 100 mg per dosage unit or not more than 2.5% in undivided preparations. The following preparations currently available are also included:

a   preparations of cocaine containing not more than 0.1% calculated as cocaine base;
b   preparations of medicinal opium, or morphine, containing not more than 0.2% calculated as anhydrous morphine base;
c   preparations of diphenoxylate containing not more than 2.5 mg of diphenoxylate calculated as base and a quantity of atropine sulphate equivalent to at least 1% of the dose of diphenoxylate (e.g. Lomotil®);

d preparations of dextropropoxyphene, for oral administration, containing not more than 135 mg of dextropropoxyphene or not more than 2.5% in undivided preparation.

A number of new substances with psychoactive properties were added to Schedules 1, 2, 3 and 4 by the Misuse of Drugs (Amendment) Regulations 2010 as part of moves to ban substances sold in 'head shops' (see section on 'Legal highs' for further details).

Although not defined in legislation, the abbreviations 'CD1', 'CD2', 'CD3', 'CD4' and 'CD5' are commonly used to denote drugs classified in the different schedules.

In a statute, interpretation can be a major problem when the classification is ambiguous. Such ambiguity in relation to the United Kingdom (UK) equivalent of the Misuse of Drugs Act was considered in the English case *R* v. *Watts*.[6] The relevant UK Act included amphetamine which it specifically listed as amphetamine and dexamphetamine, and, in a further paragraph, included stereoisomeric forms of listed substances. Dexamphetamine is one of the two stereoisomers of amphetamine, the other being levoamphetamine. In *R* v. *Watts* it was alleged that the accused possessed levoamphetamine and the question before the court was: is this a controlled drug? Under the rule *expressio unius est exclusio alterius*, the argument was put that the specific mention of the isomer dexamphetamine excluded the other isomer, which would be implied otherwise by the phrase 'stereoisomeric forms'. A further rule of statutory interpretation was also argued in this case, namely, that where something is ambiguous it should be construed in favour of the accused. The court ruled that while normally every word in a statute should be ascribed some meaning, in this instance either amphetamine or dexamphetamine was redundant. The court found it would be more in keeping with the policy of the Act that the word dexamphetamine was redundant, so that 'controlled drugs' included amphetamine and either of its isomers.

General prohibitions

A person must not produce, supply, offer to supply, import, export or possess a controlled drug unless he or she is authorised to do so.[7] A person may be authorised by virtue of a general authority (e.g. practitioners, pharmacists, etc.), a licence or registration.

---

6. *R* v. *Watts (Nigel)* (1984) 2 All E.R. 380.
7. Article 4.

Administration

It is not an offence for:

a any person to administer to another person any drug specified in Schedule 5 or
b for a registered medical practitioner, registered dentist or registered nurse to administer any Schedule 2, 3 or 4 controlled drug to a patient or
c any person, other than a registered medical practitioner, registered dentist or registered nurse

to administer a Schedule 2, 3 or 4 controlled drug to a patient, in accordance with the directions of a registered medical practitioner or registered dentist or registered nurse.[8]

The corollary of this is that administration of a controlled drug in any other circumstances is an offence.

Exemption for practitioners and pharmacists

When acting in their capacity as such for the purpose of their profession or business, the following may manufacture or compound, and supply or offer to supply any controlled drug (except Schedule 1 drugs) to any person who may lawfully have that drug in their possession:[9] a practitioner, a pharmacist or a person lawfully operating a 'retail pharmacy business' under the Pharmacy Acts.

Supply

The Misuse of Drugs Regulations specify that certain persons, when acting in their capacity as members of their class, may supply any Schedule 2, 3, 4 or 5 drug to any person who may lawfully have that drug in his or her possession.[10] The classes in question are:

a the matron (or acting matron) of a hospital or nursing home which is maintained by public funding or voluntary subscriptions, where the drug is a medical preparation. This authority applies only in the case of an institution where a pharmacist is not employed (see section on Hospitals);
b the ward sister (or acting sister) of such a hospital or nursing home, where the drug is a medical preparation and supplied to him or her in accordance with the regulations (see section on Hospitals);
c a person in charge of a laboratory, engaged in scientific education or research;
d the State Chemist;

---

8. Article 6.
9. Article 7.
10. Article 8(1).

e   the Director of the Forensic Science Laboratory of the Department of
     Justice;

f   a public analyst duly appointed;

g   the Medical Director of the IMB;

h   an inspector of the IMB;

i   a person engaged in an official drug testing scheme;

j   an inspector of the PSI.

A person who is authorised as a member of a group may, in accordance
with the terms of his or her group authority and in compliance with any
conditions attached thereto, supply or offer to supply any Schedule 2, 3, 4
or 5 controlled drug which is a medical preparation to any person who may
lawfully have that drug in his or her possession.

Owners and masters of ships are entitled to supply medical preparations
containing controlled drugs in limited circumstances (see section on Ships), as
are installation managers of offshore installations (see section on Offshore
installations).

A person whose name appears in a register kept for that purpose by the
Minister for Health and Children may supply Schedule 3, 4 or 5 controlled
drugs to any person lawfully entitled to possess them.

The Minister may grant to any person not covered by a general authorisation a licence to supply controlled drugs.[11]

Possession

Any person who is authorised to produce or supply a Schedule 2, 3 or 4
controlled drug (see previous sections) may have it in their possession.[12]

A person may have in his or her possession a Schedule 2 or 3 drug for
administration for medical, dental or veterinary purposes in accordance with
the directions of a practitioner. In the case of a patient who obtained it on foot
of a prescription, possession of the drug is an offence if the prescription was
obtained under false pretences.

A person whose name appears in a register kept for that purpose by the
Minister for Health and Children may have in his or her possession Schedule 3
or 4 controlled drugs.

The master of a foreign ship which is in an Irish port may have in his or her
possession any Schedule 2 or 3 controlled drug insofar as it is necessary for the
equipment of his ship (see section on Ships).

A person who is authorised as a member of a group may, under and in
accordance with his or her group authority and in compliance with any

---

11. Article 5.
12. Article 9.

conditions attached thereto, have any drug specified in Schedules 2 or 3 which is a medical preparation in his or her possession.

Midwives are permitted to have in their possession and to administer medical preparations containing pentazocine and pethidine subject to certain conditions (see section on Midwives).[13]

The following are entitled to have controlled drugs in their possession only when acting in the course of their duty as members of their class. They are not entitled, however, to be supplied, as individuals, except on foot of a valid prescription or otherwise as provided for in the regulations:[14]

a   a member of the Garda Síochána or an officer of the Customs and Excise;
b   a person engaged in the work of any laboratory to which the drug has been sent for forensic examinations;
c   a person authorised in writing by the Minister under Section 24 of the Misuse of Drugs Act 1997 to enforce the act and any regulations made thereunder;
d   a person engaged in conveying the drug to a person authorised to have it in his or her possession (e.g. a postman or *bona fide* carrier) (see section on Messengers);
e   a registered nurse engaged in providing palliative care;
f   an official of the Department of Agriculture and Food engaged in the sampling for analysis of crops of *Cannabis sativa* L., while monitoring and sampling for the purpose of the relevant European Union (EU) scheme involving grant aid for the production of hemp fibre;
g   a prison officer.

A person who is lawfully in possession of a controlled drug may supply that drug to a person from whom he or she obtained it.[14]

The Minister may grant to any person not covered by any of the above provisions, a licence to possess controlled drugs.[15]

With regard to the possession of controlled drugs, we have seen that certain classes of people are entitled to be in possession of them under specified conditions. In *R v. Dunbar*[16] a doctor was found in possession of controlled drugs and was charged with unlawful possession on the grounds that he had no patients and wanted the drugs to treat himself. At first instance, the judge found that the doctor could not rely on the relaxation because, with no patients except himself, he could not be acting 'in his capacity as such'. However, the Court of Appeal reversed the lower court's decision. A doctor treating himself could be acting in his capacity as such; it

13. Article 10.
14. Article 11.
15. Article 5.
16. (1981) 1 W.L.R. 1536; (1982) 1 All E.R. 188.

was for the jury to decide on the specific facts of each case whether the doctor was indeed so acting. Where a problem exists with regard to the use of controlled drugs by a medical practitioner, it is normally dealt with by the Medical Council, the registration body for medical practitioners in Ireland, which may prohibit a doctor from prescribing or possessing such substances.

Prescription requirements

A 'prescription' means a prescription issued by a registered medical practitioner for the medical treatment of an individual, a registered dentist for the dental treatment of an individual, a registered veterinary surgeon for the purpose of animal treatment or by a registered nurse for the medical treatment of an individual.[17] It is unlawful for a practitioner (i.e. registered doctor, dentist, veterinary surgeon or nurse) to issue a prescription for a Schedule 2 or 3 drug unless it complies with requirements specified in the Misuse of Drugs Regulations. The prescriber must also be satisfied as to the identity of the patient.[18]

The prescription must:[18]

a   be in ink or otherwise so as to be indelible and signed by the practitioner with his or her usual signature and dated by him or her;

b   except in the case of a health prescription (i.e. General Medical Services (GMS) prescription), specify the address of the person issuing it;

c   specify (in the prescriber's handwriting) the name and address of the person for whose treatment it is issued or, if issued by a registered veterinary surgeon, the name and address of the person to whom the prescribed drug is to be delivered. In the case of a patient in a hospital or nursing home, the address of the patient need not be specified provided the prescription is written on the patient's bed card (drug kardex) or case sheet;

d   clearly indicate the name of the person issuing it and state whether that person is a registered medical practitioner, registered dentist, registered veterinary surgeon or registered nurse (and in the case of a nurse, his or her registration number). It is noteworthy that the Medical Council's *Guide to Professional Conduct and Ethics for Registered Medical Practitioners*[19] states that prescriptions must include a doctor's registration number, although this is not a legal requirement;

17. Article 3(1) as amended by Misuse of Drugs (Amendment) Regulations 2007.
18. Article 13.
19. Medical Council. *Guide to Professional Conduct and Ethics for Registered Medical Practitioners*, 7th edn. 2009, paragraph 59.1.

e   specify a telephone number at which the prescriber may be contacted. This is not required in the case of a prescription for a patient in a hospital or nursing home which is written on the patient's bed card or case sheet (drug kardex);

f   specify (in the prescriber's handwriting):
    i   the dose to be taken,
    ii the form in the case of preparations,
    iii the strength (when appropriate),
    iv in both words and figures, either the total quantity of the drug or preparation or the number of dosage units to be supplied;

g   in the case of a prescription for a total quantity intended to be dispensed by instalments, specify the quantity, the number of instalments, and the intervals to be observed when dispensing.

Nurse prescribing

Up until 2007 only registered medical practitioners, registered dentists and registered veterinary surgeons were permitted to issue prescriptions for controlled drugs. The Misuse of Drugs Regulations were amended in 2007 to extend the definition of 'practitioner' to include registered nurses[20] and to set out the conditions under which registered nurses could prescribe controlled drugs. It should be noted that the regulatory authority for nurses and midwives, An Bord Altranais, requires registered nurses and midwives to complete an accreditation process before they may act as prescribers;[21] so although the Misuse of Drugs Regulations appears to give prescribing rights to all registered nurses, this right may only be exercised by registered nurses and midwives who have received the appropriate accreditation.

Registered nurses may prescribe Schedule 4 and Schedule 5 controlled drugs and certain drugs from Schedules 2 and 3 as listed in Schedule 8 to the Regulations (see Table 8.1), but with restrictions placed on their prescribing as follows:[22]

a   the nurse must be employed by a health service provider in a hospital, nursing home, clinic or other health service setting, including in a private home;

b   the drug prescribed must be one that is usually prescribed within the health service setting;

20. Article 3(1) as amended by Misuse of Drugs (Amendment) Regulations 2007.
21. See An Bord Altranais website www.nursingboard.ie for further information (accessed 1 March 2011).
22. Article 3A as inserted by Misuse of Drugs (Amendment) Regulations 2007.

Table 8.1 Section 2 and 3 drugs which registered nurses may prescribe (Schedule 8 to Misuse of Drugs Regulations 1988 as amended)	
Drug	Route of administration
Part I – Drugs for pain relief in hospital:	
Morphine sulphate	Oral, intravenous, intramuscular
Codeine phosphate	Oral
Part II – Drugs for palliative care:	
Morphine sulphate	Oral, subcutaneous
Hydromorphone	Oral, subcutaneous
Oxycodone	Oral, subcutaneous
Buprenorphine	Transdermal
Fentanyl	Transmucosal, transdermal
Methylphenidate	Oral
Codeine phosphate	Oral
Part III – Drugs for purposes of midwifery:	
Pethidine	Intramuscular
Part IV – Drugs for neonatal care in hospital:	
Morphine sulphate	Oral, intravenous
Fentanyl	Intravenous

c the prescription must be issued in the usual course of provision of that health service;

d drugs listed in Schedule 8 may only be prescribed in accordance with the conditions specified (relating to circumstances of use and route of administration). In the case of drugs that may be prescribed for pain relief in hospitals, nurses may only prescribe them for pain relief in the case of probable myocardial infarction, for the relief of the acute or severe pain after trauma, or for post-operative pain relief of patients who have suffered probable myocardial infarction or trauma.

A health service provider may prohibit a nurse from prescribing any drug that he or she is permitted to prescribe under these regulations. A health service provider, if allowing a nurse to prescribe, may impose further restrictions on such prescribing.

Of note is that a pharmacist, or other person supplying drugs, may refuse to supply a drug on foot of a prescription issued by a nurse if they have reasonable cause to believe that the conditions referred to above have not been satisfied.[23]

A prescription from a nurse, in addition to stating that the prescription was written by a registered nurse, must also include the registration number assigned to the nurse in the Register of Nurses established under Section 27 of the Nurses Act 1985.[24]

Forged or altered prescriptions

The Act prohibits the possession of either a forged prescription or an altered prescription except where a person does so to prevent another person from committing or continuing to commit an offence, and who intends to deliver it into the custody of the Garda Síochána or to an inspector of the PSI.[25]

Dispensing requirements

A pharmacist dispensing a prescription for a Schedule 2 or Schedule 3 drug must ensure that it conforms with the requirements for controlled drug prescriptions and that:[26]

a   the address of the prescriber as written on the prescription is one within the State;

b   he or she is acquainted with the signature of the prescriber and has no reason to believe it is not genuine, or else takes reasonable steps to ensure that it is genuine;

c   the prescription is not dispensed before the date specified on it or later than fourteen days afterwards;

d   in the case of a prescription to be dispensed by instalments, the first instalment is not dispensed later than fourteen days from the date on the prescription and no instalment is dispensed later than two months after the date on the prescription;

e   he or she is satisfied as to the identity of the patient or in the case of a representative, his or her *bona fides*;

f   the date of supply is marked on the prescription and on each occasion that an instalment is supplied;

g   the prescription is retained on the premises for two years.[27]

---

23. Article 3B as inserted by Misuse of Drugs (Amendment) Regulations 2007.
24. Article 13(d).
25. Article 24.
26. Article 14.
27. Article 19(2).

While the 1988 regulations did much to improve the Irish legislation relating to controlled drugs, a number of points give rise to problems. In particular, under prescription writing, it is questionable if any advantage can be ascribed to the inclusion of the prescriber's telephone number on the prescription. The Storkwain case[28] demonstrated that a pharmacist would be unwise to rely on a telephone number on a prescription to contact a prescriber. The facts of the case were that a forged prescription was presented in a pharmacy for dispensing. The pharmacist, suspecting something was amiss, decided to contact the prescriber by telephone. The number he dialled was the number on the prescription form (a local telephone kiosk). An accomplice was waiting to receive the call and reassured the pharmacist that everything was in order. It is now accepted pharmaceutical practice that the prescriber's telephone number from the prescription form should never be taken as fully reliable.

Labelling of controlled drugs

Except when supplied on a prescription, the bottle or package containing a Schedule 2 or Schedule 3 drug must be clearly marked with the amount of drug therein in the case of raw drugs, or in the case of preparations, either the number of dosage units and the amount of controlled drug in each, or the total amount and the percentage of each controlled drug present.[29]

Requisitions

A person who supplies a controlled drug other than on foot of a prescription to any of the following must obtain a requisition in writing before the drug is delivered:[30]

a   a practitioner;
b   the matron of a hospital or nursing home (see section on Hospitals);
c   a midwife (see section on Midwives);
d   a person who is in charge of a laboratory;
e   the owner or master of a ship (see section on Ships);
f   the manager of an offshore installation (see section on Offshore installations).

The requisition must be in writing and be signed by the recipient, state his or her name, address and occupation, specify the total quantity to be supplied and the purpose for which it is required.

---

28. *Pharmaceutical Society of Great Britain* v. *Storkwain Ltd.* (1985) 3 All E.R. 4.
29. Article 15.
30. Article 12(2)–(5).

The pharmacist must be reasonably satisfied that the signature is that of the person purporting to sign the requisition and that he or she is engaged in the occupation stated. A practitioner urgently requiring a drug and unable to supply a requisition before delivery, may be supplied on his or her giving an undertaking to furnish a requisition. Failure to furnish such a requisition within 24 hours is an offence.

Hospitals

The matron (or acting matron) of a hospital or nursing home which is wholly or mainly maintained by a public authority out of public funds or by a charity or by voluntary subscriptions, and where a pharmacist is not employed, may be supplied with controlled drugs.[31] In these circumstances, the supplier, before delivering any controlled drug, must receive a requisition which complies with the general requirements for requisitions (see above). It must also be countersigned by a doctor, dentist or registered nurse (who may be the matron or acting matron) employed or engaged in the institution concerned.[32]

The sister (or acting sister) in charge of a ward, theatre or department in a hospital or nursing home may be supplied with a controlled drug, solely for the purpose of administration to a patient in that ward, theatre, or department, in accordance with the directions of a registered medical practitioner, registered dentist or registered nurse.[31] Where the pharmacist, or matron, as the case may be, supplies a controlled drug to a ward sister in these circumstances, he or she must obtain a requisition in writing signed by the sister which specifies the total quantity of the drug to be supplied, mark the requisition in such a manner as to show it has been complied with and retain the requisition for two years in the dispensary from which it was supplied. A copy of the requisition, or a note of it, must be retained by the sister.[33]

Ward sisters, while obliged to keep a copy of the requisition form, are not required to maintain a controlled drugs register in respect of Schedule 2 drugs received and supplied by them.[34]

Midwives

A registered midwife may be supplied with pethidine and pentazocine for the practise of his or her profession,[35] provided a written order, signed by him or her and countersigned by a medical practitioner or registered nurse, who is a

---

31. Article 8(1).
32. Article 12(5)(a).
33. Article 12(6).
34. Article 16(4)(b).
35. Article 10.

practitioner, practising in their area, is received. The order must state the name and address of the midwife, the quantity to be supplied, and the purpose for which it is required. If the midwife falls within the definition of 'practitioner' then he or she may sign the written order. Midwives must keep a record of any pethidine obtained and administered,[36] and its destruction must be witnessed by an authorised person.

Ships

The owner or the master of a ship which does not carry a registered medical practitioner on board as part of her complement, or the master of a foreign ship in an Irish port, may be supplied with a controlled drug provided they furnish the pharmacist with a requisition in writing which complies with the general requirements for requisitions (see above). In the case of a foreign ship, the requisition must also contain a statement, signed by a medical officer of health for the area, that the quantity of drug to be supplied is necessary for the equipment of the ship.[37]

The owner or master of a ship which does not carry a registered medical practitioner on board as part of her complement is entitled to supply any Schedule 2, 3, 4 or 5 controlled drug which is a medical preparation to any member of the crew, to any person who may lawfully supply that drug or to a member of the Garda Síochána or a Customs and Excise officer for destruction.[38]

Offshore installations

The installation manager of an offshore installation may be supplied with a controlled drug being a medical preparation provided they furnish a requisition in writing which complies with the general requirements for requisitions (see above). The requisition must contain a statement signed by the Industrial Medical Adviser (Offshore Installations) that the quantity of drug to be supplied is the quantity necessary for the equipment of that installation.[39] The installation manager is entitled to supply any Schedule 2, 3, 4 or 5 drug which is a medical preparation to any person on the installation whether present in the course of employment or not, to any person who may lawfully supply that drug or to a member of the Garda Síochána or a Customs and Excise officer for destruction.[40]

---

36. Article 17(3).
37. Article 12(5)(b).
38. Article 8(3).
39. Article 12(5)(c).
40. Article 8(4).

Messengers

A controlled drug may be delivered either to the patient himself or herself to some responsible person on his or her behalf or to an employee of the pharmacist to be delivered to the patient. The pharmacist must be satisfied that the patient's representative is a *bona fide* representative.[41]

A person entitled to be supplied with a controlled drug otherwise than on prescription, who is unable to receive the drug personally, may send a messenger to receive it. Such a messenger may be supplied only if he or she produces, in addition to a requisition in the proper form, a statement in writing from the purchaser to the effect that the messenger is empowered to receive the drug on his or her behalf. The pharmacist must be reasonably satisfied that the document is genuine and must retain it for two years.[42]

Export

A person cannot export a controlled drug unless the transaction is properly documented and the commercial documents (e.g. invoices, cargo manifests, custom and other shipping documents) accompanying the drug include the name of the drug as set out in the relevant schedule. Where the name would not identify the drug adequately, then the international non-proprietary name must be used. The documentation must also be dated and include the total quantity being exported, the name and address of the exporter and of the importer and, if known, the name of the ultimate consignee.[43]

Registers

Every person authorised to supply Schedule 2 drugs must record every transaction (receipt and supply) in a register (commonly called a 'controlled drugs' or 'CD' register) kept for that purpose.[44] The register must be in the format set out in Schedules 6 and 7 to the regulations and be a bound book and not any form of loose-leaf register or card index.

The following entries must be made for all purchases or receipts:[45]

a   date of receipt;
b   name and address of person or firm from whom obtained;
c   amount obtained;
d   form in which obtained.

---

41. Article 14(1)(f).
42. Article 12(1).
43. Article 15A.
44. Article 16.
45. Schedules 6 and 7 to Misuse of Drugs Regulations.

The following entries must be made for all sales or supplies:

a   date on which the transaction was effected;
b   name and address of person or firm supplied;
c   particulars as to licence or authority of person or firm supplied to be in possession;
d   amount supplied;
e   form in which supplied.

A running stock balance must be recorded after each transaction.

Entries must be in ink, in chronological sequence, and be made on the day of the transaction or not later than the day afterwards. No cancellation, obliteration or alteration is permitted. Corrections, where necessary, should be made only by way of marginal note or footnote in ink and must specify the date on which the correction was made.

The class of drugs to which the entries on any page relate must be specified at the head of that page. A separate register, or a separate part of a register, must be kept for each class of drugs. However, a separate section within a register may be used in respect of different drugs or strengths of drugs within the class of drugs to which the register, or separate part, relates, but not more than one register may be kept at any time for any particular class of drugs without the approval of the Minister. The register may not be used for any purpose other than the purposes of the regulations.

The requirement to maintain a register in respect of transactions of Schedule 2 drugs does not apply to a person licensed by the Minister for Health and Children where the licence so directs or to a ward sister in a hospital or nursing home.

Retention of records

The CD register must be retained for two years from the date of the last entry, on the premises to which it relates. Prescriptions, requisitions and any other orders on foot of which controlled drugs have been supplied must also be retained for two years.[46] In the case of health prescriptions (i.e. GMS prescriptions), the duplicate copy is retained as the original must be submitted for reimbursement.

Wholesalers and suppliers

A person who supplies a Schedule 2 or Schedule 3 drug to a community pharmacy or a hospital must furnish a receipt with each consignment. This

---

46. Article 19.

must be checked by the recipient, any deviations noted, dated and signed by him or her and returned to the supplier within three working days.[47]

Retention of invoices

Producers of Schedule 3 and 5 drugs and wholesalers must retain for two years every invoice or other record issued in respect of any Schedule 3 or Schedule 5 drugs obtained or supplied by them.[48]

A pharmacist must retain for two years every invoice or other record issued in respect of any Schedule 3 drugs obtained and supplied by him or her and every invoice issued in respect of any Schedule 5 drugs obtained by him or her.[49]

Furnishing information

The following persons: a licence holder, a wholesaler, a person operating a 'retail pharmacy business' (see Chapter 12, The Pharmacy Act), a practitioner, a hospital pharmacist, the matron or acting matron (of a hospital or nursing home), a person in charge of a laboratory or a person whose name is on a register and is authorised by the Minister to supply a controlled drug, on demand made by the Minister or by any person authorised in writing by him or her, must furnish within fourteen days such particulars in respect of controlled drugs as may be requested, and produce any stock, register, book or document kept in respect of such drugs.[50]

Personal records (i.e. records from which an individual (living or dead) can be identified and relating to his or her physical or mental health) need not be disclosed[51] (e.g. patient medication records held in a card index or on computer). Registers, books, prescriptions or other documents required to be kept under these regulations are not deemed to be personal records.

Destruction of controlled drugs

The destruction of a Schedule 1 or 2 drug may be carried out only in the presence of, and in accordance with any directions given by, a person authorised by the Minister for Health and Children.[52] The classes of persons who may witness the destruction of controlled drugs include PSI inspectors. Particulars of the date of destruction and the quantity destroyed must be

---

47. Article 12(7)–(8).
48. Article 20(1).
49. Article 20(4).
50. Article 21.
51. Article 21(4).
52. Article 22.

recorded in the register and that record must be signed by the authorised person in whose presence the drug is destroyed.

The master of a ship or the manager of an offshore installation may not destroy a controlled drug but must give it to a member of the Garda Síochána, an officer of Customs and Excise or to a person who may lawfully supply it to him or her.

By virtue of the fact that a person legally in possession of a controlled drug may supply it to the person from whom they received it,[53] the regulations permit a patient to return unwanted prescribed controlled drugs to the pharmacist from whom he or she obtained them for the purposes of destruction. The destruction of returned drugs should be carried out as soon as possible after receipt and need not be witnessed. Entries in the controlled drug register are not required in this instance.

Cessation of business

A person who has ceased to operate a retail pharmacy business or who becomes the legal personal representative of such a person is obliged on demand made by the Minister for Health and Children to furnish particulars of stocks of any controlled drug in his or her possession, produce any such stocks, produce the register, books or documents in his or her possession relating to Schedule 2, 3 or 4 drugs and dispose of any such stocks in his or her possession in accordance with directions given by the Minister or a person authorised as above.[54]

Role of the IMB

Since September 2005, the IMB has managed the application and issue processes for controlled licences on behalf of the Department of Health and Children, although the licences continue to be formally issued in the name of the Minister for Health and Children.[55] The IMB carries out inspections of manufacturers and distributors to ensure compliance with the relevant requirements.

The Irish Medicines Board (Miscellaneous Provisions) Act 2006 provides for amendments to the Misuse of Drugs Act to transfer formal responsibility for licensing to the IMB, but the relevant section[56] has not been commenced at the time of writing.

---

53. Article 11(2).
54. Article 23.
55. IMB Annual Report 2005.
56. Section 7.

Storage of controlled drugs

A person operating a retail pharmacy business must ensure that all Schedule 2 and 3 drugs are kept on the premises at which he or she operates in a locked safe or cabinet which complies with the requirements of the Misuse of Drugs (Safe Custody) Regulations 1982 as amended, or if it does not meet those requirements, has been certified as providing an equivalent degree of security by a member of the Garda Síochána, not below the rank of Superintendent.[57] PSI inspectors are authorised to check that these requirements are complied with.

Any other person who has a Schedule 1, 2 or 3 controlled drug in his or her possession must ensure, insofar as circumstances permit, that it is kept in a locked, fixed receptacle which can only be opened by him or her or by a person authorised by him or her. This requirement does not apply to a person to whom the drug has been supplied by or on the prescription of a practitioner for his or her own treatment or that of another person or of an animal, couriers/carriers acting in the course of their business, a person delivering the drug to a person authorised to have it in his or her possession or to a postal worker acting in the course of his or her duty.

Methadone

Special arrangements apply to the prescribing and dispensing of methadone[58] which reflects the fact that it is most commonly used in treatment programmes for opiate dependency. Methadone is a Schedule 2 controlled drug and therefore all the usual prescription, recording and storage requirements apply, however there are some further requirements as set out below.

Where a registered medical practitioner intends to prescribe methadone for the first time to a person, he or she must notify the Eastern Health Board (now the Health Service Executive (HSE)) of the patient's name, address and date of birth, prior to issuing a prescription. The person's name is then included in the 'Central Treatment List' maintained by the HSE and a drug treatment card is issued to the patient which is valid for a maximum of one year.

Methadone may only be prescribed on special methadone forms supplied by the HSE on behalf of the Department of Health and Children and only for a patient who has a valid drug treatment card. The requirement for a name and address of the patient to be in the prescriber's own handwriting is waived if the required details are impressed upon the prescription from an embossed drug treatment card but the other prescription writing requirements for controlled drugs must be complied with in full.

---

57. Misuse of Drugs (Safe Custody) Regulations 1982 (S.I. No. 321 of 1982) as amended by Misuse of Drugs Regulations 1988.
58. Misuse of Drugs (Supervision of Prescription and Supply of Methadone) Regulations 1998 (S.I. No. 225 of 1998).

A pharmacist may only dispense methadone on foot of a prescription written on the special methadone prescription form and only to patients who have a valid drug treatment card. He or she must supply details to the Minister for Health and Children of all methadone dispensed by providing the original prescription and the details of how much was supplied and when. This information must be submitted within fourteen days of the end of the calendar month in which the supply was made. The Minister is required to maintain records of all methadone prescriptions received.

In the case of a methadone prescription to be dispensed in instalments, the normal requirement to record details of each instalment dispensed in the controlled drugs register is waived if details of each supply are written on the prescription and the total amount dispensed on foot of that prescription is entered in the register. This provision has been included in the regulations because methadone may be dispensed to patients in treatment programmes several times a week, in some cases daily, and the administrative load associated with recording each individual supply would be unduly onerous.

The 1998 regulations do not apply to methadone prescriptions issued in a hospital for administration to an inpatient or for supply in exceptional circumstances to patients who have attended the hospital for the treatment of opiate dependency.

Where methadone is being used for purposes other than the treatment of opiate dependence (e.g. pain relief) it may be initiated by a medical consultant. It must still be written on the special methadone prescription form. However, there is no need to notify the HSE to include the patient on the Central Treatment List or for the patient to have a drug treatment card.

Scheduled substances

The Misuse of Drugs (Scheduled Substances) Regulations 1993[59] implemented Council Directive 92/109/EEC on the manufacture and placing on the market of certain substances used in the illicit manufacture of narcotic drugs and psychotropic substances (being drugs to which the Misuse of Drugs Acts apply). The controls applied have their origin in the UN Convention Against Illicit Traffic in Narcotic Drugs and Psychotropic Substances 1988. The effect of these regulations is to impose restrictions on the production, supply, importation and exportation of the substances concerned, which vary according to the extent to which those substances are likely to be used for the illicit manufacture of narcotic drugs and psychotropic substances. The importation and exportation controls only apply to certain substances, and in respect of consignments destined for or originating in countries which are not EU member states.

---

59. S.I. No. 338 of 1993.

In addition, the regulations specify the classes of persons who may possess and/or supply scheduled substances and the circumstances in which such possession or supply would not be in contravention of the Misuse of Drugs Acts. Requirements are also laid down in regard to the labelling of scheduled substances and in respect of documentation, record-keeping and the furnishing of information on scheduled substances.

The purpose of the 2004 scheduled substances amendment regulations[60] was to implement Commission Directive 2003/101/EC relating to the manufacture and placing on the market of certain substances used in the illicit manufacture of narcotic drugs and psychotropic substances.

'Legal highs'

In response to growing concerns about the availability of substances with psychoactive effects that were not regulated under the Misuse of Drugs Acts, approximately 200 'legal high' substances, which had been on sale in 'head shops', were declared to be controlled drugs in May 2010. The substances controlled include synthetic cannabinoids, benzylpiperazine (BZP) and piperazine derivatives (commonly known as 'party pills'), mephedrone, methylone, methedrone, butylone, flephedrone, methylenedioxypyrovalerone (MDPV) (often sold as baths salts or plant food), and gamma-butyrolactone and butan-1,4-diol.[61]

In addition to these controls on legal highs, the Criminal Justice (Psychoactive Substances) Act 2010[62] was enacted to ensure that the sale or supply of substances which might not be specifically proscribed under the Misuse of Drugs Act, but which had psychoactive effects, would be a criminal offence.

The Minister for Health and Children has indicated that the list of controlled legal highs will be kept under review and that if individuals seek to circumvent the controls on certain legal high substances by importing other substances that are currently not subject to control under the Misuse of Drugs Act, Government approval will be sought to ban additional substances if they pose a risk to public health.[63]

---

60. S.I. No. 92 of 2004.
61. Misuse of Drugs Act 1977 (Controlled Drugs) (Declaration) Order 2010 (S.I. No. 199 of 2010), Misuse of Drugs (Amendment) Regulations 2010 (S.I. No. 200 of 2010), Misuse of Drugs (Designation) (Amendment) Order 2010 (S.I. No. 201 of 2010), the Misuse of Drugs (Exemption) (Amendment) Order 2010 (S.I. No. 202 of 2010). Copyright Houses of the Oireachtas 2010.
62. No. 22 of 2010.
63. 'Opening Statement for meeting of Joint Committee on Health and Children in relation to recent legislation made to control certain substances under the Misuse of Drugs Act 1977', 1 June 2010, www.dohc.ie (accessed 1 March 2011).

The process of introducing controls under the Misuse of Drugs Act is complex, particularly for substances which have legitimate uses but also have the potential to be misused. For example, some of the substances which have been controlled for the first time in 2010 have legitimate uses in the pharmaceutical and chemicals industries; two of the BZP derivatives are used to manufacture authorised medicines, and gamma-butyrolactone (GBL) and butan-1,4-diol (1,4-BD) are widely used in the manufacture of plastics as industrial solvents, as well as in many consumer products such as paints, toiletries, cleaning products, food products and others.

Controlling substances under the Misuse of Drugs Acts is an ongoing process which involves national and international cooperation and engagement. Substances are scheduled under the acts in accordance with Ireland's obligations under international conventions and EU Council decisions and/or where there is evidence that the substances are causing significant harm to public health in Ireland. For example, in 2006 and 2009 respectively, psychotropic ('magic') mushrooms and the party pill BZP were declared controlled drugs and their possession and sale became illegal. At a national level, the Department of Health and Children works closely with the Department of Justice and Law Reform, the Office of the Minister for Drugs, the National Advisory Committee on Drugs, the Garda Síochána, the Customs Service, the Forensic Science Laboratory, the IMB, the Health Research Board and others to monitor emerging trends in the development of new psychoactive substances. At an international level, the Department engages with the European Monitoring Centre for Drugs and Drug Addiction and the UN Office of Drug Control regarding international trends in the emergence of new substances and drug control.

Enforcement

Primary responsibility for enforcement of the Misuse of Drugs acts and regulations rests with the Garda Síochána. The Minister for Health and Children may also authorise other persons for the purpose of enforcing Misuse of Drugs legislation.[64] For example, officers of the PSI are authorised to carry out certain inspectorial duties in community pharmacies and IMB inspectors are authorised to do so in relation to manufacturers and wholesalers of controlled drugs.

The Irish Medicines Board (Miscellaneous) Provisions Act 2006 provides for amendments to the Misuse of Drugs Act 1977 to permit the IMB and the Council of the PSI, as well as the Minister, to authorise persons to enforce the Misuse of Drugs Regulations.[65] In the case of persons authorised by the PSI

---

64. Section 24 of Misuse of Drugs Act 1977.
65. Section 9.

Council, these rights will only extend to retail pharmacy businesses. The relevant section of the Irish Medicines Board (Miscellaneous) Provisions Act 2006 has not been commenced at the time of writing.

Appendix 8.1 Controlled drugs classified into five schedules

(Misuse of Drugs Regulations 1988 as amended.[66] Schedules 1–5)

Schedule 1

1 The following substances and products, namely:

a 1-(1,3-Benzodioxol-5-yl)-2-(1-pyrrolidinyl)-pentanone [Inserted by 2010 Amendment Regulations]

1-Benzylpiperazine [Inserted by No. 2 2009 Amendment Regulations and substituted by 2010 Amendment Regulations]

Bufotenine

Cannabinol, except where contained in cannabis or cannabis resin

Cannabinol derivatives

Cannabis and cannabis resin

Cathinone

Coca leaf

Concentrate of poppy-straw

[2,3-Dihydro-5-methyl-3-(4-morpholinylmethyl)pyrrolo[1,2,3-*de*]-1,4-benzoxazin-6-yl]-1-naphthalenylmethanone [Inserted by 2010 Amendment Regulations]

3-Dimethylheptyl-11-hydroxyhexahydrocannabinol [Inserted by 2010 Amendment Regulations]

Eticyclidine

Etryptamine [Inserted by 2010 Amendment Regulations]

1-(2-Fluorophenyl)-2-methylaminopropan-1-one [Inserted by 2010 Amendment Regulations]

1-(3-Fluorophenyl)-2-methylaminopropan-1-one [Inserted by 2010 Amendment Regulations]

1-(4-Fluorophenyl)-2-methylaminopropan-1-one [Inserted by 2010 Amendment Regulations]

---

66. S.I. No. 328 of 1988 as amended by S.I. No. 342 of 1993, S.I. No. 273 of 1999, S.I. No. 53 of 2006 (Copyright Houses of the Oireachtas 2006), S.I. No. 200 of 2007 (Copyright Houses of the Oireachtas 2007), S.I. No. 63 of 2009 (Copyright Houses of the Oireachtas 2009), S.I. No. 122 of 2009 (Copyright Houses of the Oireachtas 2009) and S.I. No. 200 of 2010 (Copyright Houses of the Oireachtas 2010).

9-(Hydroxymethyl)-6, 6-dimethyl-3-(2-methyloctan-2-yl)-6a,7,10,10a-tetrahydrobenzo[c]chromen-1-ol [Inserted by 2010 Amendment Regulations]

[9-Hydroxy-6-methyl-3-[5-phenylpentan-2-yl] oxy-5,6,6a,7,8,9,10,10a octahydrophenanthridin-1-yl] acetate [Inserted by 2010 Amendment Regulations]

Khat (being the leaves of *Catha edulis* (Celastraceae) [Inserted by 1993 Amendment Regulations]

Lysergamide

Lysergide and other N-alkyl derivatives of lysergamide

Mescaline

Methcathinone [Inserted by 2010 Amendment Regulations]

1-(4-Methoxyphenyl)-2-(methylamino)propan-1-one [Inserted by 2010 Amendment Regulations]

2-Methylamino-1-(3,4-methylenedioxyphenyl)butan-1-one [Inserted by 2010 Amendment Regulations]

2-Methylamino-1-(3,4-methylenedioxyphenyl)propan-1-one [Inserted by 2010 Amendment Regulations]

α-Methyl-4-(methylthio)phenethylamine [Inserted by 2010 Amendment Regulations]

1-(4-Methylphenyl)-2-methylaminopropan-1-one [Inserted by 2010 Amendment Regulations]

Psilocin, any substance, product or preparation (whether natural or otherwise) including a fungus of any kind or description which contains psilocin or an ester of psilocin [Inserted by 2006 Amendment Regulations]

Raw opium

Rolicyclidine

Tenocyclidine

N,N-Diethyltryptamine

N,N-Dimethyltryptamine

N-(1-Benzyl-4-piperidyl) propionanilide

N-(1-(2-Thenyl)-4-piperidyl) proprionanilide

2.5-Dimethoxy-α,4-dimethylphenethylamine

N-Hydroxytenamphetamine [Inserted by 1993 Amendment Regulations];

4-Methyl-aminorex [Inserted by 1993 Amendment Regulations];

b   any substance (not being a substance specified in subparagraph (a) above) structurally derived from tryptamine or from a ring-hydroxyl tryptamine by substitution at the nitrogen atom of the sidechain with one or more alkyl substituents but no other substituent;

c   any substance (not being methoxyphenamine or a substance specified in subparagraph (a) above) structurally derived from phenethylamine, an N-alkylphenethylamine, α-methyl phenethylamine, an N-alkyl-α-methylphenethylamine, α-ethylphenethylamine, or an N-alkyl-α-ethylphenethylamine by substitution in the ring to any extent with alkyl, alkoxy. alkylenedioxy or halide substituents, whether or not further substituted in the ring by one or more other univalent substituents;

d   any substance (not being a substance specified in Schedule 2) structurally derived from fentanyl by modification in one or more of the following ways, that is to say:

   i   by replacement of the phenyl portion of the phenethyl group by any heteromonocycle whether or not further substituted in the heterocycle;

   ii   by substitution in the phenethyl group with alkyl, alkenyl, alkoxy, hydroxy, halogeno, haloalkyl, amino or nitro groups;

   iii by substitution in the piperidine ring with alkyl or alkenyl groups;

   iv   by substitution in the aniline ring with alkyl, alkoxy, alkylenedioxy, halogeno or haloalkyl groups;

   v   by substitution at the 4-position of the piperidine ring with any alkoxycarbonyl or alkoxyalkyl or acyloxy group;

   vi   by replacement of the N-propionyl group by another acyl group;

e   any substance (not being a substance specified in Schedule 2) structurally derived from pethidine by modification in one or more of the following ways, that is to say:

   i   by replacement of the 1-methyl group by an acyl, alkyl, whether or not unsaturated, benzyl or phenethyl group, whether or not further substituted;

   ii   by substitution in the piperidine ring with alkyl or alkenyl groups or with a propano bridge, whether or not further substituted;

   iii by substitution in the 4-phenyl ring with alkyl, alkoxy, aryloxy, halogeno or haloalkyl groups;

   iv   by replacement of the 4-ethoxycarbonyl by any other alkoxycarbonyl or any alkoxyalkyl or acyloxy group;

   v   by formation of an N-oxide or a quarternary base;

f   any substance structurally derived from 3-(1-naphthoyl)indole or 1H-indol-3-yl-(1-naphthyl)methane by substitution at the nitrogen atom of the indole ring by alkyl, alkenyl, cycloalkylmethyl, cycloalkylethyl or 2-(4-morpholinyl)ethyl, whether or not further substituted in the indole ring to any extent and whether or not substituted in the naphthyl ring to any extent [Inserted by 2010 Amendment Regulations];

g any substance structurally derived from 3-(1-naphthoyl)pyrrole by substitution at the nitrogen atom of the pyrrole ring by alkyl, alkenyl, cycloalkylmethyl, cycloalkylethyl or 2-(4-morpholinyl) ethyl, whether or not further substituted in the pyrrole ring to any extent and whether or not substituted in the naphthyl ring to any extent [Inserted by 2010 Amendment Regulations];

h any substance structurally derived from 1-(1-naphthylmethyl)indene by substitution at the 3-position of the indene ring by alkyl, alkenyl, cycloalkylmethyl, cycloalkylethyl or 2-(4-morpholinyl)ethyl, whether or not further substituted in the indene ring to any extent and whether or not substituted in the naphthyl ring to any extent [Inserted by 2010 Amendment Regulations];

i any substance structurally derived from 3-phenylacetylindole by substitution at the nitrogen atom of the indole ring with alkyl, alkenyl, cycloalkylmethyl, cycloalkylethyl or 2-(4-morpholinyl)ethyl, whether or not further substituted in the indole ring to any extent and whether or not substituted in the phenyl ring to any extent [Inserted by 2010 Amendment Regulations];

j any substance structurally derived from 2-(3-hydroxycyclohexyl) phenol by substitution at the 5-position of the phenolic ring by alkyl, alkenyl, cycloalkylmethyl, cycloalkylethyl or 2-(4-morpholinyl) ethyl, whether or not further substituted in the cyclohexyl ring to any extent [Inserted by 2010 Amendment Regulations];

k any substance (not being a substance for the time being specified in Schedule 3) structurally derived from 1-benzylpiperazine or 1-phenylpiperazine by modification in any of the following ways:

  i by substitution at the second nitrogen atom of the piperazine ring with alkyl, benzyl, haloalkyl or phenyl groups;

  ii by substitution in the aromatic ring to any extent with alkyl, alkoxy, alkylenedioxy, halide or haloalkyl groups [Inserted by 2010 Amendment Regulations].

2 Any stereoisomeric form of a substance specified in paragraph 1.

3 Any ester or ether of a substance specified in paragraph 1 or 2.

4 Any salt of a substance specified in any of paragraphs 1, 2 or 3.

5 Any preparation or other product containing any proportion of a substance or product specified in any of paragraphs 1, 2, 3 or 4, not being a preparation specified in Schedule 5.

Schedule 2

1 The following substances and products, namely:

Acetorphine
Acetylmethadol
Alfentanil
Allylprodine
Alphacetylmethadol
Alphameprodine
Alphamethadol
Alphaprodine
Anileridine
Benzethidine
Benzylmorphine
   (3-benzylmorphine)
Betacetylmethadol
Betameprodine
Betamethadol
Betaprodine
Bezitramide
Carfentanil
Clonitazene
Cocaine
Codoxime
4-Cyano-2-dimethylamino-
   4,4-diphenylbutane
4-Cyano-1-methyl-
   4-phenylpiperidine
Desomorphine
Dextromoramide
Diamorphine
Diampromide
Diethylthiambutene
Difenoxin
Dihydroetorphine [Inserted
   by 2010 Amendment
   Regulations]
Dihydromorphine
Dimenoxadole
Dimepheptanol
Dimethylthiambutene
Dioxaphetyl butyrate
Diphenoxylate
Dipipanone

Drotebanol
Ecgonine, and any derivative
   of ecgonine which is
   convertible to ecgonine or
   to cocaine
Ethylmethylthiambutene
Etonitazene
Etorphine
Etoxeridine
Fentanyl
Furethidine
Hydrocodone
Hydromorphinol
Hydromorphone
Hydroxypethidine
Isomethadone
Ketobemidone
Levomethorphan
Levomoramide
Levophenacylmorphan
Levorphanol
Lofentanil
Medicinal opium
Metazocine
Methadone
Methyldesorphine
Methyldihydromorphine
   (6-methyldihydromorphine)
2-Methyl-3-morpholino-1,
   1-diphenylpropane-
   carboxylic acid
1-Methyl-4-phenylpiperidine-
   4-carboxylic acid
Metopon
Morpheridine
Morphine
Morphine methobromide,
   morphine N-oxide and
   other pentavalent nitrogen
   morphine derivatives
Myrophine

Nabilone
Nicomorphine
Noracymethadol
Norlevorphanol
Normethadone
Normorphine
Norpipanone
Oripavine [Inserted by
   2010 Amendment
   Regulations]
Oxycodone
Oxymorphone
Pethidine
Phenadoxone
Phenampromide
Phenazocine
Phencyclidine
Phenomorphan
Phenoperidine
1-Phenylcyclohexylamine
4-(1-Phenylcyclohexyl)
   morpholine
4-Phenylpiperidine-4-
   carboxylic acid ethyl ester

Piminodine
1-Piperidinocyclohexane-
   carbonitrile
Piritramide
Proheptazine
Properidine
Racemethorphan
Remifentanil [Inserted by
   2010 Amendment
   Regulations]
Racemoramide
Racemorphan
Sufentanil
Tapentadol [Inserted by
   2010 Amendment
   Regulations]
Thebacon
Thebaine
4-[1-(2-Thienyl)cyclohexyl]-
   morpholine
1-[1-(2-Thienyl)cyclohexyl]-
   pyrrolidine
Tilidine
Trimeperidine

2   Any stereoisomeric form of a substance specified in paragraph 1 not being dextromethorphan or dextrophan.

3   Any ester or ether of a substance specified in paragraph 1 or 2, not being a substance specified in paragraph 6.

4   Any salt of a substance specified in any of paragraphs 1, 2 or 3.

5   Any preparation or other product containing any proportion of a substance or product specified in any of paragraphs 1, 2, 3 or 4, not being a preparation specified in Schedule 5.

6   The following substances and products, namely:

Acetyldihydrocodeine
Amineptine [Inserted by 2010
   Amendment Regulations]
Amphetamine
Amphetaminil [Inserted
   by 2010 Amendment
   Regulations]
Benzphetamine
Buprenorphine
Butorphanol

Codeine
Dexamphetamine
Dextropropoxyphene
Dihydrocodeine
N-Ethylamphetamine
Ethylmorphine
   (3-ethylmorphine)
Fenethylline
Glutethimide
Lefetamine

Mecloqualone
Methaqualone
Methylamphetamine
Methylphenidate
Nalbuphine
Nicocodine
Nocodicodine
(6-nicotinoyldihydrocodeine)

Norcodeine
Phendimetrazine
Phenmetrazine
Pholcodine
Propiram
Quinalbarbitone
Zipeprol [Inserted by 2010
Amendment Regulations].

7 Any stereoisomeric form of a substance specified in paragraph 6.
8 Any salt of a substance specified in paragraph 6 or 7.
9 Any preparation or other product containing any proportion of a substance or product specified in any of paragraphs 6, 7 or 8, not being a preparation specified in Schedule 5.

Schedule 3

1 The following substances, namely
   a Cathine
     1-(3-Chlorophenyl)-4-
       (3-chloropropyl)piperazine
       [Inserted by 2010
       Amendment Regulations]
     1-(3-Chlorophenyl)-
       piperazine [Inserted by
       2010 Amendment
       Regulations]
     Chlorphentermine
     Diethylpropion
     Ethchlorvynol
     Ethinamate
     Flunitrazepam [Inserted by
       1993 Amendment
       Regulations]

   4-Hydroxybutanoic acid
     [Inserted by 1993
     Amendment Regulations]
   Ketamine [Inserted by 2010
     Amendment Regulations]
   Mazindol
   Mephentermine
   Meprobamate
   Methyprylone
   Pemoline
   Pentazocine
   Phentermine
   Pipradrol
   Temazepam [Inserted by
     1993 Amendment
     Regulations];

   b any substance (not being quinalbarbitone) structurally derived from barbituric acid by disubstitution at the 5,5 positions, whether or not there is also substitution at the 1 position by a methyl substituent.

2 Any stereoisomeric form of a substance specified in paragraph 1, not being phenylpropanolamine.
3 Any salt of a substance specified in paragraph 1 or 2.
4 Any preparation or other product containing any proportion of a substance or product specified in paragraphs 1, 2 or 3, not

being a preparation specified in Part 2 of Schedule 4 or in Schedule 5.

Schedule 4

Part 1

1   The following substances, namely:

Alprazolam	Loprazolam
Aminorex [Inserted by 2010	Lorazepam
Amendment Regulations]	Lormetazepam
Bromazepam	Medazepam
Brotizolam [Inserted by 2010	Mefenorex
Amendment Regulations]	Mesocarb [Inserted by 2010
Camazepam	Amendment Regulations]
Chlordiazepoxide	Midazolam [Inserted by 1993
Clobazam	Amendment Regulations]
Clonazepam	Nimetazepam
Clorazepic Acid	Nitrazepam
Clotiazepam	Nordazepam
Cloxazolam	Oxazepam
Delorazepam	Oxazolam
Diazepam	Pinazepam
Estazolam	Prazepam
Ethyl loflazepate	Propylhexedrine
Fencamfamin	Pyrovalerone
Fenproporex	Selegiline [Inserted by 1993
Fludiazepam	Amendment Regulations]
Flurazepam	Tetrazepam
Halazepam	Triazolam
Haloxazolam	Zolpidem [Inserted by 2010
Ketazolam	Amendment Regulations].

2   Any stereoisomeric form of a substance specified in paragraph 1.
3   Any salt of a substance specified in paragraph 1 or 2.
4   Any preparation or other product containing any proportion of a substance or product specified in any of paragraphs 1 to 3, not being a preparation specified in Schedule 5.

Part 2

Any preparation containing not more than 100 mg of methylphenobarbitone or of phenobarbitone (calculated in either case in terms of base) per dosage unit and no other controlled drug and which in the case of an undivided preparation has a concentration of not more than 0.5% of phenobarbitone (calculated as base) and no other controlled drug.

Schedule 5

1   a   Any preparation of one or more of the substances to which this paragraph applies (not being a preparation designed for administration by injection) when compounded with one or more other ingredients and which contains a total of not more than 100 mg of the substance or substances (calculated as base) per dosage unit and which in the case of an undivided preparation has a total concentration of not more than 2.5 percent of the substance or substances (calculated as base);

    b   The substances to which this paragraph applies are acetyldihyrocodeine, codeine, ethylmorphine (3-ethylmorphine), nicocodeine, nicodicodeine (6-nicotinoyldihydrocodeine), norcodeine, pholcodine and their respective salts.

2   Any preparation of dihydrocodeine (not being a preparation designed for administration by injection) containing, per dosage unit, not more than 10 mg of dihydrocodeine (calculated as base) and which in the case of an undivided preparation has a concentration of not more than 1.5% of dihydrocodeine (calculated as base).

3   Any preparation of cocaine containing not more than 0.1% of cocaine calculated as cocaine base, being a preparation which is compounded with one or more other ingredients in such a way that the cocaine cannot be readily recovered.

4   Any preparation of medicinal opium or of morphine containing, in either case, not more than 0.2% of morphine calculated as anhydrous morphine base, being a preparation which is compounded with one or more other ingredients in such a way that the opium or morphine cannot be readily recovered.

5   Any preparation of dextropropoxyphene, being a preparation designed for oral administration, containing not more than 135 mg of dextropropoxyphene (calculated as base) per dosage unit or with a total concentration of not more than 2.5%, (calculated as base) in undivided preparations.

6   Any preparation of difenoxin containing, per dosage unit, not more than 0.5 mg of defenoxin and a quantity of atropine sulphate equivalent to at least 5%, of the dose of difenoxin.

7   Any preparation of diphenoxylate containing, per dosage unit, not more than 2.5 mg of diphenoxylate calculated as base, and a quantity of atropine sulphate equivalent to at least 1%, of the dose of diphenoxylate.

8 Any preparation of propiram containing, per dosage unit, not more than 100 mg of propiram calculated as base and which is compounded with at least the same amount, by weight, of methylcellulose.

9 Any powder of ipecacuanha and opium comprising 10% powdered opium, 10% powdered ipecacuanha root, both well mixed with the remaining 80 percent consisting of any other powdered ingredient which contains no controlled drug.

10 Any mixture containing one or more of the preparations specified in this schedule, being a mixture of which none of the other ingredients is a controlled drug.

9

Poisons Act and Regulations

S Byrne and L Clarke

The term 'poison' is a legislative mechanism by which any substance is legally controlled by having it listed in Schedule 1 to the Poisons Regulations 2008[1] (see Appendix 9.1). It does not necessarily relate to its inherent toxicity in the conventional meaning of the word. Any substance so listed is deemed to be a poison. It should be noted that a reference to a poison includes a preparation or product containing that poison. Other substances, no matter how toxic, are not legally deemed to be poisons.

Poisons Act

The Poisons Act 1961 as amended[2] provides the legislative framework for the regulation and control of poisons, including those intended for use in pharmaceutical preparations and for agricultural and veterinary purposes. Both the Minister for Health and Children and the Minister for Agriculture, Fisheries and Food, have power to make regulations under the Act, the former in relation to the poisons in general and the latter in relation to poisons intended for veterinary and agricultural purposes only. Both may declare substances to be poisons. The Poisons Act has been amended by both the Misuse of Drugs Act 1977 and the Pharmacy Act 2007.

Scope of Poisons Regulations

The Poisons Regulations 2008 consolidated and replaced the Poisons Regulations 1982[3] and the amendment Regulations of 1983, 1984, 1986, 1991 and 2003.[4]

---

1. S.I. No. 511 of 2008. Copyright Houses of the Oireachtas 2008.
2. No. 12 of 1961 as amended by Act No. 12 of 1977 and Act No. 20 of 2007.
3. S.I. No. 188 of 1982.
4. S.I. No. 51 of 1983, S.I. No. 349 of 1984, S.I. No. 424 of 1986, S.I. No. 353 of 1991 and S.I. No. 351 of 2003.

Unlike the 1982 regulations, the 2008 regulations do not have effect in respect of veterinary medicines (which are legally known as 'animal remedies' in Ireland), medicinal products (for human use) and cosmetic products, as each of these product categories is now controlled as such products in their own right.

Traditionally, poisons legislation was used to regulate the retail sale and supply of a wide range of substances, including human and veterinary medicines. Human medicines containing poisons were confined to sale or supply from pharmacies or registered druggist's premises, by or under the supervision of a pharmacist or registered druggist, and this offered a useful intermediate level of control between prescription-only status and supply from non-pharmacy outlets.

However, the Poisons Regulations had become less significant as a mechanism of control over human medicines in the last two decades. The introduction of provisions in the regulations governing prescription medicines[5] which stated that (with some limited exceptions) medicines exempted from prescription control (by virtue of their dose, daily dose, strength, pack size or indication) could only be sold or supplied from a pharmacy, by or under the supervision of a pharmacist, meant that a parallel system now existed to ensure supervision of the sale of non-prescription medicines. Furthermore, no new poisons used in medicinal products had been designated as poisons since 1986, even if earlier members of the same therapeutic class had been so classified.

In relation to animal remedies, the Poisons Regulations traditionally defined the range of products that could be sold by specially licensed lay persons ('licensed sellers'), including a limited number of antibiotics for the management of bovine mastitis. However, the regulatory framework for animal remedies has been strengthened considerably with the passing of the Animal Remedies Act 1993 and the transposition into Irish law of increasingly robust European Union directives relating to veterinary medicinal products (see Chapter 10, Veterinary medicines).

The first step to narrow the scope of poisons legislation came with the complete exclusion of animal remedies from the Poisons Regulations 1982 as amended, by the Animal Remedies (Poisons Act 1961) Regulations 2007.[6] The Pharmacy Act 2007 amended the Poisons Act 1961 to prohibit the Minister for Health and Children from declaring as poisons, substances whose sole use was as a medicinal product. The Poisons Regulations 2008 then exempted human medicinal products in their entirety from the controls

---

5. Currently the Medicinal Products (Prescription and Control of Supply) Regulations 2003 as amended. The requirement for pharmacist supervision of the sale or supply of most exempted products was first introduced by the Medicinal Products (Prescription and Control of Supply) Regulations 1993.
6. S.I. No. 861 of 2007.

set out in the regulations. In tandem with this, the list of poisons in Schedule 1 to the 2008 regulations does not include substances whose sole use is medicinal.

The sale and supply of human medicinal products is now regulated under the Pharmacy Act 2007 and regulations and rules made under that Act (see Chapter 12, The Pharmacy Act), the Irish Medicines Board Acts 1995 and 2006;[7] and regulations made under Section 32 of that act, including the Medicinal Products (Prescription and Control of Supply) Regulations 2003[8] as amended and the Medicinal Products (Control of Placing on the Market) Regulations 2007[9] as amended (see Chapter 4, Placing medicines on the market and Chapter 7, Prescription and control of supply of medicines). Animal remedies have a parallel system of control under the European Communities (Animal Remedies) Regulations 2007 and 2009[10] as well as the Animal Remedies Acts 1993 and 2006 (see Chapter 10, Veterinary medicines).

Role of the Pharmacy Act 2007 in the control of poisons

The Pharmacy Act 2007 sets out a framework for the ownership, control and supervision of retail pharmacy businesses and for the keeping of open shop for the sale of poisons by registered pharmacists and druggists. Section 74 of the Pharmacy Act deals specifically with the sales of poisons and makes a number of amendments to the Poisons Act 1961. As mentioned previously, the Poisons Act now states at Section 14(3A) that the Minister for Health and Children may not declare a substance whose sole use is medicinal to be a poison. A new Section 18A has been inserted into the Poisons Act which defines who may keep open shop for the sale of poisons, including registered pharmacists and registered druggists. Section 18A also gives the Council of the Pharmaceutical Society of Ireland (PSI) the power to make rules with the approval of the Minister for Health and Children, in relation to persons keeping open shop for the sale of poisons, covering areas such the keeping of records in relation to premises and personnel and the furnishing of statements and returns.

Poisons Council (Comhairle na Nimheanna)

The Poisons Act 1961 provided for the establishment of a council known as Comhairle na Nimheanna (Poisons Council). The purpose of the Council is to

---

7. No. 29 of 1995 as amended by the Irish Medicines Board (Miscellaneous Provisions) Act 2006 (No. 3 of 2006).
8. S.I. No. 540 of 2003.
9. S.I. No. 540 of 2007.
10. S.I. No. 786 of 2007 as amended by S.I. No. 182 of 2009.

advise the Minister for Health and Children or the Minister for Agriculture, Fisheries and Food in relation to the making of regulations under the act. The functions and constitution of the Council are given in Appendix 9.2.

Schedules to Poisons Regulations

There are nine schedules to the Poisons Regulations 2008 and the following is a brief summary of their significance.

- **Schedule 1**: lists in Part 1, poisons that may only be sold by registered pharmacists or registered druggists (see Appendix 9.1) and in Part 2, those that may also be sold by licensed sellers (see Appendix 9.1);
- **Schedule 2**: lists the more dangerous poisons to which special record-keeping requirements apply (see Appendix 9.3);
- **Schedule 3**: lists poisons which are exempted from all controls. General exemptions are listed in Part 1, with specific exemptions listed in Part 2 (see Appendix 9.4);
- **Schedule 4**: sets out the form and the circumstances of sale applicable to certain Schedule 1 Part 2 poisons when sold by licensed sellers (see Appendix 9.5);
- **Schedule 5**: sets out the format of the poisons register in which sales of Schedule 2 poisons must be recorded (see Figure 9.1);
- **Schedule 6**: sets out the form of application to the Health Service Executive (HSE) for a licence to sell Schedule 1 Part 2 poisons, i.e. licensed sellers (see Figure 9.2);
- **Schedule 7**: sets out the form of licence issued by the HSE to licensed sellers (see Figure 9.3);
- **Schedule 8**: sets out the form of certificate to be given by a householder for the purchase of a Schedule 2 poison which in some cases must be endorsed by a member of the Garda Síochána (see Figure 9.4);
- **Schedule 9**: sets out the form of certificate to be given by an analyst for use as evidence in legal proceedings under the Poisons Regulations.

General restrictions on sale of poisons

The purposes of the Poisons Regulations 2008 are:

a to designate substances as poisons;
b to define where and by whom poisons may be sold; and
c to impose certain requirements in relation to their sale or supply.[11]

---

11. Regulation 5.

Date of sale	Name and quality of poison sold	Purchaser's			Purchaser's statement of the purpose for which the poison is required	Date of certificate (if any)	Name and address of person giving certificate (if any)	Signature of purchaser, or where a signed order is presented, the words 'signed order' with the appropriate reference number
		Name	Address	Trade, business or occupation				

Figure 9.1 Format of Poisons Register.

Poisons Regulations 2008
(S.I. No. 511 of 2008)

Application for a licence to sell certain poisons set out in Part 2 of Schedule 1 to the Regulations

To the Health Service Executive

I[1]... trading as[2]...

....

hereby apply for a licence in respect of the following premises namely[3]

....

....

I hereby nominate[4]...

to act as my responsible deputy(ies) for the purpose of Regulation 10(5) of the said Regulations.

Signature of applicant..

Date..

Notes:
[1] Here insert name of applicant.
[2] Here insert the name or trading style of the business or enterprise.
[3] Here insert address of the premises in respect of which licence is sought. A separate application and licence are required in respect of each premises.
[4] If so desired insert the name/s of proposed deputy/ies (not more than 2).

Figure 9.2 Application form to apply to the Health Service Executive for a licence to sell certain poisons set out in Part 2 of Schedule 1 (i.e. Licensed Seller).

These regulations provide that the retail sale of certain poisons (i.e. those specified in Part 1 of Schedule 1 – see Appendix 9.1) may only take place at retail pharmacies by or under the supervision of a registered pharmacist. The regulations also provide that certain other poisons (i.e. those specified in Part 2 of Schedule 1 – see Appendix 9.1) may be sold by retail outlets licensed for that purpose, as well as through pharmacies. These latter poisons are intended mainly for use by persons engaged in the business of agriculture, horticulture and forestry and the sellers concerned are known as 'licensed sellers'.

It should be noted that the sale of any poison from a travelling shop, vehicle or automatic vending machine is prohibited.

Licence No........................

Reference........................

Health Service Executive

Poisons Regulations 2008
(S.I. No. 511 of 2008)
Licence to sell certain poisons set out in Part 2 of Schedule 1 to the Regulations

---

The Health Service Executive hereby grants to..

a licence under Regulation 10 of the Poisons Regulations 2008, in respect of the following

premises namely...

....

The following person(s) is/are hereby specified as responsible deputy(ies) for the purpose

of Regulation 10(5) of the said Regulations..

....

This licence shall, unless sooner cancelled or suspended, continue in force until the last

day of................ 20.......

Signed on behalf of the Executive.

....

Date..

Figure 9.3   Form of licence issued to licensed seller.

The regulations define 'sell' as including offering or keeping for sale. 'Sale by wholesale' means sale to a person who buys for the purpose of selling again and cognate words are to be construed accordingly.[12]

Licensed sellers

Subject to appropriate application including the payment of an application fee (currently €100), the HSE may grant licences to persons who wish to sell poisons set out in Part 2 of Schedule 1 (i.e. licensed sellers).[13] The Poisons Regulations specify the format of the application (Schedule 6, see Figure 9.2) and that of the licence itself (Schedule 7, see Figure 9.3). The licence is valid for

---

12. Regulation 3.
13. Regulations 10 and 11.

two years, unless cancelled sooner or suspended by the HSE. It may specify up to two persons who may act as responsible deputies on behalf of the licensee.

The HSE may refuse an application for a licence in the case of a person who:

a   fails to pay the appropriate fee;
b   is, in the opinion of the HSE, for any sufficient reason relating to him or her personally, not a fit and proper person to be licensed;
c   has nominated a person to act as his or her responsible deputy who is not a fit and proper person to be a deputy;
d   has applied for a licence in respect of a premises which is not a fit and proper premises as to enable the granting of a licence.

The HSE may cancel, suspend or restore a licence. If such a decision is taken by the HSE, the person affected by the decision may appeal it to the Minister for Health and Children and where such an appeal is successful the HSE shall allow the application or shall not cancel or suspend the licence, as the case may be.

The HSE is required to keep a register of licences granted to licensed sellers and any person may, at all reasonable times, on payment of a fee (€10 at the time of writing), inspect and make copies of any entry in that register.

A licensed seller may not sell:

a   any poison listed in Part 2 of Schedule 1 (Appendix 9.1) which has, since being obtained by him or her, been subject to any form of manipulation, treatment or processing as a result of which the poison has been exposed;
b   any poison listed in the first column of Part 1 of Schedule 4 (Appendix 9.5) unless the substance or product sold is in the form specified opposite the description of the poison in the second column of Part 1;
c   any poison set out in Part 2 of Schedule 4 (Appendix 9.5) unless the purchaser is engaged in the business of agriculture, horticulture or forestry and requires the poison for that purpose.

A licensed seller is not permitted to use in connection with the premises to which the licence relates, any title, emblem or description reasonably calculated to suggest that he or she is entitled to sell any poison which he or she is not actually entitled to sell.

Restrictions on sales of certain poisons

The Poisons Regulations 2008 impose additional restrictions on the sale of certain poisons by persons entitled to sell poisons, as follows:[14]

---

14. Regulations 12 and 13.

- Strychnine, its salts or quaternary compounds or preparations containing 0.2% or more of strychnine may only be sold or supplied to a department of State, a local authority or the HSE for the purpose of destruction, or to a person or institution involved in scientific research, education or chemical analysis, for the purpose of such research, education or analysis.
- Fluoroacetic acid, its salts, fluoroacetamide, salts of thallium or zinc phosphide may only be sold or supplied to a department of State, a local authority or the HSE requiring it for the public service or in connection with the exercise of any statutory powers, functions or duties, or to a person carrying on a business of pest control for use as a rodenticide.
- A person shall not sell or supply potassium arsenites and sodium arsenites.
- Calcium cyanide, potassium cyanide or sodium cyanide may only be sold or supplied to a department of State, a local authority or the HSE requiring it for the public service or in connection with the exercise of any statutory powers, functions or duties, or to a person who requires it for the purpose of his or her trade, business or profession.
- Chlordane, chlordecone or reserpine, or any of their respective isomeric compounds may not be sold or supplied for use as a pesticide.

The restrictions described above do not apply in the case of sale or supply of any of the poisons mentioned:

a   to persons or institutions involved in scientific education, research or chemical analysis, for the purposes of such education, research or analysis;
b   to be exported to purchasers outside the State; or
c   by way of wholesale dealing.

Records for Schedule 2 poisons

A poison listed in Schedule 2 may not be sold unless the purchaser is known by the seller or by a registered pharmacist or registered druggist in the employment of the seller at the premises where the sale takes place, to be a person to whom the poison may properly be sold.[15] If the purchaser is not known to the seller, the purchaser must furnish a certificate in writing signed by a householder. If the householder that provides the certificate is also unknown to the seller, the certificate must be countersigned by a member of the Garda Síochána. The format of the certificate required is set out in Schedule 8 (see Figure 9.4) and it must be retained by the seller following completion of the sale.

---

15. Regulation 7.

Poisons Regulations 2008

(S.I. No. 511 of 2008)

For the purpose of Regulation 7 of the Poisons Regulations 2008, I, the undersigned, being a householder occupying (1)..

....

....

....

Hereby certify from my knowledge of (2)...

of (1) .... that he or she is a person to

whom (3) .... may properly be supplied

I further certify that (4) ....

is the signature of the said (2) ....

....

Signature of the householder giving certificate

Date ....

Notes

(1) Insert full postal address.

(2) Insert full name of intending purchaser.

(3) Insert name of poison.

(4) Intending purchaser to fill his or her name here.

Endorsement required to be made by a member of the Garda Síochána when the householder giving the certificate is not known to the seller of the poison to be a responsible person of good character.

I hereby certify, in so far as is known to the Gardaí of the district in which

** .... resides, that he or she is a responsible person

of good character.

Office Stamp of Garda Station

Signature of Garda................................

Rank..

Date..

*** Insert full name of householder giving the certificate.*

Figure 9.4 Form of certificate to be given by a householder for the purchase of a Schedule 2 poison.

The seller must ensure that each sale or supply of a Schedule 2 poison is recorded in a poisons register in which the following information must be entered (see Figure 9.1):

a   date of sale;

b   name and quantity of the poison sold;

c   name and address of purchaser and his or her trade, business or occupation;

d purpose for which the poison is required;

e date of the certificate (if any);

f name and address of the householder issuing a certificate (if appropriate).

The purchaser must sign the poisons register, unless a signed order has been provided (see below). It should be noted that a signature is not required for retail sales of compounds of fentin.

The signature of the purchaser is not required if the seller has obtained, before the completion of the sale, an order in writing signed by the purchaser ('signed order') stating the purchaser's name and address, trade, business or profession, the purpose for which the poison is required and the total quantity to be purchased. The seller must be reasonably satisfied that the signature is that of the person indicated to have signed the order and that that person carries on the trade, business or profession stated in the order, being one in which the poison to be purchased is used. The seller inserts in the poisons register in the space where the signature of the purchaser would normally be recorded, the words 'signed order' and a reference number by which the order can be identified.

Where a person urgently requires a poison set out in Schedule 2 for the purposes of his or her trade, business or profession, the seller may, if he or she is reasonably satisfied that the person so requires the poison and is, by reason of some emergency, unable before delivery to furnish a signed order or to attend in person to sign the poisons register, deliver the poison to the purchaser on an undertaking by the purchaser to furnish a signed order within 72 hours.

The poisons register must be preserved for two years from the date on which the last entry was made and be kept readily available for inspection by any member of the Garda Síochána or a person holding a written authorisation for the purposes of the regulations (e.g. PSI inspector).

The requirements relating to recording in the poisons register, signed orders, etc. do not apply to the sale or supply of any poison by the person who manufactures or imports it. Similarly, they do not apply to a person who wholesales poisons where the poison is sold or supplied to a person carrying on a business in the course of which poisons are regularly sold or are regularly used in the manufacture of other products and the seller or supplier is reasonably satisfied that the purchaser requires the poison for the purposes of that business.

Restrictions on sales to shopkeepers

The Poisons Regulations 2008 specifically state in relation to the sale of poisons to shopkeepers that a person shall not sell a poison by wholesale to shopkeepers unless the seller has reasonable grounds for believing that the purchaser is a person lawfully conducting a retail pharmacy business or is otherwise entitled to sell the poison (e.g. licensed seller), or he or she has received a statement signed by the purchaser, or by a person acting on his or her behalf, to the effect that the purchaser requires the poison for the purpose of his or her trade, business or profession and that he or she does not intend to sell the poison on any premises used for, or in connection, with his or her retail business.[16]

Storage

Poisons in retail shops and premises must be stored in a cupboard or drawer reserved solely for the storage of poisons; or on a shelf reserved solely for the storage of poisons and no food being kept directly underneath that shelf; or in a part of the shop or premises which is partitioned off or otherwise separated from the remainder of the shop or premises, to which customers do not have access, and in which no food is kept.[17]

Labelling of poisons

Products containing poisons typically fall within the remit of other legislation such as pesticides legislation or dangerous substances legislation which set out detailed provisions as to the labelling required. For that reason, the Poisons Regulations 2008, unlike the earlier regulations, do not include any general requirements regarding the labelling of poisons. However, for a small number of poisons, specific requirements in relation to labelling are detailed in the regulations as follows:[18]

- Compressed hydrogen cyanide cannot be sold or supplied unless the container in which it is sold or supplied is labelled with the word 'Poison' and with the words 'Warning. This container holds poisonous gas and should only be opened and used by persons having expert knowledge of the precautions to be taken in its use.'
- Salts of paraquat in liquid form for use as a pesticide cannot be sold or supplied unless the container in which they are sold or supplied is labelled with the word 'Poison' and with the words 'Keep out of the reach of children. Do not re-pack from this container. Destroy container when empty.'

The above provisions do not require the labelling of any transparent cover where the appropriate warning remains visible, or any wrapper, hamper,

16. Regulation 8.
17. Regulation 9.
18. Regulation 6.

packing case, crate or other covering used solely for the purpose of transport or delivery.

Exemptions

The controls set out in the Poisons Regulations do not apply to any poison contained as an ingredient or component in any substance, product or article listed in Part 1 of Schedule 3 (see Appendix 9.4).[19] Examples include medicinal products, animal feedingstuffs, paints and plastics.

A poison listed in the first column of Part 2 of Schedule 3 (see Appendix 9.4) is exempted from the requirements of the Poisons Regulations when contained in a substance, product or article in the circumstances referred to in the second column of Part 2 opposite the mention of the poison. In the main, this kind of exemption refers to poisons contained in products having less than a stated percentage of a poison or particular forms of products, for example, nicotine is exempt when contained in cigarettes.

The restrictions on who may sell or supply poisons (i.e. registered pharmacists or registered druggist or licensed seller as applicable) do not apply with regards to the following:

a   the sale of any poison by a person carrying on a business in the course of which poisons are regularly sold either by wholesale or for use by the purchaser thereof in his or her trade, business or profession, where the sale is to:
   i   a person who requires the poison for the purpose of his or her profession;
   ii   a person carrying on a business in the course of which poisons are regularly used in the manufacture of other products;
   iii   a department of State or a local authority or the HSE, requiring the poison for the public service or in connection with the exercise of any statutory powers, functions or duties;
   iv   a person or institution involved in scientific education, research or chemical analysis, for the purposes of such education, research or analysis;
b   the sale by wholesale of any poison by any person in the course of a business carried on by him or her.

The provisions of the regulations regarding who may sell or supply poisons (Regulation 5), the labelling of certain poisons (Regulation 6) and the restrictions on sales of poisons to shopkeepers (Regulation 8) do not apply to the sale of poisons for export to purchasers outside the State.

---

19. Regulation 14.

Enforcement

The enforcement of the Poisons Regulations and the prosecution of offences under the Poisons Act 1961 as amended, specifically under Section 17, in relation to the Poisons Regulations may be carried out:[20]

a   by officers of the Minister for Health and Children;
b   by the Council of the PSI and its officers;
c   as regards the sale or keeping for sale of poisons by persons other than those conducting a retail pharmacy business or persons to whom Section 18A(3)(a) of the Poisons Act 1961 refers, by the HSE and its officers.

The enforcement and execution of the provisions of these regulations as regards poisons set out in Part 2 of Schedule 1 (Appendix 9.1) may also be carried out by officers of the Minister for Agriculture, Fisheries and Food.

Any of the officers referred to above are required to have an appropriate written authorisation, for example, in the case of an officer of the PSI, the written authorisation of the Council of the PSI. They may, at all reasonable times, for the purpose of ascertaining whether or not there is or has been a contravention of these regulations:

a   enter premises of any class or description;
b   enter any vehicle or travelling shop;
c   inspect any substance which is stored or offered or kept for sale at such premises, vehicle or travelling shop;
d   require the production of, inspect and, if he or she thinks fit, take copies of, any document or of any entry in any book at such premises, vehicle or travelling shop;
e   take (without payment) samples of poisons or of any substances stored, or offered or kept for sale, at such premises, vehicle or travelling shop for test, examination or analysis.

These powers do not apply with respect to any of the following premises:

a   such part of any premises (not being a shop) where a registered medical practitioner, registered dentist or registered veterinary practitioner practises; or
b   a premises used only as a private dwelling.

Officers of the PSI are not allowed to enter the following premises with regards to inspection under these regulations:

a   a hospital, nursing home, clinic or similar institution;
b   the premises of a manufacturer of a poison or a person carrying on a business in the course of which poisons are regularly sold only by

---

20. Regulation 15.

wholesale or for use by the purchaser in his or her trade, business or profession;

c   a licensed seller's premises.

Officers of the HSE are not allowed to enter the following premises with regards to inspection under these regulations:

a   the premises of a manufacturer of a poison or a person carrying on a business in the course of which poisons are regularly sold only by wholesale or for use by the purchaser in his or her trade, business or profession;

b   the premises of a person conducting a retail pharmacy business.

Evidence of result of test, examination or analysis

The Poisons Regulations provide that in any proceedings for an offence under Section 17 of the Poisons Act 1961, a certificate signed by any of the following stating the result of any test, examination or analysis of a sample shall, with regard to that sample, be evidence of the matters stated in the certificate unless the contrary is proved:[21]

a   the State Chemist or another chemist employed or engaged at the State Laboratory and authorised by the State Chemist to sign the certificate;

b   a public analyst appointed under Section 10 of the Sale of Food and Drugs Act 1875 or another analyst authorised by such a public analyst to sign the certificate;

c   a chemist or analyst appointed by the Council of the PSI for that purpose.

Appendix 9.1 List of substances declared to be poisons

Poisons Regulations 2008, Schedule 1[22]

Part 1 – Poisons which may only be sold by or under the supervision of a registered pharmacist or registered druggist

Aluminium phosphide
Amyl nitrite and other alkyl nitrites
Antimony, organic compounds of
Arsenic; its compounds other than those specified in Part 2 of this Schedule
Barium, salts of, other than barium sulphate and the salts of barium specified in Part 2 of this Schedule

---

21. Regulation 16.
22. S.I. No. 511 of 2008. Copyright Houses of the Oireachtas 2008.

Bromomethane

Chloroform

Chloropicrin

Cyclohexyl nitrite

Fluoroacetic acid; its salts; fluoroacetamide

Hydrogen cyanide; metal cyanides, other than ferrocyanides and ferricyanides

Lead acetates; compounds of lead with acids from fixed oils

Magnesium phosphide

Mercury, compounds of, the following: nitrates of mercury; oxides of mercury; mercuric cyanide oxides; mercuric thiocyanate; ammonium mercuric chlorides; potassium mercuric iodides; organic compounds of mercury which contain a methyl group directly linked to the mercury atom

Nux Vomica, the dried ripe seeds of *Strychnos nux-vomica* L.

Organochlorine compounds, the following; their isomers: aldrin, chlordane, chlordecone, dieldrin, DDT

Oxalic acid

Phenols (phenol; phenolic isomers of the following: cresols, xylenols, monoethylphenols) other than those substances specified in Part 2 of this Schedule; compounds of phenols with a metal other than those substances specified in Part 2 of this Schedule

Phosphorus, yellow

Reserpine

Strychnine; its salts; its quaternary compounds

Thallium, salts of.

Part 2 – Poisons which may also be sold by licensed sellers

Aldicarb

Alpha-chloralose

Ammonia

Arsenic, compounds of, the following: calcium arsenites, copper acetoarsenite, copper arsenates, copper arsenites, lead arsenates

Barium, salts of, the following: barium carbonate, barium silicofluoride

Carbofuran

Cycloheximide

Dinitrocresols (DNOC); their compounds with a metal or a base

Dinoseb; its compounds with a metal or a base

Dinoterb

Drazoxolon; its salts
Endosulfan
Endothal; its salts
Endrin
Fenaminosulf
Fenazaflor
Fentin, compounds of
Formaldehyde
Formic acid
Hydrochloric acid
Hydrofluoric acid; alkali metal bifluorides; ammonium bifluoride; alkali metal fluorides; ammonium fluoride; sodium silicofluoride
Mercuric chloride; mercuric iodide; organic compounds of mercury except compounds which contain a methyl (CH_3) group directly linked to the mercury atom
Metallic oxalates
Methomyl
Nicotine; its salts; its quaternary compounds
Nitric acid
Nitrobenzene
Oxamyl
Paraquat, salts of
Phenols (as defined in Part 1 of this Schedule) in substances containing less than 60%, mass in mass, of phenols; compounds of phenols with a metal in substances containing less than the equivalent of 60%, mass in mass, of phenols
Phosphoric acid
Phosphorus compounds, the following: azinphos-methyl, chlorfenvinphos, demephion, demeton-S-methyl, demeton-S-methyl-sulphone, dialifos, dichlorvos, dioxathion, disulfoton, fonofos, mecarbam, mephosfolan, methidathion, mevinphos, omethoate, oxydemeton-methyl, parathion, phenkapton, phorate, phosphamidon, pirimiphos-ethyl, quinalphos, schradan, sulfotep, thiometon, thionazin, triazophos, vamidothion
Potassium hydroxide
Sodium hydroxide
Sodium nitrite
Sulphuric acid
Thiofanox
Zinc phosphide.

Appendix 9.2 Comhairle na Nimheanna/Poisons Council

Poisons Act 1961 as amended, Sections 2–13

Establishment of the Council

2.   The Minister [for Health and Children] shall by order establish as on and from a specified date a council to be called and known as Comhairle na Nimheanna to fulfil the functions assigned to it by this Act.

Functions of the Council

3.   (1)   The Council shall advise the Minister in relation to any regulations under Section 14 of this Act and the Minister for Agriculture in relation to any regulations under Section 15 of this Act.

     (2)   The Council shall advise the Minister or the Minister for Agriculture on such other matters in relation to poisons, their manufacture, storage, transport, distribution, sale and use and the regulation, limitation, control and supervision of such manufacture, storage, transport, distribution, sale and use as the Minister or the Minister for Agriculture as the case may be, shall refer to it.

     (3)   (a)   The Council shall advise the Minister in relation to any Regulations made or proposed to be made after the commencement of this section under Section 65 of the Health Act, 1947, which he refers to it.

           (b)   The provisions of subsection (17) (inserted by Section 41 of the Health Act, 1953) of Section 98 of the Health Act, 1947, shall not apply in relation to regulations made or proposed to be made under the aforesaid Section 65 which are referred to the Council under this subsection.

Constitution of the Council

4.   (1)   The Council shall consist of:
           (a)   three persons, each of whom is a registered medical practitioner, has, for a period of not less than ten years before the date of his appointment as a member of the Council, been registered, or been entitled to be registered, in the Register of Medical Practitioners for Ireland and possesses an academic qualification which is higher than the minimum qualification required for such registration and is, in the opinion of the Minister, a desirable qualification as respects membership of the Council,

(b) five persons, each of whom is a registered pharmaceutical chemist and has, for a period of not less than ten years before the date of his appointment as a member of the Council, been registered, or been entitled to be registered, in the Register of Pharmaceutical Chemists for Ireland, *and one of whom is a person with knowledge and experience of the manufacture of preparations containing poisons* [Latter section in italics inserted by Misuse of Drugs Act 1977, No. 12 of 1977],

(c) one person who is a registered dentist and has, for a period of not less than ten years before the date of his appointment as a member of the Council, been registered, or been entitled to be registered, in the Register of Dentists for Ireland,

(cc) one person who is a fellow, ordinary member or licentiate of the Institute of Chemistry of Ireland [Inserted by Misuse of Drugs Act 1977],

(d) two persons nominated by the Minister for Agriculture, each of whom is a registered veterinary surgeon,

(e) one person with special knowledge and experience of the use of poisonous substances in agriculture nominated by the Minister for Agriculture,

(f) two persons nominated by the Minister for Agriculture, each of whom is a person whose main occupation is farming,

(g) three other persons (whether or not having any qualification referred to in the foregoing paragraphs).

(2) At least two of the persons referred to in paragraph (a) of subsection (1) of this section shall be Fellows of the Royal College of Physicians of Ireland.

(3) (a) Each of three, but not more than three, of the persons referred to in paragraph (b) of subsection (1) of this section shall be a person whose main occupation is either the carrying on of the business of pharmaceutical chemist or in employment as a pharmacist and at least two of those three persons shall be persons who, on the date of their appointment as members of the Council, are members of the Council of the Pharmaceutical Society of Ireland.

(b) At least one of the persons referred to in paragraph (b) of subsection (1) of this section shall be a person whose main occupation is the teaching of pharmacy or a similar subject.

(4) One member of the Council shall be the chairman and the others shall be ordinary members.

(5) The Minister shall appoint a person to act as secretary to the Council.

Appointment of members of the Council

5. **(1)** Subject to subsection (3) of this section, the members of the Council shall be appointed by the Minister from time to time as occasion requires.

(2) Subject to subsection (3) of this section, before the establishment of the Council, the Minister shall appoint seventeen persons to be members of the Council.

(3) If, during any period when the number of persons standing appointed as members of the Council is less than seventeen, it is not, in the opinion of the Minister, practicable to appoint any other person to be a member of the Council, the Council shall, during that period, consist of the persons standing appointed as aforesaid.

Chairman of the Council

6. **(1)** The chairman of the Council shall be appointed from time to time as occasion requires by the Minister.

(2) The chairman of the Council may at any time resign his or her office by letter addressed to the Minister and the resignation shall take effect as on and from the date of the receipt of the letter by the Minister.

Determination of certain matters in relation to the Council by the Minister by order

7. **(1)** The Minister may by order determine the term of office (being a term of not more than five years) of the chairman of the Council, the term of office (being a term of not more than five years) of the ordinary members of the Council, the procedure for calling meetings of the Council and the quorum for meetings of the Council.

(2) An order under this section, including an order under this subsection, may be amended or revoked by the Minister by order under this subsection.

Meetings and procedure of the Council

8. **(1)** The Council shall hold such number of meetings as may be necessary for the due performance of its functions.

(2) The Minister may fix the date, time and place of the first meeting of the Council.

(3) Subject to the provisions of this Act, the Council may regulate, by standing orders or otherwise, the procedure and business of the Council.

(4) The functions of the Council may be exercised notwithstanding one or more vacancies among its members.

Removal of member of the Council

9. The Minister may at any time remove a member of the Council from office.

Re-appointment of members of the Council

10. A member of the Council who ceases for any reason to hold office as such member shall be eligible for re-appointment.

Resignation of members of the Council

11. A member of the Council may resign his or her office as a member of the Council by letter sent by registered post to the Council, and the resignation shall take effect at the commencement of the meeting of the Council held next after the receipt of the letter if the resignation is not withdrawn in writing before that meeting.

Casual vacancies

12. **(1)** A casual vacancy occurring among the members of the Council shall be filled by appointment by the Minister, subject to the like conditions (if any) as governed the appointment of the member occasioning the vacancy.

(2) A person appointed under this section shall hold office for the remainder of his predecessor's term.

Expenses of members of the Council

13. The Minister may, out of the moneys provided by the Oireachtas, pay to a member of the Council attending a meeting of the Council or performing any function on behalf of the Council his travelling and subsistence expenses and the payments shall be in accordance with a scale approved of by the Minister with the consent of the Minister for Finance.

Appendix 9.3 Poisons to which record-keeping requirements apply

Poisons Regulations 2008, Schedule 2[23]

Aldicarb
Alpha-chloralose other than preparations thereof specified in Part 1 of
Schedule 4
Aluminium phosphide
Antimonial poisons except substances containing less than the equivalent
of 1% of antimony trioxide
Arsenic; its compounds; except substances containing less than the
equivalent of 0.0075% of arsenic (As)
Barium, salts of (other than barium sulphate)
Bromomethane
Chloropicrin
Cycloheximide
Dinitrocresols (DNOC); their compounds with a metal or a base; except
winter washes containing not more than the equivalent of 5% of
dinitrocresols
Dinoseb; its compounds with a metal or a base
Dinoterb
Drazoxolon; its salts
Endosulfan
Endothal; its salts
Endrin
Fenaminosulf
Fenazaflor
Fentin, compounds of
Fluoroacetic acid; its salts; fluoroacetamide
Hydrogen cyanide; metal cyanides, other than ferrocyanides and
ferricyanides
Lead, compounds of, with acids from fixed oils
Mercuric chloride except substances containing less than 1% of mercuric
chloride; mercuric iodide except substances containing less than 2% of
mercuric iodide; nitrates of mercury except substances containing less than
the equivalent of 3%, mass in mass, of mercury (Hg); potassium mercuric
iodides except substances containing less than the equivalent of 1% of
mercuric iodide; organic compounds of mercury except substances, not
being aerosols, containing less than the equivalent of 0.2%, mass in mass,
of mercury (Hg)

---

23. S.I. No. 511 of 2008. Copyright Houses of the Oireachtas 2008.

Methomyl
Paraquat, salts of
Phosphorus compounds, the following: azinphos-methyl,
chlorfenvinphos, demephion, demeton-*S*-methyl, demeton-*S*-methyl-
sulphone, dialifos, dichlorvos, dioxathion, disulfoton, fonofos,
mecarbam, mephosfolan, methidathion, mevinphos, omethoate,
oxydemeton-methyl, parathion, phenkapton, phorate, phosphamidon,
pirimiphos-ethyl, quinalphos, schradan, sulfotep, thiometon, thionazin,
triazophos, vamidothion
Strychnine; its salts; its quaternary compounds; except substances
containing less than 0.2% of strychnine
Thallium, salts of
Thiofanox
Zinc phosphide.

Appendix 9.4 General and specific exemptions from requirements of Poisons Regulations

Poisons Regulations 2008, Schedule 3[24]

Part 1 – General exemptions

Adhesives; animal feedingstuffs (including medicated animal feedingstuffs)
and premixes therefor; animal remedies; anti-fouling compositions; builders'
materials; ceramics; cosmetic products; distempers; electrical valves; enamels;
explosives; fillers; fireworks; fluorescent lamps; flux in any form for use in
soldering; glazes; glue; inks; lacquer solvents; loading materials; medicinal
products; matches; motor fuels and lubricants; paints; photographic paper;
pigments; plastics; propellants; rubber; varnishes; vascular plants and their
seeds (not being Nux Vomica).

Part 2 – Specific exemptions

Poison	Substance or product in which exempted
Ammonia	Substances not being solutions of ammonia or preparations containing solutions of ammonia; substances containing less than 10%, mass in mass, of ammonia (NH_3); refrigerators; smelling bottles
Arsenic; its compounds	Pyrites ores or sulphuric acid containing arsenic or compounds of arsenic as natural impurities; in reagent kits or reagent devices, supplied for medical or veterinary purposes; substances containing less than 0.1%, mass in mass, of arsanilic acid

---

24. S.I. No. 511 of 2008. Copyright Houses of the Oireachtas 2008.

Poison	Substance or product in which exempted
Barium, salts of	Witherite other than finely ground witherite; barium carbonate bonded to charcoal for case hardening; fire extinguishers containing barium chloride; sealed smoke generators containing not more than 25%, mass in mass, of barium carbonate
Bromomethane	Fire extinguishers
Carbofuran	Granular preparations
Drazoxolon; its salts	Treatments on seeds
Formaldehyde	Substances containing less than 5%, mass in mass, of formaldehyde (H.CHO); photographic glazing or hardening solutions
Formic acid	Substances containing less than 25%, mass in mass, of formic acid (H.COOH)
Hydrochloric acid	Substances containing less than 10%, mass in mass, of hydrochloric acid (HCl)
Hydrogen cyanide	Preparations of wild cherry; in reagent kits supplied for medical or veterinary purposes; substances containing less than the equivalent of 0.1%, mass in mass, of hydrogen cyanide (HCN)
Lead acetate	Substances containing less than the equivalent of 2.5%, mass in mass, of elemental lead (Pb)
Mercuric chloride	Batteries; dressings on seeds or bulbs
Mercuric chloride; mercuric iodine; organic compounds of mercury	Treatments on seeds and bulbs
Mercury, oxides of	Canker and wound paints (for trees) containing not more than 3%, mass in mass, of yellow mercuric oxide
Methomyl	Solid substances containing not more than 1%, mass in mass, of methomyl
Nitric acid	Substances containing less than 20%, mass in mass, of nitric acid (HNO$_3$)
Nicotine; its salts; its quaternary compounds	Tobacco; in cigarettes, the paper of a cigarette (excluding any part of that paper forming part of or surrounding a filter), where that paper in each cigarette does not contain more than the equivalent of 10 mg of nicotine; preparations in aerosol dispensers containing not more than 0.2% of nicotine, mass in mass; other liquid preparations, and solid preparations with a soap base, containing not more than 7.5% of nicotine, mass in mass
Nitrobenzene	Substances containing less than 0.1% of nitrobenzene; polishes
Oxalic acid; metallic oxalates	Laundry blue; polishes; cleaning powders or scouring products, containing the equivalent of not more than 10% of oxalic acid dehydrate
Oxamyl	Granular preparations
Paraquat, salts of	Preparations in granular or pellet form containing not more than 5% of salts of paraquat calculated as paraquat ion

Phenols	Creosote obtained from coal tar; liquid disinfectants and antiseptics containing less than 5% of phenols as defined in Schedule 1; motor fuel treatments not containing phenol and containing less than 2.5% of other phenols; in reagent kits supplied for medical or veterinary purposes; solid substances containing less than 60% of phenols; tar (coal or wood), crude or refined; in tar oil distillation fractions containing not more than 5% of phenols
Phenyl mercuric salts	Antiseptic dressings on toothbrushes; in textiles containing not more than 0.01% of phenyl mercuric salts as a bacteriostat and fungicide
Phosphoric acid	Substances containing phosphoric acid, not being descaling preparations for household use containing more than 50%, mass in mass, of ortho-phosphoric acid
Phosphorus compounds, the following:	
Chlorfenvinphos	Treatments on seeds; granular preparations
Dichlorvos	Preparations in aerosol dispensers containing not more than 1%, mass in mass, of dichlorvos; materials impregnated with dichlorvos for slow release; granular preparations; ready for use liquid preparations containing not more than 1% mass in volume, of dichlorvos
Disulfoton	Granular preparations
Fonofos	Granular preparations
Oxydemeton-methyl	Aerosol dispensers containing not more than 0.25%, mass in mass, of oxydemeton-methyl
Parathion	Granular preparations
Phorate	Granular preparations
Pirimiphos-ethyl	Treatments on seeds
Thionazin	Granular preparations
Thiazophos	Granular preparations
Potassium hydroxide	Substances containing the equivalent of less than 17% of total caustic alkalinity expressed as potassium hydroxide; accumulators; batteries
Sodium fluoride	Substances containing less than 3% of sodium fluoride as a preservative.
Sodium hydroxide	Substances containing the equivalent of less than 12% of total caustic alkalinity expressed as sodium hydroxide
Sodium nitrite	Substances other than preparations containing more than 0.1% of sodium nitrite for the destruction of rats or mice
Sodium silicofluoride	Substances containing less than 3% of sodium silicofluoride as a preservative
Sulphuric acid	Substances containing less than 15%, mass in mass, of sulphuric acid (H_2SO_4); accumulators; batteries and sealed containers in which sulphuric acid is packed together with car batteries for use in those batteries; fire extinguishers
Thiofanox	Granular preparations

In Part 2 of this Schedule the expression 'granular preparation' in relation to a poison means a preparation:

a   which consists of absorbent mineral or synthetic solid particles impregnated with the poison, the size of the particles being such that not more than 4%, mass in mass, of the preparation is capable of passing a sieve with a mesh of 250 microns, and not more than 1% a sieve with a mesh of 150 microns;

b   which has an apparent density of not less than 0.4 g/mL if compacted without pressure;

c   not more than 12% of which, mass in mass, consists of one or more poisons in respect of which an exemption is conferred by this Schedule in relation to granular preparations.

Appendix 9.5 Restrictions on licensed sellers

Poisons Regulations 2008, Schedule 4[25]

Part 1 – Form to which the poisons specified are restricted when sold by licensed sellers

Poison	Form to which sale is restricted
Aldicarb	Preparations for use in agriculture, horticulture or forestry
Alpha-chloralose	Preparations intended for indoor use in the destruction of rats or mice and containing not more than 4%, mass in mass, of alpha-chloralose; preparations intended for indoor use in the destruction of rats or mice and containing not more than 8.5%, mass in mass, of alpha-chloralose, where the preparation is contained in a bag or sachet which is itself attached to the inside of a device in which the preparation is intended to be so used and the device contains not more than 3 g of the preparation
Arsenic, compounds of, the following:	
Calcium arsenites	Agricultural, horticultural and forestal insecticides or fungicides
Copper acetoarsenite	Agricultural, horticultural and forestal insecticides or fungicides

---

25.   S.I. No. 511 of 2008. Copyright Houses of the Oireachtas 2008.

Copper arsenates	Agricultural, horticultural and forestal insecticides or fungicides
Copper arsenites	Agricultural, horticultural and forestal insecticides or fungicides
Lead arsenates	Agricultural, horticultural and forestal insecticides or fungicides
Barium carbonate	Preparations for the destruction of rats or mice
Carbofuran	Preparations for use in agriculture, horticulture or forestry
Cycloheximide	Preparations for use in forestry
Dinitrocresols (DNOC); their compounds with a metal or a base	Preparations for use in agriculture, horticulture or forestry
Dinoseb; its compounds with a metal or a base	Preparations for use in agriculture, horticulture or forestry
Dinoterb	Preparations for use in agriculture, horticulture or forestry
Drazoxolon; its salts	Preparations for use in agriculture, horticulture or forestry
Endosulfan	Preparations for use in agriculture, horticulture or forestry
Endothal; its salts	Preparations for use in agriculture, horticulture or forestry
Endrin	Preparations for use in agriculture, horticulture or forestry
Fenaminosulf	Preparations for use in agriculture, horticulture or forestry
Fenazaflor	Preparations for use in agriculture, horticulture or forestry
Fentin, compounds of	Preparations for use in agriculture, horticulture or forestry
Mercuric chloride	Agricultural, horticultural and forestal fungicides, seed and bulb dressings, insecticides
Mercuric iodide	Agricultural, horticultural and forestal fungicides, treatments on seeds or bulbs
Mercury, organic compounds of	Agricultural, horticultural and forestal fungicides, treatments on seeds or bulbs, solutions containing not more than 5%, mass in volume, of phenyl mercuric acetate for use in swimming baths
Metallic oxalates other than potassium quadroxalate	Photographic solutions or materials

Poison	Form to which sale is restricted
Methomyl	Preparations for use in agriculture, horticulture or forestry
Nitrobenzene	Argicultural, horticultural and forestal insecticides
Oxamyl	Preparations for use in agriculture, horticulture or forestry
Paraquat, salts of	Preparations for use in agriculture, horticulture or forestry
Phosphorus compounds, the following: Azinphos-methyl Chlorfenvinphos Demephion Demeton-S-methyl Demeton-S-methylsulphone Dialifos Dichlorvos Dioxathion Disulfoton Fonofos Mecarbam Mephosfolan Methidathion Mevinphos Omethoate Oxydemeton-methyl Parathion Phenkapton Phorate Phosphamidon Pirimiphos-ethyl Quinalphos Sulfotep Thiometon Thionazin Triazophos Vamidothion	Preparations for use in agriculture, horticulture or forestry
Zinc phosphide	Preparations for the destruction of rats or mice

Part 2 – Poisons which may be sold by licensed sellers only to persons engaged in the business of agriculture, horticulture or forestry and for the purpose of that business

Aldicarb
Arsenic, compounds of, the following: calcium arsenites, copper acetoarsenites, copper arsenates, copper arsenates, lead arsenates
Carbofuran
Cycloheximide
Dinitrocresols (DNOC); their compounds with a metal or a base; except winter washes containing not more than the equivalent of 5% of dinitrocresols
Dinoseb; its compounds with a metal or a base
Dinoterb
Drazoxolon; its salts
Endosulphan
Endothal; its salts
Endrin
Fenaminosulf
Fenazaflor
Fentin, compounds of
Mercuric chloride; mercuric iodide; organic compounds of mercury, except solutions containing not more than 5%, mass in volume, of phenyl mercuric acetate for use in swimming baths
Methomyl
Oxamyl
Paraquat, salts of
Phosphorus compounds, the following: azinphos-methyl, chlorfenvinphos, demephion, demeton-S-methyl, demeton-S-methylsulphone, dialifos, dichlorvos, dioxathion, disulfoton, fonofos, mecarbam, mephosfolan, methidathion, mevinphos, omethoate, oxydemeton-methyl, parathion, phenkapton, phorate, phosphamidon, pirimiphos-ethyl, quinalphos, sulfotep, thiometon, thionazin, triazophos, vamidothion
Thiofanox.

10

Veterinary medicines

D Gaughan and S McCarthy

The controls applicable to the authorisation, use and control of veterinary medicines have undergone significant change and updating in recent years to ensure that the supply chain for a veterinary medicine from manufacture to delivery and subsequent employment by the end user is regulated in the interest of the health, safety and welfare of animals and the public, as well as environmental safety.

EU legislation

The legislation controlling veterinary medicines is based on European standards which have been consolidated and improved over the years and harmonised across the member states of the European Union (EU). The basis for the national legislative controls is derived from Directive 2001/82/EC as amended.[1] In 2001, the main Community legislation relating to the production, marketing, distribution and use of veterinary medicines, other than medicated feeds and feed additives, was combined into a new Directive 2001/82/EC. The aim of the directive was to harmonise the legislative provisions in place across all the member states, having due regard to the safeguarding of public health and by means which would not hinder the development of industry and trade in medicinal products within the Community. In 2004, following a review of the provisions and to facilitate the expansion of the EU, as well as the experience gained up to this time and the rapid development of knowledge and technology in the area of pharmaceuticals, the legislation was amended by Directive 2004/28/EC.

---

1. Directive 2001/82/EC of the European Parliament and of the Council of 6 November 2001 on the Community code relating to veterinary medicinal products as amended by Directive 2004/28/EC, Directive 2009/9/EC, Directive 2009/53/EC, Regulation (EC) No. 470/2009 and Regulation (EC) No. 596/2009.

Other EU legislation will be referred to below under the relevant sections, however, all EU legislation on veterinary medicines is published by the European Commission in Volume 5 of *The Rules Governing Medicinal Products in the European Union* which is modified periodically to account for updates in the legislation. This and other volumes of the same series are available on the Commission website.[2]

National legislation

The provisions relating to veterinary medicinal products as decreed in EU directives have been transposed into national legislation, primarily by the European Communities (Animal Remedies) Regulations 2007 and 2009 (the 'Animal Remedies Regulations'),[3] which provide a comprehensive legislative basis for licensing, manufacture, import and export, sale, supply, possession and administration of veterinary medicines in Ireland.

The Minister for Agriculture, Fisheries and Food has overall national responsibility in relation to the regulation of the veterinary medicines market in Ireland. The Department of Agriculture, Fisheries and Food is responsible for a number of functions including the production of legislation, issuing import and retail licences, enforcement of legislation including the taking of prosecutions, the management of the issue of retail licences and residue surveillance.[4] The department ensures appropriate controls are applied to the range of commercial outlets selling veterinary medicines, including those operated by veterinary surgeons. All such outlets at both wholesale and retail levels must meet specified standards in order to be licensed, and the holding of a current licence is a prerequisite for trading in veterinary medicines.

The Irish Medicines Board (IMB) is the competent authority in Ireland for the licensing of veterinary medicinal products and may act as a reference or concerned member state for the purposes of the mutual recognition and decentralised procedures.[5] The IMB is also responsible for the maintenance and implementation of a pharmacovigilance system,[6] and for the granting of licences in respect of the manufacturing of an animal remedy and the importation of an animal remedy from outside the EU.[7] The classification of

---

2. http://ec.europa.eu/health/documents/eudralex/vol-5/index_en.htm (accessed 1 March 2011).
3. European Communities (Animal Remedies) (No. 2) Regulations 2007 (S.I. No. 786 of 2007) (Copyright Houses of the Oireachtas 2007) as amended by European Communities (Animal Remedies) (Amendment) Regulations 2009 (S.I. No. 182 of 2009) (Copyright Houses of the Oireachtas 2009).
4. See website of Department of Agriculture, Fisheries and Food, www.agriculture.ie (accessed 1 March 2011).
5. Regulation 8, S.I. No. 786 of 2007 as amended.
6. Regulation 12, S.I. No. 786 of 2007 as amended.
7. Regulation 20, S.I. No. 786 of 2007 as amended.

products either as animal remedies requiring to be licensed or out-of-scope of the legislation is also the responsibility of the IMB.[8]

Terminology

Directive 2001/82/EC as amended[9] defines a 'veterinary medicinal product' as:

> any substance or combination of substances presented as having properties for treating or preventing disease in animals, or any substance or combination of substances which may be used in, or administered to, animals with a view either to restoring, correcting or modifying physiological functions by exerting a pharmacological, immunological or metabolic action, or to making a medical diagnosis.

In national legislation, the Animal Remedies Acts 1993 and 2006[10] use the term 'animal remedy' and define it as:

> any substance or combination of substances which (a) is intended for administration to animals, (b) may be administered to animals, or (c) is, whether expressly or by implication, presented for administration to animals, for the purpose of (i) treating, preventing or modifying disease in animals, (ii) making a medical or surgical diagnosis in animals, (iii) restoring, correcting or modifying physiological functions in animals, or (iv) except for a feedingstuff commonly known and solely used as such, otherwise improving the health or condition of animals.

The definition is broad in scope and interpretation, and therefore allows for the recognition of a wide range of products as being animal remedies.

Authorisation requirements

All veterinary medicinal products must be authorised before being placed on the market, in accordance with requirements specified under both EU and national legislation. The implementation of this requirement is provided for in the Animal Remedies Regulations with the definition of an 'animal remedies authorisation' as:[11]

a   a veterinary product authorisation within the meaning of Article 5 of Directive 2001/82/EC as amended (i.e. a marketing authorisation

---

8. Regulation 3(a)(i), S.I. No. 786 of 2007 as amended.
9. Article 1 of Directive 2001/82/EC as inserted by 2004/28/EC.
10. Animal Remedies Act 1993 (No. 23 of 1993) as amended by Irish Medicines Board (Miscellaneous Provisions) Act 2006 (No. 3 of 2006).
11. Regulation 2(1).

granted by a competent authority), or a registration following an application under Regulation 7(2) of the Animal Remedies Regulations, granted by the IMB in accordance with Regulation 9 (in respect of a homeopathic animal remedy that does not make any specific therapeutic claims);

b   a licence granted by the Minister under Regulation 16, 17 or 19 (see section on Issuing of a licence by the Minister);

c   a marketing authorisation granted under Regulation (EC) No. 726/2004 (i.e. a Community marketing authorisation granted under the centralised procedure);

d   such other document, registration, licence or authorisation deemed by the Animal Remedies Regulations to be an animal remedies authorisation.

The Animal Remedies Regulations prohibit the importation, possession, sale or supply of an animal remedy unless there is a relevant animal remedies authorisation in force. However, there are certain circumstances where exemptions are provided for. These are:[12]

a   a homeopathic animal remedy (other than an immunological homeopathic animal remedy) which, on or before 31 December 1993, was registered under the Animal Remedies (Registration of Manufacturers, Importers and Wholesalers) Regulations 1980;[13]

b   if the IMB determines (on foot of an application) that a substance does not come within the terms of Directive 2001/82/EC as amended;

c   in the case of veterinary medicinal products intended solely for aquarium fish, cage birds, homing pigeons, terrarium animals, small rodents, ferrets and rabbits kept exclusively as pets, provided that such products do not contain substances the use of which requires veterinary control and all possible measures are taken to prevent unauthorised use of the product for other animals.

Exemptions from the requirement to have an animal remedies authorisation also apply in relation to 'cross border practice', to the importation of animal remedies in certain health situations and under the 'cascade' system (see section on Exceptional authorisation/administration of an animal remedy).

Authorisation procedures

There are three routes by which a marketing authorisation may be obtained. These can be summarised as national procedure, mutual recognition or decentralised procedure, and centralised procedure.

---

12. Regulation 3.
13. S.I. No. 115 of 1980.

National procedure

This applies to products that are not already authorised in the EU and for which the authorisation is required in one member state only. The IMB operates the national procedure for an application for a veterinary product authorisation (VPA), which is utilised when it is intended to make a veterinary medicinal product available in Ireland. In the operation of the national procedure, an application is made to the IMB in the form specified and accompanied by specified particulars and documentation.[14] Information submitted in a new product application includes administrative data, the proposed summary of product characteristics (SmPC), product label and package leaflet and summaries of the dossier along with data on quality, safety and efficacy. The IMB examines the application with due regard to specified criteria in order to ensure compliance with the requirements of Directive 2001/82/EC as amended. The use of this procedure may also facilitate the future application in respect of a mutual recognition application to another member state.

Mutual-recognition or decentralised procedure

These procedures apply where an applicant wishes to obtain authorisations for a product in two or more member states. The mutual recognition procedure applies where following the granting of an authorisation for the veterinary medicinal product by one EU member state (the reference member state), the holder applies to one or more member states (the concerned member states) to issue identical authorisations. The decentralised procedure applies where there is not yet an existing authorisation for the product by any EU member state. In this case, one of the member states from among the concerned member states is chosen to be the reference member state. Following a coordinated assessment by the reference member state on behalf of all concerned member states, identical but separate authorisations are issued in each member state at the end of the procedure.[15]

Centralised procedure

Council Regulation (EC) No. 726/2004 created a centralised Community procedure for the authorisation of human and veterinary medicinal products, for which there is a single application, a single evaluation and a single authorisation allowing direct access to the single Community market. This procedure is compulsory for high-technology medicinal products, particularly those resulting from biotechnical processes and for veterinary medicinal

---

14. Regulation 4, S.I. No. 786 of 2007 as amended.
15. Articles 31–43 of Directive 2001/82/EC as amended.

products intended primarily for use as performance enhancers in order to promote the growth of treated animals or to increase yields from treated animals.[16] Applicants may at their own discretion use this procedure for medicinal products intended for use in animals containing a new active substance (i.e. one which on 20 November 2005 was not authorised in the Community for use in a medicinal product intended for use in animals), for medicinal products which constitute a significant therapeutic, scientific or technical innovation or for immunological products for the treatment of animal diseases that are subject to Community prophylactic measures.[17]

Exceptional authorisation/administration of an animal remedy

Cross-border practice

The Animal Remedies Regulations make provision for a veterinary practitioner established in another member state and providing cross-border professional services in Ireland to import, possess, sell, supply or administer small quantities of an animal remedy, notwithstanding the fact that it is not authorised in Ireland.[18] Certain conditions pertain to the animal remedy, in that the remedy must be authorised in the state in which the veterinary practitioner is established, it must be brought into Ireland by the practitioner and supplied in the manufacturer's original packaging and, when used in a food-producing animal, it must be analogous in terms of qualitative and quantitative composition to an animal remedy authorised in Ireland.

When using such a product, the veterinary practitioner must inform the owner of the animal of the appropriate withdrawal period (where applicable) and must indicate this on the label of the product supplied. The product quantity supplied must be that which would be expected to be in the possession of a practitioner in terms of the daily needs of good practice, but must not exceed five days' supply. Appropriate records must be kept by the veterinary practitioner, within the State, for a period of five years detailing the following:

a   the identity of the animal(s) treated;
b   date of examination of the animal(s);
c   number of animals treated;
d   name and address of the owner/person in charge of the animal(s);
e   the veterinary practitioner's diagnosis;
f   details of the animal remedy;
g   dosage of animal remedy;

---

16. Annex to Regulation (EC) No. 726/2004 as amended.
17. Article 2, Regulation (EC) No. 726/2004 as amended.
18. Regulation 15.

h   duration of treatment;

i   withdrawal period specified.

Such records are subject to inspection by an authorised officer.

Issuing of a licence by the Minister

There are a number of circumstances which may apply, and during which the Minister for Agriculture, Fisheries and Food may grant a licence which will provide an authority to import, possess, sell, supply or administer an animal remedy which is not authorised:[19]

a   if the health situation requires it and the animal remedy is authorised in another member state;

b   in exceptional circumstances and if the health situation requires it, the animal remedy may be one that is not authorised in either Ireland or another member state but is one which is pending consideration of an application for authorisation by the IMB or the European Medicines Agency (EMA);

c   where an immunological animal remedy is required to deal with a serious epizootic disease;

d   in exceptional circumstances where an animal is to be exported to a third country (i.e. outside the EU) and there is a need to use an immunological remedy authorised in that country.

The licence in all of the above situations will specify the route of sale of the animal remedy. If after consulting with the IMB, the Minister is of the opinion that it is more appropriate that an application for authorisation be made to the IMB, then a licence may not be granted.

The issuing of a licence by the Minister to provide an authority to manufacture, import from a third country, possess, sell or supply an animal remedy which is not authorised, in certain miscellaneous situations is provided for. This would includes situations where the animal remedy will be:[20]

a   used in a trial for research purposes;

b   supplied to the IMB or Minister to support an application for an authorisation;

c   supplied to a third-level institution or similar for educational or research purposes;

d   used for *in vitro* or other studies not involving administration to animals; or

e   exported from Ireland.

---

19. Regulation 16, S.I. No. 786 of 2007 as amended.
20. Regulation 17, S.I. No. 786 of 2007 as amended.

The `cascade'

The goal of the authorisation process is to scientifically assess a veterinary medicinal product against statutory criteria of safety, quality and efficacy when the product is used in accordance with the manufacturer's recommendations. This takes account of potential risks to animals, people who administer the medicine, those who may consume produce from treated animals and the environment. This evaluation of the benefits and the risks forms the basis for whether an authorisation is granted or not. The use of a medicine in a way that has not been authorised may pose potential risks and thus the law requires that, wherever possible, only medicines authorised for the condition and species being treated are used. However, the legislation recognises that there will be conditions affecting species for which no medicine is authorised and therefore provides exemptions in certain circumstances, subject to specified conditions. This process is referred to as the 'cascade'.[21]

A veterinary practitioner must not prescribe an animal remedy for, or administer an animal remedy to, a food-producing animal, other than in accordance with an animal remedies authorisation unless, for the animal in question, there is no licensed product indicated for the condition and species to be treated, and he or she is satisfied that the treatment is necessary to avoid unacceptable suffering to the animal. Under the cascade system, veterinary practitioners may use one of the following options:

a   a product licensed in Ireland for another condition in the same species;
b   a product licensed in Ireland for another animal species;
c   an authorised human medicinal product;
d   an animal remedy imported from another EU member state (i.e. a product authorised in another member state, for which a licence is issued by the Minister to allow for importation, possession, sale or supply by either a veterinary practitioner, a licensed wholesaler or a pharmacist);
e   if the previous conditions cannot be met, an animal remedy may be extemporaneously prepared by a veterinary practitioner or by a pharmacist or a licensed manufacturer in accordance with a prescription issued by a veterinary practitioner.

A veterinary practitioner is limited in respect to the substances that may be prescribed and administered to food producing animals under the cascade system. The pharmacologically active substances contained in the medicine must be listed in Annex I, II or III to Council Regulation (EEC) No. 2377/90.[22] In the case of an equid (i.e. horses and related animals such as donkeys) classed

---

21. Regulation 18, S.I. No. 786 of 2007 as amended.
22. Regulation (EEC) No. 2377/90 was repealed and superseded by Regulation (EC) No. 470/ 2009 which lays down Community procedures for the establishment of residue limits of pharmacologically active substances in foodstuffs of animal origin.

as a food-producing animal, substances listed in the Annex to Commission Regulation (EC) No. 1950/2006 in accordance with the conditions outlined there may also be prescribed or administered.

If a veterinary practitioner needs to prescribe or administer to a food producing animal, an unauthorised animal remedy in accordance with the criteria and conditions listed above, he or she must specify a withdrawal period to ensure that any food from the animal does not contain a residue which may be harmful to the consumer. The animal remedy or medicinal product may in some cases specify applicable withdrawal periods for the animal treated. In cases where this is not indicated, there is a requirement that the following minimum periods be observed:

- eggs from treated animals – 7 days;
- milk from treated animals – 7 days;
- meat from treated animals (including fat and offal) – 28 days;
- meat from fish – 500 degree days (the number of days treated at a particular temperature, e.g. 3 days at 4°C = 12 degree days);
- meat from an equid treated with a substance listed in the Annex to Commission Regulation (EC) No. 1950/2006 in accordance with the Conditions outlined there, at least six months.

These are the minimum periods and a longer period may be specified.

The veterinary practitioner must complete, at the time of prescribing or administering, a record which must be retained for five years at his or her premises detailing the following information:

a   date of examination of the animal;
b   identity of the animal;
c   number of animals treated;
d   name and address of owner (or person in charge of the animal);
e   diagnosis;
f   details of the substance, and the reason for its use;
g   dosage of substance;
h   duration of treatment;
i   specified withdrawal period.

The requirements for a withdrawal period and record-keeping set out above do not apply in the case of a homeopathic animal remedy which contains an active substance listed in Annex II to Regulation (EEC) No. 2377/90.[23]

The use of this system is to provide for the treatment of a specific animal(s) at a particular premises and does not provide for the general manufacture, possession, sale, supply or administration of a substance. The provisions of

---

23. Now replaced by Regulation EC (No.) 470/2009.

this system also provide that companion animals may also be treated via this mechanism, if necessary, provided the qualifying criteria are met as indicated.

Manufacture, import and export of animal remedies and starting materials

A person shall not manufacture an animal remedy or import an animal remedy from a third country unless he or she has been granted a licence ('manufacturer's licence') by the IMB.[24]

There are a number of exemptions to this, including:

a   dividing up, packaging or presenting an animal remedy, not carried out in advance, by:

   i   a pharmacist in respect of an animal remedy to be sold from a pharmacy,

   ii   a veterinary practitioner in respect of an animal remedy supplied by him or her for the treatment of an animal under his or her care,

   iii   a responsible person selling or supplying it from a premises to which an animal remedies merchant's licence relates, but only insofar as an intramammary animal remedy is concerned;

b   extemporaneous preparation in accordance with the cascade system of an animal remedy or magistral formula (provided it is not prepared in advance), by a veterinary practitioner for the treatment of an animal under his or her care or by a pharmacist in accordance with a veterinary prescription;

c   importation of an animal remedy from a third country for trans-shipment to another member state, where the animal remedy is not for sale or supply in Ireland;

d   manufacture of an animal remedy in a laboratory engaged in veterinary or pharmaceutical education, research or analysis and used in the laboratory;

e   manufacture of a medicated feedingstuff or an intermediate product under and in accordance with a licence authorising such manufacture granted by the Minister in accordance with Regulation 4 of the European Communities (Animal Remedies and Medicated Feedingstuffs) Regulations 1994.[25]

When an applicant applies for a manufacturer's licence from the IMB, he or she must provide evidence to demonstrate that:

a   they have available suitable and sufficient premises, technical equipment and trained staff as regards both manufacture and control and the storage of animal remedies or substances thereof;

---

24. Regulation 20, S.I. No. 786 of 2007 as amended.
25. S.I. No. 176 of 1994.

b   all manufacturing will be carried out in accordance with the relevant principles and guidelines;

c   the services of at least one qualified person who fulfils the requirements applicable to a qualified person are available to carry out the functions of a qualified person.

The IMB must, within 90 days of the receipt of a valid application, notify an applicant of a decision to grant a licence, or of a proposal to refuse an application.

There are a number of obligations on the holder of a manufacturer's licence.[26] He or she must keep at their premises detailed records of incoming and outgoing transactions relating to animal remedies manufactured, sold or supplied by him or her and these records must show:

a   the date;

b   name of animal remedy;

c   batch number and expiry date;

d   quantity supplied;

e   name and address of the recipient.

These records must be maintained and be available for inspection by an authorised officer for a period of not less than five years from the date of manufacture, or for a period ending one year after the labelled expiry date of the animal remedy, whichever is the longer period.

A manufacturer's licence, unless previously revoked, remains in force for three years or a shorter period if specified in the licence. It may be renewed by the IMB on the basis of an application by the holder. The manufacturer's licence granted after the renewal is then valid for an unlimited period,[27] although the IMB has the right to revoke, suspend or vary it at any time if it is established that any animal remedy to which the licence relates is not being appropriately manufactured.[28]

Restrictions on sale of animal remedies

Specific routes of sale are indicated for authorised animal remedies in the Animal Remedies Regulations as follows:[29]

- **Veterinary Practitioner Only (VPO-1)** refers to an animal remedy which may be sold or supplied only by a registered veterinary practitioner and administered by the practitioner to an animal under his or her care.

---

26. Regulation 23.
27. Regulation 24.
28. Regulation 25.
29. Schedule 1, Part I and Schedule 2, Part IV.

- **Veterinary Practitioner Only (VPO)** refers to an animal remedy which may be sold or supplied only by a registered veterinary practitioner and administered either by the practitioner, or by a person in his or her presence and under his or her direct supervision, to an animal under his or her care.
- **Prescription-Only (POM)** refers to an animal remedy which may be sold or supplied only by:
  a   a pharmacist from a pharmacy in accordance with a veterinary prescription;
  b   a registered veterinary practitioner and the animal is under his or her care and he or she has issued a veterinary prescription in respect of the animal remedy;
  c   a responsible person from a premises to which an animal remedies merchant's licence relates in accordance with a veterinary prescription in the case of the following animal remedies (if designated POM): intramammaries, antifungals, endo or ecto parasiticides, immunologicals, injectable digestive stimulants and injectable vitamins and minerals.
- **Prescription-Only-Exempt (POM(E))** refers to an animal remedy which may be sold or supplied only by a pharmacist from a pharmacy or by a registered veterinary practitioner where the animal is under his or her care.
- **Pharmacy Only (PS)** refers to an animal remedy which may be sold or supplied only from a pharmacy under the personal supervision of a pharmacist, or by a registered veterinary practitioner where the animal is under his or her care.
- **Licensed Merchant (LM)** refers to an animal remedy which may be sold or supplied only from a pharmacy, by a registered veterinary practitioner where the animal is under his or her care, or from a premises to which an animal remedies merchant's licence relates.
- **Companion Animal Medicine (CAM)** refers to an animal remedy which may be sold or supplied only from a pharmacy, by a registered veterinary practitioner, from a premises to which an animal remedies merchant's licence relates, or from a premises to which a companion animal medicine seller's registration relates.

The route of sale is assigned by the IMB and the criteria to be taken into account in assigning the different categories are detailed in Schedule 1, Part II to the Animal Remedies Regulations.

It is illegal to sell or supply an animal remedy other than in accordance with its designated route of sale.[30]

---

30. Regulation 28(1).

A person may not sell or supply an animal remedy unless he or she holds an animal remedies wholesaler's licence, an animal remedies merchant's licence or is registered in the companion animal medicine sellers register. This provision does not apply to the sale or supply of animal remedies by or under the supervision of a pharmacist from a pharmacy, the sale or supply of animal remedies by a veterinary surgeon for use in animals under his or her care or to the sale or supply by wholesale of animal remedies by the person who has manufactured them in accordance with a manufacturer's licence.[31]

A premises cannot be used for the sale or supply of animal remedies (or for the storage of animal remedies for that purpose) unless it is:[32]

a   a pharmacy;
b   a premises in respect of which there is a manufacturer's licence, animal remedies wholesaler's licence or an animal remedies merchant's licence;
c   a premises owned or operated by a person registered in the companion animal medicines seller's register;
d   a premises used by a veterinary surgeon in connection with the practice of veterinary medicine (not being a retail outlet).

As a general rule, animal remedies may only be sold from fixed premises and not through the internet or by mail order, from travelling shops, vehicles or vending machines or at trade fairs or other places where animals are exhibited or in competition. This provision does not apply to the sale or supply of an animal remedy in the course of the provision of a veterinary service by a veterinary practitioner for the treatment of an animal under his or her care. The Minister may also grant a licence to a licensed merchant or a pharmacist to sell licensed merchant or companion animal medicines by retail through the internet or by mail order.[33]

Wholesale supply of animal remedies

An animal remedies wholesaler's licence, granted by the Minister for Agriculture, Fisheries and Food, is required to lawfully sell or supply an animal remedy by wholesale.[34] This requirement does not apply to the sale or supply of an animal remedy by a pharmacist to a veterinary practitioner for use under the provisions of the cascade system or the sale or supply of animal remedies by the person who has manufactured them in accordance with a manufacturer's licence. The wholesaler's licence may apply to animal remedies in general, to animal remedies of a particular class or to one or more specific animal remedies.

31. Regulation 28(3), S.I. No. 786 of 2007 as amended.
32. Regulation 29, S.I. No. 786 of 2007 as amended.
33. Regulation 36, S.I. No. 786 of 2007 as amended.
34. Regulation 30, S.I. No. 786 of 2007 as amended.

The licence is generally valid for a period of three years, unless a shorter period is indicated, or it is suspended, varied or revoked at an earlier date.

The premises used for wholesale may not be used as a licensed merchant's premises or as a companion animal medicines retail outlet.

An animal remedies wholesaler must ensure that animal remedies are only sold to a person who is lawfully entitled to sell or supply the particular remedy. Suitable premises, equipment and staff with arrangements to avoid deterioration of an animal remedy must be available and maintained and any material change in these must be notified to the Minister within seven days. Suitable procedures must be in place in respect of storage, stock rotation and maintenance of records and these must be specified in the application for the licence. Suitable withdrawal and recall procedures must be in place.

Record-keeping must be such that incoming and outgoing transactions are recorded, detailing at least:

a   transaction date,
b   precise identity of the animal remedy inclusive of form and pack size,
c   manufacturer's batch number,
d   name and address of supplier or consignee, and
e   quantity (including any remedies received back for disposal).

Records must be retained for five years by the wholesaler and be available for inspection by authorised officers. The wholesaler must furnish a purchaser with details of the date of supply, identity of the animal remedy, quantity supplied and manufacturer's batch number.

The wholesaler must provide systems to receive back from purchasers (i.e. veterinary practitioners, pharmacists, licensed merchants or companion animal medicines sellers) any unused or expired product (i.e. gone beyond its expiry date) for subsequent return to the marketing authorisation holder or his or her agent.

At least once a year, the wholesale licence holder must carry out a detailed audit to reconcile incoming and outgoing supplies with those held in stock. Any discrepancies must be specifically recorded. These records must also be held for a period of five years and made available for inspection by authorised officers.

Licensed merchants

An animal remedies merchant's licence is an authority granted by the Minister for Agriculture, Fisheries and Food to a person to sell or supply by retail, certain animal remedies generally, animal remedies of a particular class specified in the licence or one or more specific animal remedies, in accordance with the designated route of sale or supply.[35] The licence is valid for three years or

---

35. Regulation 31, S.I. No. 786 of 2007 as amended.

for a shorter period specified in the licence, unless it is suspended, varied or revoked at an earlier date.

The holder of an animal remedies merchant's licence ('licensed merchant') must meet specific conditions associated with that licence. These are similar in nature to those required of the holder of an animal remedies wholesaler's licence.

Premises, equipment, staff and appropriate arrangements necessary to avoid deterioration of an animal remedy must be provided and maintained, with any material change being notified to the Minister within seven days. Suitable storage, stock rotation, withdrawal and recall procedures must be in place. The premises referred to in the animal remedies merchant's licence may not be also used as a wholesaler's premises.

Records must be maintained of incoming and outgoing transactions detailing certain minimum information including transaction date, precise identity of the animal remedy inclusive of form and pack size, manufacturer's batch number, name and address of supplier or consignee, quantity (including any received back for disposal), and for prescription-only products, the serial number of the veterinary prescription. The records must be retained for five years from the date of transaction at the premises of the licensed merchant and be available for inspection by authorised officers. Annual reconciliations of stocks held must be completed and documented.

The holder of the licence must provide systems to receive back from purchasers any unused or expired product for return to his or her supplier. Steps must be taken to ensure that customers are aware of this facility.

The holder of the licence must ensure that animal remedies are only sold or supplied from the premises by a responsible person, excepting animal remedies classified as companion animal medicines. The Minister approves appropriate training courses for the purpose of ensuring that responsible persons have adequate training in the proper and safe handling and storage of animal remedies.[36]

Companion animal medicines sellers

A person may not sell or supply by retail companion animal medicines unless he or she is registered in the companion animal medicine sellers register maintained by the Minister for Agriculture, Fisheries and Food. The requirement to register does not apply to pharmacists, veterinary practitioners, licensed merchants or holders of an animal remedies wholesaler's licence.

Sellers of companion animal medicines must comply with the storage requirements specified on the labelling of the product. They must also have in place arrangements to receive and return to the person from whom they

---

36. Regulation 32, S.I. No. 786 of 2007 as amended.

purchased them, unused or expired animal remedies and take steps to ensure that customers are aware of these arrangements.[37]

Veterinary prescribing

A person shall not prescribe an animal remedy unless he or she is a registered veterinary practitioner and the animal to which the veterinary prescription relates is under his or her care and he or she is satisfied that:[38]

a   the veterinary prescription will be used to treat the animal to which the prescription relates;
b   use of the animal remedy is justified for the animal;
c   administration of the animal remedy is, to the best of his or her knowledge and belief, not incompatible with a current or previous treatment (where appropriate, by consulting with any other veterinary practitioner who has responsibility for the care of the animals);
d   there is no contraindication and there will be no adverse reaction if other animal remedies have been, or are to be, administered or prescribed.

A veterinary practitioner may only prescribe a sufficient quantity of an animal remedy for the treatment of the condition in respect of which the animal remedy is prescribed subject, in the case of a food producing animal, to a maximum quantity of twelve months' supply from the date the prescription is issued.

When a veterinary practitioner prescribes or administers a veterinary practitioner-only (VPO-1), veterinary practitioner-only (VPO), or prescription-only animal remedy for or to an animal, he or she must, at the time, issue a veterinary prescription to the owner or person in charge of the animal. An exception to this rule occurs with prescribing to companion animals (other than equids) whereby the veterinary practitioner is not required to issue a written prescription if the owner or person in charge of the animal declines the offer of the prescription.[39]

A veterinary prescription must:[40]

a   be issued by a registered veterinary practitioner;
b   be written in ink or printed, legible and indelible and be signed in ink by, and include, in block capital letters, the name and address of the veterinary practitioner;

---

37.   Regulation 33, S.I. No. 786 of 2007 as amended.
38.   Regulation 43, S.I. No. 786 of 2007 as amended.
39.   Regulations 28(6) and 43(3), S.I. No. 786 of 2007 as amended.
40.   Regulation 43, S.I. No. 786 of 2007 as amended.

c be issued in triplicate. The original and one copy must be given to the owner or person in charge of the animal to be treated and the other copy retained by the veterinary practitioner; and

d contain the following information:[41]

   i details of the animal remedy to be administered, specifying the authorised name and the number of the veterinary product authorisation or any licence issued by the Minister in relation to the product under the cascade system;

   ii quantity of animal remedy prescribed;

   iii date of issue;

   iv manner and site of administration;

   v dose rate and withdrawal period to be observed;

   vi description of the animal or animals to which the prescription relates;

   vii name and address of the person to whom the prescription is granted;

   viii period during which the prescription is valid;

   ix special instructions, precautions or risks;

   x name, address and signature of the veterinary practitioner.

The prescription should also bear a serial number and contain a declaration that the prescription is granted in respect of an animal under the care of the prescribing veterinary practitioner.

A veterinary practitioner who issues a veterinary prescription must, if there is more than one authorised animal remedy suitable for treatment of the condition to which it applies, specify at least two animal remedies on the veterinary prescription.

The veterinary practitioner must retain, at his or her premises, a copy of a veterinary prescription for five years and make it available for inspection on request by an authorised officer.

Dispensing requirements for veterinary prescriptions

Veterinary prescriptions may be dispensed by a pharmacist from a pharmacy. Licensed merchants may dispense veterinary prescriptions for the following when designated as prescription-only medicines: intramammaries, antifungals, endo or ecto parasiticides, immunologicals, injectable digestive stimulants and injectable vitamins and minerals.[42]

A person who dispenses a veterinary prescription in part must immediately record on the prescription and on the copy, in a conspicuous, legible and

---

41. Schedule 3, S.I. No. 786 of 2007 as amended.
42. Schedule 1, Part I, S.I. No. 786 of 2007 as amended.

indelible manner, the quantity of an animal remedy sold or supplied by him or her on foot of the veterinary prescription and the date of each such sale or supply and then sign the prescription and retain a copy of it (which may be a photocopy).

A person who has completed dispensing a veterinary prescription must write 'dispensed' on the prescription and on the copy in a conspicuous, legible and indelible manner and sign and date it. A copy of the prescription must be returned to the person who presented it, and the person dispensing it must retain, at his or her premises, the original prescription for five years and shall make this available on request to an authorised officer.

A veterinary prescription must not be dispensed later than twelve months after the date on which it was issued.[43]

Emergency supply of prescription-only animal remedies

Similar to requests for emergency supplies of human medicines, pharmacists may supply a prescription-only animal remedy before receiving a veterinary prescription, so long as the request comes from the prescribing veterinary practitioner and the following conditions are met:[44]

a the veterinary practitioner is unable to furnish a prescription immediately due to an emergency and undertakes to do so within 72 hours;
b the animal remedy is sold or supplied in accordance with the directions of the veterinary practitioner requesting it;
c the animal remedy is not a controlled drug specified in Schedule 1 or 2 to the Misuse of Drugs Regulations 1988 as amended;
d the animal remedy is labelled in accordance with the requirements for prescription-only medicines (see section on Labelling);
e the sale or supply is recorded by the pharmacist in the usual manner (see section on Record-keeping and other requirements for veterinary practitioners and pharmacists).

If a veterinary practitioner fails to provide a prescription within 72 hours, the pharmacist must not make any further emergency supplies at the request of that veterinary practitioner.

Emergency supply of any animal remedy at the request of the owner or person in charge of an animal is not permitted in any circumstances. Similarly, emergency supply of prescription-only medicines by licensed merchants is not permitted.

---

43. Regulation 43(7)(c), S.I. No. 786 of 2007 as amended.
44. Regulation 44, S.I. No. 786 of 2007 as amended.

Labelling of animal remedies

General requirements

The outer packaging, immediate packaging, label or package leaflet of animal remedies must contain at least the following information as appropriate:[45]

a   name of the animal remedy, as approved by the IMB, followed by its strength and pharmaceutical form;

b   a statement of the active substances expressed qualitatively and quantitatively per unit or according to the form of administration for a particular volume or weight, using the common names of the active substances;

c   the manufacturer's batch number;

d   the authorisation number;

e   the name or corporate name and permanent address or registered place of business of the authorisation holder and, where appropriate, of his or her representative;

f   the species of animal for which the animal remedy is intended including the method and where appropriate, the route of administration (adequate space must be provided on the label for the prescribed dose to be indicated);

g   the withdrawal period, even if nil, in the case of an animal remedy to be administered to a food-producing animal (details must be given for each animal species and each foodstuff concerned);

h   expiry date;

i   special storage precautions;

j   special precautions relating to the disposal of an unused animal remedy or its waste particulars;

k   the words 'For animal treatment only' and where appropriate 'To be supplied only on veterinary prescription' or in the case of a homeopathic animal remedy, the words 'Homeopathic animal remedy for veterinary use'.

The pharmaceutical form and the contents by weight, volume or number of dose units have to be shown on the outer package only.

At least the following must appear on the immediate packaging:

a   name of the animal remedy;

b   quantity of the active substances;

c   route of administration;

d   manufacturer's batch number;

---

45.   Schedule 2, Parts I–II, S.I. No. 786 of 2007 as amended.

e   expiry date;

f   the words 'For animal treatment only'.

Package leaflets

The inclusion of a package leaflet in the packaging of an animal remedy is obligatory unless all the information required can be conveyed on the immediate and outer packaging. Information on the leaflet shall solely relate to the animal remedy with which it is included. It must be comprehensible and in the English or Irish language and shall include at least the following information in the order indicated:[46]

a   name or corporate name and permanent address or registered place of business of the authorisation holder and of the person responsible for marketing and of the manufacturer, if different;

b   name of the animal remedy as approved by the IMB followed by its strength and pharmaceutical form. (If the animal remedy has been authorised under the mutual recognition or decentralised procedure under different names in the concerned member states, a list of the names authorised in each member state);

c   the main therapeutic indications, contraindications and side-effects;

d   the species of animal for which the animal remedy is intended, the dosage for each species, the method and route of administration and advice on correct administration, if necessary;

e   the withdrawal period, even if this is nil, in the case of an animal remedy to be administered to a food-producing animal;

f   special storage precautions;

g   particulars required by Article 26(1) of Directive 2001/82/EC as amended (i.e. any additional precautions and warnings for the use of the animal remedy as required by the marketing authorisation to appear on the label);

h   special precautions for the disposal of unused product or waste materials.

A person must not remove or alter a label or package leaflet in relation to an animal remedy unless authorised to do so by the IMB.[47]

Additional labelling of prescription-only medicines

A person who supplies a prescription-only animal remedy must affix an additional label to the animal remedy at the time of sale or supply (in a manner

---

46.   Schedule 2, Part III, S.I. No. 786 of 2007 as amended.

47.   Regulation 11(11), S.I. No. 786 of 2007 as amended.

that does not obscure the other information appearing on the label) stating the following:[48]

a   his or her name and address;
b   serial number of the veterinary prescription;
c   name of the prescribing veterinary practitioner;
d   date of sale or supply;
e   dosage and duration of treatment (unless indicated on the proprietary label).

Record-keeping and other requirements for veterinary practitioners and pharmacists

Veterinary practitioners and pharmacists are required to keep at their premises, a record of purchases and sales of animal remedies (including quantities administered), detailing at least the following in respect of each incoming and outgoing transaction:[49]

a   date of the transaction, and in the case of a veterinary practitioner only (VPO-1), veterinary practitioner only (VPO) or prescription-only animal remedy, the serial number of the veterinary prescription;
b   precise identity of the animal remedy or in cases where the 'cascade' applies, the medicinal product, including name, pharmaceutical form and pack size;
c   manufacturer's batch number;
d   name and address of the supplier or consignee;
e   quantity received or supplied (including any quantity of unused or expired animal remedies returned to or by them or otherwise disposed of).

These records must be kept for five years from the date of receipt, sale or supply or administration of the animal remedy and be made available to an authorised officer on request. Records do not have to be kept in relation to companion animal medicines.

Veterinary practitioners and pharmacists are also required to have in place arrangements to receive from consignees and return to the person from whom they purchased them, unused or expired animal remedies. They must take steps to ensure that clients are aware of these arrangements.

Possession of animal remedies

It is illegal for a person to possess a prescription-only animal remedy unless he or she has a veterinary prescription for the animal remedy in question or is a

---

48. Regulation 28(5), S.I. No. 786 of 2007 as amended.
49. Regulation 34, S.I. No. 786 of 2007 as amended.

pharmacist or veterinary practitioner or holds a manufacturer's or animal remedies wholesaler's licence. Licensed merchants may possess those classes of prescription-only medicines that they are entitled to sell and supply. This prohibition does not apply to owners or persons in charge of companion animals (other than equids) who have declined the offer of a prescription from the veterinary practitioner who supplied the product.

A person, other than the holder of a manufacturer's licence or an animal remedies wholesaler's licence or a registered veterinary practitioner, is not permitted to have an animal remedy designated veterinary practitioner only (VPO-1) or veterinary practitioner only (VPO) in his or her possession or under his or her control unless he or she has a veterinary prescription relating to the animal remedy in question. In the case of a premises where an animal is kept, sold, supplied or slaughtered, the only person who is permitted to have these categories of animal remedies in their possession is a veterinary practitioner.[50]

Administration of animal remedies

A person must not administer:

a   cause or permit administration of an animal remedy to an animal unless there is an animal remedies authorisation in force in respect of the animal remedy;

b   the administration is carried out in accordance with that authorisation;

c   the authorisation allows the administration of the animal remedy to the animal, class of animal or species in question by the person concerned; and

d   all legal requirements are complied with.[51]

Veterinary practitioner only (VPO-1) animal remedies may only be administered to an animal by a veterinary practitioner and the animal in question must be under his or her care. Animal remedies designated 'veterinary practitioner only (VPO)' may be administered by a veterinary practitioner or by another person, provided they do so in the presence and under the direct supervision of the prescribing veterinary practitioner.

A prescription-only animal remedy may only be administered to an animal if it has been prescribed by a veterinary practitioner and the person administering the animal remedy has the relevant veterinary prescription in his or her possession.

It is illegal to import, export, sell, supply or slaughter for human consumption, a food-producing animal to which an animal remedy has been

---

50. Regulation 38, S.I. No. 786 of 2007 as amended.
51. Regulation 39, S.I. No. 786 of 2007 as amended.

administered illegally or to import, export, sell, supply or process meat, milk, eggs etc., derived from such an animal. The owner or person in charge of a food-producing animal to whom an animal remedy has been administered must ensure that the animal is not offered for slaughter and that no produce derived from the animal is disposed of with a view to being offered for human consumption before the end of the designated withdrawal period for the animal remedy in question.[52]

Animal Remedies Record

The owner or person in charge of a food-producing animal must keep at his or her premises an 'Animal Remedies Record' where details of all animal remedies purchased and administered are recorded. The Animal Remedies Record must be retained at the premises for five years after administration of the animal remedy and be made available on request to an authorised officer.[53]

The owner or person in charge of a food-producing animal is also required to keep for five years at his or her premises and produce on request to an authorised officer, a copy of each veterinary prescription issued by a veterinary practitioner in respect of VPO-1, VPO and POM animal remedies administered to an animal under his or her control.

Any unused or expired animal remedy must be returned to the person from whom he or she purchased it and a record of this must be made in the Animal Remedies Record.

Advertising of animal remedies

The advertising or other promotion of an animal remedy is only permitted if it is an authorised animal remedy.[54]

An animal remedy cannot be advertised if it contains a substance subject to restrictions resulting from the implementation of United Nations Conventions on narcotic and psychotropic substances, is designated veterinary practitioner only (VPO-1) or veterinary practitioner only (VPO) or prescription-only, or in contravention of an animal remedies authorisation. These restrictions do not apply in the case of advertisements solely directed at veterinary practitioners, pharmacists, wholesalers or licensed merchants.

Veterinary practitioners, pharmacists, licensed merchants and sellers of companion animal medicines must display a list of prices of animal remedies held in stock.

---

52. Regulation 40, S.I. No. 786 of 2007 as amended.
53. Regulation 42, S.I. No. 786 of 2007 as amended.
54. Regulation 37, S.I. No. 786 of 2007 as amended.

Control of animal remedies and their residues

The European Communities (Control of Animal Remedies and their Residues) Regulations 2009[55] implement the provisions of Council Directive 96/22/EC concerning the prohibition in stock farming of certain substances having hormonal or thyrostatic action and of beta agonists. They also implement the provisions of Council Directive 96/23/EC on measures to monitor certain substances and their residues in live animals and animal products. The regulations put in place restrictions on the import, manufacture, sale or supply of certain animal remedies. They prohibit the sale or slaughter of a farm or aquaculture animal or their meat or other food of animal origin to which a prohibited animal remedy has been administered or where an authorised animal remedy is present in the animal or product at concentrations in excess of the maximum residue limit.

Each year the Department of Agriculture, Fisheries and Food implements a residue control plan, which is one of a range of measures designed to safeguard consumers from exposure to illegal residues and to meet requirements laid down by the European Commission. The national legal basis for the residue plan is provided for in the European Communities (Control of Animal Remedies and their Residues) Regulations 2009. Under Directive 96/23/EC, each member state is required to implement residue surveillance plans and to submit their programmes annually to the European Commission for approval. Implementation of the plan involves taking samples from food-producing species at both farm and primary processing plant levels.[56]

---

55. S.I. No. 183 of 2009. Copyright Houses of the Oireachtas 2009.
56. See website of Department of Agriculture, Fisheries and Food, www.agriculture.ie (accessed 1 March 2011).

11

Methylated spirits legislation

S Byrne and P Weedle

The sale of methylated spirits is controlled under the Intoxicating Liquor (General) Act 1924.[1]

Definitions

'Spirits' means spirits of any description, and includes all liquors mixed with spirits, and all mixtures, compounds or preparations, made with spirits. 'Methylate' means to mix spirits with some substance in such a manner as to render the mixture unfit for use as a beverage, and 'methylated spirits' means spirits so mixed to the satisfaction of the Revenue Commissioners.

Mineralised methylated spirit consists of alcohol mixed with wood naphtha (9.5%) and crude pyridine (0.5%). To every 450 bulk litres of the mixture is added 1.7 L of mineral naphtha (petroleum oil) and not less than 0.7 g of methyl violet. This gives the methylated spirits its characteristic violet colour to identify that it should not be consumed.

Spiritus Methylatus Industralis BP is alcohol (95%) 19 volumes and approved wood naphtha, 1 volume. It is more commonly known as 94% volume 'industrial methylated spirits' (99% volume and 93% volume industrial methylated spirits are also available). The use of industrial methylated spirits is permitted in a number of preparations made in accordance with the British Pharmacopoeia and British Pharmaceutical Codex formulae.

Spiritus Methylatus Industralis sine Acetono BPC is of the same strength as industrial methylated spirits BP, but the denaturant used is practically free from acetone. It is compatible with iodine, with which industrial methylated spirits containing acetone yields irritating vapours. (Note that there are other industrial methylated spirits, e.g. 'power methylated spirits'.)

---

1. No. 62 of 1924, see Sections 28 and 29.

The following persons, and no others, are authorised to supply methylated spirits:

a   authorised methylators;
b   persons licensed to retail methylated spirits and referred to hereafter as 'retailers of methylated spirits'.

Conditions governing the manner of supply, the amounts supplied, the labelling requirements, etc., are imposed on authorised methylators. A retailer of methylated spirits is restricted as to the quantity he or she receives or has in his or her possession at any one time. He or she must not receive methylated spirits from a retailer of methylated spirits in a quantity exceeding 18.5 L at a time, and must not sell to or for the use of any one person more than 18.5 L at a time. On request, he or she must at all reasonable times produce his or her stock of methylated spirits for examination by an officer of the Customs and Excise and must keep an account, in the prescribed form, of his or her stock of methylated spirits and of the sale thereof.

Manufacture

If the retailer is also authorised to use methylated spirits in any sort or manufacture, he or she must obtain all his or her methylated spirits from an authorised methylator. Where it is required to receive mineralised methylated spirits in larger quantities than 18.5 L, the prior authority of the Revenue Commissioners must be obtained. Industrial methylated spirits may be received only by persons authorised by the Revenue Commissioners.

A pharmacist who wishes to use methylated spirits in any process necessary for the production of medicinal and other extracts in which no such spirits nor any derivatives thereof remain, must make special application to the Revenue Commissioners for permission to use methylated spirits for the purpose.

Essential oil or other flavouring must not, without the express sanction of the Revenue Commissioners, be added to or mixed with methylated spirits; and very severe penalties are incurred by any person who prepares, sells, uses or has in his or her possession any mixture, preparation or combination of methylated spirits for use as a beverage, or internally as a medicine. (This section does not apply to the manufacturer of sulphuric ether or chloroform, etc.)

Retail sales

The sale of methylated spirits by retail is prohibited to any person:

a   whose name and address are not either previously known to the seller or vouched for by some person previously known to him or her;
b   who does not state the purpose for which he or she requires such spirits.

Date	Name	Address	Purpose for which stated to be required	Quantity	Introduced by

Figure 11.1 Example of a methylated spirits register.

Every retailer of methylated spirits must at the time of that sale by him or her of any quantity of such spirits by retail, record in a book to be kept by him or her for the purpose (see Figure 11.1):

a   the name and address of the purchaser;
b   the purpose for which the purchaser stated he or she required the spirits;
c   the quantity of spirits so sold;
d   the date of the sale.

Good practice would also require the supplier to initial the sale and where relevant to record the name and address of the person vouching for a person not previously known to the seller.

Any officer of the Customs and Excise or any member of the Garda Síochána may at any time inspect and take extracts from the book kept by a retailer of methylated spirits as outlined in the foregoing section, and may for that purpose enter the premises of any such retailer.

Any sale of methylated spirits between the hours of nine o'clock on Saturday evening and nine o'clock on the following Monday morning is prohibited.

Every person who sells any methylated spirits:

a   at any time during which its sale is prohibited;
b   to any person to whom the sale of methylated spirits is prohibited;
c   without recording in such book as aforesaid the particulars prescribed;

and every person who obstructs any officer of Customs and Excise or any member of the Garda Síochána in the exercise of his or her rights of inspection and taking extracts, shall be guilty of an offence and shall be liable on summary conviction to a fine.

Every person who drinks methylated spirits shall be guilty of an offence and shall be liable on summary conviction to imprisonment for a term not exceeding six months.

12

The Pharmacy Act

D Dowling

Any good doctor or pharmacist diagnosing or treating a patient will not just examine the site of the sickness or injury, but will do it in the context of the overall person. In the same way, if one were simply to view the Pharmacy Act 2007[1] (the 'Act') in isolation and outside its context, then any understanding gained would only be a shallow one. Contextualising the Act in terms of its origin and its place in the canon of laws which deal with medicines and human health is informative and worthwhile.

As with a great deal of legislation, the passing of a law by a government is often done in response to a demand from society, and so it is with health law. Experience has shown that sick people or people desiring health gain can very easily become the prey of charlatans and quacks who seek to profit out of another's misery. This is as true today as it was some 700 years ago when attempts were made on a commercial basis via the old Guilds to control the purity of drugs. Some 200 years later, in the mid-sixteenth century, the first English law was enacted by a sovereign parliament to permit the protection of the public and the destruction of corrupted medicines (see Chapter 2, Historical development of pharmacy and medicines law).

As the understanding and knowledge of medicines and healthcare progressed, so too did the development and emergence of the various branches of the healthcare professions; physicians, barber surgeons and apothecaries. The practice of medicine, in the sense of the direct treatment of patients, developed in Ireland under the aegis of the College of Physicians. The emerging class of healthcare professionals engaged in the compounding and sale of drugs and medicines was first statutorily regulated under the Apothecaries' Hall Act 1791.[2] This Act served to crystallise in legislative form the distinction between the one profession which prescribed medicines for patients and the other

---

1. No. 20 of 2007. Copyright Houses of the Oireachtas 2007.
2. 31 Geo. 3, c. 34.

which compounded and dispensed those prescriptions. About this time a further class of persons existed who were referred to as druggists. Druggists were entitled to sell poisons and miscellaneous medicines but could not dispense prescriptions. Their conduct was not regulated in any way by statute. This was a time of unhappy relationships between physicians, surgeons, apothecaries and druggists. The public were confused and vulnerable.

In response to these health needs and to complete the separation of prescribing and dispensing, Parliament passed an act entitled the Pharmacy Act in 1875.[3] In the preamble to the Act, it was stated that the purpose of the Act was:

> to enable persons who, although they do not desire to practise the art and mystery of an apothecary, desire and are qualified to open shop for the retailing, dispensing and compounding of poisons and medical prescriptions, to keep open shop for the purposes aforesaid.

Section 4 of this Act established a society of members called the Pharmaceutical Society of Ireland. The purpose of the Pharmaceutical Society of Ireland, as expressed in the preamble of the Act, was *inter alia*:

> for the examination of persons desiring to keep open shop for the purposes aforesaid, and for the registration of such of the said persons as may be found, on examination, to possess a competent practical knowledge of pharmaceutical and general chemistry and other branches of useful knowledge, as fit persons to keep open shop for the dispensing and compounding of prescriptions of duly qualified medical practitioners.

The Pharmaceutical Society of Ireland was created by Parliament as a body corporate, in other words, it had a legal identity and *persona* separate and distinct from the various legal identities and personae of its individual human members. It was prescribed in the 1875 Act that the Pharmaceutical Society would be run by a Council. The members of the first Council of the newly formed Society were individually named in the Act. They included medical doctors, surgeons and licentiates of Apothecaries' Hall. The first person to be appointed President of the newly constituted Council was Sir Dominic Corrigan, Baronet, 'Physician in Ordinary to the Queen in Ireland'.

In addition to a Council, the 1875 Act also provided for the appointment of 'a fit and proper person as a Registrar'.

It was the job of the Council to conduct examinations of all persons who wished to be registered as pharmaceutical chemists. The Act mandated that they would be examined:

> with respect to their knowledge of the Latin and English languages, of arithmetic, of botany, of materia medica, of pharmaceutical and

---

3. Pharmacy Act (Ireland) Act 1875. 38 & 39 Vict., c. 57.

general chemistry, of practical pharmacy, of the British pharmacopoeia, and of such other subjects as may from time to time be prescribed by any regulations made in pursuance of this Act.

By way of illustration of the clearly defined distinctions between the healthcare professions, the Act also provided that no examination could include the theory and practice of medicine, surgery or midwifery. A person passing an examination was entitled to a certificate from the examiners, testifying to their qualification and skill to be registered as pharmaceutical chemists. Every person who was so certified by the examiners was then entitled to apply to the Registrar to have their name registered under the Act as a pharmaceutical chemist. The Act then went on in Section 30 to make it unlawful for any person:

> to sell or keep open shop for retailing, dispensing or compounding of poisons . . . or medical prescriptions, unless such person be registered as a pharmaceutical chemist . . . under this Act, or to assume or use the title of pharmaceutical chemist . . . .

The above remained the position for some 132 years until the passing of the 2007 Act. There were in the intervening years some modifications of the 1875 Act. These modifications and reforms were accomplished by the Pharmacy Act (Ireland) 1875 Amendment Act 1890 (the '1890 Act'),[4] the Pharmacy Act 1951 (the '1951 Act')[5] and the Pharmacy Act 1962 (the '1962 Act').[6]

The 1890 Act repealed certain sections of the 1875 Act. It established a register of druggists entitled to keep open shop for the sale of poisons but did not confer on such persons any right to compound medical prescriptions. The 1890 Act also empowered the Council to hold examinations for the purpose of examining assistants to pharmaceutical chemists. The 1890 Act protected the titles of registered druggist or chemist, making it a criminal offence to use these titles unless so registered. It imposed a requirement that shops for the sale of poisons or compounding of medical prescriptions had to be personally managed by the owner who in turn had to be qualified and registered as such with the Society. The 1890 Act also gave power to the Registrar of the Society to require the proprietor of a pharmacy to provide him with certain information concerning the pharmacy under pain of prosecution.

The 1951 Act established a register of dispensing chemists and druggists and specified that registered druggists were entitled to seek registration in that register upon passing an examination set by the Council for that purpose. Registered dispensing chemists and druggists were granted the same rights as

---

4. 53 & 54 Vict., c. 48.
5. No. 30 of 1951.
6. No. 14 of 1962.

pharmaceutical chemists to compound medical prescriptions and sell poisons and to keep open shop.

The 1962 Act provided a mechanism and legitimacy for pharmacies to be run by limited companies, by the legal personal representatives of a proprietor pharmacist who had died and by trustees in bankruptcy or the committees of persons of unsound mind. It gave power to the Council to make regulations concerning record-keeping in pharmacies and the filing with the Society of annual returns. It also permitted the making of regulations concerning the training and examinations of intending pharmacists and the recognition of foreign qualifications.

Although the 2007 Act enjoys the rather all-embracing title of the Pharmacy Act 2007, it would be a great mistake to think it sets out all the laws that relate to pharmacy. The Act is only one part of a much larger legislative picture. It is very important to appreciate the Act in this context. The practice of pharmacy and the development and provision of medicinal products to and for the general public constitutes an enormous global endeavour. It forms part of the global economy. For economic reasons and, as stated earlier, in order to protect people who are vulnerable as a consequence of being sick, national governments and international law-making bodies such as the European Union (EU) have promulgated and enforced an enormous body of interrelated 'medicine-related' laws and regulations. Consider, for example, the legal requirements of patient protection which exist in the areas of:

a   research and development;
b   product safety and the licensing of 'medicinal products'. (In this regard it is significant to decide what is or is not a 'medicinal product' as opposed to, for example, a medical device, a cosmetic or a foodstuff. If something is not a medicinal product, then a different and, in some cases, less onerous set of protections apply);
c   manufacturing processes and authorisations;
d   distribution/wholesaling processes and authorisations;
e   advertising;
f   packaging and labelling;
g   end-user provision or sale.

These topics are covered elsewhere in this book in the chapters dealing with medicines legislation.

There is also a whole body of 'medicine' laws that are more commercially orientated. These include:

a   the intellectual property rights in medicinal products or the component parts thereof;
b   patent law and proprietary medicines;

c   competition law and proprietary medicines;
d   competition law and monopolies;
e   government purchasers or subventors of medicinal products;
f   global trade issues including conflict of laws;
g   taxation and tariffs.

The Act aims only to legislate directly in a very small subset of the areas described above. It may 'on the ground' have a more profound and pervasive indirect effect, in that every person who wishes to be or remain registered as a pharmacist must conduct themselves in accordance with the Code of Conduct for Pharmacists (see Appendix 12.1) which has been drawn up under Section 7(2)(a)(iii) of the Act.

If a person is registered as a pharmacist in Ireland, then regardless of where in the world they work or in what branch or area of pharmacy, they are obliged to practise their profession in a manner which respects the principles of the Code of Conduct. In the event that they fail to do so, they can be made accountable under the provisions of Part 6 of the Act, Complaints, Inquiries and Discipline (see Chapter 14, The pharmacy disciplinary system).

As with so much domestic legislation, the law relating to medicines and the practice of pharmacy has significant EU antecedents and drivers. The Act is in part a product of those antecedents.

The opening recitals of Directive 2001/83/EC, which codifies a number of prior EU pharmaceutical directives dating from January 1965 to September 1992 (Directive 2001/83/EC has itself been amended several times since 2001[7]) states at recital number 2: 'The essential aim of any rules governing the production, distribution and use of medicinal products must be to safeguard public health.' It would be hard to find any individual or organisation disagreeing with this proposition. Recital number 3, however, modifies the proposition somewhat by stating: 'However this objective [the objective recited in recital number 2 above] must be attained by means which will not hinder the development of the pharmaceutical industry or trade in medicinal products within the community.' It is interesting to note that even at the highest level, the therapeutic/commercial tensions which existed in the supply of medicines over 700 years ago still remain (see Chapter 3, Historical development of medicines and pharmacy law).

It is also important to make reference to Directive 2005/36/EC as amended, sometimes referred to as the Recognition of Professional Qualifications Directive. This Directive concerns the recognition by member

---

7. Amended by Directive 2002/98/EC, Directive 2003/63/EC, Directive 2004/24/EC, Directive 2004/27/EC, Directive 2008/29/EC, Directive 2009/53/EC, Directive 2009/120/EC, Regulation (EC) No. 1901/2006 and Regulation (EC) No. 1394/2007.

states of professional qualifications acquired in other member states. It recognises that the facilitation of such a process has to be ensured in a context of strict respect for public health and safety and consumer protection. Recital 19 of the preamble to this Directive states:

> Freedom of movement and the mutual recognition of the evidence of formal qualifications of doctors, nurses responsible for general care, dental practitioners, veterinary surgeons, midwives, pharmacists and architects should be based on the fundamental principle of automatic recognition of the evidence of formal qualifications on the basis of coordinated minimum conditions for training. In addition access in the Member States to the professions of doctor . . . pharmacist should be made conditional upon the possession of a given qualification ensuring that the person concerned has undergone training which meets the minimum conditions laid down. This system should be supplemented by a number of acquired rights from which qualified professionals benefit under certain conditions.

Recital 25 states:

> Holders of qualifications as a pharmacist are specialists in the field of medicines and should, in principle, have access in all Member States to a minimum range of activities in this field. In defining this minimum range, this Directive should neither have the effect of limiting the activities accessible to pharmacists in the Member States, in particular as regards medical biology analyses, nor create a monopoly for those professionals, as this remains a matter solely for the Member States.

In accordance with public health and safety requirements, Article 44 of the Professional Qualifications Directive provides that, for the purposes of recognition, evidence of formal qualification of a pharmacist should attest to training of at least five years' duration, including at least four years' full-time theoretical studies and practical training at a university or equivalent higher institute and a six-month traineeship in a pharmacy which is open to the public (or in a hospital). The training cycle must include at least a programme described in the Directive.[8] This article has significant implications throughout the EU in the area of the harmonisation of pharmacy qualifications and the facilitation of the free movement of the holders of those qualifications.

The Recognition of Professional Qualifications Directive is relevant to the Act in that the 2007 Act seeks to give it effect in national law. The relevant provisions in the Act were further updated in 2008 by the European Communities (Recognition of Professional Qualifications Relating to the

---

8. Annex V, Point 5.6.1.

Profession of Pharmacy) (No. 2) Regulations 2008.[9] The way in which this is accomplished in the Act in its current form and its manner of expression is complicated and sometimes difficult to understand. It is helpful when applying the Act and the 2008 Regulations to have regard to the policies and principles as set out in the Directive.

Turning specifically to the Act it is useful to have an understanding of some of the principal reasons for its introduction. These serve to give a better perspective on the content of the Act. In the first place, governmental and public thought on how professions generally should be regulated has developed considerably in the 130 or so years since the first Pharmacy Act was passed. The old concept of a society of members who regulated themselves and who were not accountable to the people whom they served and from whom they earned their livelihoods (the general public) had become unacceptable. This was particularly so since the original Act effectively created a trading monopoly. The operation of the old style regulatory processes by the various professions has been criticised. In truth it left the professions open to the accusation that even if the system of regulation itself was sound (which was doubted), then the people who were operating it did not do so in a fair, open and unbiased manner.

The second reason (at least in the area of pharmacy practice) was that there was no legislative authority under which the Pharmaceutical Society of Ireland could discipline registrants. The 1875 Act and succeeding (and analogous) legislation provided simply for control of the profession by the creation of criminal offences. The Pharmaceutical Society of Ireland was authorised to prosecute these offences in a court of law where penalties would be imposed by a judge as in any other criminal or quasi-criminal matter. This was a very blunt and often ineffective instrument of control. With the growth of community pharmacy businesses and the concomitant growth in the number of transactions and relationships with patients, the Society's records began to show a growth in the level of complaints against pharmacists. Both the profession and the government appreciated the need to put in place a proper system which would enable objective practice standards to be promulgated and to have complaints dealt with impartially, fairly, proportionately and speedily.

The third principal reason for the passing of the Act was that the government was anxious to fulfil its EU obligations in the matter of the free movement of pharmacists to and from this State. The old legislation did not permit this to happen in a coherent and properly regulated manner. Finally, the profession itself had been seeking a new Pharmacy Act since the early 1970s. After almost 40 years of engagement with government on the issue, the profession had increased pressure and was taking the issue into the public forum.

---

9. S.I. No. 489 of 2008. Copyright Houses of the Oireachtas 2008.

The passing of the 2007 Act

From the date when the first draft of the Bill was published in early 2007, it proceeded with considerable pace through the legislative process and was signed into law by the President on 21 April 2007. The entire Act did not become fully operational on that date, rather the Act envisaged as per Section 1 that it would be implemented on a phased basis and would:

> come into operation on such day or days as the Minister may appoint by order or orders either generally or with reference to any particular purpose or provision and different days may be so appointed for different purposes or provisions.

The entire Act has now been commenced.

The Act is comprehensive and relatively complex. In order to avoid getting caught up in the minutiae and not seeing the Act as a whole it is worth reciting the preamble thereto which states:

> An Act to make new provision for the regulation of pharmacy, including provision for the dissolution of the Pharmaceutical Society of Ireland and the setting up of a new Pharmaceutical Society of Ireland, for the establishment, constitution and functions of the new Society's Council, for a new system of registration of qualified pharmacists, druggists and pharmaceutical assistants and of pharmacies, for the creation of certain offences relating to pharmacy and for the setting up of new procedures to ensure that pharmacists are and continue to be fit to practise and to prevent pharmacists, pharmacy owners and medical practitioners from entering into certain inappropriate relationships; and to provide for related matters.

Overview of how the 2007 Act works

The Act accomplishes its mandate to protect public health by continuing to employ the concept of registration, as created by the 1875 Act. The Act has made the registration system more robust and up-to-date but the principles remain the same. In very simple terms, a person cannot act as a pharmacist unless they are registered and a person cannot be registered unless and until they satisfy certain criteria. These criteria are set out in Section 14 of the Act. The system of registration is supplemented by a complaints system. If a registered pharmacist is 'accused' of poor professional performance or professional misconduct, they will be subjected to the complaints, inquiries and disciplinary process (see Chapter 14). This is a process administered by the Society through a series of independent committees established under Part 6 of the Act.

The business of the Society is carried on by a Council of 21 persons. There must be a majority of non-pharmacists on the Council. The Council in turn employs people who comprise the permanent administration of the Society. The affairs of the Society and the work of the permanent administration are placed under the charge of a chief executive officer, known as the Registrar. In order to better assist it in the discharge of its functions, the Act confers on the Society substantial investigative powers. The Act also places in the responsibility of the Society the function of specifying the standard of education and training required for persons who seek to become and remain registered as pharmacists. The Society is also charged under the Act to provide information and advice (about pharmacy) to the Minister for Health and Children. It is constituted as a competent authority for the purposes of the mutual recognition of pharmacy qualifications obtained in EU member states and also obtained in third countries (i.e. all other countries).

The Act confers on the Society and its constituent parts (including the Council, the Registrar and its employees) all the powers necessary to accomplish the foregoing. These functions and powers have been conferred on the Society, not to perpetuate or serve or preserve a commercial monopoly for the members of a healthcare profession, but rather for the purpose stated in Section 7(1)(a) of the Act: 'to regulate the profession of pharmacy in the State having regard to the need to protect, maintain and promote the health and safety of the public'.

Insofar as the Society (or any of its constituent parts) ignores Section 7(1)(a) of the Act and purports to act in a manner which is not in the interests of the health and safety of the public, then it may find that it has acted *ultra vires*[10] with all the legal and practical negative consequences which that entails.

The various functions, powers and constituent parts of the Society are all interdependent and interrelated, and in one sense there is in operation within the Society what might be termed a mini-version of the doctrine of separation of powers. In other words no one constituent part of the Society (be it the Council, the Registrar, the registrants, the authorised officers or the employees) is capable of acting in an unchecked and unilateral way to the detriment of the others, or the members of the public, whom they are in office to serve.

For a better understanding of the Act, it makes sense to set out the following commentary according to the parts into which the Act has been divided and in (more or less) the same order. This will give a more coherent overview of the Act and its operation. It is not appropriate in this treatment of the subject to provide a detailed analysis of each individual section of the Act. This treatment is designed to inform in a general way how each part of the Act operates, what the most important aspects of each part of the Act are and how they relate and interact with the other parts. Some of the matters governed by

---

10. Means outside its powers.

the Act are dealt with outside the Act by way of statutory rules or regulations. These rules and regulations are dealt with in more detail in Chapter 13.

Preliminary and general (Part 1)

The 'long title' to the Act sets out what the Act intends to accomplish, and was outlined earlier in this chapter. This should not be lost sight of, particularly when dealing with some of the more complex and convoluted provisions of the Act. It often helps to recall what the purpose of any act is when teasing out any particular 'local' problems in individual sections of the act.

As mentioned previously, the Act has already been amended. The amendment was effected under and by virtue of the European Communities (Recognition of Professional Qualifications Relating to the Profession of Pharmacist) (No. 2) Regulations 2008.[11] These regulations also revoked the earlier European Communities (Recognition of Professional Qualifications Relating to the Profession of Pharmacist) Regulations 2008[12] and limited the application to the profession of pharmacist of the Recognition of Professional Qualifications (Directive 2005/36/EC) Regulations 2008.[13] Rather than deal with the European Communities (Recognition of Qualifications Relating to the Profession of Pharmacist) (No. 2) Regulations 2008 at this point, they will be dealt with in terms of the amendments which they make to the Act as and where those amendments appear in the amended Act itself.

Some definitions used within the Act

Section 2 of the Act sets out the various definitions which are used during the course of the Act. Some of these definitions are more important than others. A 'medicinal product' is defined as having the same meaning as in Directive 2001/83/EC as amended[14] (except that until 30 April 2011, it does not include herbal or homeopathic medicinal products)

---

11. These regulations replaced Sections 16(4), 16(5) and amended 16(8) of the 2007 Act. They also inserted a new subsection Section 16(10) and new Sections 21A, 24A and 24B. They substituted several paragraphs in Schedule 2 to the Act.
12. S.I. No. 167 of 2008.
13. S.I. No. 139 of 2008.
14. Article 1.2 of Directive 2001/83/EC defines a medicinal product as '(a) any substance or combination of substances presented as having properties for treating or preventing disease in human beings; or (b) any substance or combination of substances which may be used in or administered to human beings, either with a view to restoring correcting or modifying physiological functions by exerting a pharmacological, immunological or metabolic action or to making a medical diagnosis.' The Directive also contains definitions of the words 'substance', 'immunological medicinal products', 'homeopathic medicinal products' and 'herbal medicinal product'.

A 'pharmaceutical assistant' is also defined. A pharmaceutical assistant is a member of a class of people who work within the profession of pharmacy. Pharmaceutical assistants were first 'recognised' in Section 19 of the 1890 Act which permitted the Council of the Society to hold examinations for the purposes of examining assistants to pharmaceutical chemists. Such assistants having passed such examinations were then deemed to be competent 'to transact the business of a licentiate of the Pharmaceutical Society in his temporary absence but shall not be entitled to conduct or manage a business or to keep open shop on their own account'. Section 19 has been repealed and accordingly 'pharmaceutical assistants' are now a closed class of persons within the profession.

Section 2 of the Act introduced an entirely new concept by providing a definition of a 'retail pharmacy business'. This is stated to be:

> a business (not being a professional practice carried on by a registered medical practitioner or a registered dentist) which consists of or includes the sale or supply of medicinal products other than medicinal products on a general sales list (whether or not such products on such list are also sold or supplied in the course of the business).

The word 'sale' which is employed in this definition is itself defined as effectively meaning sale by retail. The word 'supply' is defined in terms of a supply other than by way of sale to a person who receives the medicinal product for a purpose other than sale or supply or administering it in the course of a business or profession. 'Medicinal products on a general sales list' are defined as medicinal products which may be sold under regulations made by the Minister pursuant to Section 32(2)(m)(ii) of the Irish Medicines Board Act 1995.[15]

The concept of a 'retail pharmacy business' is new and significant. In order lawfully to operate a retail pharmacy business, the business must be registered with the Society.[16] Prior to the coming into operation of the Act there was no formal definition of a retail pharmacy business and certainly no obligation to register it before one could trade. There was a requirement to notify the Society of a new opening of a shop within three months of the date of opening and to submit annual statements of return. Under Section 2 of the 1962 Act it was sufficient that a person keeping open shop for the dispensing or compounding of medical prescriptions would ensure that there was an authorised person present and that the dispensing and

---

15. Section 32(2)(m)(ii) of the Irish Medicines Board Act 1995 (No. 29 of 1995) as substituted by Irish Medicines Board (Miscellaneous Provisions) Act 2006 (No. 3 of 2006).
16. See Section 17 of the Act.

compounding was personally supervised by such a person. An authorised person was defined in Section 2(3) of the Pharmacy Act 1962 as including a registered pharmaceutical chemist, a registered dispensing chemist and druggist, a licentiate of Apothecaries' Hall and certain other narrower classes of persons as set out therein.

The introduction of a system for the registration of retail pharmacy businesses provides a new safeguard for members of the public in the commercial healthcare marketplace. It will be seen later in this chapter that if a business constitutes a retail pharmacy business then there are considerable obligations placed upon the proprietors which go with the enjoyment of that particular status.

The Pharmaceutical Society of Ireland (Part 2)

Part 2 of the Act deals with the dissolution of the old Society which had been established in 1875 and the establishment of a new Society in its place which has the same name. The Society continues at least from one perspective to be a Society of members and under Section 5(3) of the Act every registered pharmacist is a member of the Society. As has already been stated, the members of the Society are no longer in full control of the affairs of the Society. Under Section 11 of the Act, the functions of the Society are performed on its behalf by a Council. The Council, by virtue of Section 10 of the Act, must have a non-pharmacist majority.

Section 5 of the Act transfers from the old Society to the new Society all the rights, property and liabilities of the old Society. In the same way, employees of the old Society became employees of the new Society. The new Society is substituted for the old Society in any court or other proceedings and in any legal contracts or agreements. The new Society (in the same way as the old Society) is a body corporate with a legal life and persona of its own distinct from its members. It can acquire, hold and transfer lands. It can sue and be sued and it has an official seal.

The most important section in Part 2 of the Act is Section 7. This sets out the functions, duties and powers of the Society. The principal functions of the Society as set out in Section 7(1) are to:

a   regulate the profession having regard to the need to protect, maintain and promote the health and safety of the public;
b   promote and ensure high standards of education and training in the profession;
c   ensure those persons and pharmacists obtain appropriate experience;
d   ensure practising pharmacists undertake appropriate continuing professional development, including the acquisition of specialisation;
e   supervise compliance with the Act.

Section 7(2)(a) deals with the duties of the Society. These include:

a   keeping the registers;
b   determining and applying criteria for registration;
c   drawing up codes of conduct for pharmacists;
d   determining, approving and reviewing programmes for education;
e   providing advice and information to the Minister;
f   acting as competent authority for the purposes of the Professional Qualifications Directive;
g   improving the profession of pharmacy.

Section 7(2)(b) confers various powers on the Society so as to enable it to carry out its duties and accomplish the functions for which it was established.

Sections 8 and 9 of the Act permit the Minister to confer additional functions and ancillary powers respectively upon the Society.

The Council of the Society (Part 3)

Section 11(1) of the Act provides that 'subject to this Act the functions of the Society shall be performed on its behalf by the Council'. The Council is composed as per Section 10(2) of 'a group of 21 persons appointed by the Minister'. Section 10(3) specifies the basis upon which that appointment is made (i.e. on the basis of the nomination of appointees to and by the Minister). The persons entitled to be nominated in accordance with Section 10(3) comprise:

a   a nominee of the Irish Medicines Board – as a representative of the management of the regulation of medicinal products;
b   a nominee by the Health Service Executive – as a representative of the management of the public health sector;
c   a Minister's nominee to represent the provision of the continuing professional development in pharmacy;
d   three nominees of the Minister possessing such qualifications, expertise, interests or experience as would enable them to make a substantial contribution to the performance by the Society of its functions;
e   eleven nominees of the Minister who are not and never have been pharmacists;
f   nine members of the Society who have been selected by its members [in accordance with the provisions of the Pharmaceutical Society of Ireland (Council) Rules 2008];[17]
g   a member of the Society selected as a representative of third-level pharmacy educational and training establishments.

---

17. S.I. No. 492 of 2008.

The manner in which the Council conducts itself and the rules relating to its procedures and processes are set out (at least in part) in Schedule 1 to the Act.

It should be noted that Schedule 1 is not exhaustive and further provisions are set out in the Pharmaceutical Society of Ireland (Council) Rules 2008 (see Chapter 13). Schedule 1 of the Act provides that the term of office of a Council member shall be four years from the date of appointment. A person may cease to be qualified to hold office as a Council member for various reasons including bankruptcy, conviction of an indictable offence or an offence involving fraud or dishonesty or if they have been sentenced to a term of imprisonment. The Minister can remove a Council member from office if the Minister is satisfied that the member has become incapable of performing his or her functions or has committed a stated misbehaviour or if removal of the member appears necessary so as to enable the Council to perform its functions effectively.

Paragraph 4 of Schedule 1 provides that a President and vice-President shall be elected from among those members of Council who are registered as pharmacists. The President and vice-President each hold office for one year and the mechanism for their election is set out in Part 4 of the Pharmaceutical Society of Ireland (Council) Rules 2008.

The Council is obliged to hold at least four meetings in every twelve-month period. Questions which fall to be determined at meetings are, in the absence of agreement, decided by way of vote, the Chair having a casting vote. Paragraph 6(7) of Schedule 1 obliges the Council to record the business done at its meetings and those of its committees.

Paragraph 7 of Schedule 1 permits the Council to establish committees and determine their terms of reference. Section 11(8) of the Act permits the Council to delegate any of its functions to any of its committees and where such function has been delegated the remit of the committee is extended accordingly. This power has been extensively availed of by the Council. Quite clearly the Council and its members (in the same way as a minister of government) could not as a matter of practicality deal with every item of the Society's business. The Council has established a number of advisory committees including the:

- Administration, Finance and Corporate Governance Committee;
- Inspection and Enforcement Committee;
- Professional Development and Learning Committee;
- Registration and Qualification Recognition Committee;
- Pharmacy Practice Development Committee;
- Audit Committee.

The Council has delegated to those committees the task of dealing with much of the work which arises in their heading areas. Details of the work, members and remit of these committees can be found on the Society's website.[18]

Part 5 of the Pharmaceutical Society of Ireland (Council) Rules 2008 deals with the management and administration of the Council and of its committees.

A member of the Council of the Society or an employee of the Society who becomes a member of the Oireachtas or who is elected to the European Parliament, in the case of a Council member, ceases to be a member of the Council or in the case of an employee, stands seconded and shall not be paid any remuneration by the Society.

A member of Council or an employee of the Society has certain obligations in the event that they have an 'interest' in what is referred to as a 'specified matter'. A specified matter is defined in paragraph 9 of Schedule 1 to the Act as an arrangement to which the Council is a party or a proposed such arrangement or a contract or other agreement with the Council or a proposed such contract or agreement.

Generally speaking when such an event occurs, the member or employee is obliged to disclose the nature of their 'interest'. They may not seek to influence the decision or vote thereon and must absent themselves from the affected part of any meeting and generally may not take part in any further deliberations on the issue in which they have an interest.

Paragraph 11 of Schedule 1 makes it an offence for a member of Council or one of its committees or an advisor or consultant or employee of the Society to disclose 'confidential information'. Confidential information is information which is declared by the Council to be confidential or proposals of a commercial nature or tender submitted to the Council.

The Council is obliged to keep proper accounts which must be audited at least once a year. Not later than three months after the end of each financial year the Council is obliged to submit copies of the accounts and the auditor's certificate and report to the Minister for Health and Children. The Minister is then obliged to lay them before each House of the Oireachtas. In the same vein, the Council is obliged to submit an annual report to the Minister and to have it printed and published.

Paragraph 20 of Schedule 1 authorises the Society with the approval of the Minister to charge fees for various 'services', including registration, continued registration, the issue of certificates of registration, the alteration of the register and restoration of a name to the register. The levels of fees charged are regulated by the Pharmaceutical Society of Ireland (Fees) Rules 2008 and 2010.[19]

In the event that the Council fails to perform any of its functions then the Minister is empowered to direct it to do so. If the Council does not comply

---

18. www.thePSI.ie (accessed 1 March 2011).
19. S.I. No. 496 of 2008 as amended by S.I. No. 257 of 2010.

with the direction of the Minister, the Minister may remove the Council or any of its members from office.

Section 11 of the Act empowers the Council to make rules for various purposes so as to enable it to carry out its functions under the Act. A draft of any proposed rules must be published with an invitation to the public to comment thereon within a reasonable time. The rules are subject to the consent of the Minister and must then be laid before each House of the Oireachtas and published.

Code of Conduct

Section 7(2)(a)(iii) of the Act obliges the Society to draw up a code of conduct for pharmacists. Once again there must be public consultation on the draft of any code. Before giving effect to such code, a draft also has to be submitted to the Competition Authority for its opinion as to whether any of the provisions of the draft code would be likely to prevent, restrict or distort competition. Assuming the Competition Authority does not have any objection, the draft code is then submitted to the Minister for his or her consent. The same provisions apply to any proposed amendment of a code of conduct. Once a code of conduct or any amendment thereto has been given effect, it must be published and submitted to the Minister for Health and Children for laying before each House of the Oireachtas. In compliance with these provisions, the Council has introduced a 'Code of Conduct for Pharmacists' (set out in Appendix 12.1).

The Code of Conduct for Pharmacists is a very significant document. A breach of the code falls within the definition of professional misconduct contained in Section 33 of the Act. If a registered pharmacist is found to have committed professional misconduct, they can be sanctioned under Part 6 of the Act, even if there is no breach of any legislative provision governing the practice of pharmacy or the supply of medicinal products. The effect of the code is that the conduct of a registered pharmacist (regardless of where or in what branch of pharmacy they work) is always open to scrutiny, amenable to complaint, subject to inquiry and, if necessary, discipline.

The Society as an educator

Section 7(1)(b) and (c) of the Act declare, respectively, that it is a function of the Society 'to promote and ensure a high standard of education and training for persons seeking to become pharmacists' and also 'to ensure that those persons and pharmacists obtain appropriate experience'. Section 7(2)(a)(iv) imposes a duty on the Society to determine, approve and keep under review programmes of education and training. Section 7(2)(b) confers certain powers on the Society including the power to conduct or arrange for the conduct of examinations of persons who are applying or might apply for registration. Section 9 of the Act also confers on the Society all such powers as are necessary for the performance by it of any of its functions.

Pursuant to its obligations under the Act the Society has made rules entitled the Pharmaceutical Society of Ireland (Educational and Training Rules) 2008.[20] These rules deal *inter alia* with the recognition and approval of programmes of education and training leading to the award of a degree in pharmacy. They also deal with the in-service practical training programme and the professional registration examination. The Society is obliged as a minimum to ensure that the standard and content of its educational courses meet with the requirements of the annex to the Professional Qualifications Directive.

Insofar as continuing pharmaceutical education is concerned, the Society has conducted an overview of this area with a view to introducing formal requirements for registrants in this regard and in October 2010, announced details of the proposed framework for continuing professional development (CPD) for pharmacists, which will become mandatory in due course.

The pharmaceutical registration system (Part 4)

Part 4 is one of the most important parts of the Act. The registration system is the most effective and substantive system provided by the Act for the protection of public health. Generally speaking no person can practise as a pharmacist or use that title unless they are registered. By the same token and in very simple terms, a retail pharmacy business cannot be operated unless it is registered. When a registered retail pharmacy business is operating, the management and administration thereof, the supervision of the services provided in each business premises, and the sale and supply of medicinal products therein must be conducted or carried out respectively by registered pharmacists with certain minimum levels of experience. Failure to comply with these requirements constitutes a criminal offence under the Act. At the time of writing, under Section 72 of the Act, a person guilty of an offence under the Act or any regulation made thereunder is liable, on summary conviction (i.e. for a minor offence), to a fine not exceeding €3000 or imprisonment for a term not exceeding six months, or to both. Upon conviction on indictment (i.e. for a serious offence) a person, in the case of a first such offence, is liable to a fine not exceeding €130 000 or to imprisonment for a term not exceeding five years, or to both. In the case of second or subsequent such offences, the maximum fine rises to €320 000 and the maximum term of imprisonment to ten years.

In addition to the foregoing, unless there are special and substantial reasons for not doing so, a court will order the convicted person to pay the costs and expenses of any prosecution brought against them.

---

20. S.I. No. 493 of 2008.

It is also worth remarking on Section 72(3) of the Act, which is designed to prevent people from hiding behind 'companies'. Section 72(3) provides:

> where an offence under this Act is committed by a corporate body and is proved to have been so committed with the consent, connivance or approval of, or to have been attributable to any wilful neglect on the part of, any person being a director, manager, secretary or any other officer of the corporate body or a person who was purporting to act in any such capacity, that person, as well as the corporate body, is guilty of an offence and is liable to be proceeded against and punished as if he or she were guilty of the first mentioned offence.

Part 4 of the Act obliges the Council to set up a register for each of the following class of persons:

a   pharmacists – Part A and Part B (visiting pharmacists from relevant EEA (European Economic Area) states[21]);
b   druggists;
c   pharmaceutical assistants;
d   retail pharmacy businesses.

The Society has under and by virtue of the Pharmaceutical Society of Ireland (Registration) Rules 2008[22] established these registers, and has entered therein all the relevant details concerning registrants. The Council is obliged to publish the registers electronically[23] and in hard copy and to update them at intervals of not more than twelve months.

Registration of pharmacists

The procedure and criteria for registration as a pharmacist are set out in Section 14 of the Act. The criteria and procedure for registration of a retail pharmacy business are set out in Section 17 of the Act.

Under and by virtue of Section 14 the Council is obliged to register in the Pharmacists Register (Part A) a person who complies with certain criteria. In broad terms these include:

a   completing the prescribed application form and providing the required information;
b   satisfying the Council that the person is fit to be registered;
c   holding a qualification appropriate for practice;

---

21. European Economic Area (EEA) comprises all EU member states plus Norway, Liechtenstein and Iceland.
22. S.I. No. 494 of 2008.
23. This requirement is met by publication of searchable versions of the registers on the PSI's website www.thePSI.ie (accessed 1 March 2011).

d   not being an undischarged bankrupt;
e   in the case of persons not being a national of the State or of another EU member state, satisfying the Council that he or she is linguistically competent;
f   paying the prescribed fee.

There are a number of phrases or expressions used in these criteria which require further elaboration. What is 'a qualification appropriate for practice'? How is a person 'fit' to be registered as a pharmacist? By the same token, how might they be found unfit to be so registered?

A 'qualification appropriate for practice' is set out in Section 16 of the Act. In simple terms, Section 16 provides for three classes of qualification, firstly those held by persons who have received in the State the prescribed training and education and have the prescribed qualifications (an Irish qualification); secondly, qualifications held by persons who are nationals of a 'relevant state' (i.e. a state within the EEA and Switzerland), and who satisfy the Council as to the requirements set out in Section 16(3)–(5) and (8) of the Act relating to evidence of qualifications; thirdly, qualifications held by persons who have received such training and education and have passed such examinations and obtained such qualifications in a third country (any country other than a 'relevant state') and which are in the opinion of the Council of a standard not lower than the standard of those necessary for practice in Ireland.

In respect of the second type of qualifications ('EU Qualifications'), applicants must satisfy the Council in respect of a complex number of 'alternative' requirements. The nature and interaction of these 'alternative' requirements are too complex to paraphrase and they can be examined in the Act.

The other expression in Section 14(1) which requires comment is the obligation on an applicant to satisfy the Council that the person is 'fit' to be a registered pharmacist. Clearly if in the preceding twelve months a registered pharmacist has been found guilty of professional misconduct or poor professional performance under Part 6 of the Act and if penalties have been imposed under that part, then issues may arise as to whether they are fit to be registered. In the same way Section 14(2) deals with the position of persons who under the laws of another state may have been prohibited from acting as a 'pharmacist' or who have been prohibited from carrying on any other practice, profession or occupation consisting mainly of the provision of healthcare or social care or services. The position of people who are applying for first registration is more complex. In general terms, they must provide a certificate from their medical practitioner confirming that he or she is not aware of any reason or grounds of physical or mental health why the applicant might be unable to discharge their responsibilities as a registered pharmacist. The applicant must also swear a declaration attesting to their good character and repute in a form published by the Society.

The detailed rules on registration are to be found in the Pharmaceutical Society of Ireland (Registration) Rules 2008.

Section 15 of the Act migrates automatically the names of all persons who were registered or entitled to be registered on the registers of the old Pharmaceutical Society of Ireland onto the new registers.

Registration of retail pharmacy business

We now turn to the Register of Retail Pharmacy Businesses. The criteria for registration of a retail pharmacy business are set out in Section 17 of the Act. This permits registration provided the applicant:

a   is the pharmacy owner;
b   specifies the name of the retail pharmacy business and the premises where it will be carried on;
c   specifies the name of the registered pharmacist who is or is to be in whole time charge of the carrying on of the business there;
d   complies with any requirements of the Council in relation to verifying the application or providing further information;
e   pays the prescribed fee;
f   satisfies the Council that the retail pharmacy business will be conducted in accordance with regulations made under Section 18 of the Act.

Where a pharmacy owner carries on business in two or more premises, each premises is regarded as a separate retail pharmacy business and each premises must be registered.

It is important to note that under Section 17(4) of the Act a change in ownership of a retail pharmacy business operates to cancel its registration. Furthermore, where the owner of a retail pharmacy business (or a joint owner) dies, registration is cancelled with effect from three months after the date of death. In all other cases cancellations take effect 28 days after the change of ownership. In the case of limited companies, a change of ownership is deemed to happen if shares amounting in value to more than half of those issued by the company change ownership.

Section 18 of the Act confers on the Minister for Health and Children the power to make regulations in respect of the operation of retail pharmacy businesses. These regulations must be made for the purposes of the health, safety and convenience of the public. Such regulations have been made and cover matters such as the manner in which medicinal products are to be sold and supplied and the precautions to be taken, the disposal of medicinal products, the establishment of patient counselling areas and the requirement for patient records. If the owner of a retail pharmacy business breaches one of the regulations made pursuant to Section 18, they are committing a criminal offence. The current regulations are entitled Regulation of Retail Pharmacy Business Regulations 2008[24] (see Chapter 13).

Section 20 of the Act provides for a further and important registration-based safeguard to the public, namely the issuing of annual certificates of registration. As soon as practicable after their registration, the Council is obliged to issue to a pharmacist and to the owner of a retail pharmacy business, a certificate of registration. The certificate of registration remains in force for a period of twelve months from the date of registration. This means that every pharmacist and retail pharmacy business must register annually with the Society if they wish to continue to practise and operate respectively. As part of the annual registration process the Society proactively checks the status of each applicant. If, for example, an applicant has in the intervening twelve months been found guilty of a criminal offence or professional misconduct or poor professional performance then their registration will not be automatically renewed. This constitutes a significant public health protection over the old regime where the only requirement for the maintenance of registration was the payment of an annual fee.

The certificate of registration contains certain designated information and enables members of the public to identify the current status of their pharmacist and the retail pharmacy business which is selling or supplying medicinal products to them. Certificates of registration are more particularly dealt with in Part 4 of the Pharmaceutical Society of Ireland (Registration) Rules 2008. Sections 27, 28 and 29 of the Act oblige, respectively, the owner of a retail pharmacy business and any pharmacist working there to display their certificates of registration conspicuously. Failure so to do may give rise to an offence under Section 26 (which deals with offences relating to retail pharmacy businesses).

In the event that the Council refuses an application for registration from either a pharmacist or a retail pharmacy business or fails to determine such an application within the specified time limit (generally three months), the aggrieved person (owner or pharmacist as the case may be) may appeal to the High Court against the refusal or failure. This appeal must be brought within a period of three months of notification of refusal or three months from the expiry of the time laid down for making the decision. The High Court is given very wide powers as to what orders it can make in those circumstances.

Section 22 of the Act obliges the Council to ensure that the registers are accurate and up-to-date. Any alteration to the registers must be notified to the registrant or their next of kin as the case may be. Insofar as a registrant is concerned, they are obliged to notify the Council in writing of any error in their entry or any change in circumstance likely to have a bearing on the

---

24. S.I. No. 488 of 2008.

accuracy of the entry. This might arise for example if the size of the pharmacy premises is materially increased or decreased.

Visiting pharmacists

Section 24A and Section 24B of the Act are new 'standalone' sections. They have been inserted into the Act by the European Communities (Recognition of Professional Qualifications Relating to the Profession of Pharmacist) (No. 2) Regulations 2008. These amendments deal with the position of visiting European pharmacists (explained below) and their registrations. In essence, the Act provides that the Council shall not for any reasons related to professional qualifications restrict a person who is legally established in another relevant state in the profession of pharmacy from providing the same services in Ireland on a temporary and occasional basis. The Council is obliged to assess the temporary and occasional nature of the provision of professional services on a case by case basis. The more detailed requirements and compliance obligations are set out in Section 24A. In circumstances where a check demonstrates that there is a substantial difference between the professional qualifications and training of the person seeking access and the professional activities of a registered pharmacist in this State, the Council is obliged to give the person an opportunity to show that he or she has acquired any knowledge or competence which may be lacking. A person providing services under this section is subject to the statutory and administrative rules applicable to those pursuing the profession of a registered pharmacist in the State.

Under Section 24B of the Act, the Council must open a second part to the register known as Part B which is entitled 'Visiting Pharmacists from Relevant EEA States'. The Council is obliged to enter into Part B of the register of pharmacists the names of persons who are visiting the State in order to provide the services of a registered pharmacist on a temporary and occasional basis and who have satisfied the requirements of Section 24A.

Offences (Part 5)

Part 5 of the Act creates the core criminal offences. In simple terms, if a registered retail pharmacy business is carried on by a natural person (i.e. a pharmacist) or by a body corporate or by the legal personal representative of a deceased pharmacist, then under Section 26 of the Act certain conditions must be met. The conditions for a natural person are set out in Section 27. The conditions for a body corporate are set out in Section 28 and the conditions for a legal personal representative are set out in Section 29. If the provisions of Section 26 are not complied with, a criminal offence is committed and the offender is liable to a fine and/or imprisonment. Similarly, the directors and officers of a body corporate may also be committing an offence.

In the case of natural persons or partnerships of natural persons the conditions laid down in Section 27 are (briefly) that:

a   the owner (or if there is a partnership, all the owners) are registered as pharmacists;

b   the management and administration of the sale and supply of medicinal products is carried out under the personal control of a registered pharmacist who has three years' minimum post-registration experience;

c   there is a registered pharmacist (who has three years' minimum post-registration experience) in whole-time charge of the premises where the business is carried on. If there is more than one premises then each premises must be in the whole-time charge of a registered pharmacist with three years' minimum post-registration experience;

d   the sale and supply of medicinal products in the premises in which the business is carried on (or in each or all of them if there is more than one premises) is conducted under the personal supervision of a registered pharmacist (such pharmacists do not have to have three years' minimum post-registration experience);

e   the name and certificate of registration of the registered pharmacist and the certificate of registration of the business must be conspicuously displayed at the premises where the business is carried on or if there is more than one premises, at each of those premises.

The position in relation to a body corporate or a limited company which wishes to carry on a registered retail pharmacy business is substantially similar. The part of the business that consists of management and administration of the sale and supply of medicinal products must be carried out under the personal control of a registered pharmacist who has three years' minimum post-registration experience. Both the company which owns the business and that pharmacist must provide to the Registrar a statement specifying the name of such pharmacist and whether he or she is an office holder (i.e. director or company secretary) within the company. If the business is being carried on in two or more premises, then each premises must be in the whole-time charge of a registered pharmacist who has at least three years' post-registration experience.

The sale and supply of medicinal products in each or any premises must be conducted by or under the personal supervision of a registered pharmacist (once again, three years' experience is not necessary for simple 'sale and supply'). Finally, the name and certificate of registration of the pharmacist who is in whole-time charge of the business in the premises (and the certificate of registration of the business itself) must be conspicuously displayed.

The position in relation to a retail pharmacy business owned by a pharmacist where the pharmacy proprietor has died is that the Registrar must be notified of the name and address of the legal personal representative of the pharmacist in question. Thereafter, the same provisions as apply to private individuals and bodies corporate must be complied with. Trading by a legal personal representative or other representative is generally permitted to endure for periods of three or five years depending on the circumstances (e.g. death of pharmacist owner or pharmacist adjudicated bankrupt or made a ward of court or subject to power of attorney due to mental incapacity). It has been previously noted as to the effect which death has on the registration status of a retail pharmacy business.

The combined effect of Sections 26 to 29 can best be understood by reference to the concepts of a 'superintendent pharmacist' a 'supervising pharmacist' and a 'duty pharmacist'. The superintendent pharmacist must have a minimum of three years' post-registration experience and is in charge of the management and administration of that part of the business that consists of the sale and supply of medicinal products. For example, a chain of ten pharmacies might have a single superintendent pharmacist acting for the entire group. Every premises in which a registered retail pharmacy business is conducted must have a supervising pharmacist. The supervising pharmacist must have three years' minimum post-registration experience and their job is to personally control the management and administration of the sale and supply of medicinal products within the premises.

The third requirement of Section 27 of the Act is that any sale or supply of medicinal products in the premises of a retail pharmacy business must be conducted by or under the personal supervision of a registered pharmacist. This pharmacist may be referred to as a 'duty pharmacist'. There is no three years' experience qualification required in the case of a 'duty pharmacist'. In the case of an owner operated pharmacy, provided the pharmacist in question has the requisite three years' experience, they may act in all the capacities of superintendent pharmacist, supervising pharmacist and duty pharmacist.

Section 30 of the Act permits a registered pharmaceutical assistant to act on behalf of a registered pharmacist during the temporary absence of the registered pharmacist from the premises.

Section 31 creates an offence for a non-pharmacist knowingly to provide skilled assistance to a registered pharmacist. Skilled assistance is defined as any assistance which consists of or includes the exercise of the knowledge, ability, judgement and other qualities necessary of a person who is a pharmacist or a pharmaceutical assistant while not actually being one.

Section 32 of the Act makes it an offence for a person other than a registered pharmacist to hold himself or herself out as a registered pharmacist. The same offence is created in the case of a business holding itself out as a registered retail pharmacy business when it is not so registered. In that instance the owner of the business would be prosecuted. It is an offence to publicly describe oneself as a pharmacist, a dispensing chemist, a pharmaceutical chemist or as a member of the Pharmaceutical Society of Ireland or MPSI or to use any emblem or device from which the public might reasonably infer that a person is a registered pharmacist. The Act also sets out a number of reserved expressions which may only be used by registered pharmacists or druggists in describing themselves publicly. These expressions include pharmacy, medical stores, drug stores, drug hall, medical supply stores, medical hall and chemist.

Complaints, inquiries and discipline (Part 6)

Part 6 of the Act deals with complaints, inquiries and discipline. It comprises some 33 separate sections and is entirely new to the profession of pharmacy. At the heart of Part 6 are the expressions 'professional misconduct' and 'poor professional performance'. Professional misconduct is defined in Section 33 as:

> In relation to a registered pharmacist, any act, omission or pattern of conduct that:

a is a breach of the Code of Conduct for registered pharmacists;

b is infamous or disgraceful in a professional respect (notwithstanding that, if the same or like act, omission or pattern of conduct were committed by a member of another profession, it would not be professional misconduct in respect of that profession);

c involves moral turpitude,[25] fraud or dishonesty of a nature or degree which bears on the carrying on of the profession of a pharmacist;

d if the registered pharmacist has been granted a licence, certificate or registration by a body outside the State relating to the practice of pharmacy, is a breach of standard of conduct, performance or ethics that:

   i applies to a person holding that licence, certificate or registration, and

   ii corresponds to a standard contained in the code referred to in paragraph (a) or a standard breach of which amounts to conduct of the kind mentioned in paragraphs (b) or (c),

but does not include an act, omission or pattern of conduct that consists of a wrongly but honestly formed professional judgement.

Poor professional performance is defined in Section 33 as:

> In relation to a registered pharmacist . . . any failure of the registered pharmacist to meet the standards of competence that may be reasonably expected of a registered pharmacist.

---

25. Means conduct that is considered contrary to community standards of justice, honesty or good morals.

Section 35 of the Act provides that in the event that a complaint is made to the Council about a registered pharmacist under a number of stated grounds, including professional misconduct or poor professional performance, the Council is obliged to take all reasonable steps to ensure that the complaint is processed in a timely manner. Other grounds for complaint include physical or mental ailments, emotional disturbances, addiction to alcohol or drugs, failure to comply with conditions of registration or undertakings provided to the Society, contravention of the Act or the rules made thereunder and conviction of an indictable offence.

Section 36 of the Act deals with complaints about registered retail pharmacy businesses, as opposed to complaints against registered pharmacists. These complaints can include complaints that the pharmacy owner or an employee or partner of the pharmacy owner has been convicted of an offence under the Act or under the Misuse of Drugs Acts 1977 to 2006,[26] the Irish Medicines Board Acts 1995 and 2006,[27] the Poisons Acts 1961 and 1977[28] or the Animal Remedies Acts 1993 and 2006.[29] Complaints may also be made on the basis that the pharmacy owner or any employee or business partner of the pharmacy owner has been convicted of any other offence or the commission of misconduct such that were the person applying to the Council for registration as a pharmacist the Council would be likely to refuse to register the person.

In order to deal with complaints, the Act obliges the Council to establish the following statutory committees:

- Preliminary Proceedings Committee;
- Professional Conduct Committee;
- Health Committee.

These are statutory committees, unlike the committees of Council referred to earlier. They are governed by very clear rules and procedures which are laid down in the Act. The President of the Society is not eligible to be appointed to these committees. The majority of such committee members must be persons other than registered pharmacists and at least one person must be appointed to represent the interests of the public. At least one third of such committee members must be registered pharmacists and at least two of the members must be registered pharmacists who are pharmacy owners. The members of these

---

26. Misuse of Drugs Act (No. 12 of 1977) as amended by Misuse of Drugs Act 1984 (No. 18 of 1984) and by Irish Medicines Board (Miscellaneous) Provisions Act 2006 (No. 3 of 2006).
27. Irish Medicines Board Act 1995 (No. 29 of 1995) as amended by S.I. No. 304 of 2001, S.I. No. 444 of 2001, S.I. No. 576 of 2002, Act No. 3 of 2006 and S.I. No. 542 of 2007.
28. Poisons Act 1961 (No. 12 of 1961) as amended by the Misuse of Drugs Act 1977. The Poisons Act was also amended by Section 74 of the Pharmacy Act 2007.
29. Animal Remedies Act 1993 (No. 23 of 1993) as amended by Irish Medicines Board (Miscellaneous) Provisions Act 2006.

committees are given much the same protections and immunities as a Judge of the High Court. The Council is also entitled to appoint a registered medical practitioner with relevant experience to advise the Health Committee.

As soon as practical after receiving a complaint, the Council is obliged under Section 38(1) to refer it to a Preliminary Proceedings Committee for its advice on whether there is sufficient cause to warrant further action being taken. The Preliminary Proceedings Committee investigates the complaint in a preliminary way. This committee does not adjudicate on issues nor does it make any findings. It is a 'look/see' committee only. It refers matters forward. The committee is entitled to require the registered pharmacist or pharmacy owner to give such information in relation to the complaint as it specifies. The person or persons complained against are entitled to make observations to the committee. The Preliminary Proceedings Committee then considers whether there is sufficient cause to warrant further action and provides the Council with its advice and refers the matter on to other committees if appropriate. If there is no basis for the complaint or if the complaint is trivial, vexatious or made in bad faith then, subject to review by the Council, the committee may effectively dismiss it and take no further action.

If there is a sound basis for the complaint then the type of further action which may be taken may include:

a   referral by the committee of the complaint for resolution by mediation pursuant to Section 37 of the Act;
b   referral by the committee of the complaint to the Professional Conduct Committee;
c   referral by the committee of the complaint to the Health Committee.

In relation to a referral of a complaint to mediation, Section 37(3) of the Act provides that 'no attempt may be made to resolve a complaint by mediation without the consent of the complainant and the registered pharmacist or pharmacy owner.' If the parties consent to mediation then the process is embarked upon and in due course the mediator reports the terms of resolution to the Council or the fact that the mediation has failed, in which event the complaint is referred on to the Professional Conduct Committee or the Health Committee. The mediation process is governed by Section 37 of the Act.

If the Preliminary Proceedings Committee or the Council are of the view that the complaint is not one which is appropriate for resolution by mediation, the complaint may be referred to the Professional Conduct Committee or to the Health Committee. These committees are 'committees of inquiry'. Under Section 41 of the Act, the formal complaint including any supporting evidence provided and the entitlement of the registered pharmacist or pharmacy owner and his or her representative to attend the committee and to be heard must be notified to them by the relevant committee of inquiry.

Thereafter it is the duty of such committees to arrange a hearing and to fix a time, date and place for it.

In general, a hearing before the Professional Conduct Committee is held in public and a hearing before the Health Committee is held in private. This is not exclusively the case. They may be held in private and in public respectively if a request is made by the complainant or pharmacist or pharmacy owner and the relevant committee is satisfied that it would be appropriate to agree to such a request.

The hearing before a committee of inquiry is not the same as a trial in a court of law but the Act does provide that the rules of natural and constitutional justice are adhered to. Section 42(5) of the Act provides that any person with the leave of the committee may lead evidence in support of the complaint. This will generally be an officer of the Society. The testimony of witnesses must be given under oath or affirmation. There is a full right to cross-examine witnesses and call evidence in defence and reply. The Professional Conduct Committee may transfer a complaint to the Health Committee and vice versa provided that both committees are satisfied that it is appropriate so to do. The committee of inquiry is given all the powers, rights, privileges and duties of a court in relation to:

a   enforcing the attendance of witnesses;
b   examining witnesses under oath or otherwise;
c   compelling the production or inspection of records or other documents or property;
d   awarding and authorising the recovery of costs.

A witness before a committee of inquiry has the same immunities and privileges as a witness before a court. If a person fails to respond to a summons to attend before a committee of inquiry or, without reasonable excuse, refuses to cooperate in certain ways with the committee, they can be charged with a criminal offence under Section 43(7) of the Act. All parties are entitled to be legally represented before a committee of inquiry but the intention would be that representation would be availed of in more serious cases only. It is to be hoped that, consistent with the principles of justice, the complaints process will not be turned into a court of law with all the attendant procedure, expense, delay and formality. There may also be substantial cost implications for the parties depending upon the duration and calibre (e.g. an eminent Senior Counsel) of the representation. Overly legalistic approaches to professional regulation are a problem which have been experienced by other regulatory authorities. If the government had intended that professional regulation should be dealt with in a court of law (with all which that entails) they would have so provided in the legislation.

If a complaint is withdrawn, the committee of inquiry considering it may, with the Council's agreement, decide that no further action be taken or it may decide to proceed as if the complaint had not been withdrawn.

Temporary suspension and closure orders

Section 45 of the Act confers on the Council the power to make an application to the High Court seeking an order to suspend the registration of a registered pharmacist or a registered retail pharmacy business against whom a complaint has been made and/or seeking an order for the closure of the premises in which the business has been carried on. Such an application would only be made in the most serious of cases. Upon such an application the High Court may make a 'closure order' if it considers that there is a risk to the health and safety of the public, which is of such magnitude that the registration of the pharmacist or the retail pharmacy business should be suspended pending further action under Part 6 of the Act.

Penalties

On completing an inquiry, a committee of inquiry must make a full report to the Council. The Council must within 30 days of receipt of the report either dismiss the complaint (if it has not been substantiated) or impose one or more of the following disciplinary sanctions:

a   admonishment or censure;
b   attachment of conditions to registration;
c   suspension of registration for a specified period;
d   cancellation of registration;
e   prohibition for a specified period on applying for restoration to the register.

As soon as practicable after deciding to impose a disciplinary sanction, the Council must notify the registered pharmacist or the pharmacy owner and the complainant of the date of its decision, the sanction imposed and the reasons for its imposition. The imposition of a disciplinary sanction other than admonishment or censure cannot take effect until it is confirmed by the High Court. Sections 51 and 52 of the Act permit the High Court on the application of either the registered pharmacist or pharmacy owner or the Council to cancel, confirm or vary a disciplinary sanction. A registered pharmacist or pharmacy owner must make their court application within 30 days after receipt of the notification of the decision from the Council. The Council is allowed a period of 60 days within which it must do so. Under Section 56 of the Act the Council is obliged to notify the Minister for Health and Children as soon as practicable of any disciplinary sanctions imposed.

Under Section 57 of the Act the Council shall, if satisfied that it is within the public interest so to do, give public notice of the imposition of various sanctions. It is likely that all sanctions will be notified to the public. They will certainly be noted in the registers of the Society and will impact on the issue of certificates of good standing for the persons concerned.

Section 59 of the Act permits the Council to cancel a registration of a pharmacist or a retail pharmacy business upon request but without prejudice to any complaint which is being investigated. The investigation will generally continue. Section 60 permits the Council to cancel a registration if a registrant fails to pay a registration fee. This matter is dealt with in more detail in the Pharmaceutical Society of Ireland (Registration) Rules 2008.

Improper relationships between pharmacists and doctors

Sections 63 and 64 of the Act deal with this difficult issue. They are designed to prohibit the creation of certain improper economic relationships between pharmacists or pharmacy owners and doctors and between retail pharmacy businesses and medical practices. From a common sense standpoint, it is clear that the two healthcare professions of doctor and pharmacist should be independent of each other in the treatment of sick people. The pharmacist as a healthcare professional, in his or her own right, has a duty to be more than a mere conduit for medicinal products. They must bring their professional knowledge and skills in the area of medicines to bear. If they have concerns in relation to what a doctor has prescribed or what non-prescription medicine a patient may be taking, they have a professional duty to raise and, if necessary act upon those concerns. It is for this reason, principally, that Sections 63 and 64 seek to separate and prohibit any improper commercial relationship between pharmacists and doctors.

A pharmacist should not have any 'interest' in the commercial success of a doctor's practice and vice versa with doctors and pharmacy practices. If this were permitted, the scope for abuse and risk to patient safety would inevitably increase. This in turn would result in a loss of patient trust in their healthcare professionals, with consequent fundamental damage to the reputation of the respective professions. Once again, the tension between unbiased patient healthcare and commercial self-interest rears its head.

Section 63 declares that it is professional misconduct by a registered pharmacist or a registered medical practitioner if he or she has a beneficial interest in the medical practice or registered retail pharmacy business of the other. Beneficial interest is defined in Section 63(5) as including the interest of a director or a shareholder in a company or the interest of a member in a corporate body which is not a company. An 'interest' also includes the interest of the landlord in the rent (or other consideration) of a leased premises in circumstances where the rental value and/or the consideration is not an open market one or where the rent or consideration is ascertained by reference to the receipts or profits of the pharmacy business or medical practice as the case might be. The definitions and requirements are quite technical and are not dealt with in this chapter.

Section 64 provides that a registered retail pharmacy business and a medical practice shall not be carried on in the same premises as each other or in separate premises which are so organised that public access to the one is only available through the other and where there is an arrangement between them which provides for, acknowledges or regulates a financial benefit to any of them arising from or facilitated by the relevant co-location or juxtaposition.

Section 64 also prohibits the improper recommendation of patients between medical practitioners and registered pharmacists or pharmacy owners and prohibits the payment of 'commissions' by pharmacists to doctors or vice versa. Section 64(6) imposes a duty on a registered pharmacist or pharmacy owner to report a contravention of Section 64 to the Society.

Powers of investigation (Part 7)

Part 7 of the Act confers on the Society very considerable powers of investigation. Section 67 enables the Council to appoint persons as authorised officers. An authorised officer when so appointed is given various powers for the purposes of ascertaining whether any offence has been committed under the Act or whether there has been any breach of the Code of Conduct or other professional misconduct.

The powers conferred upon authorised officers include the right to:

a   at all reasonable times to enter a premises by use of reasonable force if necessary;
b   inspect and take copies of any books, records or other documents which he or she finds in the course of his or her inspection together with;
c   remove same from the premises and detain them for such period as is reasonably necessary for the purposes of carrying out its functions.

An authorised officer also has the right to carry out such tests, examination, analysis and inspections on premises or any equipment, machinery, plant or other item found there which might be relevant to their investigation. He or she can require any person at the premises or the owner or the person in charge or any employee to give him or her such assistance and information and to produce to him or her such books, records and other documents as are in that person's possession or which he or she could reasonably obtain. The authorised officer may take samples of anything found at the premises and direct that certain specified items should not be sold or distributed or moved from the premises without the consent of the authorised officer. The authorised officer is further entitled to secure for later inspection any premises or any part of a premises. They may also inspect and copy or extract information from any data within the meaning of the Data Protection Acts 1988 and 2003.[30] They may require a person having authority so to do to break open any container or package or to open any machine or to make available facilities such as post office boxes, telecommunications or electronic mail addresses or like facilities.

Under Section 71 of the Act, when an authorised officer has completed his or her investigations, they must provide a written report to the Council, which may do whichever of the following that it considers appropriate:

a   take no action;
b   commence disciplinary proceedings;
c   bring summary proceedings for the commission of a criminal offence and/ or direct the Registrar to take a specified action;
d   take such other action as it considers appropriate.

The offences to be prosecuted might include *inter alia* offences committed under this Act, under the Irish Medicines Board Acts 1995 and 2006, under the Poisons Act 1961 as amended or any regulations made thereunder.

Miscellaneous (Part 8)

Part 8 of the Act deals with miscellaneous general matters including the restriction of the powers conferred by the Apothecaries' Hall Act of 1791, the amendment of the Poisons Act 1961 (see Chapter 9, Poisons Acts and Regulations), and some transposition of provisions from the old Act into the new Act in relation to nomenclature.

The Registrar

It is worth remarking on the office known as the Registrar. Paragraph 13 of Schedule 1 to the Act obliges the Council to appoint a chief officer who will be known as the Registrar. The Registrar is charged with keeping the registers, managing and controlling the administration and business of the Society and the Council and performing such other functions as may be determined by the Council.[31] The Registrar by virtue of his or her office enjoys certain expressed and implied powers. The expressed powers include taking custody of a certificate of registration;[32] issuing certificates for the

---

30. Data Protection Act 1988 (No. 25 of 1988) as amended by Data Protection (Amendment) Act 2003 (No. 6 of 2003).
31. Paragraph 13(4) of Schedule 1 to the Act.
32. Section 20(6).

purposes of legal proceedings;[33] receiving notification and statements;[34] making a complaint about a registered pharmacist to the Council;[35] and taking specified action for the purposes of Section 71(1)(c) of the Act.[36] In addition, and as already stated, the Council may from time to time delegate to the Registrar certain functions. The Registrar and his or her 'office' (i.e. the other employees of the Society) are effectively the executive arm of the Society. It would be quite impossible for the Council and its members personally to accomplish all that is required of the Society. The accomplishment of tasks is for the most part performed by the Registrar and his or her 'office'.

By reason of the foregoing, the implied powers and actions of the Registrar's 'office' are considerable. They are the people who run the day-to-day affairs of the Society. The Registrar is *de facto* the accountable person in much the same way as the Secretary General of a Department of Government under the Public Service Management Act 1997.[37] The Registrar in turn acts through the employees of the Society and under the Carltona Doctrine ('the decision of such an official is the decision of the Minister'), the Society, via the Council, the Registrar and its employees, continues under the law to be the accountable person.

Conclusion

The purpose and intention of this chapter was to provide a relatively uncomplicated overview of the 2007 Act. The Act's genesis has been briefly traced and some legal 'DNA' identified which goes back over 700 years. In addition to the genesis of the Act, it is also important to recall that it forms only one section of a much larger legal canvas upon which is found all the other protections and requirements in international and national law concerning healthcare in the area of medicines. It would be unwise to believe that all the law on medicines and pharmacy is to be found in the 2007 Act.

For the future much will depend upon how effectively the Pharmaceutical Society of Ireland operates the Act, how well the profession responds and how aware the public becomes of the new safeguards and protections which the Act has afforded them. As the Act is rolled out, there will be a raising of standards within the profession and the growth of a healthy intolerance both inside and outside the profession of standards and behaviours which fall short of required norms.

---

33. Section 23.
34. Under Sections 28 and 29 of the Act.
35. Section 35(3).
36. Action at the request of the Council where it appears from the report of an authorised officer that an offence has been committed.
37. No. 27 of 1997.

The Act has confirmed in the twenty-first century a certain commercial advantage and exclusivity for registered pharmacists in the market of supplying medicinal products. There is a price to be paid by the profession for such continuing commercial privilege. The price is the raising and maintenance of standards, the improvement of professional behaviour, a focus on patient and public health needs and accountability to the people for whom the profession exists to serve. On the basis of past performance, it would appear that the public has good grounds to be optimistic that the profession of pharmacy will rise to the challenge. It is interesting to note that after 700 years the old tensions between private commercial gain and patient motivated healthcare have not gone away.

Appendix 12.1 Pharmaceutical Society of Ireland Code of Conduct for Pharmacists

Foreword

The Pharmacy Act 2007 has brought significant and important changes to the regulation of pharmacy and pharmacists in Ireland, including the adoption of a statutory Code of Conduct for pharmacists.

Under the Act, it is a duty of the Pharmaceutical Society of Ireland (PSI), as the pharmacy regulator, to draw up a code of conduct for pharmacists. During 2008 the draft code underwent extensive consultation with the pharmacy profession and sector, and the wider public, as well as submission to the Competition Authority for its opinion, as per the statutory requirement. Following approval by the Minister for Health and Children, Ms Mary Harney TD on 14 November 2008, this Code was laid before the Houses of the Oireachtas in February 2009.

Every pharmacist has an obligation to comply in full with the statutory Code of Conduct. Superintendent and supervising pharmacists have vitally important roles and are expected to ensure and support compliance with the Code. This six-principle Code is a critical element of the new professional regulatory system. It is a public declaration of the principles and ethical standards which govern pharmacists in the practice of their profession, and which the public, patients, other healthcare professionals and society generally require and expect from professional pharmacists as key frontline health professionals. Every pharmacist and pharmacy in the country should regularly consult this important document and ensure that their professional practice is guided and supported by these six principles.

The health, wellbeing, care and safety of their patients is the primary concern of every pharmacist and this is now clearly mandated. Every pharmacist has a responsibility to enhance and improve the reputation and status of the profession, and this Code enables and empowers all in the profession.

Dr Ambrose McLoughlin
PSI Registrar/CEO

Index of contents

The nature and purpose of the Code of Conduct for Pharmacists

As healthcare professionals, practising pharmacists are required not only to display full technical competence in their chosen profession but also to behave with probity and integrity and to be accountable in this regard for their actions (or omissions). The qualities of competence, probity, integrity and accountability which a pharmacist must demonstrate are underwritten by a Code of Conduct to which all pharmacists must subscribe. This Code of Conduct is a public declaration of the principles and ethical standards which govern pharmacists in the practice of their profession. A person dealing with a pharmacist (whether as a patient, a healthcare professional or a member of the general public) is entitled to expect that a pharmacist will conduct himself/herself in accordance with the principles laid down in the Code of Conduct. The Code of Conduct is one of a number of regulatory devices employed by the PSI so as to ensure that any person employing the services of a pharmacist can expect to encounter the highest professional standards in the delivery of pharmacy care, treatment or service.

This Code of Conduct sets out the core principles in accordance with which pharmacists must act and by which they will be judged whilst so acting in the provision of their professional services. The Code of Conduct sets out the principles for professional practice and behaviour which patients, members of the public, other healthcare professionals and society generally require and expect from pharmacists who are registered with the PSI. The Code of Conduct also provides support and guidance to pharmacists as they discharge their professional duties. Pharmacists are expected to exercise their professional judgement in the light of the principles set out in the Code of Conduct.

Every pharmacist is personally responsible under the Code of Conduct for his/her own acts or omissions. Pharmacists may also be responsible under the Code for the acts or omissions of persons operating in the area of pharmacy under their direction, control or supervision.

Principles of the Code of Conduct

The Code of Conduct comprises and is contained in the six principles as follows:

1   The practice by a pharmacist of his/her profession must be directed to maintaining and improving the health, wellbeing, care and safety of the patient. This is the primary principle and the following principles must be read in light of this principle.
2   A pharmacist must employ his/her professional competence, skills and standing in a manner that brings health gain and value to the community and the society in which he/she lives and works.
3   A pharmacist must never abuse the position of trust which they hold in relation to a patient and in particular, they must respect a patient's rights, including their dignity, autonomy, and entitlements to confidentiality and information.
4   A pharmacist must conduct himself/herself in a manner which enhances the service which their profession as a whole provides to society and should not act in a way which might damage the good name of their profession.
5   A pharmacist must maintain a level of competence sufficient to provide his/her professional services effectively and efficiently.
6   A pharmacist must be aware of his/her obligations under this Code and should not do anything in the course of practising as a pharmacist, or permit another person to do anything on his/her behalf, which constitutes a breach of this Code or impairs or compromises his/her ability to observe this Code.

For the purposes of this Code of Conduct, a patient includes a person or persons who stand in such a degree of relationship to a pharmacist that the pharmacist ought to reasonably apprehend that such a person or person's health, wellbeing and care are likely to be affected by the acts or omissions of that pharmacist.

Legislative background

The Pharmacy Act 2007 ('the Act') requires and enables pharmacists to practise in their profession in a regulated, controlled and safe environment in a manner that is focussed on the safety and interests of their patients. Section 7(2)(a)(iii) of the Act requires the PSI to draw up a Code of Conduct for pharmacists. The Code of Conduct applies to all pharmacists whether they practise in community, hospital, industry, regulatory or administrative environments or in any other form of professional practice.

It is the responsibility of all pharmacists to make every reasonable effort to ensure that everything that they do (or that is done under their supervision, or in their name, by any other individual under their jurisdiction) conforms with the principles laid down in the Code of Conduct.

Pharmacists should note that Section 33 of the Act defines 'professional misconduct' *inter alia* as 'any act, omission or pattern of conduct that is a breach of the Code of Conduct for registered pharmacists . . . .' If there is a finding of professional misconduct against a pharmacist, then under Section 48 of the Act, the Council can impose certain penalties on the offending pharmacist including: admonishment or censure, the attachment of conditions to the registration of the pharmacist, the suspension of registration for a specified period, the cancellation of registration, a prohibition for a specified period on applying for restoration to the register.

The operation and application of the Code of Conduct for Pharmacists

The following part of the document is illustrative rather than prescriptive. It seeks to establish some practical conduct templates for pharmacists in respect of each of the six principles of the Code of Conduct. These templates are intended to direct and guide pharmacists on the proper use of the Code in terms of their relationships and interactions with patients, other healthcare professionals (including fellow pharmacists), pharmacy students, employees (including fellow employees), employers, their Regulatory Authority (PSI) and the general public.

It sets out some of the main practical considerations which pharmacists should take into account when applying the principles of the Code of Conduct. The guidance notes are neither exhaustive nor exclusive. Every circumstance in the professional life of a pharmacist is governed by the application of the principles of the Code of Conduct. Decisions must be made on a case-by-case basis. The professional conduct of a pharmacist in any given situation will be judged by a reference to the principles set out in the Code of Conduct.

Principle One

The practice by a pharmacist of his/her profession must be directed to maintaining and improving the health, wellbeing, care and safety of the patient. This is the primary principle and the following principles must be read in light of this principle.

In order to fulfil his/her obligations under this principle a pharmacist should:

- Ensure the health of the patient is their primary focus.
- Be cognisant of the wellbeing of the patient, including non-medical holistic needs.
- Endeavour to ensure the safety of the patient in all circumstances by decision-making, which may at times conflict with the stated requirements of the patient.
- Provide a proper standard of practice and care to those for whom they provide professional services.
- Use their professional skills, competence and specialised knowledge about medicines, health-related products, medicinal and non-medicinal therapies for the benefit of patients.
- Not purchase or supply any product, including a medicinal product, where there is reason to doubt its safety, efficacy or quality or where a product may impose a hazard to a patient's health or wellbeing.
- Encourage the rational and proper use of medicines.
- Ensure suitable controls and accountability mechanisms are in place, appropriate to the area of practice, to govern the management of the supply and distribution of medicinal products which have a potential for abuse or dependency.
- Promote compliance with effective medicine and treatment regimes, and seek to address issues that may impinge on a patient obtaining the best result from his treatment.
- Ensure that all professional activities undertaken are covered by appropriate professional indemnity arrangements.
- Ensure that in instances where they are unable to provide prescribed medicines or pharmacy services to a patient they must take reasonable action to ensure these medicines/services are provided and the patient's care is not jeopardised.
- Honour commitments, agreements and arrangements for the provision of professional service having due regard to their competence and other options for assistance available to a patient.

This list is neither exhaustive nor exclusive.

Principle Two

A pharmacist must employ his/her professional competence, skills and standing in a manner that brings health gain and value to the community and the society in which he/she lives and works.

In order to fulfil his/her obligations under this principle a pharmacist should:

- Be cognisant of societal requirements for the provision of a pharmacy service.
- Ensure discriminatory practices are not demonstrated towards any class of patient or sector of the community.
- Support positive changes in the healthcare system.
- Actively influence and participate in health policy development, review and revision.
- Safeguard society as a whole by ensuring that the protection of vulnerable individuals is given due significance and any cases of mistreatment or abuse referred to the appropriate authorities.
- Take care when disposing of medicinal products and hazardous substances.
- Raise concerns with the appropriate authority if policies, systems, working conditions or the actions, professional performance or health of others compromise patient care or public safety.
- Support the advancement of knowledge and practice by conducting and supporting research and development and promoting pharmacy education and training, wherever possible.
- Comply with medicines legislation, the directive of the Irish Medicines Board and law enforcement agencies including An Garda Síochána and Customs and Excise.
- Support cost-effective therapies and prudent use of healthcare resources.
- Ensure all information provided to the public is legal, truthful and rational.
- Serve the patient and public interest and never improperly confer an advantage or disadvantage on any individual.

This list is neither exhaustive nor exclusive.

Principle Three

A pharmacist must never abuse the position of trust which they hold in relation to a patient and in particular, they must respect a patient's rights, including their dignity, autonomy, and entitlements to confidentiality and information.

In order to fulfil his/her obligations under this principle a pharmacist should:

- Ensure the position of trust they hold in respect of a patient is never abused.
- Ensure the patient is treated with courtesy, dignity, integrity and honesty.
- Ensure that the patient receives all his/her entitlements.
- Ensure the patient's confidentiality and privacy is respected.
- Avoid arrangements with prescribers, other pharmacists or other healthcare professionals that could affect any individual's independent professional judgement or interfere with the patient's right to choose a treatment, care or pharmacy service.
- Recognise and endeavour to avoid conflicts of interest and declare any personal or professional interests to those who may be affected.
- Not accept inducements, gifts, offers or benefits that could be reasonably perceived as affecting their independent professional judgement.
- Ensure that their professional judgement is not impaired by personal or commercial interests including incentives, targets or similar measures.
- Seek to involve patients in decisions regarding their health and should explain options available to help patients make informed decisions regarding service and treatment options.
- Not allow their personal views to prejudice care and treatment of patients.
- Provide honest, relevant, accurate, current and appropriate information to patients regarding the nature, cost, value and benefit of medicines, health-related products and services provided by them.
- Comply with all relevant laws, regulations, rules, professional standards.
- Recognise the entitlement of the patient to appropriate information and disclose material risks associated with medication therapy.
- Ensure the patient is at all times acknowledged as a person.

This list is neither exhaustive nor exclusive.

Principle Four

A pharmacist must conduct himself/herself in a manner which enhances the service which their profession as a whole provides to society and should not act in a way which might damage the good name of their profession.

In order to fulfil his/her obligations under this principle a pharmacist should:

- Respect the expertise and care delivery of other healthcare professionals.
- Work effectively with other healthcare individuals.
- Practise within relevant legislative and professional regulatory guidance.

- Accept responsibility for all of his or her professional activities, and for all activities undertaken under their direct supervision.
- Report and make disclosures to relevant authorities on matters affecting or having the potential to impact on patient safety and wellbeing.
- Endeavour to ensure that each patient is assisted in a manner which facilitates the care and treatment that they may be receiving from another recognised healthcare professional.
- Not practise under conditions which compromise their ability to exercise their professional judgement and integrity or the quality of their practice.
- Ensure that information obtained in the course of professional practice is used only for the purpose for which it was obtained.
- Maintain patient confidentiality unless detrimental to a patient's safety and welfare, and ensure that all persons who operate under their direction and supervision conserve this confidentiality.
- Be aware of the limitations of their professional knowledge and refer patients to other appropriate healthcare avenues when required.
- Respond honestly, openly and courteously to complaints and criticisms.
- Co-operate with inspections and investigations into their or another healthcare professional's fitness to practise, and the operation of a retail pharmacy business.
- Respect the integrity, skills and expertise of colleagues and other healthcare professionals, and maintain and promote professional relationships to ensure patients' needs are met.
- Not impose conditions on other pharmacists or health professionals which compromise their professional judgement, integrity or quality of service or impinge on the ability to meet professional and legal obligations for patient care and safety.
- Disclose any concerns adversely affecting patient care and safety to the PSI.

This list is neither exhaustive nor exclusive.

Principle Five

A pharmacist must maintain a level of competence sufficient to provide his/her professional services effectively and efficiently.

In order to fulfil his/her obligations under this principle a pharmacist should:

- Maintain, develop and update competence and knowledge of evidence-based learning, which includes CPD (continuing professional development) and CE (continuing education).
- Ensure reasonable due care and expertise is employed before providing a product or service.

- Seek all relevant information required to assess the patient's needs and where necessary refer the individual to other relevant health professionals, services and organisations.
- Communicate and work effectively with patients and other health professionals, and ensure individuals who work and deliver patient care under their supervision and direction have sufficient competence and communication skills.
- Undertake regular reviews, audits and risk assessments, both to improve quality of service and to inform learning requirements and possible deficits.
- Be accurate and impartial when teaching others and when providing or publishing information, to ensure they do not mislead others or make claims that cannot be justified.

This list is neither exhaustive nor exclusive.

Principle Six

A pharmacist must be aware of his/her obligations under this Code and should not do anything in the course of practising as a pharmacist, or permit another person to do anything on his/her behalf, which constitutes a breach of this Code or impairs or compromises his/her ability to observe this Code.

In order to fulfil his/her obligations under this principle a pharmacist should:

- Ensure he/she displays awareness, application and adherence to the principles of the Code.
- Ensure he/she is aware of all current regulations, standards and guidance governing the practice of pharmacy.
- Ensure active participation and interaction with the regulator.
- Display and perform appropriate stewardship in respect of the partnership management of a patient's health needs.
- Ensure that clearly defined parameters and accountabilities are specified and understood by all individuals in the practice environment.
- Ensure that he/she is objective in behaviour and decision-making.
- Ensure that he/she takes account of the views of those under their jurisdiction, but reaches his/her own conclusions and decisions.
- Ensure that he/she does not impose any constraint, financial, tangible or intangible on any individual bound by these principles which would impact that person's objectivity and judgement.
- Ensure that he/she practises, and encourages others to operate, in as open and transparent a manner as possible.

- Ensure that he/she promotes and supports the principles of the Code by leadership and by example.
- Ensure the maintenance of and adherence to a sound system of internal controls in the practice environment, to manage risk and promote safety.
- Ensure, in accordance with his/her role, that an optimal practice environment and required resources are evaluated and provided.
- Ensure that work practices inconsistent with professional practice as governed by the principles of the Code do not occur.

This list is neither exhaustive nor exclusive.

13

Pharmacy Act – regulations and rules

L Clarke, P Weedle and D Dowling

The Pharmacy Act 2007 (the 'Act') was commenced in a planned and phased manner over a three-year period to ensure the proper operation of the legislation. In total, there were four commencement orders, with the last one being made by the Minister for Health and Children on 1 May 2010.[1] The Minister is also empowered by virtue of Section 8 of the Act to confer by order, additional (but connected) functions and powers on the Pharmaceutical Society of Ireland (PSI). No such orders have been made at the time of writing.

The Pharmacy Act 2007 provides at Section 18 that the Minister may, for the purposes of the health, safety and convenience of the public, make regulations regarding the operation of retail pharmacy businesses. The Act further provides under Sections 11, 30 and 74 that the Council of the PSI may make rules to set out in greater detail the procedures and requirements which will be operated by the Council in carrying out its various functions under the Act. Regulations and rules have been made under a number of these sections in tandem with the phased implementation of the Act itself and they are discussed in this chapter.

The PSI also had a duty imposed on it by virtue of Section 7(2)(a)(iii) of the Pharmacy Act to draw up a code of conduct for pharmacists (see Appendix 12.1). The promulgation of regulations, statutory rules and a code of conduct,

---

1. Pharmacy Act 2007 (Commencement) Order 2007, S.I. No. 243 of 2007; Pharmacy Act 2007 (Commencement) Order 2008, S.I. No. 487 of 2008; Pharmacy Act 2007 (Commencement) Order 2009, S.I. No. 281 of 2009; Pharmacy Act 2007 (Section 64(9)) Order 2009, S.I. No. 282 of 2009.

when taken in conjunction with the provisions of the Act, provide a framework to ensure that criteria are established and met in:

i   the operation of each retail pharmacy business;
ii   the carrying out by pharmacists of their professional obligations;
iii the conduct by PSI of its affairs.

Regulation of retail pharmacy businesses regulations

The Regulation of Retail Pharmacy Businesses Regulations 2008 (the 'Regulations'),[2] which were made by the Minister for Health and Children under Section 18 of the Pharmacy Act, set out certain requirements to be complied with by persons carrying on retail pharmacy businesses. They also lay down requirements in respect of the sourcing, sale, supply and keeping of records in respect of medicinal products for human and veterinary use. Requirements in respect of staff, premises, equipment and procedures are also laid down, including certain responsibilities that must be discharged by superintendent and supervising pharmacists.

The Regulations reinforce many of the obligations that apply to pharmacists under legislation governing matters such as human and veterinary medicines, controlled drugs, animal remedies and poisons. However, they also put on a statutory footing many aspects of good pharmaceutical practice which did not previously have any legislative basis, relating to matters such as review of prescriptions, counselling of patients and disposal of medicines. The Regulations also introduce the titles of 'superintendent pharmacist' and 'supervising pharmacist' to describe the different categories of pharmacist responsible for managing and supervising retail pharmacy businesses as provided for in Sections 27–29 of the Pharmacy Act 2007 and provide some additional detail on their respective responsibilities. Further new requirements include the obligation to have a separate, designated patient consultation area in the pharmacy and to maintain a contemporaneous 'duty register'.

Staff, premises, equipment and procedures

The Regulations set out various responsibilities for pharmacy owners in relation to staff, premises, equipment and procedures in order to avoid the deterioration of any medicines stored, dispensed, compounded or sold.[3] Pharmacy services may only be delivered from the premises registered with the PSI and the layout of the premises must facilitate the supervision by a pharmacist of all the professional activity taking place there. The disposal of

---

2. S.I. No. 488 of 2008. Copyright Houses of the Oireachtas 2008.
3. Regulation 4.

any medicines in the pharmacy must not result in any danger or risk to public health or the environment. Controlled drugs must be stored in a safe or cabinet that meets the requirements of the Misuse of Drugs (Safe Custody) Regulations 1982 as amended[4] and which is sufficiently big to hold the quantity of such drugs to be stored.

Finally, a separate and designated area for patient counselling is required.

Management and supervision of retail pharmacy businesses

The management and supervisory requirements pertaining to a retail pharmacy business are specified in the Regulations and the particular responsibilities held by the pharmacy owner, the superintendent pharmacist and the supervising pharmacist are delineated as follows.[5]

The part of the retail pharmacy business that consists of the management and administration of the sale and supply of human and veterinary medicines must be carried out in accordance with all legal requirements and under the personal control of the superintendent pharmacist. Each premises where the retail pharmacy business is carried on must be in the whole-time charge of a supervising pharmacist who has at least three years' post-registration experience. The certificate of registration of the supervising pharmacist must be conspicuously displayed in the pharmacy. A record of the pharmacists on duty must be maintained in a contemporaneous, ongoing retrievable form (i.e. a 'duty register').

The sale or supply of all medicines in the pharmacy, including veterinary medicines and general sale medicines, and the dispensing and compounding of prescriptions for human and veterinary medicines, must be carried out by or under the personal supervision of a registered pharmacist. Prescription-only medicines, both human and veterinary, and prescription-exempt products which are classified as CD5 (controlled drugs, Schedule 5) under the Misuse of Drugs Regulations 1988 as amended[6] must not be accessible to the public for self-selection. Cooperation with directions of authorities such as the Irish Medicines Board (IMB) in relation to product withdrawals and recalls is required.

The superintendent pharmacist and pharmacy owner must be satisfied as to the identity and registration status of any pharmacist employed in the pharmacy. They must also ensure that all pharmacists and other staff in the

---

4. Misuse of Drugs (Safe Custody) Regulations 1982 (S.I. No. 321 of 1982) as amended by Misuse of Drugs Regulations 1988 (S.I. No. 328 of 1998).
5. Regulation 5.
6. Misuse of Drugs Regulations 1988 (S.I. No. 328 of 1988) as amended by S.I. No. 342 of 1993, S.I. No. 273 of 1999, S.I. No. 53 of 2006, S.I. No. 200 of 2007, S.I. No. 63 of 2009, S.I. No. 122 of 2009 and S.I. No. 200 of 2010.

pharmacy have the knowledge, skills (including language skills) and general fitness to practise required to discharge the duties assigned to them.

Medicinal products: sourcing, storage, sale and supply

All medicinal products sourced by a retail pharmacy business must be obtained from an authorised manufacturer or wholesaler in Ireland or in another state within the European Economic Area (EEA).[7] Provision is made in the Regulations for the acceptance of returned stock previously dispensed or supplied on the understanding that this would never be reused but disposed of appropriately. Allowance is made for the occasional transfer of stock between retail pharmacy businesses to meet the immediate prescription needs of an individual patient. The quality of human and veterinary medicines being handled by the pharmacy should be assured by adhering to the storage conditions specified in the marketing authorisation or any other applicable standards.[8] The Regulations prohibit[9] the sale of medicinal products that do not have a current marketing authorisation or fall into the category of exempted medicinal products provided for in Regulation 6(4) of the Medicinal Products (Control of Placing on the Market) Regulations 2007.[10]

Review of medicine therapy and patient counselling

It is a requirement of the Regulations that prescriptions be reviewed and patients counselled when supplying medicinal products on foot of a prescription.[11] A pharmacist, prior to the dispensing of a prescription and supply of a medicinal product, must review the prescription having regard to its pharmaceutical and therapeutic appropriateness for the patient. The nature of the review is indicated in broad professional and patient safety terms and following its completion, the pharmacist must ensure that the patient has sufficient information and advice for the proper use and storage of the prescribed medicinal product. The pharmacist must offer to discuss with the patient or his or her representative such matters as he or she, exercising professional judgement, deems significant.

---

7. Regulation 6.
8. Regulation 7.
9. Regulation 8.
10. S.I. No. 540 of 2007 as amended by S.I. No. 3 of 2009 and S.I. No. 287 of 2010. This prohibition does not apply until 30 April 2011 to herbal medicinal products and homeopathic medicinal products to which regulation 11 of the Medicinal Products (Control of Placing on the Market) Regulations 2007 apply (see Chapter 4, Placing medicines on the market).
11. Regulation 9.

Counselling when supplying medicinal products other than on foot of a prescription is also provided for in the Regulations.[12] In particular, the pharmacist must be satisfied that the purchaser is aware of the appropriate use of the product, that the product is being sought for that use and, insofar as the pharmacist is aware, the product is not intended for abuse or misuse.

Other requirements

The Regulations also specify that veterinary medicinal products must be sold or supplied in accordance with the applicable animal remedies regulations.[13]

The Regulations reinforce the requirement to comply with the record-keeping requirements provided for in the Medicinal Products (Prescription and Control of Supply) Regulations 2003 as amended,[14] and the Misuse of Drugs Regulations 1988 as amended, and also require the keeping of appropriate patient medication records. Provision is made for the validation and certification of computer software used to maintain any of these records. The keeping of records, marking of prescriptions and other related matters applicable to veterinary medicines are also addressed.[15]

The Council of the PSI may publish, with the prior approval of the Minister for Health and Children, detailed guidelines to facilitate compliance with the regulations.[16] Guidelines published to date deal with matters such as patient consultation areas[17] and the sale and supply of codeine-containing products.[18]

Finally, designated offences are specified.[19]

Pharmaceutical Society of Ireland rules

As stated in the introduction, the Council of the PSI may make rules relating to its functions under Sections 11, 30 and 74 of the Pharmacy Act 2007. Section 11 empowers the Council to make rules generally relating to the Act; Section 30, in relation to the activities of pharmaceutical assistants; and Section 74, in relation to the keeping of open shop for the sale of poisons. The Council may not make rules for any purpose for which the Minister for Health and Children may make regulations under Section 18[20] and any statutory rules

---

12. Regulation 10.
13. Regulation 11.
14. S.I. No. 540 of 2003 as amended by S.I. No. 510 of 2005, Act No. 3 of 2006, S.I. No. 201 of 2007, S.I. No. 540 of 2007, S.I. No. 512 of 2008, S.I. No. 442 of 2009.
15. Regulations 12 and 13.
16. Regulation 14.
17. Guidelines on Patient Consultation Areas in Retail Pharmacy Businesses, PSI, May 2010.
18. Non-Prescription Medicinal Products Containing Codeine: Guidance for Pharmacists on Safe Supply to Patients, PSI, May 2010.
19. Regulation 15.
20. Section 11(4), Pharmacy Act 2007.

made by the Council require the consent or approval of the Minister.[21] At the time of writing, the Council has made the following statutory rules:

- Council Rules;[22]
- Education and Training Rules;[23]
- Registration Rules;[24]
- Retail Pharmacy Businesses Registration Rules;[25]
- Fee Rules.[26]

Council Rules

The Council Rules[22] lay down the procedures to be followed for the selection of members of the PSI for appointment to the Council by the Minister for Health and Children under Section 10(3)(f) of the Pharmacy Act 2007. They also lay down the procedure for the filling of casual vacancies which may arise on the Council and for the election of a President and vice-President of the Council. The procedures to be followed in relation to Council meetings are also described and deal with matters such as the frequency of meetings, setting of agendas, recording of minutes, motions and voting.

In addition, the rules provide for the appointment of advisory committees by the Council and describe how they are to be managed and their reporting relationship to the Council. The rules also set out requirements relating to financial and resource management of the PSI, which include the obligation to submit a corporate strategy and an annual service plan to the Minister. The rules also require the Council to adopt and publish a governance framework, which may include a code of conduct for members of the Council, its advisory committees and the PSI staff, and standing orders and procedures for Council meetings.

Education and Training Rules

The Education and Training Rules[23] impose upon the Council an obligation to prepare, adopt and publish a framework document setting out certain

---

21. Sections 11(5), 30(2) and 74(4), Pharmacy Act 2007.
22. Pharmaceutical Society of Ireland (Council) Rules 2008, S.I. No. 492 of 2008. Copyright Houses of the Oireachtas 2008.
23. Pharmaceutical Society of Ireland (Education and Training) Rules 2008, S.I. No. 493 of 2008. Copyright Houses of the Oireachtas 2008.
24. Pharmaceutical Society of Ireland (Registration) Rules 2008, S.I. No. 494 of 2008. Copyright Houses of the Oireachtas 2008.
25. Pharmaceutical Society of Ireland (Retail Pharmacy Businesses) (Registration) Rules 2008, S. I. No. 495 of 2008. Copyright Houses of the Oireachtas 2008.
26. Pharmaceutical Society of Ireland (Fee) Rules 2008 and 2010, S.I. No. 496 of 2008 as amended by S.I. No. 257 of 2010. Copyright Houses of the Oireachtas 2008 and 2010.

designated learning and competencies which a person must demonstrate before he or she can become registered as a pharmacist. The Council is obliged to review and update the designated learning and competencies at least every five years to take account of advancements in pharmacy and healthcare internationally and national policy in the areas of pharmacy, healthcare practice and higher education. The schedule to the rules specifies the minimum designated learning and competencies that must be acquired as part of an educational programme leading to obtaining qualification as a pharmacist.

The rules specify the type of qualifications which are considered appropriate for practice for the purposes of Section 16(1) of the Pharmacy Act. Part 3 of the rules permits the Council to 'recognise' a degree in pharmacy as being a qualification appropriate for practice provided it meets with certain requirements, including imparting to the student the designated learning and competencies. The Council is required to publish criteria for the recognition and approval of pharmacy degree programmes and to review them at least every five years.

The rules lay down the procedure to be followed by an educational institution seeking recognition and approval of a pharmacy degree programme. It is the duty of the Council to review approved degree programmes at least every five years to ensure that they continue to comply with the requirements of these rules and the Pharmacy Act. The rules specify the manner in which such reviews and 'visits' to educational institutions should be conducted.

Parts 4 and 5 of the rules deal with the in-service practical training programme and the Professional Registration Examination that must be undertaken by trainee pharmacists.

Registration Rules

The Registration Rules[27] set out the mechanics by which a person who wishes to become registered as a pharmacist may do so. The four schedules to these rules set out respectively, the particulars which must accompany an application for first registration by a pharmacist; an application for continued registration by a pharmacist; an application for continued registration by a pharmaceutical assistant; and an application for recognition of a third-country qualification (i.e. not one gained in Ireland or elsewhere in the EEA or Switzerland) as a qualification appropriate for practice.

The rules also set out the information which must be recorded in the various registers which the Council is obliged to maintain under Section 13 of the Pharmacy Act (i.e. register of pharmacists, register of pharmaceutical assistants, register of druggists and register of retail pharmacy businesses). The rules confirm that that part of the register of pharmacists other than

---

27. Pharmaceutical Society of Ireland (Registration) Rules 2008.

Part B (where details of visiting pharmacists from other EEA states are entered under Section 24B of the Act) is to be known as 'Part A' of the register.

These rules prescribe the format of certificates of registration for pharmacists, pharmaceutical assistants and for retail pharmacy businesses. Procedures for the removal of registrants from the registers for failure to apply for continued registration or to pay fees are set out in the Rules.

Part 6 of the rules describe the circumstances in which a pharmacist qualification obtained in a third country may be recognised as a qualification appropriate for practice in Ireland.

Retail Pharmacy Business Registration Rules

The Retail Pharmacy Business Registration Rules[28] set out the procedures to be followed by a person wishing to register a retail pharmacy business pursuant to Section 17 of the Pharmacy Act 2007. The rules set out the particulars to be provided to the PSI with the application. They provide for the notification of material changes to premises and of certain personnel, for the cancellation of registration and for restoration to the register of retail pharmacy businesses. They also set out certain time limits within which registration issues must be dealt with and the procedure to be followed if the Council proposes to refuse an application for registration of a retail pharmacy business.

Fee Rules

The Fee Rules[29] set the procedure for the charging of fees by the PSI and for approval of those fees by the Minister for Health and Children. They set out the amount of the fees payable by applicants for registration, continued registration, and restoration to the various registers maintained by the PSI. They also provide for fees for cancellation from, and for the notification of changes to, the relevant registers.

The rules also set out the amount of the fees to be paid in the case of removal of conditions attaching to registration, and fees for replacement certificates of registration and for the issue of other certificates. Fees in respect of the in-service practical training programme, the Professional Registration Examination, the recognition of third-country qualifications and other related fees are also set out in these Rules. These fees may be varied from time to time by the Council with the approval of the Minister.

---

28. Pharmaceutical Society of Ireland (Retail Pharmacy Businesses) (Registration) Rules 2008.
29. Pharmaceutical Society of Ireland (Fees) Rules 2008 and 2010.

14

The pharmacy disciplinary system

F Crean and P Weedle

One of the novel features of the Pharmacy Act 2007[1] (the 'Act') is the fitness to practise regime and the disciplinary apparatus that is to be operated by the Pharmaceutical Society of Ireland (PSI). Professional disciplinary proceedings aim to secure three important objectives:

i   the protection of members of the public;
ii the declaration and maintenance of standards within the profession;
iii the deterrence of future misconduct through the imposition of sanctions on practitioners.[2]

Members of the disciplinary committees when exercising disciplinary functions perform tasks often undertaken by judges, such as deciding whether facts have been proved, applying the rules to those facts and determining sanctions. The exercise of these 'quasi-judicial'[3] functions by committees established under the Act can have very serious consequences for pharmacists. The operation of disciplinary tribunals by professional bodies has been endorsed by the courts. In *R* v. *General Medical Council Ex. p. Nicolaides*,[4] Tucker J. stated:

> Most, if not all professions, are self-regulatory and self-regulating. They establish their own domestic tribunals for the purpose of disciplining their members and controlling their affairs. It is far more satisfactory that they should do so rather than the court's time should be taken up or any other external body should be involved. It is

---

1. No. 20 of 2007. Copyright House of the Oireachtas 2007.
2. *Dey* v. *General Medical Council* [2001] UKPC 44 at para. 11.
3. *Allbutt* v. *GCMER* (1889) 23 Q.B.D. 400 at p. 409.
4. [2001] Lloyd's Rep. 525 at para. 34.

appropriate that the professions should set their own standards and decide whether or not they have been breached in any particular case, and if so, what disciplinary measures are required. Provided these tribunals are independent and impartial both in fact and in appearance, they do not offend against the rules of natural justice which have long been a feature of our common law.

Overview of disciplinary system

The disciplinary apparatus introduced by the Pharmacy Act 2007 operates at a number of levels. The Council of the Pharmaceutical Society of Ireland (the 'Council') is empowered to deal with certain categories of complaints and to impose specified sanctions in respect of complaints that are upheld. In order to discharge its statutory functions, the Council establishes a number of committees.

The first stage in the process is the making of a complaint. The Act provides for a filtration mechanism in respect of complaints whereby a preliminary assessment is made of each complaint in order to decide whether it should proceed further. This stage of the process is carried out by the Preliminary Proceedings Committee (PPC). If a complaint proceeds beyond this stage, it can be resolved either by a hearing before a committee of inquiry or by mediation where appropriate. There are two types of committee of inquiry that are empowered to hear such a complaint, depending on the nature of the complaint: the Professional Conduct Committee (PCC) and the Health Committee. After the resolution of the complaint, a report is made to the Council which acts on the findings of the committee or the mediator, as appropriate. The Council has the power to impose certain sanctions. Where more serious sanctions are recommended, these do not have any legal effect until they are confirmed by the High Court.

Structure of disciplinary apparatus

The Council is required by the Act to appoint three disciplinary committees: a Preliminary Proceedings Committee, a Professional Conduct Committee and a Health Committee.[5] The composition of these disciplinary committees is prescribed in detail by Section 34 of the Act and by paragraph 7 of Schedule 1 to the Act. Each disciplinary committee must have a majority of non-pharmacist members,[6] though at least a third of the committee must be registered pharmacists and at least two committee members must be pharmacy owners.[7]

---

5. Pharmacy Act 2007, Section 34(1).
6. Section 34(3).
7. Section 34(4) and (5).

A disciplinary committee is chaired by a committee member nominated by the Council.[8] The quorum of a disciplinary committee[9] considering a complaint against a pharmacy owner must include at least one registered pharmacist who is a pharmacy owner.[10] At least one member of each committee must be appointed to safeguard the interests of the public.[11] Concurrent membership of more than one disciplinary committee is not permitted[12] and the President of the Society is ineligible for membership of a disciplinary committee.[13]

Making a complaint

The disciplinary process is set in motion once a complaint is received by the Society. A complaint, in writing, or in another form acceptable to the Council,[14] may be made by or on behalf of any person or by the Registrar;[15] there is no requirement of *locus standi* to make a complaint. Material that may give rise to a complaint can arise in a number of ways. It appears that evidence given in confidence to the Garda Síochána may be disclosed by them to the Society once they are persuaded that the material in question is relevant to an inquiry being held by the Society.[16] This is so even if there is no request from the Society. In addition, a judge may make a complaint arising out of a pharmacist's conduct as a witness in the course of a trial in an appropriate case.[17]

The Council must inform the pharmacist or pharmacy owner in question of the fact that a complaint has been made against him or her and must give the pharmacist or pharmacy owner a copy of the complaint.[18] Although a complaint may be withdrawn after having been made, the committee of

---

8. Paragraph 7(5) of Schedule 1.
9. The quorum is fixed by the Council pursuant to paragraph 7(6) of Schedule 1.
10. Section 34(6).
11. Section 34(3).
12. Section 34(7). In O'Callaghan v. *The Disciplinary Tribunal* [2002] 1 I.R.1 it was held that there was nothing unfair in a commonality of membership of a preliminary practices committee involved in screening a particular complaint and a committee of inquiry that heard the substantive complaint. Nonetheless, such an issue will not now arise under the 2007 Act.
13. Section 34(2).
14. Section 35(2).
15. Section 35(3).
16. *Woolgar* v. *Chief Constable of Sussex Police* [2000] 1 W.L.R. 25 at p. 36 D-F. This disclosure may be made in the public interest provided that confidentiality will be maintained over the material in question and that it will be used solely for the purposes of the inquiry. In that case, the regulatory body concerned did not make a request for information.
17. *Meadow* v. *GMC* [2007] 1 Q.B. 462. In that case, it was held that the common law immunity from suit enjoyed by witnesses did not necessarily extend to professional disciplinary matters.
18. Section 35(4) and Section 36(2).

inquiry, acting in concert with the Council, may still proceed with a hearing on foot of that complaint.[19]

The Preliminary Proceedings Committee

The first stage in the processing of a complaint is the referral of same to the Preliminary Proceedings Committee (PPC). The function of the PPC is to consider whether the complaint warrants further action being taken and to advise the Council accordingly.

In order to reach a decision, the PPC has a number of powers to gather written evidence within a specified time frame.[20] The PPC may require the complainant to verify his or her complaint by way of affidavit[21] and may also require the complainant to provide further information.[22] The PPC may also invite the registered pharmacist or pharmacy owner about whom the complaint is made to submit observations or to give specified information in relation to the complaint. Indeed, the registered pharmacist or pharmacy owner may supply information and submit observations to the PPC without being required or invited to do so.[23] The PPC must consider all of the information it has gathered and must decide whether the complaint is frivolous, vexatious, made in bad faith, or whether it merits further action.[24] The PPC must then advise the Council of its decision.

The purpose of the screening process in the context of professional disciplinary proceedings has been held by the courts to involve two fundamental considerations. The primary purpose of this stage of the disciplinary process is to provide a 'protective filter'[25] and 'an essential safeguard' to ensure that a practitioner is not harassed by groundless complaints.[26] This purpose is achieved by ensuring that such frivolous or vexatious complaints are summarily disposed of.[27]

---

19. Section 44(b).
20. Section 38(2) and (3).
21. Section 38(2)(a).
22. Section 38(2)(b). The PPC may require such further information to be in the form of a statutory declaration.
23. Section 38(4). In *O'Callaghan* v. *Disciplinary Tribunal* [2002] 1 I.R.1, it was held that the decision to hold an inquiry into the professional misconduct of any person was so grave as to entitle that person to be put on notice of any preliminary inquiry. Similarly, in Ó *Ceallaigh* v. *An Bord Altranais* [2000] 4 I.R. 54, the Supreme Court held that as the Nurses Act 1985 carried with it the presumption of constitutionality, its provisions also carried the presumption that the powers and functions granted by it would be exercised in accordance with fair procedure.
24. Section 38(5).
25. *R* v. *General Medical Council; Ex parte Gee* [1986] 1 W.L.R. 226 at p. 238E.
26. *The Law Society* v. *Walker* [2007] 3 I.R. 581; *R* v. *General Medical Council; Ex parte Gee* [1986] 1 W.L.R. 1247 at 1257A.
27. *The Law Society* v. *Walker* [2007] 3 I.R. 581 at para. 30.

In *R* v. *GMC ex parte Toth*,[28] it was held by Lightman J. that the screening process fulfilled two functions:

> The Act and Rules set out to provide a just balance between the legitimate expectation of the complainant that a complaint of serious professional misconduct will be fully investigated and the need for legitimate safeguards for the practitioner, who as a professional person may be considered particularly vulnerable to and damaged by unwarranted charges against him.

In *The Law Society* v. *Walker*[29] Finnegan P. (as he then was) provided guidance as to how the screening process should be fulfilled. In that case, the court considered the procedures of the Disciplinary Tribunal of the Law Society. The then President outlined the functions and duties of that tribunal as follows:

> I am satisfied that the function of the Tribunal is to consider all matters on Affidavit before it. While at this stage of the procedures the Tribunal is not the fact finding body it may for the purposes of deciding on whether a *prima facie* case is disclosed make findings of fact where the facts are clear, for example, where the complaint is based on a clear misapprehension as to the facts or the law. Subject to this the Tribunal should consider all the material before it and determine whether the application has any real prospect of being established at an inquiry any doubt being resolved in favour of an inquiry being held.[30]

Finnegan P. held that a factor to be considered in determining whether a *prima facie* case is disclosed is the fact that the applicable standard of proof is the criminal standard.[31] It is likely that these remarks, though concerning the disciplinary procedures of the Law Society, apply with equal force to the PPC. It has been held that a preliminary screening committee should be slow to dispose of a complaint when the decision may be inconsistent with the decision made by another public body with medical personnel or input, such as a coroner, and reasons should be given for any departure from the reasoning of such other decision.[32]

If a complaint relating to the conduct of a pharmacist is deemed by the PPC to disclose a *prima facie* case, it is likely that additional evidence of such conduct can be put before a committee of inquiry without further reference to the PPC provided that all other aspects of fair procedures are afforded to the accused. It has been held that the rules governing the General Medical Council

28. [2000] 1 W.L.R. 2209.
29. [2007] 3 I.R. 581.
30. Ibid. at para. 39.
31. Ibid. at para. 31.
32. *Woods* v. *GMC* [2002] EWHC 1484 Admin.

allow its Professional Conduct Committee to deal with additional evidence of a course of conduct constituting the subject matter of a complaint but which had come to light since referral from its Preliminary Proceedings Committee as long as the evidence to be put in support of the complaint is notified to the accused in accordance with the rules.[33]

Referral from the PPC

Once the Council receives the advice of the PPC, it must decide whether it will take further action. The Council does not have the power to decline to proceed with a complaint if the PPC recommends that further action is warranted.[34] If the PPC advises that the complaint warrants further action being taken, or if the Council decides of its own motion that such further action is warranted,[35] the next phase of the disciplinary process is engaged. If the Council decides that no further action is warranted, it must inform the complainant, the registered pharmacist or pharmacy owner and the PPC of its decision.[36]

If the Council decides that the complaint does warrant further action being taken, the PPC must refer the complaint to the appropriate committee of inquiry or to mediation within the meaning of the Act.[37] The relevant committees of inquiry are the Professional Conduct Committee and the Health Committee. The Health Committee is advised by a registered medical practitioner who is appointed by the Council[38] but who does not have voting rights on the committee.[39]

If a complaint is referred for mediation, that is not necessarily the end of the matter. If the mediator indicates that the matter cannot be resolved by mediation within the meaning of the Act, or that the matter can be more appropriately resolved by a committee of inquiry, then the matter is remitted to the PPC, which must then refer the matter to the appropriate committee of inquiry.[40]

As soon as is practicable after a complaint has been referred to a committee of inquiry, the committee concerned must notify the registered

---

33. *Gee* v. *General Medical Council* [1987] 1 W.L.R. 564 at p. 577.
34. It appears that the power of the Council to decide whether to take further action in Section 39(1) is qualified by the provisions of Section 40(1).
35. Section 40(1).
36. Section 39(2). In *Singapore Medical Council* v. *GMC* T.L.R., it was held that the procedural rights enjoyed by a complainant in this regard do not necessarily extend to a body acting in the public interest. In that case the court considered that such a body was more properly classified as an informant rather than a complainant.
37. Section 40(1). It would appear that the Council can form this view even if the PPC recommends that no further action be taken.
38. Section 34(9).
39. Section 34(10).
40. Section 40(2).

pharmacist or pharmacy owner of such referral,[41] and provide the registered pharmacist or pharmacy owner with the subject matter of the complaint, as well the particulars of any evidence provided in support of such complaint.[42] Where the complaint constitutes separate allegations of misconduct, it should be formulated as separate charges so long as proof of an individual allegation would not aggravate the seriousness of another.[43] The committee must also apprise the registered pharmacist or pharmacy owner of their entitlement to be heard and represented before the committee.[44] After such notification, the committee must then fix a time, date and place for the hearing of the complaint[45] and give the complainant and the registered pharmacist or pharmacy owner at least 30 days' written notice of the same.[46]

Mediation

Section 37 of the Act provides for resolution of complaints by alternative dispute resolution mechanisms such as mediation. The Act does not envisage the resolution of every type of complaint by way of mediation. The Council is required to produce guidelines outlining, *inter alia*, the types of disputes that are appropriate for resolution by mediation.

These guidelines were not available at the time of writing. It is likely that these guidelines will aim to exclude the possibility of recourse to mediation in circumstances where a private agreement by way of mediation cannot vindicate the public interest. Such circumstances might arise where there are serious lapses of professional standards or where there is an allegation of dishonesty.

The consent of all parties is required before the mediation process can be embarked upon.[47] If the parties resolve the complaint through mediation or otherwise within the ambit of this section, the mediator must report the terms of the resolution to the Council.[48] Where the terms of resolution correspond to one or more of the disciplinary sanctions set out in Section 48(1)(b), the Council may impose the relevant sanction(s) as if under Section 48(1). Any statements made during the mediation process are confidential and may not be used in subsequent civil, criminal or disciplinary proceedings.[49] If the

---

41. Section 41(1)(a).
42. Section 41(1)(b).
43. *Reza* v. *General Medical Council* [1991] 2 W.L.R. 939.
44. Section 41(1)(c). The right to be represented at the committee is not expressly conferred by the Act but is implied in the wording of the subsection.
45. Section 41(2).
46. Section 41(3).
47. Section 37(3). The consent of the pharmacist or pharmacy owner concerned does not amount to an admission of liability pursuant to Section 37(4).
48. Section 37(5).
49. Section 37(7).

mediator is of the opinion that the complaint cannot be resolved by mediation or is not appropriate for resolution in this manner, the PPC must be informed of this and must then refer the matter to a committee of inquiry for hearing.

Accordingly, a pharmacist or pharmacy owner may face disciplinary sanction arising out of mediation, but will not be penalised for attempting to resolve a complaint made against him or her through the process.

Interim suspension of registration

Section 45 of the Act provides for the suspension of the registration of a registered pharmacist or a registered retail pharmacy business against whom a complaint has been made, pending the processing of that complaint. Such an order may be made by the High Court on application by the Council.[50] An application for interim suspension of registration of a registered pharmacist or registered retail pharmacy is made on notice[51] and is heard *in camera*. The Act does provide that the respondent registered pharmacist or registered retail pharmacy owner may apply to have the matter held in public.[52] Where the order is sought against a registered retail pharmacy, the order may provide for the closure of the premises in which that registered retail pharmacy business was carried on.[53] An order may only be made under Section 45 in circumstances where warranted by the magnitude of the risk to health and safety of the public.[54] The Act does not prescribe criteria by reference to which the discretion of the court should be exercised.

The courts have considered the nature of a similar power created by Section 51 of the Medical Practitioners Act 1978.[55] That section created a power to suspend the registration of a medical practitioner where it was in the public interest to do so. Accordingly, there are similarities between the power under the Pharmacy Act and that under Section 51 of the Medical Practitioners Act 1978 and the jurisprudence in relation to the latter may be of relevance to applications made under Section 45 of the Act.[56]

In *Casey* v. *The Medical Council*,[57] Kelly J. considered the nature of such an application and how the potentially draconian powers ought to be

---

50. Section 45(1).
51. Section 45(3).
52. Section 45(5). In Ó *Ceallaigh* v. *An Bord Altranais* [1999] 2 I.R. 552, it was held that persons with a proper interest, such as expert witnesses, were permitted to attend a private disciplinary hearing pursuant to the Nurses Act 1985. Such expert witnesses should be allowed to hear the expert evidence given on behalf of the Board to allow them to assess the same.
53. Section 45(2).
54. Section 45(4).
55. No. 4 of 1978. This Act has now been repealed and replaced by the Medical Practitioners Act 2007 (No. 25 of 2007).
56. One important difference between the two Acts is that Section 51(3) of the Medical Practitioners Act 1978 provided for the application to be made *ex parte*.
57. [1999] 2 I.R. 534. See also Ó *Ceallaigh* v. *An Bord Altranais* [2000] 4 I.R. 54.

exercised in the context of the disciplinary scheme. The learned judge emphasised that the power to suspend the registration of a practitioner must be reserved for exceptional cases:

> It seems to me that Section 51 is reserved for exceptional cases where a doctor has to be suspended from practice because it is in the public interest that he should be. There must be cases where the Council would, from the point of view of protecting the public, wish to bring about an improvement in the standards of an individual practitioner. It would be absurd that in every such case where the Council desired so to do it would have to invoke the provisions of Section 51.[58]

In *The Medical Council* v. *PC*,[59] the Supreme Court held that such an order can only be made when, on all the evidence available, 'the public interest requires that this be done and that the public interest outweighs the constitutional right of the medical practitioner concerned to carry on his or her practice and earn his or her livelihood as a doctor'.[60] The court may award the costs of such an application, pursuant to its inherent jurisdiction.[61]

In *The Medical Council* v. *PC*, Keane C.J. indicated a number of factors at pp. 693–694 that were of relevance in assessing whether the balance lay in favour of making the order sought under Section 51 of the Medical Practitioners Act 1978:

a   the gravity of the threat to public health arising out of the practice of the respondent;
b   whether the respondent's practice can continue if an interim order is made;
c   the time frame before the likely completion of the disciplinary process;
d   whether the matter has entered the public domain;
e   whether the respondent acknowledges guilt in respect of any of the allegations against him;
f   the particular problems inherent for a doctor in the closure of his practice.

The High Court, on hearing an application under Section 45 of the Act, will have to consider whether there is evidence probative of a risk to public health and safety, that that risk is occasioned by a respondent's practice, and that the risk is of such magnitude that the suspension of registration or closure

---

58. Ibid. at p. 549.
59. [2003] 3 I.R. 600.
60. Ibid. at p. 602. In *Ó Ceallaigh* v. *An Bord Altranais* [2000] 4 I.R. 54, the Supreme Court construed a similar provision of the Nurses Act 1985 literally. That Act provided for an application to the High Court for the suspension of a nurse's registration where it was in the public interest to do so.
61. *The Medical Council* v. *PAO* [2004] 2 I.R. 12. Section 45 of the Pharmacy Act does not make express provision for the costs of such an application.

order is waranted. After having so considered, the court must then consider whether the public interest in suspension of the respondent's registration is outweighed by the respondent's constitutional right to earn a livelihood or his or her right to a good name.

Procedure before a committee of inquiry

The procedure to be followed at committees of inquiry set up under the Act is provided for by Section 42 of the Act. The Act provides that, *prima facie*, a hearing before the Professional Conduct Committee shall be held in public[62] and a hearing before the Health Committee shall be held in private.[63] If, however, either party can satisfy the committee that it would be appropriate to do so, a hearing before the Professional Conduct Committee may be held in private[64] and a hearing before the Health Committee may be held in public.[65]

Hearings before a committee of inquiry set up under the provisions of the Act are formal in nature. Any person, with the leave of the committee, may lead evidence in support of his or her complaint.[66] All testimony is to be on oath or affirmation,[67] which oath or affirmation may be administered by any member of the committee.[68] A registered pharmacist or pharmacy owner, against whom a complaint is made, may cross-examine witnesses called by the complainant and may lead evidence to meet the complaint.[69]

Transfer of hearing of complaint

The Act provides for the transfer of the hearing of a complaint between different committees of inquiry in specified circumstances. Such transfer may be made before or after the hearing of evidence, as long as both committees are satisfied that it is appropriate to transfer the hearing[70] and that the registered pharmacist or pharmacy owner will not be prejudiced by the transfer.[71] The committee of inquiry to which the hearing is transferred under this provision may rely on a transcript of evidence before the original committee of inquiry[72] or may rehear any evidence taken before

---

62. Section 42(1).
63. Section 42(3).
64. Section 42(2).
65. Section 42(4).
66. Section 42(5)(a).
67. Section 42(5)(b).
68. Section 42(6).
69. Section 42(5)(c).
70. Section 42(7)(a).
71. Section 42(7)(b).
72. Section 42(8)(a).

the other committee of inquiry if it considers, in the interests of fairness, that it is necessary to do so.

Powers of committee of inquiry

Section 43 of the Act gives each committee of inquiry extensive powers in relation to the manner in which hearings are conducted. The committee is allocated the same powers as the High Court to compel the attendance of witnesses,[73] to conduct the examination of witnesses on oath,[74] to compel the production of documentary or other evidence,[75] and to make appropriate awards of costs.[76]

The committee of inquiry is also specifically empowered to issue a summons for the purpose of compelling the attendance of a witness or the production of evidence,[77] without prejudice to the generality of the committee's powers in this area.[78] The committee is bound to act judicially and has powers to take evidence by various means. Hearsay evidence cannot be included on the sole basis that a witness is unwilling to attend.[79] Section 11 of the Act permits the Council to make rules to provide for the taking of evidence before the committees of inquiry. Subject to these rules, and to the requirement that fair procedures be followed, evidence may be given to the committee orally,[80] by way of statutory declaration[81] or by live video link or other modes of transmission.[82]

A witness before a committee of inquiry shall have the same immunities and privileges as a witness before the High Court.[83] The Act provides that it shall be an offence to do anything that would, if the inquiry was held in a court, amount to a contempt of court.[84] The Act also provides that it shall be an offence to fail, without providing a reasonable excuse, to attend before the committee having been summoned to do so,[85] to refuse to take an oath or make an affirmation,[86] to refuse to produce evidence the committee has required that person to produce or to refuse to answer a question that the person is lawfully required to answer.[87] In addition to the above defaults

---

73. Section 43(1)(a).
74. Section 43(1)(b).
75. Section 43(1)(c).
76. Section 43(1)(d).
77. Section 43(2).
78. Section 43(3).
79. *Borges* v. *The Medical Council* [2004] 1 I.R. 103.
80. Section 43(4)(a).
81. Section 43(4)(b).
82. Section 43(4)(c).
83. Section 43(5).
84. Section 43(7).
85. Section 43(7)(a).
86. Section 43(7)(b)(i).
87. Section 43(7)(b)(ii) and (iii).

constituting statutory offences, the Council may apply to the High Court for an order to deal with the default. The Council may apply for an order compelling the attendance of a witness before the committee of inquiry,[88] compelling a person to perform any thing that he or she refused to perform before the committee of inquiry,[89] make such interim or interlocutory orders as appear necessary[90] or authorise an award of costs[91] as appropriate.

The committee of inquiry may request the registered pharmacist or registered retail pharmacy owner to consent to one or more of a specified number of courses of action before the determination of the hearing. The committee of inquiry may request that the respondent do one or more of the following:

a   undertake not to repeat the conduct which is the subject matter of the complaint;

b   undertake to attend specified educational or training courses;

c   consent to undergo medical treatment;

d   consent to being admonished or censured by the Council.

The respondent pharmacist or pharmacy owner is entitled to refuse to comply with the request, in which case, the hearing will proceed as if the request had not been made.[92]

At the conclusion of the hearing, the committee must send a written report to the Council[93] stating the subject matter of the complaint, the evidence presented and the findings of the committee,[94] together with any additional matters the committee deems appropriate.[95]

Obligation to give reasons

Though the Act does not require a committee of inquiry to give reasons for its decisions, such a duty is implied by the common law and in some cases the European Convention on Human Rights (ECHR). The provision of reasons is necessary to ensure that the Superior Courts can exercise their jurisdiction to enquire into and if necessary to correct decisions of administrative bodies.[96]

---

88. Section 43(8)(a).
89. Section 43(8)(b).
90. Section 43(8)(c).
91. Section 43(8)(d).
92. Section 46.
93. Subsection 47(1).
94. Subsection 47(2).
95. Subsection 47(3).
96. *Rajah* v. *Royal College of Surgeons* [1994] 1 I.R. 385. Kelly J confirmed that decisions of the Fitness to Practise Committee of the Medical Council are subject to this obligation in *Prendiville & Murphy* v. *The Medical Council* [2007] IEHC 427 Unreported, Kelly J 14 December 2007 at p. 90.

Reasons must be given to enable the determination of whether a disciplinary charge was made out and to examine the decision reached on the question of penalty.[97] In *Prendiville & Murphy* v. *The Medical Council*,[98] Kelly J. confirmed that the Fitness to Practise Committee of the Medical Council was subject to an obligation to give reasons for its decisions. The obligation to give reasons also extends to the Health Committee.[99] A discursive statement of reasons is not required.[100]

In *Prendiville & Murphy* v. *The Medical Council*, however, Kelly J. held that the Fitness to Practise Committee of the Medical Council is subject to a 'basic obligation to give a general explanation of the basis for its determination on questions of serious professional misconduct'.[101] It is likely that the obligation on a committee of inquiry under the Pharmacy Act is identical to that identified by Kelly J. in the case cited above.

Where a person's civil rights and obligations are being determined by a tribunal, Article 6 (1) of the ECHR requires that reasons be given.[102] Insofar as proceedings before a committee of inquiry determine the right of a pharmacist to practise his or her profession, such a committee is a tribunal which determines a civil right of a pharmacist.[103] In such circumstances, the protection of Article 6(1) is engaged in respect of proceedings before a committee of inquiry.[104] The European Court of Human Rights has held that disciplinary proceedings 'do not normally' lead to a dispute over civil rights and obligations for the purposes of Article 6.[105]

Costs

The power of the committee to award and authorise the recovery of costs is not mirrored by any provision of the Nurses Act 1985, the Veterinary Practitioners Act 2005 or the Medical Practitioners Act 2007. The decision to award costs and the amount of costs awarded will be a matter for the committee's discretion. As no inquiries have yet taken place at the

---

97. *Selvanathan* v. *GMC* [2001] Lloyd's Med. Rep. 1.
98. [2008] 3 I.R. 122.
99. In *Stefan* v. *General Medical Council* [1999] 1 W.L.R. 1293, it was confirmed that a Health Committee of the General Medical Council was subject to this obligation.
100. *FP* v. *Minister for Justice* [2002] I.R. 164; Followed by Kelly J in respect of decisions of the Fitness to Practise Committee of the Medical Council in *Prendiville & Murphy* v. *The Medical Council* [2007] IEHC 427.
101. [2008] 3 I.R. 122 at p. 172.
102. *Van De Hurk* v. *The Netherlands* (1994) 18 E.H.R.R. 418 at p. 501.
103. *Chaudhury* v. *General Medical Council* [2002] UKPC 41 at para. 20.
104. *Ghosh* v. *General Medical Council* [2001] 1 W.L.R. 1915 at p. 1922-1923. In *Chaudhury* v. *General Medical Council* [2002] UKPC 41, the Privy Council reserved its position as to whether the doctrine of proportionality has any direct application to orders for interim suspension of registration or for suspension of registration of a medical practitioner.
105. *Le Compte, Van Leuven and Meyere* v. *Belgium* (1982) 4 E.H.R.R. 1.

time of writing, there is no body of jurisprudence regarding whether or in what circumstances costs will be awarded to practitioners at fitness to practise inquiries. The experience with disciplinary tribunals in other jurisdictions may provide some guidance in this regard.

In *Baxendale-Walker* v. *The Law Society*,[106] it was held that the ordinary rules of costs in civil matters did not apply to professional disciplinary proceedings.[107] There is no presumption that an order for costs should be made in favour of a professional who had successfully defended an allegation of professional misconduct. It has been held that costs will be awarded against the regulator where the proceedings 'were a shambles from start to finish'[108] or where an allegation of dishonesty was improperly made.[109] In *Baxendale-Walker*, it was held that an order for costs should not be made against the Law Society unless the complaint had been improperly brought.[110]

If a practitioner is acquitted of a professional disciplinary charge, it appears that costs should only be awarded against him or her in limited circumstances. Before such an award can be made, there must be some element of default on the part of the practitioner concerned and a causal connection between that default and the incurring of costs.[111]

A further issue relates to the scope of costs orders that can be made. It is unclear whether the costs that can be awarded are limited to the costs of the hearing, or whether the costs of an investigation required to prosecute the charge are also recoverable. It has been held in a number of cases that the costs of an investigation must be paid by a convicted person.[112] The fact that the investigating officer is salaried makes no difference to the power to award costs in respect of his or her time.[113] An award of costs made by the committee of inquiry may be appealed to the District Court within 21 days of the order being made.[114]

Categories of complaints

The Act prescribes the jurisdiction of the disciplinary committees of the Council. The Council is empowered to deal with certain categories of

---

106. [2008] 1 W.L.R. 426.
107. Ibid. at para. 34.
108. *R (Gorlov)* v. *Institute of Chartered Accountants in England and Wales* [2001] EWHC 220 Admin. at para. 37.
109. *Law Society* v. *Adcock* [2007] 1 W.L.R. 1096 at para. 42.
110. Ibid. at para. 49.
111. *Hayes* v. *The Law Society* [2004] EWHC 1165 (Admin) at para. 23.
112. *Neville* v. *Gardner Merchant Ltd.* (1983) 9 Cr.App.R.(S.) 349; *R* v. *Associated Octel Ltd.* [1997] 1 Cr.App.R.(S.) 435.
113. *Attorney General* v. *Shillibeer* (1849) 4 Exch. 606.
114. Section 43(6).

complaints. The categories of complaints that may be referred to a committee of inquiry differ depending on whether the respondent is a registered pharmacist or a registered retail pharmacy business. There are seven subsets of complaints that may be dealt with by a committee in respect of a registered pharmacist. These are set out in Section 35(1) of the Act:

a   poor professional performance;
b   professional misconduct;
c   impairment of a registered pharmacist's ability to practise owing to a physical or mental ailment, an emotional disturbance or an addiction to alcohol or drugs;
d   failure to comply with a condition of registration;
e   failure to comply with an undertaking or to take any action specified in a consent given in response to a request under Section 46;
f   a contravention of the Act or rules made by the Council under the Act;
g   a conviction within the State for an offence triable on indictment, or an act or omission outside the State which, if done or made within the State, would constitute an offence triable on indictment.

The complaints that may be made against a registered retail pharmacy business are set out in Section 36(1) of the Act as follows:

a   the pharmacy owner or an employee or partner of the pharmacy owner has been convicted of an offence under the Act, any Act repealed by the Act, or Regulations made under the Act or any such repealed Act, the Misuse of Drugs Acts 1977 to 2006, the Irish Medicines Board Acts 1995 and 2006, the Poisons Acts 1961 and 1977 or the Animal Remedies Acts 1993 and 2006;
b   the pharmacy owner or an employee or a partner of the pharmacy owner has been convicted of any other offence or has committed misconduct and the nature of that offence or misconduct is such that, were the person applying to the Council for registration as a pharmacist, the Council would be likely to refuse to register the person;
c   in a case where the business has been carried on as mentioned in Sections 26 and 29 of the Act by a representative, the representative or any person engaged by the representative in connection with the carrying on of the pharmacy (whether or not for the purposes of Section 29) has:
  i   been convicted of an offence mentioned in paragraph (a); or
  ii been convicted of an offence or committed misconduct the nature of which is as mentioned in paragraph (b).

For the purposes of such complaints, the activities of a director of the retail pharmacy business concerned attract the same scrutiny as those of a pharmacy owner.[115] Many of these categories of complaint speak for themselves and matters that may fall within these categories will be discussed below.

Many of these matters have already arisen before the disciplinary apparatus of the Royal Pharmaceutical Society of Great Britain (the RPSGB).

The RPSGB's functions in relation to fitness to practise and disciplinary matters were transferred in September 2010 to the new UK pharmacy regulations, the General Pharmaceutical Council (GPhC). At the time of writing, the GPhC has only considered a small number of fitness to practise cases. In order to assess the relevance of decisions made by the committees of the RPSGB, it is necessary to briefly consider the procedures that operated pursuant to the legislation and the rules that governed the RPSGB.

Fitness to practise system for pharmacists in the UK

The RPSGB's disciplinary scheme for pharmacists was operated for many years by the Statutory Committee, which was superseded in recent years by the Disciplinary Committee. Over the course of that period, a body of case law accumulated which provides guidance on what might be considered professional misconduct and is instructive in terms of how the disciplinary jurisdiction of the PSI might be exercised under the Act. Decisions of the Statutory Committee and of the Disciplinary Committee of the RPSGB were reported in the *Pharmaceutical Journal*. Determinations of fitness to practise cases heard by the GPhC are published on the GPhC's website.

In assessing the relevance of these UK decisions, it is necessary to bear in mind that many of these cases deal with breaches of the Code of Conduct published by the RPSGB. In addition, two particular features of the operation of the Statutory Committee ought to be borne in mind when considering the potential relevance of decisions made by it. A finding of professional misconduct against a pharmacist such as to render him or her unfit to be on the Register of Pharmaceutical Chemists did not automatically result in the removal of the pharmacist in question from the register; it vested a discretion in the Statutory Committee whether to direct the erasure of that person's name from the register.[116] However, there was a statutory presumption that a finding of professional misconduct by a pharmaceutical chemist automatically carried with it the penalty of removal from the register. Accordingly, penalties imposed by the Statutory Committee are of limited precedental

---

115. Section 36(3).
116. *R v. Royal Pharmaceutical Society of Great Britain Ex. Parte Panjawani* [2002] EWHC 1127 Admin.

value. In addition, the adverse findings that could be made by the Statutory Committee were limited to misconduct and the proof of a conviction. The array of findings that may be made by the PCC is far broader and accordingly it is difficult to say for certain whether a finding of misconduct by the Statutory Committee would be repeated by the PCC on similar facts. Arising out of these differences, examples from the jurisprudence of the Statutory Committee and the Disciplinary Committee are cited sparingly below.

Poor professional performance

Section 33 of the Act states that poor professional performance: 'in relation to a registered pharmacist, means any failure of the registered pharmacist to meet the standards of competence that may be reasonably expected of a registered pharmacist.'

An act, pattern of conduct or omission that consists of a wrongly, but honestly formed professional judgment, does not amount to misconduct.[117] It appears that such an act, pattern of conduct or omission may instead be considered within the rubric of poor professional performance.

A number of matters have arisen before the Statutory Committee and the Disciplinary Committee which may ground a finding of poor professional performance by the PCC. Examples include:

a   failure to diagnose a minor ailment correctly and prescribing inappropriate treatment;[118]
b   supply of medicines on foot of a forged prescription where errors on the prescription should have alerted him;[119]
c   emergency supply of prescription-only medicines without fulfilling the proper procedure;[120]
d   failure to ensure the safe disposal of out-of-date and/or returned medicines;[121]
e   failure to keep adequate records;[122]
f   failure to ensure that medicines are stored properly;[123]
g   dispensing out-of-date medication.[124]

---

117. Section 33.
118. *Re Price*, Statutory Committee, 23 February 2006. It seems that such an error could also be considered professional misconduct depending on the circumstances of the case..
119. *Re Solola*. Pharm J 2004; 272(7296): 524–526.
120. *Re Shah*. Pharm J 2002; 269(7227): 829–831. Such an act would probably be considered professional misconduct if the emergency supplies concerned controlled drugs (*Re Shah*. Pharm J 2000; 264(7084): 290).
121. *Re Proctor*. Pharm J 2000; 264(7080): 129.
122. *Re Shah*. Pharm J 2002; 269(7227): 829–831.
123. *Re Loiacono*. Pharm J 2005; 275(7357): 66–67.
124. *Re Nicholson*. Pharm J 2005; 275(7358): 69.

In *Re Iqbal*,[125] the respondent was found to have committed a serious dispensing error, whereby he dispensed gliclazide 80 mg instead of, and labelled as, bumetanide 1 mg tablets. The patient took the medication according to the directions on the label and became seriously ill. There was no evidence of a systemic failure of dispensing procedures and the Disciplinary Committee found that the error in question did not amount to misconduct, but was a case of human error falling short of misconduct. It is unlikely that a finding of poor professional performance could be made by the PCC in respect of a single simple dispensing error. In the case of a serious error or of a number of repeated errors, a matter that is likely to be considered of particular relevance to the nature of the disciplinary charge is whether or not the pharmacist in question had in place a standard operating procedure for dispensing and whether he or she adhered to the same.

The PSI has published practice notes regarding the dispensing and storage of certain medicines where serious consequences might attach to a dispensing error. Accordingly, it appears that failure to conform to the standard set out in these practice notes is a matter to which a disciplinary committee would have regard.

Professional misconduct

The term 'professional misconduct' is defined in Section 33 of the Act as any act, omission or pattern of conduct that:

a   is a breach of the Code of Conduct for registered pharmacists;
b   is infamous or disgraceful in a professional respect (notwithstanding that, if the same or like act, omission or pattern of conduct were committed by a member of another profession, it would not be professional misconduct in respect of that profession);
c   involves moral turpitude, fraud or dishonesty of a nature or degree which bears on the carrying on of the profession of a pharmacist;
d   if the registered pharmacist has been granted a licence, certificate or registration by a body outside the State relating to the practice of pharmacy is a breach of a standard of conduct, performance or ethics that:
    i   applies to a person holding that licence, certificate or registration; and
    ii   corresponds to a standard contained in the Code referred to in paragraph (a) or a standard breach of which amounts to conduct of the kind mentioned in paragraphs (b) or (c),

---

125. Disciplinary Committee, 13 July 2007.

but does not include an act, omission or pattern of conduct that consists of a wrongly but honestly formed professional judgment.

This effectively adopts the definition provided by Keane J. in the case of *Ó Laoire* v. *The Medical Council*.[126]

Each of the categories of acts or omissions that constitute professional misconduct is considered below.

Breach of the code of conduct for registered pharmacists

The Society has drawn up a Code of Conduct in accordance with Section 7(2) of the Act (see Appendix 12.1). This statutory Code of Conduct outlines the principles and standards which govern pharmacists in the practise of their profession. The Code of Conduct represents the point of departure in considering whether conduct alleged as against a registered pharmacist amounts to professional misconduct. The applicable standard is subject to any modification of the Code of Conduct published by the Society in accordance with the provisions of Section 7(2) of the Act and in force at any given time.[127] The Code of Conduct is contained in six broad principles. The Society has also published an illustrative guide as to how a registered pharmacist should act in order to comply with each of the six principles comprised in the Code of Conduct. The list of suggestions provided by the Society in each case is not intended to be exhaustive or exclusive and it remains to be seen how these principles will be interpreted in practice.

First principle

The practice by a pharmacist of his/her profession must be directed to maintaining and improving the health, wellbeing, care and safety of the patient. This is the primary principle and the following principles [of the Code] must be read in light of this principle.

It is well established that the prescription of excessive quantities of controlled drugs with a known propensity for addiction constitutes professional misconduct for a doctor.[128] It is likely that the supply of excessive quantities

126. Unreported, High Court, Keane J., 27 January, 1995 at p. 106. The statutory definition of professional misconduct differs slightly from the definition provided by Keane J. in *Ó Laoire*. In particular, the fifth limb of the definition provided by Keane J., which identified professional misconduct as being conduct connected with his or her profession in which a practitioner has 'seriously fallen short, whether by omission or commission of the standards of practice expected amongst registered medical practitioners' is omitted. It is submitted that this omission will not be of any great significance in practice. The code of conduct for registered pharmacists is broad and prescribes the standard of conduct expected amongst registered pharmacists. A breach of the provisions of the code of conduct can amount to professional misconduct.
127. *Prendiville* v. *The Medical Council* [2008] 3 I.R. 122 at p. 165.
128. *Medical Council* v. *Murphy* Unreported, High Court, Finlay P., 29 June 1984.

of substances with a known potential for misuse by a pharmacist is also a matter which could be considered misconduct by a pharmacist in certain circumstances.[129] In this regard, the provisions of the Regulation of Retail Pharmacy Businesses Regulations 2008[130] oblige community pharmacists to ensure that medicinal products are not sold for the purposes of misuse or abuse. The PSI guidelines – 'Non-Prescription Medicinal Products Containing Codeine: Guidance for Pharmacists on Safe Supply to Patients, May 2010' – which came into operation on 1 August 2010 are also relevant here. In order to fulfil their duties in this area, it is submitted that pharmacists and retail pharmacies would have to demonstrate that staff received sufficient training and that appropriate standard operating procedures were in place.

A pharmacist has a duty to satisfy himself of the correctness of any prescriptions dispensed by him.[131] In many cases, a pharmacist who fails to make proper inquiries in respect of a prescription is likely to be guilty of poor professional performance rather than professional misconduct. A pharmacist, who dispenses a prescription he or she reasonably suspects to be a forgery, or to have been altered, runs the risk of a finding of professional misconduct being made against him or her. In addition, consistent oversupply of medication, albeit on foot of valid prescriptions can amount to professional misconduct.[132]

Second principle

A pharmacist must employ his/her professional competence, skills and standing in a manner that brings health gain and value to the community and the society in which he/she lives and works.

In this regard, pharmacists who make repeated dispensing errors and who fail to review their dispensing procedures are liable to have their registration cancelled.[133]

Third principle

A pharmacist must never abuse the position of trust which they hold in relation to a patient and in particular, they must respect a patient's rights, including their dignity, autonomy, and entitlements to confidentiality and information.

It is well settled that the abuse of a patient's confidence constitutes professional misconduct.[134]

---

129. *Re Parmar*, Disciplinary Committee, 29 June 2006.
130. S.I. No. 488 of 2007.
131. *Horton* v. *Evans* [2006] All E.R. (D) 134.
132. *Re Salako* Disciplinary Committee, 28 September 2007.
133. *Re Ganpatsingh* Pharm J 2002; 269(7222): 658-660.
134. *Roylance* v. *General Medical Council* [2000] A.C. 311 at p. 331.

Fourth principle

A pharmacist must conduct himself/herself in a manner which enhances the service which their profession as a whole provides to society and should not act in a way which might damage the good name of their profession.

Blatant disregard for the system of registration is likely to be considered professional misconduct. In *Gupta* v. *General Medical Council*,[135] it was held that the purpose of the system of registration is 'to safeguard the interests of patients and to maintain high standards within the profession'[136] and any attempt to undermine the system is a grave matter which is likely to constitute professional misconduct.

Fifth principle

A pharmacist must maintain a level of competence sufficient to provide his/her professional services effectively and efficiently.

It has been held that seriously negligent treatment can constitute professional misconduct; there is 'a duty to protect the public from the genially incompetent as well as the deliberate wrongdoers'.[137] The negligence involved in this regard must be more grave than ordinary negligence. In *Preiss* v. *General Dental Council*,[138] the following was stated at p. 1936:

It is well settled that serious professional misconduct does not require moral turpitude. Gross professional negligence can fall within it. Something more is required than a degree of negligence enough to give rise to civil liability but not calling for the opprobrium that inevitably attaches to the disciplinary offence.

If the negligence complained of is attributable to a single incident, it will be more difficult to cross the threshold into professional misconduct.[139] If a complaint is based on several episodes of clinical errors or on a course of conduct, a finding of professional misconduct will often follow.[140] A single episode of misconduct can merit cancellation of registration if it is accompanied by aggravating factors such as the failure to co-operate with an investigation into that incident.[141]

---

135. [2002] 1 W.L.R. 1691.
136. Ibid. at para. 20.
137. *McCandless* v. *General Medical Council* [1996] 1 W.L.R. 167 at p. 169. This passage was quoted with approval by O'Donovan J. in *Perez* v. *An Bord Altranais* [2005] 4 I.R. 298 at p. 300.
138. [2001] 1 W.L.R. 1926.
139. *Rao* v. *General Medical Council* [2002] UKPC 65 at para. 17.
140. As in *Norton* v. *General Medical Council* [2002] UKPC 6 where complaints were received from three patients on whom the doctor concerned had performed cosmetic surgery.
141. *Subramanian* v. *General Medical Council* [2002] UKPC 64.

Sixth principle

A pharmacist must be aware of his/her obligations under this Code and should not do anything in the course of practising as a pharmacist, or permit another person to do anything on his/her behalf, which constitutes a breach of this Code or impairs or compromises his/her ability to observe this Code.

Conduct that is infamous or disgraceful in a professional respect or involving moral turpitude, fraud or dishonesty

Conduct which is infamous or disgraceful involves some element of moral turpitude, fraud or dishonesty.[142] In order for professional misconduct to be established, there must be some connection between the conduct complained of and the profession.[143] In *Petitions of Lynch and Daly*,[144] each of the petitioners was accused of conduct disgraceful to him in a professional respect. Kenny J. explained the nature of misconduct of this type as follows at p. 11:

> The conduct must be of a kind which brings disgrace upon the person primarily in the eyes of the members of his profession, but also in those of the public. 'Disgraceful' implies an element of conscious wrongdoing or the doing of something which a professional person by reason of his training must have realised would cause him to incur shame in the eyes of his professional colleagues. The conduct must also be in a professional respect and so it must relate to something which he does when carrying on his profession and in the course of the performance of the duties which it imposes.

Behaviour may, however, constitute professional misconduct even although it does not occur within the actual course of the carrying on of the person's professional practice. There is no doubt, for example, that the abuse of a patient's confidence or the making of some dishonest private financial gain[145] would constitute professional misconduct. In cases of moral turpitude, the profession is entitled to be concerned that 'the public reputation of the profession may suffer and public confidence in it may be prejudiced'.[146] In *A County Council v. W. (Disclosure)*,[147] Cazalet J. held that a finding that a doctor had sexually abused his daughter 'demonstrated conduct disgraceful to him as reflecting on his profession and/or indeed conduct disgraceful to him as

---

142. *Ó Laoire* v. *The Medical Council,* Unreported, High Court, Keane J., 27 January 1995.
143. *Doughty* v. *General Dental Council* [1988] A.C. 164 at p. 173.
144. [1970] I.R. 1.
145. *Roylance* v. *General Medical Council* [2000] A.C. 311 at p. 331.
146. Ibid. at p. 331.
147. [1997] 1 F.L.R. 574.

a practising doctor'. In *Marten* v. *Royal College of Veterinary Surgeons Disciplinary Committee*,[148] Marten was found, on account of his work as a farmer, to be guilty of conduct disgraceful to him as a practising veterinary surgeon in circumstances whereby he was found to have failed to give adequate care to his animals.

In *Patel* v. *General Medical Council*,[149] it was held that for professional persons, 'a finding of dishonesty lies at the top end of the spectrum of gravity of misconduct'. A number of matters have arisen in the context of the fraudulent submission of claims for payment in respect of drugs supplied by the pharmacist in question. The following matters have been held to amount to misconduct before the Disciplinary Committee of the RPSGB:

a   submission of claims for reimbursement in respect of medicines not dispensed;[150]

b   inflation of claims submitted for reimbursement to the payment authority;[151]

c   acceptance of payment in the form of prescriptions from a doctor and subsequently submitting the same for reimbursement;[152]

d   dispensing of patient returned medicines and claiming payment in respect of the same;[153]

e   consistent oversupply of medication, albeit on foot of valid prescriptions.[154]

Professional misconduct relating to the practice of pharmacy outside the State

Subsection (d) of the statutory definition of professional misconduct provides that certain acts, omissions or patterns of conduct will constitute professional misconduct for a registered pharmacist notwithstanding that the acts, omissions or pattern of conduct complained of did not occur in the State. This subsection applies to registered pharmacists who have been granted a licence, certificate or registration from a body outside the State relating to the practice of pharmacy. Any act or omission or pattern of conduct that constitutes a breach of standard of conduct, performance or ethics for a person holding such a licence, certificate or registration and would constitute professional misconduct if the act, omission or pattern of conduct occurred in the State, will be professional misconduct notwithstanding that the act, omission or pattern of conduct complained of occurred outside the State.

---

148. [1966] 1 Q.B. 1.
149. [2003] UKPC 16.
150. *Re Black*, Statutory Committee, 24 February 2005.
151. *Re Patel (Bijal)* 13 December 2006.
152. *Re Ul Haq* Pharm J 2001; 266(7151): 780-781.
153. *Re Mistry (Ramanlal)* 24 January 2007.
154. *Re Salako* 28 September 2007.

Conflicts of interest

Sections 63 to 65 of the Act are directed to preventing conflicts of interest arising out of professional relationships between registered pharmacists or pharmacy owners and medical practitioners. To that end, the Act provides that it shall be professional misconduct for a registered pharmacist[155] or a pharmacy owner[156] to have a beneficial interest in a medical practice. Any beneficial interest held by a business partner or employee of a registered pharmacist or pharmacy owner, with the knowledge of the latter, is imputed to the pharmacist[157] or pharmacy owner[158] concerned. A beneficial interest that is imputed to a registered pharmacist or pharmacy owner in this manner does not amount to professional misconduct if the Society is notified in the prescribed manner.[159] To avail of this exemption, the pharmacist or pharmacy owner must, within 21 days of finding out that his business partner has a beneficial interest in a medical practice, notify the Society of the nature and extent of that interest. Any beneficial interest held by the spouse or by a dependant child of a pharmacist or pharmacy owner is also imputed to the pharmacist or pharmacy owner concerned.[160]

A beneficial interest can arise in two ways *viz.* (a) ownership of a share in a medical practice; and (b) the provision of premises for use and occupation by a medical practice.

Ownership of a share in a medical practice

The interest of a director or a shareholder in a medical practice owned by a company[161] or of a member of a body corporate other than a company which owns a medical practice[162] can constitute a beneficial interest for the purposes of the Act. It would appear, however, that an interest in ownership of a medical practice or part thereof does not of itself constitute a beneficial interest within the meaning of the Act.[163] Where that interest in ownership benefits the pharmacist or pharmacy owner in the practice of his or her profession however, the provisions of the Act are engaged and the pharmacist or pharmacy owner will be considered to have a beneficial interest in the medical practice in question.

---

155. Section 63(1)(a).
156. Section 63(2)(a).
157. Section 63(1)(b).
158. Section 63(2)(b).
159. Section 63(6).
160. Section 63(5).
161. Section 63(5)(a)(i)(I). A pharmacist or a pharmacy owner who owns up to 0.5% or the shares of a medical practice is not a shareholder for the purposes of the Act.
162. Section 63(5)(a)(i)(II).
163. Section 63(4).

Provision of premises

A pharmacist or pharmacy owner who provides an indirect benefit to a medical practice by providing business premises to a medical practice at a favourable rate[164] is deemed to have a beneficial interest in the medical practice as a result. This is the case whether the premises are provided by way of lease, licence or any similar arrangement for use or occupation by a medical practice.[165] If the discrepancy between the rent actually charged and the market rental value of the property 'may reasonably be attributed to the existence of a commercial relationship between the parties other than that of landlord and tenant',[166] the registered pharmacist or pharmacy owner will be deemed to have a beneficial interest in the medical practice. In addition, if the rents or charges levied on a medical practice by a pharmacist or pharmacy owner vary with the financial performance of the medical practice or retail pharmacy business concerned, the pharmacist is deemed to have a beneficial interest in that medical practice.[167] It would appear, however, that it would be difficult to justify the provision of premises at below market rent to a medical practice by reference to non-commercial criteria.

Improper commercial practices

Section 64 of the Act provides that it shall be professional misconduct for a registered pharmacist and misconduct for a pharmacy owner to engage in certain commercial practices.

A registered pharmacist or a pharmacy owner may not recommend a medical practice or medical practitioner to a member of the public otherwise than in the exercise of his or her professional judgment as a pharmacist[168] or in the proper course of carrying on business.[169] A recommendation is not made in the proper course of carrying on the business of a pharmacy if it is intended to result in a financial benefit from the medical practice or registered medical practitioner concerned.[170] Similarly, a medical practitioner may only recommend a registered pharmacist or retail pharmacy on the basis of his or her professional judgment.[171] A registered pharmacist who is aware of any improper recommendation contrary to Section 64 is obliged to report it to the Society[172] and a medical practitioner who becomes aware of such an improper commercial practice is similarly obliged to report it to the Medical Council.[173]

---

164. Section 63(5)(a)(ii)(I).
165. Section 63(5)(b).
166. Section 63(5)(a)(ii)(I).
167. Section 63(5)(a)(ii)(II).
168. Section 64(3).
169. Section 64(3) and (5).
170. Section 64(4).
171. Section 64(5).
172. Section 64(6).
173. Section 64(7).

In addition, the Act provides that a medical practice and a registered retail pharmacy business cannot be carried on in the same premises, or in separate premises that share common public access or where public access to one is available only by way of the other premises, in circumstances where there is an 'arrangement' between the parties that 'provides for, acknowledges or regulates' a financial benefit accruing to either party arising out of the proximity of the pharmacy and the medical centre in question.[174]

The definition of premises in the context of these provisions is unclear. Section 2(3) of the Act distinguishes between the concepts of 'premises' and 'building' and provides that two distinct premises can exist in a single building. However, Section 2(4) of the Act provides that this definition does not apply to Sections 63 and 64 of the Act. It seems likely that for the purposes of Section 64 of the Act, a building cannot contain more than one premises; any building that houses both a retail pharmacy and a medical practice could attract scrutiny under this section.

It is important to note that such a degree of proximity between a medical practice and a registered retail pharmacy does not of itself amount to professional misconduct on the part of a registered pharmacist or to misconduct by a pharmacy owner. In the absence of an arrangement between the parties that alludes to a financial benefit to either party, a pharmacist or pharmacy owner does not fall into misconduct.

Section 65 is a saving provision for existing property interests. It prevents any issue arising as to the validity of existing titles to, leases of, or planning permission appurtenant to property as a result of these provisions. In addition, a pharmacist or pharmacy owner is not prevented from dealing with property in any way that does not give rise to a beneficial interest in a medical practice or constitute an 'arrangement' within the meaning of the Act. The exact meaning of this provision is unclear. A number of meanings are possible. It could mean, that a lease or other means whereby title to property is held are not affected by the provisions of the Act if they pre-exist it. On the other hand, it could merely mean that, whilst the validity of the instrument under which the property in question is held cannot be impugned by the provisions of the Act, disciplinary consequences could still flow from a disciplinary offence that arises from the holding of such property. It is submitted that the latter is the more likely interpretation, having regard to the provisions of Section 64(9) of the Act.

Impairment of ability to practise on health grounds

It is envisaged that complaints under this category will be heard *in camera* before the Health Committee rather than the PCC. The Health Committee is

---

174. Section 64(1).

advised by a registered medical practitioner appointed by the Council but who does not have any voting rights on the committee.[175] In *Richardson* v. *Redpath Brown & Co. Ltd.*,[176] the role of a medical advisor was considered. Viscount Simon L.C. held that the role of a medical assessor is not that of an 'unsworn witness in the special confidence of the judge',[177] rather:

> He is an expert available for the judge to consult if the judge requires assistance in understanding the effect and meaning of technical evidence. He may, in proper cases, suggest to the judge questions which the judge himself might put to an expert witness with a view to testing the witness's view or to making plain his meaning. The judge may consult him in case of need as to the proper technical inferences to be drawn from proved facts, or as to the extent of the difference between apparently contradictory conclusions in the expert field.[178]

The precise role of a medical advisor to a Health Committee, at the time of writing, awaits clarification by way of rules of procedure. Some guidance as to the approach to be taken where the evidence of experts retained by a pharmacist conflicts with the evidence of the medical advisor to the Health Committee was provided in *Watson* v. *GMC*.[179] In that case, Stanley Burnton J. held that it was desirable that the medical advice given to the panel by a medical assessor should be given in the presence of all of the parties and that those parties should be given an opportunity to address that advice.[180] The learned judge further held that a committee of inquiry should be cautious in preferring a diagnosis of a medical assessor based on reading of the papers in a case and on his impression of expert practitioners giving their evidence, to the evidence of expert practitioners having examined the patient concerned.[181] In *Watson*, the court considered that adherence to proper procedures in this regard is a constituent of the right to a fair trial guaranteed under Article 6 of the ECHR.[182]

Whether a registered pharmacist's ability to practise has been impaired on grounds of health will be a matter for medical evidence in each case.

---

175. Sections 34(9) and (10).
176. [1944] A.C. 62.
177. Ibid. at p. 70.
178. Ibid. at pp. 70–71. In *Watson* v. *GMC* [2006] I.C.R. 113, p. 123, para. 43, Stanley Burnton J. considered that this constituted the starting point for the consideration of the role of a medical assessor and that 'their role and questions of procedure must be determined by the rules applicable to the procedure in question'.
179. [2006] I.C.R. 113. Stanley Burnton J. held that the rules of procedure of the committee in question should be the primary reference for the role of a medical assessor to that committee.
180. Ibid. at p. 127, para. 57.
181. Ibid. at p. 130, para. 72.
182. Ibid. at p. 124, para. 48.

Convictions for drink driving offences have led the Disciplinary Committee and the Statutory Committee of the RPSGB to remove pharmacists from the register,[183] unless the committee was satisfied that the pharmacist's work was not affected.[184] Offences under Sections 49 and 50 of the Road Traffic Act 1961 are not indictable offences in this jurisdiction and the fact of such a conviction could not, of itself, give rise to a complaint pursuant to the Act. The facts found proved before recording the conviction could, however, form the basis of a complaint under this category. Findings that a pharmacist was intoxicated whilst at work have lead to removal from the register.[185] By contrast, in *Re Karagiannis*,[186] the Health Professionals Disciplinary Tribunal in New Zealand imposed a fine on a pharmacist who admitted being drunk whilst working in a pharmacy and who allowed an unqualified person to dispense prescriptions without checking them.

Conviction

One of the complaints that can be made about a pharmacist is that he or she has been convicted of an indictable offence. The experience in other jurisdictions provides some assistance in predicting the likely outcome of such complaints. The fact of a conviction cannot ground a complaint against a registered pharmacist unless the conviction is for an indictable offence. If a practitioner is removed from the register or has his registration suspended as a result of a criminal conviction, it has been held that he or she should not be allowed to resume practice before the satisfactory completion of his sentence.[187]

This limb of the jurisdiction of the PCC does not extend to criminal cases wherein a practitioner is acquitted or given the benefit of the Probation Act.[188] However, the acquittal of a registered pharmacist on a criminal charge does not operate as a bar to a complaint being made in respect of the conduct out of which the criminal charge arose.[189] A disciplinary inquiry on foot of a complaint presented in accordance with the Act is undertaken in a different context and with different objectives to the criminal charges brought against

---

183. *Re Finch* Pharm J 1999; 263(7076): 978-979.
184. *Re Tucker* Pharm J 2001; 267(7162): 276-277.
185. *Re Davison* Pharm J 2003; 271(7267): 386-388.
186. Decision 181/Phar08/91P.
187. *CRHP* v. *General Dental Council and Fleischmann* [2005] EWHC 87 (Admin) at para. 54. In that case Newman J. held that this principle would not apply in respect of sentences consisting of periods of disqualification from driving or to time allowed by a court for the payment of a fine.
188. *R.* v. *Statutory Committee of the Pharmaceutical Society of Great Britain; ex parte Pharmaceutical Society of Great Britain* [1981] 1 W.L.R. 886.
189. *A.A.* v. *Medical Council* [2003] 2 I.R. 1.

him or her. As such the principle of double jeopardy does not apply.[190] By analogy, it is submitted that the facts found proved before recording a conviction for a summary offence or before applying Section 1(1) of the Probation of Offenders Act 1907 may form the subject matter of a complaint of professional misconduct against a registered pharmacist.

Whether a conviction will result in cancellation of registration

The conviction of a pharmacist or pharmacy owner for an offence cannot constitute grounds for the cancellation of the registration of the pharmacist or retail pharmacy business, unless in the Council's opinion, the nature of the offence or the circumstances in which it was committed are such that, if the pharmacist or pharmacy owner was applying for registration, registration would be refused.[191]

Any person applying to be registered as a pharmacist must satisfy the Council that he or she is fit to be a registered pharmacist. The statutory criteria to which the Council must have regard in determining whether an applicant is fit to be a registered pharmacist in considering whether to register him or her as such are set out in Sections 14 and 16 of the Act. The Council is entitled to conclude that the applicant is unfit to be registered if the applicant has:

a   been prohibited from practising as a pharmacist in another state;
b   been prohibited from carrying on a retail pharmacy business in another state;
c   been convicted in another state of an offence which renders the applicant unfit to be a registered pharmacist;
d   been convicted of an offence in the State that renders the applicant unfit to be a registered pharmacist; or
e   committed misconduct that renders the applicant unfit to be a registered pharmacist.

Some guidance in this regard may be gleaned from the procedures adopted by the Registration Appeals Committee of the RPSGB and from its decisions. The Registration Appeals Committee used a document entitled 'Good Character Assessment Framework' to facilitate assessment of character. The procedure that was adopted by the RPSGB was to consider in the first instance whether there was any evidence concerning the applicant's character. Such evidence could include testimonials or references concerning the applicant, convictions or findings by a regulator of a health or social care profession or convictions. The RPSGB then considered whether evidence of conduct or behaviour committed by an applicant was inconsistent with the standards published by the RPSGB.

---

190. *Shine* v. *Fitness to Practice Committee of the Medical Council* [2009] 1 I.R 283.
191. Section 48(2).

It is submitted that in considering whether a pharmacist is rendered unfit to practise by reason of a conviction, the Council must consider:

a   the seriousness of the conviction;
b   the relevance of the conviction to the practice of pharmacy;
c   the relevance of the conviction to the honour and dignity of the profession of pharmacy;
d   the recency of the conduct or behaviour referable to the conviction;
e   the applicant's age at the time when the acts in question were committed;
f   the applicant's personal mitigation in respect of the conduct or behaviour concerned;
g   the applicant's efforts or lack of efforts to rehabilitate himself or herself since the conduct or behaviour referable to the conviction was committed;
h   the applicant's insight or lack of insight in to the conduct or behaviour concerned;
i   the extent to which the conduct or behaviour is counterbalanced by testimonials and character references about the applicant's subsequent and recent conduct and behaviour;
j   the extent to which the conduct or behaviour is characteristic of the applicant or indicative of a propensity by the applicant to commit such conduct or behaviour in the future;
k   the extent to which the applicant disclosed, or failed to disclose, the conduct or behaviour during the application process; and
l   the extent of co-operation or lack of co-operation, by the applicant with any enquiries into the conduct or behaviour by the Society.

When considering the seriousness of a conviction, the following aggravating factors will generally qualify the conviction as serious:

a   conviction of an offence involving dishonesty, fraud or misrepresentation;
b   conviction of an offence indicating drug or alcohol dependency;
c   conviction of an offence involving violence exhibiting intentional or deliberate disregard of human life;
d   conviction of an offence involving non-consensual sexual acts;
e   conviction of an offence involving any sexual acts with children;
f   conviction of an offence involving trafficking in or illegally manufacturing any controlled drug;
g   conviction of an offence that poses a serious threat to public health, safety or welfare;
h   conviction of an offence indicating a blatant disregard for the law or the system of registration.

In cases where a criminal penalty has been imposed and satisfied, the Council, when imposing sanction, must bear in mind that it would be unjust to punish the pharmacist concerned again.[192]

The Council must consider whether, in the circumstances, a conviction warrants cancellation of registration. The conviction of a pharmacist of an offence involving dishonesty would be likely to ground cancellation or suspension of registration. In *Manzur v. General Medical Council*,[193] the Privy Council held that an admonition or censure would be too lenient in a case involving dishonesty. The Statutory Committee and the Disciplinary Committee of the RPSGB have considered a number of such cases. Conviction for theft and fraud offences,[194] even on a small scale[195] and especially offences relating to fraudulent processing of claims for payment[196] have warranted removal from the register. Theft from an employer has also been considered a serious breach of trust which is worthy of removal from the register.[197] Conviction for tax evasion has also resulted in removal from the register.[198]

By contrast, the Health Practitioners Disciplinary Tribunal[199] in New Zealand has tended to suspend the registration of the pharmacist concerned for number of months and impose a fine in such cases.[200]

The decisions of the Statutory Committee and the Disciplinary Committee of the RPSGB have repeatedly emphasised the importance of the pharmacist's role in the community as a custodian of controlled drugs. Convictions for theft and possession of methadone,[201] for possession of cannabis with intent to supply[202] and for conspiracy to illegally import steroids[203] have resulted in pharmacists being removed from the register. Convictions for possession of drugs *simpliciter* have resulted in suspension of registration.[204] Conversely, conviction for unsupervised supply of medicines has not generally resulted in removal from the register as long as procedures have improved by the time of the disciplinary hearing.[205]

---

192. *Bolton* v. *The Law Society* [1994] 1 W.L.R. 512 at p. 518.
193. [2001] UKPC 55.
194. *Re Imafidon* Pharm J 1999; 263(7063): 852-854.
195. *Re Daffu* Pharm J 2000; 264(7086): 366-367.
196. *Re Patel* Pharm J 1999; 263(7076): 978-979.
197. *Re Joshi* Pharm J 2002; 269(7205): 38-39.
198. *Re Nicholson* Pharm J 2008; 280(7490): 227.
199. Established pursuant to the provisions of the Health Practitioners Competence Assurance Act 2003.
200. *Re Winefield* Decision 60/Phar06/30P; *Re Burton* Decision 142/Phar07/78P.
201. *Re Buchanan* Pharm J 1999; 263(7063): 852-854.
202. *Re Crawford* Pharm J 2000; 265(7110): 262.
203. *Re Abdul* Pharm J 2000; 265(7123): 750.
204. *Re Parsi* Disciplinary Committee, 15 August 2008.
205. *Re Sarna* Pharm J 2005; 274(7335): 158-160.

Convictions for certain offences have been held to be such an affront to the dignity and honour of the profession, and to be so inconsistent with its aims as to warrant removal from the register. The Statutory Committee and the Disciplinary Committee of the RPSGB have considered that conviction for false imprisonment and assault,[206] for indecent assault,[207] for breach of the terms of a community service order,[208] for driving whilst disqualified and uninsured[209] and for possession of child pornography[210] were so serious as to warrant removal of a pharmacist from the register. Conviction for Health and Safety at Work and environmental offences has also resulted in removal from the register.[211]

Other complaints

Section 35 of the Act provides that a number of other types of complaints may be made about a registered pharmacist. The Society is empowered to impose conditions on the registration of pharmacists pursuant to a number of provisions of the Act. The failure to comply with any such condition is a matter which can give rise to a complaint pursuant to Section 35 of the Act. If a condition is imposed whereby a practitioner has to achieve certain targets and effect certain improvements within a specific time frame, the expiry of the relevant period of time does not render the practitioner's obligations at an end. Instead, the practitioner in default and he or she is thus rendered 'not in compliance' and can be said to be 'failing to comply' as a result.[212]

A committee of inquiry is empowered, under Section 46 of the Act to request a registered pharmacist to undertake not to repeat conduct to which a complaint relates, to undertake to attend specified courses, to consent to undergo medical treatment or to consent to being admonished or censured. The failure to comply with any such undertaking or to take any action previously consented to can also form the subject matter of a complaint to the Society pursuant to Section 35 of the Act.

Contravention of the Act or of rules made by the Council under the Act

Section 35 of the Act provides that it shall be professional misconduct for a registered pharmacist to contravene any provision of the Act or any rule made

---

206. *Re Arif* Pharm J 1999; 263(7063): 852-854.
207. *Re Wilson* Pharm J 2004; 272(7295): 490.
208. *Re Rodkoff* Pharm J 2002; 269(7222): 658-660.
209. *Re Haider* Pharm J 2000; 265(7123): 750.
210. *Re Wyatt* Pharm J 2002; 269(7229): 891-892.
211. *Re Panesar* Pharm J 2008; 280(7488): 156-157.
212. *Sadler* v. *General Medical Council* [2003] 1 W.L.R. 2259.

by the Council under the Act. This is a general provision which potentially embraces a broad spectrum of conduct.

Standard of proof required

The standard of proof required to ground a finding bearing on the fitness to practise of a pharmacist is of critical importance. In *Ó Laoire* v. *The Medical Council*,[213] Keane J. held that the appropriate standard of proof was proof beyond reasonable doubt. This finding was the distillate of the consideration of a wide range of authorities. The standard of proof in the professional misconduct regime for solicitors[214] and for nurses[215] is proof beyond a reasonable doubt.

In *Georgopoulus* v. *Beaumont Hospital Board*,[216] Hamilton C.J. stated that the facts on which allegations are based should be proved on the balance of probabilities bearing in mind that the probability required should always be proportionate to the nature and gravity of the issues investigated. However, the *Georgopoulus* case involved an internal inquiry in a hospital and not a fitness to practise inquiry. In *Millett-Johnston* v. *The Medical Council*,[217] Morris P. held that the issues involved in the *Georgopoulus* case were different to those in *Ó Laoire* and that the appropriate standard of proof in professional disciplinary proceedings continued to be beyond a reasonable doubt.

Before a finding of professional misconduct against a practitioner can be made, every factual element of a charge preferred against a practitioner must be proved beyond a reasonable doubt and it must then be established that the facts as proven constitute professional misconduct.

Sanctions

The imposition of sanctions under the Act is the function of the Council, acting on the findings of the committee of inquiry.[218] The Council must act within 30 days after considering the report of the committee of inquiry. The more serious sanctions[219] do not have any legal effect until they are confirmed by the High Court.[220] In imposing sanction, the Council must consider the misconduct and the mitigation in the case and decide what sanction is appropriate.[221]

---

213. Unreported, High Court, Keane J., 27 January 1995.
214. *Law Society of Ireland* v. *Walker* [2007] 3 I.R. 581.
215. *Perez* v. *An Bord Altranais* [2005] 4 I.R. 298.
216. [1998] 3 I.R. 132.
217. Unreported, High Court, Morris P., 12 January 2001.
218. Section 48.
219. This procedure applies to all sanctions except for admonishment and censure.
220. Section 50.
221. *Giele* v. *The Medical Council* [2006] 1 W.L.R. 942.

Mitigation

The factors which may be taken into account in mitigation of a professional about whom a finding has been made as a result of which a sanction may be imposed are set out in *Bolton* v. *The Law Society*.[222] The following passage is the *locus classicus* in relation to mitigation in professional disciplinary matters, and bears setting out in full:

> Because orders made by the tribunal are not primarily punitive, it follows that considerations which would ordinarily weigh in mitigation of punishment have less effect on the exercise of this jurisdiction than on the ordinary run of sentences imposed in criminal cases. It often happens that a solicitor appearing before the tribunal can adduce a wealth of glowing tributes from his professional brethren. He can often show that for him and his family the consequences of striking off or suspension would be little short of tragic. Often he will say, convincingly, that he has learned his lesson and will not offend again. On applying for restoration after striking off, all these points may be made, and the former solicitor may also be able to point to real efforts made to re-establish himself and redeem his reputation. All these matters are relevant and should be considered. But none of them touches the essential issue, which is the need to maintain among members of the public a well-founded confidence that any solicitor whom they instruct will be a person of unquestionable integrity, probity and trustworthiness. Thus it can never be an objection to an order of suspension in an appropriate case that the solicitor may be unable to re-establish his practice when the period of suspension is past. If that proves, or appears likely, to be so the consequence for the individual and his family may be deeply unfortunate and unintended. But it does not make suspension the wrong order if it is otherwise right. The reputation of the profession is more important than the fortunes of any individual member. Membership of a profession brings many benefits, but that is a part of the price.[223]

It has been held that references or testimonials are of more value in the case of a doctor than in that of a solicitor.[224] Considering the integral role played by pharmacists in the health system, it is submitted that

---

222. [1994] 1 W.L.R. 512.
223. Ibid. at p. 519.
224. *CRHCP* v. *GMC and Southall* [2005] EWHC 579 (Admin.). This was on the basis that honesty was a fundamental requirement for practice as a solicitor. If an allegation of dishonesty could be proved, evidence of professional excellence could not be attached too much weight.

references given by colleagues, fellow healthcare professionals and patients should be relevant regarding the work done by a pharmacist in such a situation.

Sanctions that may be imposed

If the committee of inquiry finds that the complaint is not substantiated, the Council must dismiss the complaint.[225] If the committee of inquiry finds that the complaint is substantiated, the Council may impose on the pharmacist or pharmacy owner one or more of the following sanctions specified in Section 48(1)(b) of the Act of 2007:

a   an admonishment or a censure;

b   the attachment of conditions to the registration of the pharmacist or retail pharmacy business, which may include restrictions on practice or, as the case may be, the carrying on of the business;

c   the suspension of the registration for a specified period;

d   the cancellation of the registration;

e   a prohibition for a specified period on applying for restoration to the Register.

The legislation gives the Council a discretion that is unconfined and unfettered in respect of the choice of sanction it deems appropriate in any particular case. This is subject to the requirement that the sanction imposed be proportionate to the disciplinary offence.[226] The power to impose a sanction must, however, reflect the proper purpose of sanctions in the context of professional disciplinary proceedings. In addition, guidance may be gleaned from a number of decisions of the courts and of the Statutory Committee and the Disciplinary Committee of the RPSGB regarding sanctions that are appropriate to meet the justice of any particular case.

Purpose of disciplinary sanctions

The purpose of sanctions in professional disciplinary matters has been considered extensively by the courts. Sanctions must be imposed with the aim of making these ends manifest. The purpose of fitness to practise proceedings is not primarily punitive, but to seek to ensure that no unfit person should be allowed to continue to practise the profession.[227] The leading case in this

---

225. Section 48(1)(a). Under Section 48(1)(b), the Council must impose one of the specified sanctions if a committee of inquiry finds that the complaint is substantiated. The Council does not appear to have jurisdiction to revisit the merits of the complaint.

226. *Manzur* v. *General Medical Council* [2001] UKPC 55.

227. *A.A.* v. *The Medical Council* [2002] 3 I.R. 1 at p. 32.

regard is that of *Bolton* v. *The Law Society*.[228] In that case the objectives of disciplinary sanctions were considered by Bingham M.R. as being directed to achieve one or both of the following purposes:

> One is to be sure that the offender does not have the opportunity to repeat the offence. This purpose is achieved for a limited period by an order of suspension; plainly it is hoped that experience of suspension will make the offender meticulous in his future compliance with the required standards. The purpose is achieved for a longer period, and quite possibly indefinitely, by an order of striking off. The second purpose is the most fundamental of all: to maintain the reputation of the solicitors' profession as one in which every member, of whatever standing, may be trusted to the ends of the earth. To maintain this reputation and sustain public confidence in the integrity of the profession it is often necessary that those guilty of serious lapses are not only expelled but denied re-admission. . . . A profession's most valuable asset is its collective reputation and the confidence which that inspires.[229]

In *The Medical Council* v. *Dr. Michael Murphy*,[230] Finlay P. held that the sanction imposed should also point out to other members of the profession the gravity of the offence of professional misconduct.

For offences at the lower end of the scale, the Council may impose a sanction primarily directed towards correcting the behaviour of a practitioner; in more serious cases, the protection of the public is paramount to the approach of the Council.[231] It has been recognised that there is necessarily a degree of punishment involved in the imposition of a sanction by a professional disciplinary tribunal and that the seriousness of the misconduct in question must be marked.[232] Concern over the public confidence in the profession should not, however, be carried to the extent of feeling it necessary to sacrifice the career of an otherwise competent and useful professional who presents no danger to the public 'in order to satisfy a demand for blame or punishment'.[233] Having considered all of the evidence in light of the above principles, the court must assist the pharmacist or pharmacy owner with as much leniency as possible in the circumstances.[234]

---

228. [1994] 1 W.L.R. 512.
229. Ibid. at pp. 518–519.
230. Unreported, High Court, Finlay P. 29 June 1994 at p. 5.
231. *Hermann* v. *The Medical Council* Unreported, High Court, Charleton J. 23 November 2010 at para. 9.
232. *CRHP* v. *General Medical Council and Leeper* [2004] EWHC 1850.
233. *Bijl* v. *The General Medical Council* [2002] Lloyd's Med. Rep. 60 at p. 62.
234. *The Medical Council* v. *Michael Murphy* Unreported, High Court, Finlay P. 29 June, 1994.

Selection of sanction

It appears that the Act envisages admonishment in cases where a registered pharmacist or registered pharmacy owner has been found guilty of professional misconduct or poor professional performance which posed little danger to the public. In cases where the category of misconduct or lack of competence is more serious, the Council must consider a censure in writing or whether to impose conditions on registration. In the most serious cases, suspension of registration, cancellation of registration and a prohibition for a substantial time against a practitioner applying for restoration to the register can be considered.[235] These serious sanctions are appropriate where a pharmacist is found to be unqualified or unfit to practise.

The Act does not contain a definition of what is meant by the term 'unfit to practise'. It is clear, however, that a finding of professional misconduct need not necessarily result in cancellation of registration. In *Cohen* v. *The General Medical Council*,[236] Silber J. stated the following in the context of an inquiry under the provisions of the Medical Act 1983:

> There must always be situations in which a Panel can properly conclude that the act of misconduct was an isolated error on the part of a medical practitioner and that the chance of it being repeated in the future is so remote that his or her fitness to practise has not been impaired.

In *Cheatle* v. *The General Medical Council*,[237] Cranston J. stated the following:

> [A] finding that fitness to practise is impaired is a two step process. First, there must be a finding of serious misconduct. Secondly, the Panel must conclude that, as a result, the doctor's fitness to practise is impaired. In coming to a conclusion on impairment, the authorities make clear that the Panel must look forward. It must consider whether, in the light of what happened, and of evidence as to the doctor's conduct and ability demonstrated both before and after the misconduct, fitness to practise is impaired by the particular events.

In *Cohen* v. *The General Medical Council*,[238] Silber J. identified a further relevant factor:

---

235. *Hermann* v. *The Medical Council* Unreported, High Court, Charleton J. 23 November 2010 at para. 9.
236. [2008] EWHC 581 (Admin) at para. 64.
237. [2009] EWHC 645 (Admin) at para. 63.
238. [2008] EWHC 581 (Admin) at para. 70.

the ease with which misconduct can be remedied is relevant to the issue of whether a doctor's fitness to practise has been impaired. Thus if misconduct is *incapable* of being easily remedied – say because, for example, of the doctor's psychiatric problems – this is of great importance at stage 2; similarly if the misconduct is easily remediable, this must be very relevant and merit very serious consideration by the Panel.

In *Yeong* v. *The General Medical Council*,[239] Sales J. considered that regard must be had to evidence about the insight of the practitioner into the source of his misconduct and any remedial steps which have been taken since the misconduct occurred, and assess the risk of recurrence of the misconduct. Whilst these decisions concerned professional disciplinary proceedings conducted within the rubric of a different statutory framework, it is submitted that the principles they espouse will be of assistance to the Council in deciding whether a practitioner has been rendered unfit to practise as a result of professional misconduct.

Upon proof of a disciplinary complaint in respect of a registered pharmacist, the Council must impose a sanction that is proportionate in the circumstances. Bearing in mind the weight that may be attached to mitigation in any given case, it is difficult to advise in the abstract on what would constitute professional misconduct rendering a pharmacist unfit to practise. Considering the scheme of the Act, the decisions from the disciplinary bodies of the RPSGB and the precedents from other professions, it seems that the following matters could potentially constitute misconduct rendering a pharmacist unfit to practise:

a   proof of dishonesty in the course of practice;
b   proof of supply of excessive quantities of controlled drugs or of emergency supply of controlled drugs without following proper procedures;
c   blatant disregard for the system of registration;
d   the abuse of a patient's confidence;
e   failure to review dispensing procedures after a number of dispensing errors have occurred;
f   proof of commission of acts which did not result in a criminal conviction but which nonetheless represent an affront to the dignity of the profession;
g   proof of gross negligence;
h   conviction of a serious offence. In this regard, the factors considered by the Registration Appeals Committee regarding the *indicia* of a serious offence are of assistance;

---

239. [2009] EWHC 1923 (Admin) at para. 21.

i improper recommendations of medical practitioners;

j an improper arrangement; or

k failure of a supervising and/or superintendent pharmacist to ensure, despite warning, compliance with their duties pursuant to the Act and the Regulations.

Once one of these matters is proved, the Council must have regard to a number of other matters including:

a the pharmacist's insight into the misconduct that was committed;

b the risk of recurrence of the misconduct;

c the pharmacist's conduct and ability before and after the misconduct occurred;

d how easily the misconduct can be remedied;

e any remedial steps taken by the pharmacist concerned.

Thereafter, any evidence of good character and of personal mitigating circumstances must be considered. These matters must be weighed and balanced against the purpose of professional disciplinary sanctions, which seek to ensure:

a the protection of the public;

b the maintenance of public confidence in the profession;

c that the pharmacist concerned and other pharmacists are effectively deterred from committing such misconduct in the future.

At all times, the Council must bear in mind the weight that can be attached to mitigation in the context of professional disciplinary proceedings. The Council must ensure that any penalty imposed is proportionate in the circumstances to the misconduct that has been proved.

Attaching conditions on registration

The Council appears to have a wide discretion regarding the attachment of conditions to a pharmacist's registration. Conditions may be attached to registration after a period of suspension of registration.[240] It would appear that this sanction will be particularly appropriate when the pharmacist has been proved to lack sufficient competency.[241] In *Whitefield* v. *General Medical Council*[242] a ban on the consumption of alcohol by the appellant

---

240. This was endorsed in respect of the Solicitors Disciplinary Tribunal in England in the case of *Camacho* v. *The Law Society* [2004] 1 W.L.R. 3037. It would appear that the wording of Section 48 permits such an approach to be taken by the Council.

241. *Hermann* v. *The Medical Council* Unreported, High Court, Charleton J, 23 November 2010.

242. [2002] UKPC 62.

doctor was imposed as a condition attaching to his registration for reasons of physical and mental health. Dr Whitefield claimed this was in breach of his right to private life pursuant to Article 8.1 of the ECHR. This claim was rejected. The appellant's claim to respect for private life was limited to the extent that, as a doctor, he had brought and was likely to bring his private life into contact with public life or into close connection with other potential interests. His right to an unrestricted social life had to give way to the wider public interest in ensuring that he did not present a risk to his patients. Even if there was a breach of Article 8.1, it was permissible if it satisfied the proportionality requirement under Article 8.2.[243]

Prohibition on applying for restoration

In *Gosai* v. *General Medical Council*[244] the Privy Council rejected an argument that the prohibition on the right to apply for registration for a specified period should be restricted to very clear cases or should be regarded as exceptional.

Suspension of registration

When a pharmacist's registration is suspended, it appears that the Council can indicate specific areas of training that the pharmacist should undergo during that period.[245]

Imposition of sanction

After deciding to impose a sanction, the Council has to notify the respondent of the sanction imposed on him or her, the reasons for the imposition of the sanction and the date of the sanction.[246] Where the sanction is an admonishment or censure, that is the end of the matter. In all other cases, the respondent must be informed of the time allowed for him or her to apply to the High Court for an order cancelling the decision of the Council, and of the time within which the Council must apply to the High Court for an order confirming the decision.[247]

Role of the High Court

An application to the High Court to cancel a decision of the Council must be made within 30 days after receipt of notification of the decision by the

---

243. *Bruggeman and Scheuten* v. *Federal Republic of Germany* 3 E.H.R.R. 244.
244. [2002] UKPC 31.
245. *Otote* v. *General Medical Council* [2003] UKPC 71.
246. Section 49(1).
247. Section 49(2).

pharmacist or pharmacy owner concerned.[248] The High Court may consider any evidence put before it in support of the application, whether or not such evidence was put before the committee of inquiry.[249] Any person of good standing within the profession is entitled to give expert evidence as to what constitutes poor professional performance or professional misconduct.[250] The High Court may make any order it considers just in the circumstances and may issue a direction to the Council if it considers it appropriate to do so.[251] Such a direction may request the Council to impose another sanction.[252]

If no application is made by a pharmacist or retail pharmacy owner to cancel a sanction imposed on them within the time allowed, the Council has a further 30 days to apply to the High Court for an order confirming the sanction. The High Court has discretion whether to accede to the Council's application.[253] The decision of the High Court is final, save where an issue of law of public importance arises.[254]

The role of the High Court on an appeal from a disciplinary tribunal has been considered in a number of cases. The ultimate decision regarding the disciplinary finding and of the penalty imposed in consequence of the same must rest with the High Court, save where minor penalties are in issue. This construction is necessary in order that the provisions of Articles 34.1 and 37 of the Constitution are complied with.[255]

The procedure on appeal to the High Court will vary according to the nature of the issues arising on appeal. Where the question as to whether the practitioner is a fit person to remain as a registered pharmacist depends on the truth or falsity of the evidence as to his or her conduct, the matter must proceed to a full hearing before the High Court.[256] Conversely, where there is no factual dispute, the necessity for oral evidence may not arise.[257] Indeed, it is open to the practitioner to appeal against sanction only.[258] It would appear

---

248. Section 51(2).
249. Section 51(3).
250. Section 53.
251. Section 51(4).
252. Section 51 and Section 59(2)(c).
253. Section 52(3).
254. In this instance, Section 54 provides for an appeal to the Supreme Court.
255. In *Re Solicitors Act 1954* [1960] I.R. 239; *M v. The Medical Council* [1984] I.R. 485.
256. *K. v. An Bord Altranais* [1990] 2 I.R. 296.
257. Ibid. Examples of recent cases where a full hearing has not taken place include *Brennan* v. *An Bord Altranais* [2010] IEHC 193 (Unreported, High Court, Dunne J., 20 May, 2020). In *Hermann v. The Medical Council* Unreported, Charleton J., 23 November, 2010, the appellant, who did not contest the findings of fact, adduced evidence before the High Court to support her appeal of the sanction that had been imposed on her by the Medical Council.
258. *Hermann* v. *The Medical Council* Unreported, Charleton J., 23 November 2010.

that where a dispute arises as to how the hearing should proceed, an application seeking the court's directions can be made.[259]

On appeal to the High Court, the onus rests with the Council to prove the alleged misconduct and the appropriateness of the penalty imposed. Finlay P. (as he then was) succinctly explained the position as follows:[260]

> The Council must present to the Court such evidence as it may see fit in order to discharge the onus which is upon it, first, to establish the facts which it alleges prove the misconduct, secondly, to establish that such facts do constitute misconduct and, thirdly, to support the decision it has made. The applicant is entitled to present such evidence on all these topics as he shall see fit. The Court must then, it seems to me, proceed to reach a conclusion as to whether professional misconduct has been proved.

If the High Court affirms a finding of professional misconduct, the practitioner concerned must be given an opportunity to address the court on the appropriate penalty.[261] The High Court must exercise its own analysis of whatever evidence as to sanction is put before it to impose a sanction that is proportionate in the circumstances. In the case of an appeal of sanction only, the Council bears the onus of proving that the sanction imposed was correct.[262] In deference to the experience and expertise of the Council in dealing with such matters, it appears that where the level of sanction imposed is justified by the material before the Council, the court would require a specific reason for altering it on the evidence presented to the court on the appeal.[263]

Given that the proceedings before the Council are not final and binding save in respect of minor matters, they are not likely to constitute administration of justice and are not thus repugnant to the Constitution.[264] The powers conferred on the Council that are final and binding; to request an undertaking from, censure or admonish a practitioner are 'functions so

---

259. *Brennan* v. *An Bord Altranais* [2010] IEHC 193 (Unreported, High Court, Dunne J., 20 May, 2020) at p. 9.
260. *In re M, a doctor* [1984] I.R. 479 at pp. 483–484.
261. *In re M, a doctor* [1984] I.R. 479.
262. *Hermann* v. *The Medical Council* Unreported, High Court, Charleton J. 23 November 2010 at para. 12.
263. Ibid. At paragraphs 39 and 41 of his judgment, Charleton J. declined to alter the sanction imposed by the Medical Council, having found that (a) the Council had proved that the penalty imposed was not disproportionate and (b) the evidence adduced on appeal did not provide any reason to alter the sanction.
264. In *M* v. *The Medical Council* [1984] I.R. 485 at pp. 498–499. In that case, Finlay C.J. considered analogous provisions of the Medical Practitioners Act 1978.

limited in their effect and consequence' that they are constitutionally permissible.[265]

Functions of the Council after the imposition of sanction

After the confirmation or cancellation of the Council's sanction by the High Court, the Council must notify the pharmacist or pharmacy owner of the effect of the High Court order.[266] The Council must also report the imposition of any sanction, as well as the expiry of any suspension of the registration of a pharmacist or retail pharmacy business to the Minister for Health and Children.[267]

The Council is also obliged to report to the Minister similar matters of which it becomes aware that occur in other states.[268] The Council must notify the employer of any pharmacist about whom it has had to report to the Minister,[269] when it is aware of the identity of the employer. The Council is also empowered to give public notice of any such matters where it considers it to be in the public interest to do so.[270]

Cancellation and restoration of registration by the Council

On the application of a pharmacist or pharmacy owner

A pharmacist or the owner of a retail pharmacy business may apply to the Council to have their registration cancelled. The Council has no jurisdiction to accede to the application if there is a complaint pending against the applicant.[271] If a complaint is made but the Council decides not to proceed with it, the complaint is not considered pending for the purposes of the Act.[272] The pharmacy or pharmacist is entitled to be restored to the register if he or she applies to be so restored, pays the appropriate fee and, if necessary, undertakes to comply with any conditions imposed by the Council.[273]

---

265. [1984] I.R. 485 at p. 499. These remarks were made in respect of the provisions of the Medical Practitioners Act 1978 but it is likely that they are of equal force with respect to the Council's powers.
266. Section 55.
267. Section 56(1).
268. Section 56(2).
269. Section 56(3).
270. Section 57.
271. Section 59(1). Section 59(2) provides that where a complaint has not been upheld, or has been upheld but not confirmed by the High Court, it is not considered 'pending' for the purposes of the Section.
272. Section 59(2).
273. Section 61(1)(a).

Failure to pay fees

The Council is empowered to cancel the registration of a pharmacy or pharmacist who fails, despite receiving two reminders, to pay a registration fee levied by the Council.[274] However, that pharmacy or pharmacist is entitled to be restored to the register if an application is made within six months of the fees becoming due and upon payment of all fees.[275]

Restoration to the register

There is no entitlement to be restored to the register following cancellation of registration in accordance with Section 59 or 60 of the Act if evidence emerges that would entitle the Council to refuse to register the pharmacist or pharmacy on grounds that the pharmacist in question is not fit to be registered, does not hold a suitable qualification or that the retail pharmacy business concerned would not be conducted in accordance with Ministerial regulations made under Section 18 of the Act to safeguard public health.[276]

Restoration after cancellation arising out of disciplinary proceedings

The Council has the power to restore the registration of a pharmacist or registered retail pharmacy business whose cancellation has been confirmed by the High Court. The Council must give the pharmacist or retail pharmacy business in question the opportunity to put forward evidence in relation to the matter[277] and must notify the pharmacist or pharmacy in question of any decision made in relation to a restoration to the register.[278] The consent of the High Court to such an action must be obtained before the restoration can be completed.[279]

The following passage from the judgment of Bingham M.R. in the leading case of *Bolton* v. *Law Society*[280] (cited previously in this chapter but equally pertinent to the current topic) should inform the approach of a professional disciplinary tribunal to an application for restoration to the register:

> It often happens that a solicitor appearing before the tribunal can adduce a wealth of glowing tributes from his professional brethren. He can often show that for him and his family the consequences of striking off or suspension would be little short of tragic. Often he will

---

274. Section 60.
275. Section 61(1)(b).
276. Section 61(2).
277. Section 61(4).
278. Section 61(6).
279. Section 61(3).
280. [1994] 1 W.L.R. 512.

say, convincingly, that he has learned his lesson and will not offend again. On applying for restoration after striking off, all these points may be made, and the former solicitor may also be able to point to real efforts made to re-establish himself and redeem his reputation. All these matters are relevant and should be considered. But none of them touches the essential issue, which is the need to maintain among members of the public a well-founded confidence that any solicitor whom they instruct will be a person of unquestionable integrity, probity and trustworthiness.

The Disciplinary Committee of the RPSGB previously produced a document dealing with applications for restoration to the register. This document deals with the principles to be applied and listed the matters that would be taken into account by the Disciplinary Committee on such an application.[281] It is to be noted that the rules governing the Disciplinary Committee did not empower the Disciplinary Committee to hear an application for restoration to the Register until five years had elapsed from the date of the applicant's removal. Further, an applicant had to make a 'strong case' and must demonstrate his or her suitability to be restored to the register in order for his or her application to succeed. Despite these differences between the system operated pursuant to the Pharmacy Act and that operated by the Disciplinary Committee, it is submitted that the following factors are equally relevant to an application for restoration to the Register pursuant to the Act:

a   the seriousness of the original offence of misconduct[282] and the degree of insight shown by the applicant of the gravity of the original offence of misconduct;

b   whether the applicant has made real efforts to demonstrate suitability to be restored to the register, including attempts to keep up to date in terms of knowledge and skills and with development of practice;

c   whether public confidence in the profession would be maintained if the applicant were to be restored to the register;

d   the length of time that has elapsed since removal from the register and/or any previous application for restoration;

e   the conduct of the applicant since removal from the register and any previous application for restoration;

f   testimonials, character references in support of the application and any representation received from patients or victims affected by the original misconduct.

---

281. 'Guidance on the Consideration of Applications for Restoration to the Register.' Approved by Disciplinary Committee on 7 March 2007.
282. *Gosai* v. *General Medical Council* [2003] UKPC 31.

References supplied can be of considerable importance in any application for restoration to the register. In *CRHCP* v. *GMC and Southall*,[283] Collins J. stated:

> Testimonials which establish that a doctor is, in the view of eminent colleagues and of nursing staff who have worked with him, one who is not only competent but whose loss to the profession and to his potential patients would be serious indeed can, in my opinion, be accorded substantial weight.[284]

It is likely that these observations apply with equal force to pharmacists insofar as pharmacists practise within the healthcare system and contribute to the care of patients who present to them.

Applications regarding conditions on registration

A pharmacist or pharmacy who has a condition attached to their registration may apply to the Council to have the condition removed.[285] The pharmacist or pharmacy is entitled to submit oral or written evidence in support of their application.[286] If the Council agrees to the application, it may remove or amend the condition in question or substitute another condition for it.[287] If the Council decides not to remove the condition, the pharmacist or pharmacy owner in question may appeal this decision to the High Court within three months of notification.[288]

Conclusion

At the time of writing, no inquiries have been held under the disciplinary system established by the Pharmacy Act 2007. It is submitted, however, that the committees of inquiry established pursuant to the Act are likely to be guided by the approach taken by the RPSGB and by other professional bodies when adjudicating on the complaints presented to them. The long established rules of natural and constitutional justice will inform the procedures to be adopted by such bodies. When the Council and the High Court are called upon to impose or confirm sanctions on foot of findings made by committees of inquiry, the experience which has accrued in this jurisdiction and in others in dealing with professional disciplinary matters is likely to be of considerable assistance.

---

283. [2005] EWHC 579 (Admin.).
284. Ibid. at para. 14.
285. Section 62.
286. Subsection 62(2).
287. Subsection 61(3).
288. The provisions of Section 21 of the Act in this regard are invoked by Section 62(5). The three-month period begins to run from the date of receipt of notification of the pharmacist concerned of the Council's decision.

15

Liability of community pharmacists in negligence and for defective products

F Crean

Community pharmacies provide a broad array of services in addition to the sale and supply of medicines. Patients routinely present at community pharmacies for treatment and advice regarding minor ailments. This chapter considers the liability of pharmacists in negligence arising out of the services they render and the products they supply. The relevance of the Liability for Defective Products Act 1991 for pharmacists, and the principles of contract law that apply to the sale of medicinal products and the provision of professional advice in relation to the same are also discussed.

Negligence

A tort is a civil wrong that the law will remedy. The tort of negligence involves a duty of care, a breach of that duty and resulting damage, with the link between the breach of duty and the damage not being too remote. A patient suing a pharmacist for compensation for an alleged negligent act must therefore prove three things in order to succeed:

- the pharmacist owed a duty of care to take reasonable care to avoid causing the patient to suffer reasonably foreseeable injury or loss;
- the pharmacist was in breach of that duty;
- the breach of duty caused the injury for which compensation is being claimed.[1]

---

1. *Donoghue* v. *Stevenson* [1932] A.C. 562.

A number of discrete areas of a pharmacist's professional activities could attract an action in negligence. It is established that a patient is owed a duty of care by a pharmacist who dispenses medicines to him or her,[2] or who diagnoses a minor ailment and prescribes over the counter (OTC) treatment for the patient.[3]

Once the existence of a duty of care is established, negligence occurs with the failure to conform to the required standard of behaviour (i.e. the standard of care in any given set of circumstances). The standard of care is generally expressed in terms of the conduct that is expected of a 'reasonable man', exercising ordinary care and prudence in the circumstances. The standard of care expected of professionals is assessed by comparison with the conduct expected of a similarly qualified professional exercising reasonable care in the circumstances. The nature of the duty of care owed by pharmacists and the standard of care to which their actions must conform are considered in detail below.

Supply of medicinal products on foot of a prescription

Patients can experience avoidable outcomes of care as a result of adverse drug reactions or of dispensing errors. In primary care, medication errors give rise to 22% of claims made.[4] At common law, a pharmacist owes a duty of care to a patient who has presented a prescription for dispensing. When dispensing medication, a pharmacist has a duty to ensure the safe supply of medicinal products to patients. This involves the exercise of professional skill, as well as the adherence to robust and safe dispensing procedures in order to eliminate errors.

A pharmacist has a duty to ensure that any prescription or order pursuant to which he or she is requested to dispense medicines is signed by an appropriately qualified person before dispensing the medicines in question.[5] A pharmacist must exercise independent judgment to ensure that the dose[6] and the identity[7] of the medicinal product dispensed conform to the prescriber's requirements. The pharmacist must also satisfy himself or herself that the medicinal product dispensed is suitable for the patient.[8]

---

2. *Horton* v. *Evans* [2006] All E.R. (D) 134.
3. *Jones* v. *Fay* (1865) 4 F & F 525.
4. Donaldson L. Making Amends: a consultation paper setting out proposals for reforming the approach to clinical negligence in the NHS, June 2003, London: Department of Health, p. 40, para. 23.
5. *Collins* v. *Hertfordshire County Council* [1947] K.B. 598 at pp. 613–614.
6. *Collins* v. *Hertfordshire County Council* [1947] K.B. 598.
7. *Prendergast* v. *Sam & Dee Ltd.* [1989] 1 Med. L.R. 36; *Dwyer* v. *Roderick* (1983) 127 Sol Jo 805.
8. *Horton* v. *Evans* [2006] All E.R. (D) 134.

The suitability of the dose of medication prescribed for the patient concerned may be assessed by reference to the therapeutic dose range of the medicinal product concerned. This assessment may not always suffice. If the patient is a regular customer of the pharmacy and presents with a prescription for an increased dose of his or her prescribed medication, albeit within the normal therapeutic range, the pharmacist must query the patient and inquire as to whether the dose increase is intended and, if necessary, contact the prescriber in relation to the issue.[9] It is not sufficient in this instance to attempt to deal with the issue by dispensing the medical product at the prescribed dose and labelling it 'as directed'. Similarly, if a prescription is silent about the frequency of dosage of the medication prescribed, the pharmacist has a duty to inquire as to the prescribed dose; it does not suffice to dispense the quantity of medication prescribed and label it 'as directed'.[10]

In this regard, a number of breaches of duty by pharmacists have come before the courts. For example, in *Dwyer* v. *Roderick*,[11] the plaintiff was prescribed an excessive quantity of Migril® tablets, two to be taken every four hours as necessary. The dose prescribed was a clear mistake and was dispensed as prescribed. The pharmacy where the medication was dispensed was held liable for the plaintiff's resultant injuries. In *Prendergast* v. *Sam & Dee Ltd.*,[12] a similar dispensing error was at issue. In that case, the plaintiff's general practitioner prescribed a course of the antibiotic Amoxil® for the plaintiff. The prescription was written to a poor standard of legibility. On presentation to the defendant's premises, the prescription was misread and 21 Daonil®[13] tablets were dispensed. The plaintiff suffered a hypoglycaemic coma. The pharmacist concerned was held to have breached his duty of care to the plaintiff and was held liable for his injuries.[14]

Diagnosis and over the counter treatment

Community pharmacists, owing to their expertise, experience and accessibility are regularly consulted by patients regarding minor ailments and other unexplained symptoms. The range of products that may be recommended for treatment by a community pharmacist is limited to products authorised for sale over the counter without a prescription. Community pharmacists are required to decide in each case whether the patient who presents is suffering

---

9. *Horton* v. *Evans* [2006] All E.R. (D) 134 at para. 43.
10. *Horton* v. *Evans* [2006] All E.R. (D) 134 at paras. 36–37. In that case, however, Keith J. held that the pharmacist's omission in this regard did not result in any damage to the plaintiff.
11. (1983) 127 Sol Jo 805.
12. [1989] 1 Med. L.R. 36.
13. Contains glibenclamide, an oral sulphonylurea antidiabetic agent, with a hypoglycaemic effect.
14. In that case, the prescriber's poor handwriting was held to have contributed to the error and 25% of the liability for the patient's fatal injuries was found to rest with the prescriber.

from a minor ailment that can be safely and appropriately treated with over the counter medication, or has a more serious condition that requires referral to a general practitioner for further diagnosis and treatment. Pharmacists owe a duty of care even if they give professional advice free of charge.[15] The Regulation of Retail Pharmacy Businesses Regulations 2008[16] impose an additional duty on community pharmacists to ensure that medicinal products are not sold for the purposes of misuse or abuse.[17]

It is suggested that the duty of the pharmacist in respect of diagnosis and treatment is to distinguish between minor ailments and symptoms of a more serious condition.[18] A pharmacist also has a duty to keep reasonably up to date in his or her sphere of practice so he or she will be in a position to give a good standard of care to his or her patients.[19] In diagnosing a patient's symptoms, a pharmacist must take into account everything which might bear on a patient's condition and must question the patient appropriately to this end.[20] Any available medical records should be checked and known drug allergies and any potential adverse drug reactions should be screened for before any over the counter treatment is prescribed by the pharmacist.[21] When the alleged breach of duty is that a wrong diagnosis was made, the mistaken diagnosis is not, of itself, evidence of negligence.[22] It must be established that the pharmacist omitted to carry out an examination or test, or make an inquiry which the symptoms indicated as necessary,[23] or that he or she reached a conclusion that no reasonably competent pharmacist would have made. A number of recognised protocols and questioning techniques exist that facilitate eliciting of information regarding these matters[24] and many pharmacists will have standard operating procedures in place to ensure that these are followed in each case by all members of staff. Following these practices in all cases is advisable as it minimises the chances of omitting a relevant question.

---

15. *Goode* v. *Nash* (1979) 21 S.A.S.R. 419.
16. S.I. No. 488 of 2008. Copyright Houses of the Oireachtas 2008.
17. Regulation 10.
18. McMahon BME, Binchy W. *Law of Torts*, 3rd edn. Dublin: Tottel Publishing, 2000, para. 14.31. This definition is offered in respect of the duty of care of general practitioners in diagnosis. It is submitted that these remarks apply with equal force to the duty of care of a community pharmacist in this regard.
19. *Hughes* v. *Staunton* Unreported, High Court, Lynch J., 16 February 1990 at p. 53. Lynch J. expressed the duty of a medical practitioner in these terms but it seems that pharmacists are subject to the same duty as other healthcare professionals.
20. *Collins* v. *Mid Western Health Board* [2000] 2 I.R. 154.
21. *Chin Keow* v. *Government of Malaysia* [1967] 1 W.L.R. 813.
22. Tettenborn A. Professional liability. In: Dugdale AM, Jones MA, Simpson M, eds. *Clerk & Lindsell on Torts*. London: Sweet and Maxwell, 2006, para. 10.64.
23. *Marriott* v. *West Midlands H.A.* [1999] Lloyd's Med. Rep. 23.
24. e.g. 2WHAM – Who is the medicine for? What is the medicine for? How long have the symptoms been present? Action already taken? Medicines taken for other reasons, prescribed or otherwise?

A person who represents to others that he or she is possessed of skill and knowledge must exercise all of the skill which is to be reasonably inferred from his or her representation.[25] Accordingly, a pharmacist who holds himself or herself out as having medical skill is required by law to have the skill and competence which he or she has claimed. It is prudent for a pharmacist who recommends a course of over the counter treatment to a patient to advise the patient to seek medical advice if his or her symptoms fail to resolve. This is illustrated by *Jones* v. *Fay*.[26] In that case, the defendant pharmacist had recommended an over the counter preparation to the plaintiff to treat 'painter's colic'. The plaintiff purchased the preparation, Bluepill, on several occasions. The plaintiff asked whether he should seek medical advice in relation to his ongoing complaint and was advised that he need not do so. It was held that a person who holds himself out to be a medical practitioner is liable as though he was one even though he is actually a pharmacist.

As a result of the above, a pharmacist must be careful in the advice they and their staff give.[27] It is difficult to envisage circumstances in which liability could attach to a pharmacist for referring a patient for medical attention when there was no need to do so. Common sense dictates that if in doubt regarding the nature and gravity of a presenting patient's symptoms, the pharmacist should refer the patient to his or her general practitioner. In all cases where treatment is recommended in respect of minor ailments, the patient should be advised to consult a medical practitioner within a short period if the symptoms fail to resolve. In so doing, the pharmacist implicitly represents that he or she has been unable to make an exhaustive diagnosis of the patient's ailment and prescribes a course of treatment consistent with his or her probable diagnosis.

Regulation of Retail Pharmacy Business Regulations 2008: additional duties

The Regulation of Retail Pharmacy Business Regulations 2008 (the '2008 Regulations')[28] impose certain standards that must be met in the sale of over the counter medicinal products to patients, as well as in the supply of

---

25. *Brogan* v. *Bennett* [1955] 1 I.R. 119 at pp. 127–129.
26. (1865) 4 F & F 525.
27. The Regulation of Retail Pharmacy Businesses Regulations 2008 require all professional activity carried on in a pharmacy to be supervised by an appropriately experienced pharmacist. Regulation 10 renders the supervising pharmacist responsible for ensuring the patient is properly counselled as to the appropriate use of any medicinal product purchased over the counter. In addition, Regulation 5(1)(h) obliges the superintendent pharmacist to ensure that all pharmacists and other pharmacy staff have the required skills and fitness to perform the work for which they are responsible. As a result, a pharmacist is liable for the consequences of erroneous advice given by his or her staff as if he or she had given the advice himself or herself.
28. S.I. No. 488 of 2008.

medicinal products on foot of a prescription. The regulations govern all aspects of the sale and supply of medicinal products from the sourcing of medicinal products,[29] to the process of dispensing or sale of those medicinal products, and describe the counselling services that must be offered after the dispensing or sale has been completed.[30] While the full impact of the 2008 regulations is considered in Chapter 13 (Pharmacy Act – regulations and rules), they are considered here insofar as they supplement the common law duties owed by pharmacists to their patients.

Over the counter sales

The 2008 Regulations provide that all sales of over the counter medicinal products must be supervised by a registered pharmacist[31] who must be satisfied the purchaser wishes to purchase the medicinal product for therapeutic use, rather than for misuse or abuse, and is aware of the appropriate use of the medicinal product concerned.[32] A number of medicinal products available over the counter are liable to misuse or abuse; for example, products containing codeine, laxatives, etc. have known therapeutic benefits, together with the potential for misuse in certain cases.

Supply of medicinal products on foot of a prescription

The 2008 Regulations impose a number of additional requirements regarding the dispensing of prescriptions. Regulation 9 provides that, prior to the dispensing of every prescription and prior to the supply of the medicinal products prescribed, the prescription must be reviewed by a pharmacist to assess the therapeutic and pharmaceutical appropriateness of the medicinal products prescribed for the patient.[33] This process involves screening for potential therapy problems arising from the use of any product prescribed, including:

- therapeutic duplication;
- interactions with other medicinal products (including serious interactions with over the counter medicines, herbal products and foods);
- incorrect dosage;
- incorrect duration of treatment;
- allergic reactions;
- clinical abuse or misuse.[34]

---

29. Regulation 6.
30. Regulations 9 and 10.
31. Regulation 5(1)(d).
32. Regulation 10. See also guidance produced by the PSI entitled 'Non-Prescription Medicinal Products Containing Codeine: Guidance for Pharmacists on Safe Supply to Patients'. This guidance has been in force since 1 August 2010.
33. Regulation 9(1). This effectively restates the common law duty of care.
34. Regulation 9(2).

After completing this review, the pharmacist has a duty to ensure that each patient has sufficient information to ensure the proper use and storage of their medicines. The pharmacist must offer to discuss with the patient or his or her carer all matters the pharmacist deems significant.[35] A designated patient counselling area must be made available for counselling patients in relation to the use of all medicinal products.[36]

Maintaining patient medical records

The primary focus of all of a pharmacist's professional activities is the patient. In order to safely dispense medication and prescribe over the counter treatment, a pharmacist has a duty to maintain such records as are necessary for the continued care of the patient on a properly informed basis.[37] This obliges the pharmacist to record any known drug allergies as well as recording all medicines dispensed. Most dispensing systems available to community pharmacists facilitate the recording of allergies, adverse drug reactions and interventions made by a pharmacist in respect of some aspect of a patient's care.

Checking a patient's medical history before sale or supply of medicinal products

In any case in which a medicinal product is being dispensed, sold or supplied, pharmacists must take care to check for drug–drug, drug–disease, drug–food and drug–patient interactions. Pharmacists must be alert to common drug reactions and must actively seek relevant information from patients.[38] It also appears that a pharmacist cannot rely only on what he or she has been told when it is reasonable to ask further questions.[39]

The importance of attending to such matters is illustrated by the facts of *Chin Keow* v. *Government of Malaysia*.[40] In that case, the plaintiff was allergic to penicillin and this was recorded on her records. In the course of her treatment in hospital, she was injected with penicillin and died as a result. The hospital concerned was held liable for her death; had her medical records been checked, treatment could have been modified accordingly.

---

35. Regulation 9(3). The matters to be discussed are left to the discretion of the pharmacist. A list of such matters which may, depending on the circumstances, be appropriate to discuss, is provided in Regulation 9(3).
36. Regulation 4(3).
37. *Hughes* v. *Staunton* Unreported, High Court, Lynch J. 16 February 1990 at p. 55. The duty at common law is mirrored by that imposed by Regulation 12 of the Regulation of Retail Pharmacy Businesses Regulations 2008.
38. *Collins* v. *Mid Western Health Board* [2000] 2 I.R. 154 at p. 162.
39. Ibid.
40. *Chin Keow* v. *Government of Malaysia* [1967] 1 W.L.R. 813.

The duty to patients in this regard exists regardless of whether the patient is buying medicinal products over the counter or having medicinal products dispensed to him or her on foot of a valid prescription. The duty exists in all cases where a known potential for clinically significant interaction with a medicinal product arises.

The ambit of the duty of care owed by a community pharmacist will also be informed by the provisions of the Regulation of Retail Pharmacy Businesses Regulations 2008. Regulations 9 and 10 set out certain criteria that must be adhered to in the dispensing of medicines and in the counselling of a person who has been dispensed medicinal products on foot of a prescription or sold medicinal products over the counter.

Sale and dispensing of medicinal products in pregnancy and lactation

The normal range of treatment options available to a pharmacist or doctor are greatly reduced in pregnancy and lactation (i.e. women who are breastfeeding). Most drugs are not authorised for use in pregnancy and some are contraindicated owing to their possible teratogenic effects. Great care must be taken with selling or supplying medicinal products to pregnant patients as a result. The loss of a pregnancy through negligence is actionable.[41] In addition, a child who suffered a pre-natal injury because of a negligent act during the mother's pregnancy has a cause of action at birth and can recover damages suffered since birth as a result of the pre-natal injuries.[42] Accordingly, any supply of medicinal products or giving of advice to pregnant women is an area in which great care should be exercised.

Conversely, it has been held that a sterilisation procedure which failed because the procedure was negligently carried out and after which the patient and her husband were advised that contraceptive measures were no longer necessary, entitled the patient to damages for personal injuries for the pain, suffering and inconvenience of pregnancy and childbirth.[43]

---

41. *Cunningham* v. *Governor and Guardians of the Coombe Lying-in Hospital* [2005] IEHC 354 (Unreported, High Court, Macken J. 5 September 2005).

42. *Burton* v. *Islington Health Authority* [1993] Q.B. 204.

43. *McFarlane* v. *Tayside Health Board* [2000] 2 A.C. 59. In that case, the House of Lords also held that the patient was entitled to damages to compensate for the cost of caring for the child born as a result of the failed sterilisation procedure. In *Byrne* v. *Ryan* [2004] IEHC 207 (Unreported, High Court, Kelly J. 20 June 2007), Kelly J. held that, as a matter of public policy, damages were not recoverable in this jurisdiction for the upbringing of children. The learned judge awarded damages for the pain, suffering and inconvenience of childbirth on the basis that it was conceded that such damages could be recovered if negligence was established. Kelly J. expressly reserved the question of principle as to whether there is in the law of Ireland an entitlement to such damages.

A number of drugs are known to interact with oral contraceptives resulting in loss of, or a significant reduction in, contraceptive efficacy. There can be no doubt that failing to warn a patient of the consequences of a clear drug–drug reaction falls short of the standard that is to be expected of a competent pharmacist exercising reasonable care. It is submitted that it is reasonably foreseeable for a pharmacist who fails to warn of the possible loss of contraceptive efficacy when dispensing medication to expect that an unplanned pregnancy would ensue. As the law stands, the patient whom the pharmacist neglected to warn could be entitled to an award of damages for personal injuries for the pain, suffering and inconvenience of pregnancy and childbirth.

Liability of supervising and superintendent pharmacists and pharmacy owners

The Pharmacy Act 2007 has established the roles of supervising and superintendent pharmacists in the management of the supply of pharmacy services. The 2007 Act and the Regulation of Pharmacy Businesses Regulations 2008 impose a number of duties and responsibilities on supervising and superintendent pharmacists in this regard. The additional areas of responsibility assigned to supervising and superintendent pharmacists are supervisory and administrative in nature respectively.

The role of a superintendent pharmacist

A superintendent pharmacist is responsible for the administration of the sale and supply of medicinal products in a pharmacy[44] and is accountable for the proper management of a retail pharmacy business.[45] To this end, the superintendent pharmacist must devise the appropriate clinical management structures and professional policies.[46] The superintendent pharmacist, who must have a minimum of three years' post-qualification experience, may act in this capacity for a number of retail pharmacy businesses. The roles of supervising and superintendent pharmacists may rest in one individual. It should be noted that the pharmacy owner, if different to the superintendent pharmacist, shares these responsibilities.

The role of a supervising pharmacist

A supervising pharmacist is responsible for the supervision of the sale and supply of medicinal products in a pharmacy and must ensure that all necessary

---

44. Sections 27(b), 28(a) or 29(b) of the Pharmacy Act 2007, depending on the corporate structure of the pharmacy business concerned.
45. Regulation 5, S.I. No. 488 of 2008.
46. Initial guidance on the performance of the duties of superintendent pharmacists and supervising pharmacists is provided by the PSI in Guidance on the roles and responsibilities of superintendent and supervising pharmacists. *Ir Pharm J* 2008; 86: 194–196.

systems are in place for this purpose.[47] The supervising pharmacist is in full-time charge of the operation of the pharmacy and must have at least three years' post-qualification experience. A registered pharmacist must personally supervise the sale and supply of medicinal products at the pharmacy. He or she must implement the professional policies and clinical management structures devised by the superintendent pharmacist.

Consequences in practice

The responsibilities attaching to these roles are extensive and continue, in the case of the superintendent and supervising pharmacist, even when the individuals concerned are absent from the retail pharmacy premises. The policies in place in each pharmacy must take account of specific care issues in the dispensing of particular products, having due regard to the stock held and the dispensing profile of a particular pharmacy.[48]

Accordingly, as the supervising pharmacist is liable to supervise the sale and supply of medicinal products, he or she bears responsibility for any dispensing errors that occur.[49] This responsibility arises whether by reason of his or her failure to supervise properly, or to implement properly, a safe and robust dispensing procedure. The superintendent pharmacist is responsible for the design of clinical management procedures in a pharmacy.[50] If the dispensing procedure in place suffers from obvious defects, the superintendent pharmacist runs the risk of being held liable for any injuries suffered by a patient as a result of adherence to that system. Similarly, if a patient suffers injury as a result of the use of a medicinal product sold over the counter, the supervising pharmacist bears responsibility if the medicinal product was not appropriate for that patient.[51]

If the retail pharmacy premises is being covered by a locum for a period of time, the superintendent pharmacist must be satisfied that the locum has the requisite skills, knowledge and fitness to practise to discharge his or her professional duties in the retail pharmacy in question.[52] If a dispensing error occurs when the pharmacy is staffed by a locum, the supervising pharmacist

---

47. Sections 27(b), 28(a) or 29(b) of the Pharmacy Act 2007, depending on the corporate structure of the pharmacy business concerned.
48. Guidance on the roles and responsibilities of superintendent and supervising pharmacists. *Ir Pharm J* 2008; 86: 194–196.
49. Regulation 5(1)(b) and 5(1)(d), S.I. No. 488 of 2008.
50. Regulation 5(1)(a) S.I. No. 488 of 2008; Guidance on the roles and responsibilities of superintendent and supervising pharmacists. *Ir Pharm J* 2008; 86: 194–196 at 196. In this regard, it is to be noted that adherence to a defective system will not absolve the dispensing pharmacist of liability (*Dunne (an infant)* v. *National Maternity Hospital* [1989] I.R. 91). This is discussed more fully later in the chapter.
51. Regulation 5(1)(b), S.I. No. 488 of 2008.
52. Regulation 5(1)(h), S.I. No. 488 of 2008.

continues, as the person in whole-time charge of the retail pharmacy, to bear overall responsibility for the error.[53]

The standard of care

If a task requires some special skill, a reasonable person would not attempt to perform it unless they possessed the skill in question. A pharmacist is an expert in the science of medicines, including their development, supply and use.[54] The standard of care that must be provided by a pharmacist in carrying out his or her professional duties is that of an ordinarily competent pharmacist, exercising reasonable care.[55] In *Dunne (an infant)* v. *National Maternity Hospital*,[56] the standard of care that must be provided by a professional person in treatment and diagnosis was set out. The principles established in that case are adaptable to the pharmacy profession and are relevant to a number of spheres of a pharmacist's professional activity.[57] Those principles are as follows:[58]

- Negligence in diagnosis or treatment on the part of a medical practitioner is established when it is shown that he or she has been proved to be guilty of such failure that no other medical practitioner of equal specialist or general status and skill would be guilty of if exercising ordinary care.
- Proof of deviation from a general and approved practice by a medical practitioner will not of itself establish negligence unless no other medical practitioner of equal specialist or general status and skill would have taken this course if exercising ordinary care.
- Following a general and approved practice will not constitute a defence to an action in negligence if it is shown that this practice has inherent defects which ought to be obvious to any person giving the matter due consideration.
- An honest difference of opinion between practitioners as to which is the better of two courses of treatment does not prove that a person who had followed one course rather than the other had been negligent.
- The function of the court is to decide whether the course of treatment followed complied with the careful conduct of a medical practitioner of like specialisation and skill to that professed by the defendant.

---

53. Regulation 5(1)(b), S.I. No. 488 of 2008.
54. Guidance on the roles and responsibilities of superintendent and supervising pharmacists. *Ir Pharm J* 2008; 86: 194.
55. *Lanphier* v. *Phipos* (1838) 8 C & P 475.
56. [1989] I.R. 91.
57. Indeed, actions against apothecaries and surgeons have been decided on the same principles at common law, i.e. *Slater* v. *Baker & Stapleton* (1767) 2 Wils. K.B. 359.
58. Ibid. at pp. 108–110.

The standard of care expected of a pharmacist in the exercise of his or her professional duties will also be informed by practice guidelines from the Pharmaceutical Society of Ireland (PSI) or requirements set out in the Pharmacy Act 2007 and the Regulation of Retail Pharmacy Businesses Regulations 2008. In particular, the following are matters to which regard should be had:

- Regulations 9 and 10 of the Regulation of Retail Pharmacy Businesses Regulations 2008;[59]
- any relevant entries in the PSI *Pharmacy Practice Guidance Manual*;[60]
- any relevant practice notice published by the PSI.[60]

The degree of care required when undertaking any task must have regard to the seriousness of the consequences of an error.[61] In this regard, the PSI has published practice notices for good dispensing practice in relation to some such drugs with known serious side-effects and contraindications, for example, methotrexate, and failure to adhere to the standards prescribed in these practice notices would be a matter relevant in determining whether a pharmacist had performed his or her duties to the required standard.

An error of judgement will not constitute negligence, provided the error is not an unreasonable one. In this regard, if a pharmacist's judgement is 'honest and considered and if, in the circumstances known to him at the time, it can fairly be justified',[62] it will not be actionable if it subsequently emerges to be erroneous. Inexperience is not a defence to a claim against a professional[63] and a newly qualified pharmacist will be judged by the same standards as a pharmacist with 30 years' experience.

Accordingly, in defending an action in negligence, proving adherence to the common practice of the profession is a useful starting point. The *Dunne* principles are of considerable relevance in a case involving diagnosis and treatment of a patient by a pharmacist and to the exercise of independent judgement by a pharmacist in respect of a prescription presented to him or her for dispensing.[64]

In the case of a simple dispensing error where a pharmacist has misread a prescription, however, the situation is different. In addition to this exercise of professional skill, it is essential that good dispensing practice be adhered to in

---

59. S.I. No. 488 of 2008.
60. Available at www.thePSI.ie (accessed 1 March 2011).
61. *Paris* v. *Stepney Borough Council* [1951] A.C. 562.
62. *Daniels* v. *Heskin* [1954] I.R. 73 at pp. 86–87.
63. *Wilsher* v. *Essex Area Health Authority* [1987] Q.B. 730.
64. In *Horton* v. *Evans* [2006] All E.R. (D) 134, Keith J. considered that the pharmacist's failure to adhere to the requirements of the standard operating procedures for dispensing contained in his branch manual was a relevant factor in finding the pharmacist had breached his duty of care to the patient.

order to ensure that errors do not arise. In this regard, prescribed medicines must be 'delivered in a manner which reflects diligence and care in the receipt, review, assembling, checking, recording and dispatch of the product'.[65] Such an error can arise in one of two ways. Either the system[66] to which the pharmacist adhered was defective in that it allowed such an error to arise, or the system was not properly adhered to, resulting in the error. There is no defence for a pharmacist to an action by a patient who suffers an injury as a result of such an error.

Apportionment of liability and causation

Having established a duty of care and that the defendant is at fault, it is then necessary for the plaintiff to prove that the fault caused an injury in respect of which compensation is claimed. If a pharmacist, through oversight, misreads a properly written prescription and fails to supply a patient with the medicine prescribed for him, the pharmacist is liable for any injury suffered by the patient as a result.

A doctor has a duty to write a prescription clearly and legibly. If the default on the doctor's part results in an error in dispensing the prescription, the prescribing doctor is also liable for any injuries suffered by the patient as a result of the dispensing error. In *Prendergast* v. *Sam & Dee Ltd.*,[67] the prescription was written to a poor standard of legibility, the wrong medication was dispensed and the plaintiff was fatally injured as a result. In that case, the prescribing doctor was found to be 25% liable for the plaintiff's injuries and 75% of the liability was found to rest with the pharmacy.

If the prescription was dispensed as prescribed, but the dose prescribed was unsuitable for the patient, both the prescribing doctor and the pharmacist will be liable for any injuries suffered by the plaintiff as a result. In *Dwyer* v. *Roderick*,[68] the plaintiff was prescribed an excessive quantity of Migril® tablets, two to be taken every four hours as necessary. The pharmacist who dispensed the prescription was held to be 40% liable, the general practitioner who wrote the prescription was found to be 45% liable, and the general practitioner's partner who should have spotted the error, was found to be 15% liable in respect of the injuries suffered by the plaintiff as a result.

---

65. Pharmaceutical Society of Ireland, Practice Notice, Good dispensing policy – methotrexate. Available at www.thePSI.ie (accessed 1 March 2011).
66. It is unlikely that such a system could be considered a 'medical practice' for the purposes of *Dunne (an infant)* v. *National Maternity Hospital* [1989] I.R. 91. In *Collins* v. *Mid Western Health Board* [2000] 2 I.R. 154, Keane J. distinguished between medical practices and systems of work, such as an admissions system.
67. [1989] 1 Med. L.R. 36.
68. (1983) 127 Sol Jo 805.

Causation and remoteness of damage – possible ramifications of an error

A dispensing error constitutes a breach of duty of care by a pharmacist. If a patient sustains injuries arising out of a dispensing error, the pharmacist is liable for the patient's injuries. In addition, a pharmacist who incorrectly dispenses medication runs the risk of perpetuating his or her error. In *Horton* v. *Evans*,[69] the court concluded that the purpose of a label affixed to dispensed medicinal products is twofold:

> the primary purpose of the label on a bottle of tablets is to let the patient know the medication he or she is taking and what the dose is … the label has a secondary purpose, namely 'to facilitate what the dosage was to any other health professional, e.g. a doctor who may wish to rely upon such information'.[70]

Accordingly, if a label incorrectly represents the dosage, quantity or strength of medication prescribed for a patient, the pharmacist responsible for the error risks being held liable for any injury suffered by the patient as a result of repeat prescriptions which were written in reliance on the dispensing label produced by a pharmacist.[71]

Compensation

Once liability has been established and it is proved that the breach of duty has caused the plaintiff to suffer injury, the plaintiff is entitled to an award of damages in compensation for his or her injury. The general rule is that an injured party, entitled to compensation, is awarded a sum of money to reimburse any actual loss sustained, together with a sum in general damages to take account of pain and suffering, insofar as these elements can be measured financially.[72]

---

69. [2006] All E.R. (D) 134.
70. Ibid. at para. 57.
71. Ibid. at para. 58. Keith J held that the subsequent actions of a doctor in writing a repeat prescription on foot of the dispensing label was not a *novus actus interveniens* that would operate to absolve the pharmacist concerned from liability for injury suffered by the plaintiff.
72. Section 3(d) of the Personal Injuries Assessment Board Act 2003 (No. 46 of 2003, Copyright Houses of the Oireachtas 2003) precludes the application of the provisions of that act to any injuries sustained 'arising out of the provision of any health service to a person'. Accordingly, actions for damages for personal injuries against pharmacists for professional activities will not be processed through the Personal Injuries Assessment Board. However, Section 22(1) of the Civil Liability and Courts Act 2004 (No. 31 of 2004, Copyright Houses of the Oireachtas 2004) provides that the court shall, in assessing damages in a personal injuries action, have regard to the Book of Quantum prepared by the Personal Injuries Assessment Board under the 2003 Act.

Defective products

There are, broadly speaking, two categories of complaint that can be made about a product:

i   that it is dangerous and has injured the purchaser or damaged other property of his or her; or
ii that it cannot be put to optimal use, because it does not work properly or safely, and the purchaser has suffered loss as a result.[73]

Claims of the former type are prosecuted in the law of tort and under the Liability for Defective Products Act 1991. Claims within the latter category are founded on contract law.[74]

There is a great deal of public concern about the safety of medicines. The thalidomide tragedy[75] is an early example. In the 1970s difficulties arose with the use of practolol and, in more recent years, serious adverse effects associated with the use of rofecoxib and oral nimesulide were reported. All of these products have since been removed from the market. There may be a perception that if a medicine causes injury to a person, he or she should be compensated. This perception does not necessarily reflect the reality, however, and seeking such compensation can involve substantial effort and prolonged legal proceedings.

There are two categories of claim that may be brought in tort to recover damages for loss or injury caused by defective products: an action in negligence; or a claim under the Liability for Defective Products Act 1991.

The tort of negligence and defective products

Liability in tort for injury due to negligence in the production of goods is based on the foreseeability of damage to persons through defectively manufactured articles. Liability for negligent production of goods applies to products generally, and is of clear relevance to dispensing of extemporaneous preparations compounded by pharmacists. It is the duty of pharmacists supplying medicinal products to take reasonable care to avoid causing injury to the consumer by their acts or omissions. The degree of care involved must have regard to the seriousness of the consequences of failure.[76] The duty of care extends to supplying the product in a safe container[77] and affixing an appropriate[78]

---

73. Tettenborn A. Product liability and consumer protection. In: Dugdale AM, Jones MA, Simpson M, ed. *Clerk & Lindsell on Torts*. London: Sweet and Maxwell, 2006, para. 11.02.
74. *Colgan* v. *Connolly Construction Co. (Ireland) Ltd.* [1980] I.L.R.M. 33 at p. 37.
75. Teff H, Munro C. *Thalidomide: The Legal Aftermath*. London: Saxon House, 1976.
76. *Paris* v. *Stepney Borough Council* [1951] A.C. 562.
77. *Fisher* v. *Harrods Ltd.* [1966] 1 Lloyd's Rep. 500.
78. The warning must make the user as safe as reasonably possible. *Thompson* v. *Johnson & Johnson* [1991] 2 V.R. 449.

warning label[79] to the product container.[80] Manufacturers of medicinal products must also ensure that these products comply with relevant standards regarding potency and toxicity.[81]

When a medicinal product is placed on the market for sale to a patient, it will generally be packaged in a manner that intentionally excludes interference with, or examination of, the product by anyone other than the end user. The community pharmacist must undertake a reasonable inspection and isolate obvious defects in any proprietary medicinal products he or she dispenses (e.g. products that are obsolete, have passed their expiry date, or are damaged in such a way that they are hazardous).[82] A community pharmacist should not, therefore, be liable for manufacturing or design defects in a medicinal product unless he or she could have discovered their existence by a reasonably practical inspection or testing.[83] Pharmacists may also be exposed to claims in respect of hazards they have created or to which they have contributed (e.g. by failing to supply product leaflets intended by the manufacturer to be passed on to the patient).[84]

Conversely, when compounding an extemporaneous preparation, a duty of care is owed to the consumer to ensure that any dilutions or other acts conducted are such as to render the formulation safe and fit for use. In such a case, the pharmacist has taken a number of manufactured articles and compounded them, using his or her professional skill, for sale as a medicinal product. The acts of the pharmacist are such as to bring himself or herself into direct relationship with the patient who will use the product. He or she is duty bound to consider the users of the product when compounding it and must exercise care to ensure that the product is safe for its intended use.

---

79. The duty to warn is limited to dangers that should have been apparent at the time the product left the producer's hands, hindsight being left out of account. *Roe* v. *Ministry for Health* [1954] 2 Q.B. 66.
80. *Worsley* v. *Tambrands Ltd.* [1999] EWHC 273 (QB) (3 December 1999).
81. *Best* v. *Wellcome Foundation* [1993] 3 I.R. 422.
82. Powers MJ, Harris NH, Barton A, eds. *Clinical Negligence*, 4th edn. London: Tottel Publishing, 2008, at para. 24.111.
83. *Watson* v. *Buckley, Osborne, Garrett & Co. Ltd.* [1940] 1 All E.R. 174 at 182; *Donoghue* v. *Stevenson* [1932] A.C. 562 at 603.
84. Powers MJ, Harris NH, Barton A, eds. *Clinical Negligence*, 4th edn. London: Tottel Publishing, 2008, at para. 24.112. The failure to supply a package leaflet supplied by the manufacturer, if the original pack is dispensed, is in breach of Regulation 9(3) of the Medicinal Products (Prescription and Control of Supply) Regulations 2003 (S.I. 540 of 2003). It would also appear to be a breach of Regulation 4 of the European Communities (General Product Safety) Regulations 1997 (S.I. No. 197 of 1997). Supplying a medicinal product without a package leaflet where there is one or where the labelling or leaflet do not comply with Title V of Directive 2001/83/EC as amended is in breach of Regulation 16(1) and (2) of the Medicinal Products (Control of Placing on the Market) Regulations 2007 (S.I. No. 540 of 2007).

The Liability for Defective Products Act 1991

The regime of strict liability for damage or injury caused by defective products instituted by Directive 85/374/EEC[85] was transposed into Irish law by the Liability for Defective Products Act 1991.[86] The genesis for this Directive was the thalidomide tragedy in the late 1960s. In claims for compensation for injuries caused by the teratogenic effects of thalidomide, the manufacturers successfully argued that they had not been negligent in putting the medication on the market. This defence aroused public dissatisfaction with the state of the law and provided the impetus for Directive 85/374/EEC.[87]

The Liability for Defective Products Act 1991 as amended supplements the existing remedies in tort and contract[88] and provides that a producer shall be liable for damage[89] caused wholly or partly by a defect in his or her product.[90] Liability under the Act is triggered by the existence of a defect in the product concerned; no proof of negligence on the part of the producer is required.

Product

A product for the purposes of the Act is widely defined and extends to all 'movables even though incorporated into another product or into an immovable'.[91] A dichotomy has been drawn between standard and non-standard products,[92] but the importance of this classification remains open to doubt. A standard product is a product that is and performs as the producer intends. A non-standard product differs from the standard product in the existence of a flaw by reason of a manufacturing fault. However, non-standard products are not automatically defective. If a standard product is unsafe, it is likely to be because of an error in the design of the product. A non-standard product is flawed because of its deviation from the norm. Accordingly, it would appear that the safety of a non-standard product that is alleged to be defective would be assessed by comparison with the relevant

---

85. As amended by Directive 1999/34/EC.
86. No. 28 of 1991. The 1991 Act was subsequently amended by the European Communities (Liability for Defective Products) Regulations 2000 (S.I. No. 401 of 2000). The provisions of the Act must be construed so as to be consistent with Directive 85/374/EEC. (*Case C-300/95 European Commission* v. *United Kingdom* [1997] All E.R. (EC) 481.)
87. For a discussion on the history of implementation of the Directive, see Feldschreiber P, ed. *The Law and Regulation of Medicines*. Oxford: Oxford University Press, 2008, at para. 8.19 *et seq.*
88. Article 13 of Directive 85/74/EEC.
89. Damage for the purpose of the 1991 Act includes death, personal injury or damage to other private, non-commercial property.
90. Section 2(1).
91. The definition of 'product' in the 1991 Act was amended by the European Communities (Liability for Defective Products) Regulations 2000 (S.I. No. 401 of 2000) to include primary agricultural products.
92. *A* v. *National Blood Authority (No. 1)* [2001] 3 All E.R. 289 at 317.

standard product. Conversely, the safety of a standard product that is alleged to be defective might be assessed by comparison with similar standard products available in the market. However, it is clear that the overarching criterion by which defectiveness will be measured is whether the product provides the level of safety an informed member of the public is entitled to expect.[93]

Producer

A producer includes the manufacturer of a finished product, the producer of any raw material and the manufacturer of a component part or any person who, by putting his name, trade mark, or other distinguishing feature on the product holds himself or herself out to be the producer. In addition, the supplier of a product can be deemed the producer if he or she fails to inform the injured party of the identity of the producer, having been requested to do so, in circumstances whereby the injured party cannot identify the producer.[94] The Liability for Defective Products Act 1991 envisages that more than one person in the chain of supply of medicinal products may be liable for the same injury on a joint and several basis.[95]

A pharmacist will not be the producer of a medicinal product unless he or she manufactures his or her own medicines, imports them directly from outside the European Union (EU) or fails to keep proper records identifying the product supplied or the immediate supplier of the product. Accordingly, in most cases, the manufacturer of a pharmaceutical preparation will be the producer for the purposes of the Act. There are, however, a number of ways in which liability could attach to community pharmacists under the 1991 Act.

As a producer can be any person who has branded himself or herself so as to hold himself or herself out as producer, a pharmacist who extemporaneously compounds or dispenses a bulk produced product in a smaller container with a customised label on it could be deemed a producer for the purposes of the Act.[96] So, in *Case C-203/99 Veedfald* v. *Århus Amstkommune*,[97] organ-cleansing fluid prepared by a pharmacist in the defendant's hospital for the purposes of preparing a kidney for transplant was held to have been produced by the defendant. The organ-cleansing fluid proved to be defective and rendered the kidney unsuitable for transplant. The plaintiff was entitled to an

---

93. *A* v. *National Blood Authority (No. 1)* [2001] 3 All E.R. 289 at 318.
94. Section 2 of 1991 Act. This section also provides that any person who has imported the product from outside the EU is deemed a producer for the purposes of the act.
95. Powers MJ, Harris NH, Barton A, eds. *Clinical Negligence*, 4th edn. London: Tottel Publishing, 2008, at para. 24.52.
96. Feldschreiber P, ed. *The Law and Regulation of Medicines*. Oxford: Oxford University Press, 2008, at para. 8.72 *et seq.*
97. [2001] E.C.R. I-3569.

award of damages from the defendant pursuant to Directive 85/374/EEC as amended.

Liability for defective products

The purpose of Directive 85/374/EEC as amended is to achieve a higher and consistent level of consumer protection throughout the EU and render recovery of compensation easier by removing the need to prove negligence.[98] In deciding whether a product is defective, it is irrelevant whether the hazard which had caused the damage had come, or ought reasonably to have come, to the attention of the producer before the accident occurred[99] and whether steps could have been taken to reduce the risk of the defect emerging.[100]

A product is defective if it fails to provide the safety which a person is entitled to expect, taking all the circumstances into account. This is assessed from the perspective of an informed representative of the public at large.[101] The onus is on the plaintiff to prove that the damage suffered was caused by a defect in the product.[102] Section 5 of the Act of 1991 provides a number of examples of circumstances of relevance in assessing whether a product can be considered safe:

- the presentation of the product;[103]
- the use to which it could reasonably be expected the product would be put;
- the time when the product was put into circulation.

The use to which a product is expected to be put is a matter of critical importance. If a product is required to be dangerous in respect of its expected use (e.g. a knife), then complaint cannot be made of that dangerousness. However, complaint can be made of different dangerousness (e.g. if the knife spontaneously exploded). Finally, if a product is not expected to be dangerous in respect of its expected use, but the use to which it was put is unexpected, it may not be defective.[104] Accordingly, it would be difficult for a plaintiff to succeed in a case against the producer of a medicinal product for an injury caused by a known side-effect of the product, about which the plaintiff had been adequately warned.[105]

---

98. *A* v. *National Blood Authority (No. 1)* [2001] 3 All E.R. 289 at 311j.
99. *Abouzaid* v. *Mothercare* Times Law Reports, 20 February, 2001.
100. *A* v. *National Blood Authority (No. 1)* [2001] 3 All E.R. 289 at 342.
101. *A* v. *National Blood Authority (No. 1)* [2001] 3 All E.R. 289 at 311.
102. Section 4 of the 1991 Act.
103. This includes warnings provided and the price of the product. *A* v. *National Blood Authority (No. 1)* [2001] 3 All E.R. 289 at p. 314a.
104. Ibid. at pp. 313–314.
105. *A* v. *National Blood Authority (No. 1)* [2001] 3 All E.R. 289 at p. 312.

Failure to heed instructions or warnings supplied with the medicinal product is a matter to which the court will have regard.[106] A potentially dangerous product can be rendered safe with appropriate warnings and instructions.[107] In *Worsley v. Tambrands Ltd.*,[108] a general warning on a box of tampons, together with a detailed warning on the information leaflet inside the box concerning the dangers of toxic shock syndrome, were held to render the product safe. Dangers obvious to the user do not need to be warned against.[109] Impracticability, cost or difficulty of taking precautionary measures to prevent any particular defect, or the social benefits of a product as opposed to its risks, are not relevant considerations in assessing whether a product is defective.[110]

Failure to include a patient information leaflet, if there is one, with a medicinal product could deprive the patient of the instructions he or she requires to use the product safely and could render a pharmacist liable for any injuries suffered by any party as a result.[111]

Defences

It is not possible to 'contract out' of the provisions of the Liability for Defective Products Act 1991.[112] The defences available to a producer in a claim pursuant to the 1991 Act are set out in Section 6 of the act, which provides that a producer will not be liable if he or she proves:

a   that he or she did not put the product into circulation;[113]

---

106. *Richardson* v. *LRC Products Ltd.* [2000] Lloyd's Med. Rep. 280.

107. *Worsley* v. *Tambrands Ltd.* [1999] EWHC 273 (QB) (3 December 1999). The duty of the producer is to supply the warning to the consumer. If the consumer loses or disregards the warning, liability will not attach to the producer providing the information constituting the warning was supplied.

108. Ibid.

109. *Bogle* v. *McDonalds Restaurants* [2002] All E.R. (D) 436.

110. *A* v. *National Blood Authority (No. 1)* [2001] 3 All E.R. 289.

111. These leaflets are supplied by the manufacturer for distribution to the patient in satisfaction of the manufacturer's duty to provide appropriate warnings or instructions to the patient as set out in *Worsley* v. *Tambrands Ltd.* [1999] EWHC 273 (QB) (3 December 1999) and under Regulation 16 of the Medicinal Products (Control of Placing on the Market) Regulations 2007. Failure on the part of a pharmacist to pass these on to the patient could entitle the producer to an indemnity against the pharmacist in respect of any damages awarded arising out of unsafe use of the medicinal product that would have been avoided by reference to the manufacturer's instructions.

112. Section 10 of the Liability for Defective Products Act 1991.

113. A product is put into circulation when it leaves the manufacturing process operated by the producer and enters the marketing process in the form in which it is offered for sale to the public to be used or consumed. *Case C-127/04 O'Byrne* v. *Sanofi Pasteur MSD Ltd.* [2006] E.C.R. I-1313; [2006] 1 W.L.R. 1606.

b   that, having regard to the circumstances, it is probable that the defect did not exist at the time the product was put into circulation or came into being afterwards;

c   that the product was neither manufactured by him or her for sale or any form of distribution for economic purpose, nor manufactured or distributed by him or her in the course of his or her business;[114]

d   that the defect is due to compliance of the product with mandatory regulations issued by the public authorities;

e   that the defect could not have been discovered due to the state of scientific and technical knowledge when the product was put into circulation – the 'state of the art' defence;[115]

f   in the case of a manufacturer of a component, that the defect is attributable to the design of the product in which the component has been fitted or to the instructions given by the manufacturer of the product.

A partial defence will be available in the form of contributory negligence by the plaintiff.[116] Section 7 of the 1991 Act also prescribes limitation periods within which claims must be brought.

In this regard, the 'state of knowledge' includes 'all data in the information circuit of the scientific community as a whole, bearing in mind, however, on the basis of a reasonableness test, the actual opportunities for the information to circulate'.[117] In order to successfully raise such a defence, the producer must prove that the objective state of technical knowledge when the product was put into circulation was not such as to enable the existence of the defect to be discovered.[118] It is the state of scientific knowledge that is relevant rather than the practices and standards operating in the industry at the time.[119]

Contract law

Sale of goods and supply of services

The Sale of Goods Act 1893 as amended governs the sale of goods in Ireland. This Act recognises the imbalance in bargaining power between sellers of goods on the one hand and consumers on the other. It attempts to redress this imbalance and protect the interests of consumers by implying certain

---

114. This defence does not arise where a medicinal product is supplied or administered in the course of publicly funded medical treatment for which the injured party does not have to pay. *Veedfald* v. *Àrhus Amstkommune* [2001] E.C.R. I-3569.

115. This refers to the most advanced state of scientific knowledge available that is accessible and in circulation. *A* v. *National Blood Authority (No. 1)* [2001] 3 All E.R. 289 at p. 326.

116. Section 9 of 1991 Act.

117. *Commission* v. *United Kingdom* [1997] All E.R. (EC) 480 at p. 491.

118. Ibid. at p. 495.

119. Ibid. at p. 489.

terms into consumer contracts. Accordingly, any medicinal product sold over the counter or dispensed on foot of a prescription must meet certain standards. The Sale of Goods Act 1893 as amended[120] provides that the following conditions form part of a contract for the sale of goods:

a   the seller has a right to sell the goods;[121]
b   the goods sold will correspond to their description;[122]
c   the goods sold are of merchantable quality;[123]
d   the goods sold are fit for the purpose for which they are required.[124]

Claims made in a manufacturer's promotional material do not of themselves provide the user with a contractual remedy based on a warranty that these claims were true.[125]

In addition, Section 39 of the Sale of Goods and Supply of Services Act 1980[126] implies the following terms into any contract for the supply of a service:

a   the supplier has the necessary skill to render the service;
b   he or she will supply the service with due skill, care and diligence;
c   where materials are used, they will be sound and reasonably fit for the purpose for which they are required;
d   where goods are supplied under a contract, they will be of merchantable quality.

As a result of the Acts of 1893 and 1980, these conditions form part of every contract for the sale of goods or the supply of services. Liability for breach of contract will attach to the seller or service provider regardless of whether he or she knew of any defect in the goods sold. The 1893 Act as amended imposes a regime of strict liability; it is no defence for a seller to say that he or she exercised reasonable care in the supply of the goods.[127] If goods

---

120. 56 & 56 Vict. c. 71 as amended by the Sale of Goods and Supply of Services Act 1980 (No. 16 of 1980).
121. Section 12 of the 1893 Act as amended. This condition is breached when the seller has no right to dispose of the property. If, for example, a pharmacist compounds an extemporaneous medicinal product which breaches the provision of a trademark of a third party, the condition will be breached. *Microbeads* v. *Vinhurst* [1975] 1 W.L.R. 218.
122. Section 13 of the 1893 Act as amended.
123. Section 14 of the 1893 Act as amended. This requires that the goods are reasonably fit for the purposes for which such goods are commonly purchased and reasonably durable.
124. Section 14(4) of the 1893 Act as amended. In this regard, if instructions supplied with the goods regarding their use are not followed, any claim that the goods were not fit for the purpose for which they were required, or that they were not of merchantable quality, will be defeated. *Wormell* v. *R.H.M. Agriculture (East) Ltd.* [1987] 1 W.L.R. 1091.
125. *Lambert* v. *Lewis* [1978] 1 Lloyd's Rep. 610 at pp. 628–629.
126. No. 16 of 1980.
127. *Frost* v. *Aylesbury Dairy Co. Ltd.* [1905] 1 K.B. 608.

sold or services supplied fail to comply with these statutory conditions, the buyer is entitled to repudiate the contract.

Consequences of breach of contract

Any award of damages for breach of contract is primarily designed to put the plaintiff in substantially the same position as though the contract had been performed.[128] This is generally assessed by reference to the difference between the position that the plaintiff would have occupied had the contract been performed and the position that the plaintiff is actually in as a result of the breach of contract.[129]

In *Hickey* v. *Health Service Executive*,[130] Finlay Geoghegan J. considered the unilateral reduction of the rate paid to pharmacists in reimbursement of the cost of medicines supplied on community drugs schemes. It was held that the reduction in reimbursement was in breach of the HSE's contract with community pharmacy contractors; the contract provided for a mechanism for the unilateral reduction of payments to community pharmacy contractors following consultation with the Minister for Health. This contractual procedure for variation was not followed before reducing the relevant payments. The community pharmacy contractors concerned were held to have been entitled to be paid the sums that had been deducted from their payments in breach of contract, together with interest, as this represented the loss that had been sustained as a result of the HSE's actions.[131]

Privity of contract

The doctrine of privity of contract provides that contracts affect only the parties to them, and do not bind third parties. Accordingly, a contract for the benefit of a third party cannot be enforced by that party.[132] This represents an important restriction on contractual liability to patients for drugs dispensed to them by pharmacists as outlined below.

Contract law and the supply of medicines on foot of a prescription

A number of schemes operated by the Health Service Executive (HSE) provide for the supply of medicines to eligible patients free of charge.[133] The Health

---

128. *Vandeleur* v. *Dargan* [1981] I.L.R.M. 240 at p. 242.
129. McDermott PA. *Contract Law*. Dublin: LexisNexis, 2001, paras. 22.08 *et seq.*
130. [2009] 3 I.R. 156.
131. [2008] IEHC 373 (Unreported, High Court, Finlay Geoghegan J. 19 December 2008).
132. *Dunlop Pneumatic Tyre Co. Ltd.* v. *Selfridge & Co. Ltd.* [1915] A.C. 847 at p. 853.
133. Schemes such as the General Medical Services (GMS) scheme, the Long Term Illness (LTI) scheme, the Health Amendment scheme, the Psychiatric Medicines scheme and the Hardship scheme would fall into this category.

Act 1970 provided for the introduction of the General Medical Services (GMS) scheme. Section 59(1) of the 1970 Act obliged the health boards to make arrangements for the supply, without charge, of medicines to persons eligible for a medical card. The administration of this scheme and the other community drugs schemes are governed by a contract between the pharmacy or pharmacist who dispenses the medicines and the HSE[134] which provides for remuneration of the pharmacist by the HSE. This contract clearly benefits the patients who are eligible to receive medicines free of charge, or subject to a limited co-payment. These patients are not, however, party to the contract for the supply of medicines.

The supply of drugs to a patient on a GMS prescription does not amount to a sale. This is the case where no payment[135] or a nominal payment[136] is supplied by the patient in return for the prescription. The nature of community pharmacy contractor agreements in this jurisdiction has been addressed in recent decisions.[137] In Hickey v. Health Service Executive[138] Finlay Geoghegan J. held that remuneration provided to community pharmacy contractors was for the administration of community drugs schemes. This remuneration includes an element of reimbursement of the cost price of medicines dispensed on these schemes.

It is clear that dispensing a private prescription is a sale; remuneration is provided in full by the patient concerned. Though the payment of 'a prescribed nominal charge' by the patient does not alter the character of the transaction, the current monthly threshold on the Drugs Payment Scheme could scarcely be classified as nominal. Community pharmacy contractors have an agreement with the HSE regarding the administration of the Drugs Payment Scheme whereby each patient who receives medication under that scheme must pay a sum of up to €120.[139] Accordingly, it seems that the

---

134. These contracts were originally entered into with the relevant health board. Pursuant to Section 63 of the Health Act 2004 (No. 42 of 2004), these contracts have effect as if the HSE was substituted for the relevant health board and are enforceable against the HSE. The provisions of these contracts were analysed in detail by Clarke J. in *The Irish Pharmaceutical Union* v. *The Minister for Health* [2007] IEHC 222 (Unreported, High Court, Clarke J 29 June 2007); by the Supreme Court on appeal (*The Irish Pharmaceutical Union* v. *The Minister for Health* [2010] IESC 23 (Unreported, Supreme Court, 29 April 2010)) and by Finlay Geoghegan J. in *Hickey* v. *Health Service Executive* [2009] 3 I.R. 156.

135. *Appleby* v. *Sleep* [1968] 1 W.L.R. 948 at 954. The supply of medicines in this case is a supply pursuant to a contract for services with the NHS. Though there is a supply of goods, there is no sale either to the patient or to the NHS.

136. *Pfizer Corporation* v. *Minister for Health* [1965] A.C. 512.

137. Hickey v. Health Service Executive [2009] 3 I.R. 156; The Irish Pharmaceutical Union v. The Minister for Health [2007] IEHC 222 (Unreported, High Court, Clarke J. 29 June 2007); and The Irish Pharmaceutical Union v. The Minister for Health [2010] IESC 23 (Unreported, Supreme Court, 29 April 2010).

138. [2009] 3 I.R. 156.

139. Correct as at 1 March 2011.

supply of medicines on foot of a prescription privately and perhaps on the Drugs Payment Scheme amounts to a contract of sale, and that remedies in contract law are available to purchasers as a result.

Disclosure of risks and informed consent

A manufacturer's obligations to warn in respect of any possible dangers associated with the use of his or her product may, in certain cases, be discharged by supplying a warning to professional intermediaries, rather than to the end consumer.[140] This is particularly important in the case of medicinal products, where the end user may not be qualified to take proper account of any warning given. Accordingly, a pharmacist may have a duty to give a warning regarding the nature of proposed treatment.

It is recognised that a doctor has a duty to warn in respect of elective surgery[141] and in respect of drug treatment.[142] It is submitted that, in certain circumstances, a pharmacist will also have a duty to provide an appropriate warning to a patient. If, for example, a patient has been prescribed medication that is safe to use, but that is likely to have a particular side-effect, a warning should be given by the pharmacist. For example, if a patient who has a regular prescription for a combined oral contraceptive presents with a prescription for amoxicillin, as long as the dose is appropriate and the patient is not allergic to penicillin, there is no impediment to dispensing the prescription. Penicillins are, however, known to interfere with the efficacy of combined oral contraceptives. In such a case, it is submitted that the risk of contraceptive failure should be warned against, and appropriate advice given before dispensing the prescription.

In order to discharge the duty to warn, the medical professional must warn and advise the patient in relation to the inherent risks and side-effects of the treatment[143] and in relation to any alternative treatment available.[144] The warning must be given to the patient concerned or to a parent, if appropriate.[145] A medical professional must give a warning of any material risk which is a known complication of the treatment administered. A risk is material if, however remote, grave consequences could follow from the treatment.[146] The

---

140. *Holmes* v. *Ashford* [1950] 2 All E.R. 76.
141. *Geoghegan* v. *Harris* [2000] 3 I.R. 536.
142. Tettenborn A. Professional liability. In: Dugdale AM, Jones MA, Simpson M, eds. *Clerk & Lindsell on Torts*. London: Sweet and Maxwell, 2006, para. 10.69; *Buckle* v. *Delaunay* (1970) 2 Lancet 145.
143. *Chatterton* v. *Gerson* [1981] Q.B. 432 at 443; *Sidaway* v. *Bethlehem Hospital* [1985] A.C. 871.
144. *Williamson* v. *E London & City H.A.* [1998] 1 Lloyd's Med. Rep. 6.
145. *Thompson* v. *Bradford* [2005] EWCA Civ 1439.
146. *Walsh* v. *Family Planning Services Ltd.* [1994] 1 I.R 496 at p. 521.

failure to warn of any risk that would affect the judgement of a reasonable prudent patient constitutes a breach of the medical professional's duty of care.[147] It is submitted that a pharmacist's duty to warn would be identical to the above when it arises.

147. *Fitzpatrick* v. *White* [2008] 3 I.R. at p. 551.

List of statutes

Index